Your **Research**
Project 2nd edition

A step-by-step guide for the first-time researcher

Nicholas **Walliman**

SAGE Publications
London ● Thousand Oaks ● New Delhi

SAGE Publications Ltd
1 Oliver's Yard
55 City Road
London EC1Y 1SP

SAGE Publications Inc.
2455 Teller Road
Thousand Oaks, California 91320

SAGE Publications India Pvt Ltd
B-42, Panchsheel Enclave
Post Box 4109
New Delhi 110 017

British Library Cataloguing in Publication data

A catalogue record for this book is available from the British Library

ISBN 1 4129 0131 6   ISBN-13 978-1-4129-0131-4
ISBN 1 4129 0132 4 (pbk)   ISBN-13 978-1-4129-0132-1(pbk)

Library of Congress Control Number 2004099489

Typeset by C&M Digitals (P) Ltd., Chennai, India
Printed on paper from sustainable resources
Printed in Great Britain by The Alden Press, Oxford

Summary of Contents

Contents   vii
Acknowledgements   xiii

Introduction   1

1 **Research and the Research Problem**   6

2 **Information, and How to Deal with It**   48

3 **Types of Research**   92

4 **Nature and Use of Argument**   146

5 **More about the Nature of Research**   186

6 **Research Quality and Planning**   232

7 **Research Methods**   268

8 **Honesty and Research Ethics**   334

9 **Preparing the Research Proposal and Starting to Write**   370

Key Words Glossary   429

References   440

Index   444

CONTENTS

INTRODUCTION   1

1 RESEARCH AND THE RESEARCH PROBLEM   **6**

AIMS   7

INTRODUCTION   7

THE RESEARCH APPROACH   8

What is research?   8

Scientific method in research   12

The interpretist alternative   16

STARTING YOUR OWN RESEARCH   22

Types of research degree   22

Overview of the research process   23

The research problem   26

Some common mistakes   28

Aids to locating and analysing problems   30

CONCLUSIONS   36

THE NEXT STEPS: FINDING YOUR RESEARCH
PROBLEM AREA   37

CHECKLIST OF ACTIVITIES THAT WILL PROGRESS YOUR RESEARCH   37

Consolidation and assessment   40

Key words   40

Further reading   40

ANSWERS TO EXERCISES   41

2 INFORMATION, AND HOW TO DEAL WITH IT   **48**

AIMS   49

INTRODUCTION   49

FINDING THE INFORMATION   50

Sources of information   51

The internet   53

Search techniques for on-line catalogues, databases and the net   56

DEALING WITH INFORMATION   58
   Reading   59
   Note-taking   62
DOING A LITERATURE REVIEW   75
   Critical reading skills   76
   Doing the review   77
   Style and content of the review   80
CONCLUSIONS   83
THE NEXT STEPS: DEVISING YOUR OWN INFORMATION SYSTEM
   AND WRITING YOUR LITERATURE REVIEW   83
CHECKLIST OF ACTIVITIES THAT WILL PROGRES YOUR RESEARCH   83
   Consolidation and assessment   85
   Key words   86
   Further reading   86
   Answers to exercises   88

3 **TYPES OF RESEARCH**   **92**
AIMS   93
INTRODUCTION   93
CONCEPTS AND THEORY   94
   Models   94
   Concepts   94
   Concept measurement   98
   Quantification of concepts   101
   Theory   105
TYPES OF RESEARCH   112
   Historical   113
   Comparative   114
   Descriptive   115
   Correlation   116
   Experimental   117
   Evaluation   119
   Action   121
   Ethnogenic   122
   Feminist   122
   Cultural   123
CONCLUSIONS   135
THE NEXT STEPS: WHICH TYPE OF RESEARCH FOR YOUR TOPIC?   136
CHECKLIST OF ACTIVITIES THAT WILL PROGRESS YOUR RESEARCH   136
   Consolidation and assessment   138
   Key words   138
   Further reading   139
ANSWERS TO EXERCISES   139

4 **NATURE AND USE OF ARGUMENT**   **146**
   AIMS   147
   INTRODUCTION   147
   LANGUAGE   148
      Three uses of language   148
      Statements: existent and relational   149
   ARGUMENT   155
      Deductive and inductive arguments   158
      Logic in argument   161
      Fallacies in argument   168
      Classification and analogy in argument   171
   CONCLUSIONS   175
   THE NEXT STEPS: WHAT ARGUMENT WILL YOU PURSUE?   175
   CHECKLIST OF ACTIVITIES THAT WILL PROGRESS YOUR RESEARCH   176
      Consolidation and assessment   177
      Key words   178
      Further reading   178
   ANSWERS TO EXERCISES   179

5 **MORE ABOUT THE NATURE OF RESEARCH**   **186**
   AIMS   187
   INTRODUCTION: THE DEBATE ABOUT THE NATURE OF
   KNOWLEDGE AND THE PHILOSOPHY OF RESEARCH   187
   POSITIVISM AND SCIENTIFIC ENQUIRY   189
      Pure induction   190
      Deduction and the principle of falsification   193
      The hypothetico-deductive method   195
   THE DEBATE ABOUT THE STRUCTURE OF SCIENCE AND
      THE NATURE OF KNOWLEDGE   197
   POSITIVISM AND INTERPRETIVISM IN SOCIAL RESEARCH   202
      The positivist approach   203
      The interpretivist approach   204
      The reconciliatory approach   206
   HYPOTHESES: DO YOU NEED THEM?   211
      A closer look at hypotheses and their formulation   211
      Operationalizing hypotheses   214
      Alternatives to hypotheses   217
   CONCLUSIONS   220
   THE NEXT STEPS: PHILOSOPHY IN THE RESEARCH PROJECT   220
   CHECKLIST OF ACTIVITIES THAT WILL PROGRESS YOUR RESEARCH   221
      Consolidation and assessment   224
      Key words   224
      Further reading   224
   ANSWERS TO EXERCISES   226

6	**RESEARCH QUALITY AND PLANNING**	**232**
	AIMS	233
	INTRODUCTION	233
	GOOD RESEARCH	234
	Objectives of research	234
	Desirable characteristics of research findings	235
	The research process	237
	The nature and role of data	240
	Quantitative and qualitative data	246
	PLANNING A RESEARCH PROJECT	248
	Choosing a research strategy	249
	Planning research projects	250
	CONCLUSIONS	259
	THE NEXT STEPS: PLAN YOUR OWN RESEARCH PROJECT	259
	CHECKLIST OF ACTIVITIES THAT WILL PROGRESS YOUR RESEARCH	260
	Consolidation and assessment	261
	Key words	262
	Further reading	262
	ANSWERS TO EXERCISES	264
7	**RESEARCH METHODS**	**268**
	AIMS	269
	INTRODUCTION	269
	Data collection and analysis	270
	Quantitative and qualitative research	270
	Research strategies	271
	The links between perspectives	272
	COLLECTING SECONDARY DATA	273
	COLLECTING PRIMARY DATA	275
	Sampling	275
	Questionnaires and diaries	281
	Interviews: structured, semi-structured and open	284
	Standardized scales and tests	286
	Accounts	286
	Observations and physical surveys	287
	Using the internet for primary research	288
	COMBINED DATA GENERATION AND ANALYSIS	291
	Experiments	292
	Models	295
	ANALYSING DATA	301
	Why analyse data?	301
	Quantitative analysis	302
	Qualitative analysis	308

CONCLUSIONS   321
THE NEXT STEPS: WHICH RESEARCH METHODS WILL YOU USE?   321
CHECKLIST OF ACTIVITIES THAT WILL PROGRESS YOUR RESEARCH   321
   Consolidation and assessment   324
   Key words   324
   Further reading   325
ANSWERS TO EXERCISES   330

8   HONESTY AND RESEARCH ETHICS   **334**
AIMS   335
INTRODUCTION   335
HONESTY IN YOUR WORK   336
   Intellectual ownership and plagiarism   336
   Citation and acknowledgement   336
   Responsibility and accountability of the researcher 337
   Data and interpretations   337
   Where do you stand? epistemology   339
SITUATIONS THAT RAISE ETHICAL ISSUES   340
   Research aims   340
   Means and ends   341
   Ethics in relation to other people   342
   Participants   344
   Carrying out the research   347
   Dissemination   353
ETHICS, POLICIES, PERMISSIONS AND COMMITTEES   354
   Organizations   354
   Ethics committees   358
CONCLUSIONS   360
THE NEXT STEPS: PLAN YOUR CODE OF ETHICS   361
CHECKLIST OF ACTIVITIES THAT WILL PROGRESS YOUR RESEARCH   361
   Consolidation and assessment   365
   Key words   365
   Further reading   365
ANSWERS TO EXERCISES   367

**9   PREPARING THE RESEARCH PROPOSAL AND
STARTING TO WRITE**   **370**
AIMS   371
INTRODUCTION   371
THE RECIPE FOR A SUCCESSFUL RESEARCH PROPOSAL   372
   Types of research proposal   372
   The main ingredients and sequence   374

Finalizing your proposal	379
Proposals for funded research	385
HOW TO GET STARTED WITH WRITING	400
The writing process	401
Forming the structure and preparing an outline	402
Retrieving and organizing notes	404
Drafting and redrafting	406
Presentation	412
Bibliographies, references and footnotes	413
CONCLUSIONS	418
THE NEXT STEPS: YOUR RESEARCH PROPOSAL	419
CHECKLIST OF ACTIVITIES THAT WILL PROGRESS YOUR RESEARCH	419
Consolidation and assessment	421
Further reading	422
ANSWERS TO EXERCISES	424

Acknowledgements

My grateful thanks go to Dr Rowland Newman and Professor Mike Jenks, who originally gave me inspiration to write this book; to Dr Bousmaha Baiche for his help; to Mrs Margaret Ackrill, Mrs Val Bacon and the postgraduate research students of the Department of Architecture, Oxford Brookes University, for their comments and suggestions; and to my wife and family for their unfailing support.

My thanks go to the following people and organizations for permission to reproduce material in this book: Dr Roland Newman, Margaret Ackrill, Dr Lawdy Wong, Dr Nigel Hiscock, Mark Austin, Dr Suanne Gibson, Dr Ruth Bartlett, Robert Illes, Alison Chisholm, Dr Louise Waite, Harry Dodd, R. K. Yin, Sage Publications Ltd and L. Cohen and L. Manion, ITPS Ltd, Routledge. Specific acknowledgement is made where the material appears.

I have greatly appreciated the guidance and help afforded by all the editorial team at Sage, in particular Patrick Brindle and Vanessa Harwood for their encouragement and patience.

Introduction

There is a real problem for students and practitioners embarking on a research project of knowing how to start researching and how to develop a research proposal in their chosen subject which will satisfy the requirements of their superiors, educational organizations and funding bodies. In general, supervisors and bosses have little or no time to instruct their students and employees in the theory and practice of research, so it is left to the novice researchers to wade through the bewildering variety of theoretical and technical books about research in order to try and develop a credible research proposal related to their interest. This must be done when the skills of the student or practitioner are often very rudimentary, and when he/she finds it difficult to make the connection between the general theory and practice of research and his/her own research interest.

The main objective of this book is to guide novice researchers, who are beginning to do research in any subject to do with social sciences, the environment, business studies, education and the humanities, towards writing a successful research proposal – a crucial document, as its approval is the condition for continuing research and often for obtaining funding. Most students beginning to study for a research degree, or attempting their first dissertation, have little knowledge or experience of research and are often not clear as to the exact subject they wish to research. Practitioners are also under pressure to work efficiently and in a well focused manner.

The objective of this book is achieved by systematically imparting a basic understanding of the theory of and approaches to research while at the same time helping the student/practitioner to develop the subject of his/her research, encouraging the formation of a high level of trained intellectual ability, critical analysis, rigour and independence of thought, fostering individual judgement and skill in the application of research theory and methods, and developing skills required in writing research proposals, reports and theses.

PARTICULAR FEATURES OF THE BOOK

The particular features of this book are the way it:

- combines the explanation of practical and theoretical aspects of research directly with the progressive development of the reader's ideas about his/her individual research topic
- always refers to the researcher's subject of study, with no dry theorizing which is difficult to relate to his/her individual research interests
- is divided into chapters with clearly limited objectives, requiring the researcher to apply the aspects of research he/she has learned in each chapter to the next stage in developing the proposal
- sets points for contemplation about the applicability of the learned aspects to the individual project and gives a framework for issues to be discussed with tutors and colleagues
- uses a direct approach, leading the reader step-by-step through the book with interesting and amusing self-assessed exercises to test and develop his/her knowledge.

STRUCTURE AND OUTLINE OF THE BOOK

The structure of the book is based on a combination of three sequential approaches. The first is a cumulative approach which introduces, step-by-step, the features of, and debate about, the academic subject of research theory and methods. This is offered in parallel with a problem-centred sequence which involves the researcher in the practical work of developing the skills needed to devise a good quality research proposal. There is thirdly an element of a spiral sequence, whereby concepts and techniques are reiterated and developed during the book as the researcher's understanding increases.

There are nine chapters in the book, which are designed to be worked through consecutively. The main sections in each chapter are devised to explain a major aspect of research theory or approach. These sections contain informative, discursive text, regularly interspersed with exercises for the researcher to consolidate and assess his/her understanding of the subjects presented.

There then follows a section ('the next steps') which consists of application to the reader's own area of research of the specific topics discussed in the earlier sections. Aims are set out and tasks are defined. This section is always exploratory in nature, and it is expected that the researcher will devise a range of alternative solutions to the tasks. The results of this work should, ideally, then be discussed with fellow students, colleagues, a tutor or a supervisor, who will wish to see that the researcher has understood the issues in the chapter and how they can be applied in practice. Decisions made at the end of each chapter consolidate progress towards writing the research proposal.

Each chapter concludes with a summary of the chapter's key words, suggestions for further reading (see later), and answers to the assessment exercises.

The wide range of approaches to the subject of research makes writing an introduction to research rather difficult. It is not possible within the scope of this book to cover every research strategy which might be relevant to the readers' interests. Therefore the book has been limited to explaining the characteristics of the major research approaches, and mentioning alternatives where appropriate. The reader will become aware that the subject of research is widely debated, and therefore a prescriptive approach is not appropriate. There is, however, a range of basic research techniques which it is essential to acquire, whatever the reader's subject, for example: analytical reading and thinking, note-taking and referencing skills, and writing skills.

Depending on the student's/practitioner's previous research experience and language skills, particularly if English is a foreign language, he/she might need to spend 10–20 hours on each chapter. It is important for the researcher to remember that he/she should continue to read widely in the chosen research subject while following this book, as specialist knowledge on the chosen subject will be required in order to fulfil the tasks set.

In this second edition short sections have been added at suitable points to recognize the differing needs of students at different levels of doing research projects. This book is aimed at the postgraduate readership, but there are significant differences about what is expected from taught Masters, MPhil and PhD students. It is assumed that most student readers are new to the research process and the demands made on research students.

An explanatory overview of the whole research process and the logic behind it has been inserted into Chapter 1; this section highlights some of the crucial decision stages and choices that need to be made. In Chapter 9, a summary of the steps required to produce a proposal has also been added, with references to sections in the book relevant to each step.

The layout has been redesigned to make it more accessible for students. There are now boxes with crucial information throughout the text, and detailed step-by-step checklists of activities at the end of each chapter. A full table of contents is given at the beginning of the book, and a glossary, based on the key words that appear at the end of each chapter, has been added at the end. As this book cannot go into detail about every aspect of research, an annotated bibliography has been added at the end of each chapter as a guide to further reading. In Chapter 7, on research methods, this section guides students to texts on specific methods, such as evaluation, conversation analysis, discourse analysis, and various forms of experiment.

A new chapter has been added (Chapter 8) which considers research ethics in more detail. The consideration of ethical matters, particularly in research that involves human beings, is getting ever more important in student research and is subject to vetting by relevant research ethics committees. An extended section on critical reading skills and writing literary reviews has been added to Chapter 2, as this is an essential aspect of research. I have also added a couple of new proposals in full in Chapter 9, as commendable and successful examples from the disciplines of social science and healthcare.

1

Research and the Research Problem

Introduction
The Research Approach
  What is Research?
  Scientific Method in Research
  The Interpretivist Alternative
Starting Your Own Research
  Types of Research Degree
  Overview of the Research Process
  The Research Problem
  Some Common Mistakes
  Aids to Locating and Analysing Problems
Conclusions
The Next Steps: Finding Your Research Problem Area
Checklist of Activities That Will Progress Your Research
Consolidation and Assessment
Key Words
Further Reading
Answers to Exercises

- To explain what research is and what it is not, the criteria for research and the different types of research approach.
- To present some aspects of the debate about the nature of knowledge and the value of scientific method.
- To introduce the concept at the heart of any research project – the research problem – and to discuss what a researchable problem is.
- To warn of common mistakes.
- To describe how a research problem is found and stated.

INTRODUCTION

The shortest way of describing the contents of this chapter is to say that it provides a starting point for your research efforts.

It introduces the concept of research as understood in the academic world, and contrasts it to the loose way the word 'research' is used in everyday speech. However, even in the academic world, the nature of research is the subject of a great deal of debate. The characteristics of scientific method are briefly explained, and some aspects of the debate are outlined. These are treated in much greater detail in Chapter 5.

An essential early step in the process of research is to find a research problem. What a research problem is, and how to find one, are explained. The nature of your problem will, in its turn, influence the form of your research. It is this quest for a problem which forms the task in the final section, where what you have learned in the earlier sections is applied to your own subject.

Key words are shown in bold and are repeated in the margin so you can scan through the chapter to check up on their meaning.

THE RESEARCH APPROACH

What is research?

'Research' is a term loosely used in everyday speech to describe a multitude of activities, such as collecting masses of information, delving into esoteric theories, and producing wonderful new products. It is important that a student or practitioner embarking on a programme of academic or practical research has a clear idea of what the word 'research' really means, and clears away any misconceptions which might exist owing to its common use in other fields.

It is, therefore, worth looking at a few of the ways that the word is used in common language to describe activities, often called research, which are *not* research in its real meaning, and also at some of the emotive language that surrounds the term.

These are some of the ways in which the term 'research' is wrongly used:

1 *As a mere gathering of facts or information*   'I'll go and do a bit of research into the subject.' This usually means quickly reading through a few books or magazines to become better informed about something. Such information can be collected in other ways too, e.g. by asking people questions in the street or by recording the number of vehicles driving along a road. This kind of activity may more accurately be called 'collection of information', and can be carried out in a systematic and thorough way. It certainly can be seen as an important *part* of research.

2 *Moving facts from one situation to another*   'I have done my research, and come up with this information which I present in this paper.' It is easy to collect information and reassemble it in a report or paper, duly annotated and referenced, and think of it as research. However, even if the work is meticulously carried out, and brings enlightenment about the subject to the author and the reader, one vital ingredient of the research process is missing – the interpretation of the information. One might call this form of activity 'assembly of information'. This is, as with the collection of information, an important component of research, but not its entirety.

3 *As an esoteric activity, far removed from practical life*   'He's just gone back into his laboratory to bury himself in his research into the mysterious processes of bimolecular fragmentation.' While many research projects deal with abstract and theoretical subjects, it is often forgotten that the activity of research has greatly influenced all aspects of our daily lives and created our understanding of the world. It is an activity which is prompted by our need to satisfy our natural curiosity and our wish to make sense of the world around us.

4 *As a word to get your product noticed*   'Years of painstaking research have produced this revolutionary, labour-saving product!' Very often the term 'research'

is used in an emotive fashion in order to impress and build confidence. If you ask for evidence of the research process and methodology, you are likely to be faced with incomprehension, muddled thinking, and possibly even worse: the product may be the outcome of mere guesswork!

So how can true research be defined? Box 1.1 suggests some alternatives.

Box 1.1   Definitions of research

The *Oxford Encyclopedic English Dictionary* defines research as:

   (a)   the systematic investigation into the study of materials, sources etc. in order to establish facts and reach new conclusions
   (b)   an endeavour to discover new or collate old facts etc. by the scientific study of a subject or by a course of critical investigation.

Leedy defines it from a more utilitarian point of view:

   Research is a procedure by which we attempt to find systematically, and with the support of demonstrable fact, the answer to a question or the resolution of a problem. (1989, p. 5)

Dominowski is so terse in his definition that he seems to miss the point (see above):

   Research is a fact-finding activity. (1980, p. 2)

Kerlinger uses more technical language to define it as:

   the systematic, controlled, empirical and critical investigation of hypothetical propositions about presumed relations among natural phenomena. (1970, p. 8)

You could go on finding definitions of research, which would, as in the examples in the box, differ in emphasis and scope. What is certain is that there are many different opinions about and approaches to research. However, as a means of achieving a greater comprehension of our world, research distinguishes itself from the two other basic and more ancient means, those of experience and reasoning.

Briefly, **experience** results in knowledge and understanding gained either individually or as a group or society, or shared by experts or leaders, through day-to-day living. Reflective awareness of the world around us, present to a degree even in other mammals, provides invaluable knowledge. The most immediate form of experience is personal experience, the body of knowledge gained individually through encountering situations and events in life. A child learns to

experience

Figure 1.1 Knowledge gained from experience forms an essential aid to our understanding and activities in everyday life

walk by trial and error, and an adult gets adept at decorating jobs in the house after renovating several rooms. When solutions to problems are not to be found within the personal experience of an individual, then he or she may turn to those who have wider or more specialist experience for advice, for example a solicitor in legal matters. Beyond this are the 'experts' who have written books on partic-ular subjects, e.g. health care or the finer points of playing golf.

Knowledge gained from experience forms an essential aid to our understand-ing and activities in everyday life. However, it does have severe limitations as a means of methodically and reliably extending knowledge and understanding of the world. This is because learning from experience tends to be rather haphazard and uncontrolled. Conclusions are often quickly drawn and not exhaustively tested, 'common sense' is invoked as self-evident, and the advice of experts is frequently misplaced or seen as irrelevant. Despite these shortcomings, experience can be a valuable starting point for systematic research, and may provide a wealth of questions to be investigated and ideas to be tested.

reasoning   **Reasoning** is a method of coming to conclusions by the use of logical argument. There are three basic forms of reasoning: deductive, inductive and a combination of both called inductive/deductive. Deductive reasoning was first developed by the Ancient Greeks, and was refined by Aristotle through his deductive syllogisms. An argument based on deduction begins with general statements and, through logical argument, comes to a specific conclusion. A syllogism is the simplest form of this kind of argument and consists of a major general premise (statement), followed by a minor, more specific premise, and a conclusion which follows logically. Here is a simple example:

All live mammals breathe.
This cow is a live mammal.
Therefore, this cow breathes.

Inductive reasoning works the other way round. It starts from specific observations and derives general conclusions therefrom. Its logical form cannot be so neatly encapsulated in a three-line format, but a simple example will demonstrate the line of reasoning:

> All swans which have been observed are white in colour.
> Therefore one can conclude that all swans are white.

The value of inductive reasoning was revealed by Bacon in the 1600s. By careful and systematic observation of the events in the world around us, many theories have been evolved to explain the rules of nature. Darwin's theory of evolution and Mendel's discovery of genetics are perhaps the most famous theories claimed (even by their authors) to be derived from inductive reasoning.

However, deductive reasoning was found to be limiting because it could only handle certain types of statement, and could become increasingly divorced from observation and experience. Purely inductive reasoning proved to be unwieldy and haphazard, and in practice was rarely applied to the letter. Medawar (1969, pp. 10–11) quoted Darwin himself in his sixth edition of *Origin of Species* where he wrote of himself that he 'worked on true Baconian principles, and without any theory collected facts on a wholesale scale', but later on admitted that he could not resist forming a hypothesis on every subject.

But when inductive and deductive reasoning were combined to form inductive/ deductive reasoning, the to-and-fro process of developing hypotheses (testable theories) inductively from observations, charting their implications by deduction, and testing them to refine or reject them in the light of the results, formed a powerful basis for the progress of knowledge, especially of scientific knowledge.

It is the combination of experience with deductive and inductive reasoning which is the foundation of modern scientific research. Three characteristics of research can be seen to distinguish it from gaining knowledge purely by experience or reasoning, as shown in Box 1.2.

Box 1.2   Three characteristics of research

1   Gaining experience is an uncontrolled and haphazard activity, while research is systematic and controlled.
2   Reasoning can operate in an abstract world, divorced from reality, while research is empirical and turns to experience and the world around us for validation.
3   Unlike experience and reason, research aims to be self-correcting. The process of research involves rigorously testing the results obtained, and methods and results are open to public scrutiny and criticism.

In short:

> Research is a combination of both experience and reasoning and must be regarded as the most successful approach to the discovery of truth. (Cohen and Manion, 1994, p. 5)

When we talk about this type of systematic research, it is usually assumed that it makes use of the rigorous and questioning techniques of scientific enquiry. This form of enquiry is called scientific method.

Scientific method in research

Scientific method is the discipline which forms the foundation of modern scientific enquiry. It is therefore important to mention some of the main assumptions made in this method of enquiry, and to describe some of its major characteristics.

Scientific method has been applied, to a greater or lesser extent, to research in some areas not principally thought of as 'scientific', such as sociology, psychology and education, although some scientists question the appropriateness of doing this. For example, Medawar writes: 'I doubt very much whether a methodology based on the intellectual practices of physicists and biologists (supposing that methodology to be sound) would be of any great use to sociologists' (1969, p. 13).

Assumptions

According to Cohen and Manion (1994, pp. 12–16) there are five major assumptions underlying scientific method.

order

The first major assumption is the belief that there is some kind of **order** in the universe, and that it is possible for us to gain some understanding of this order. This is linked with the idea of determinism, the assumption that events have causes, and that the links between events and causes can be revealed. This regularity enables some predictions to be made about future events (e.g. if gravity causes apples to fall today, it will also cause them to fall tomorrow). Scientists do admit, however, that owing to imperfect knowledge, predictions of varying levels of probability often result.

external reality

The second assumption is that, in order to enable us to gain this understanding of the world, there must be an agreement between people that **external reality** exists, and that people recognize the same reality, a public or shared reality. It is hardly necessary to point out that much philosophic debate has been devoted to the nature of reality. Nevertheless, scientific enquiry relies on the acceptance of the reliability of knowledge gained by experience to provide empirical evidence (evidence which is verifiable by observation) to support or refute its theories.

reliability

The third assumption is the **reliability** of human perception and intellect. Despite the many ways in which our senses can be tricked, researchers depend on their senses to record and measure their work reliably. Reasoning is an important method of organizing data and ideas, and is regarded, if used correctly, as a dependable tool of research. Human memory also plays a major role in research. To avoid questioning at every single stage, some credence must be given to the power of memory to provide reliable knowledge.

The fourth assumption is the principle of **parsimony**. Phenomena should be explained in as economic a manner as possible. Needless complexity is abhorred, and scientists aim to achieve the most elegant and simple theories.

parsimony

The fifth assumption is that of **generality**. This is the assumption that there can be valid relationships between the particular cases investigated by the researcher and the general situation in the world at large. It is accepted that these relationships can be relatively unproblematic in some sciences (e.g. chemistry and physics) but that in others, with a larger number of unknown factors (e.g. sociology), there is a weaker chance of generality.

generality

Characteristics of research which uses scientific method

Accepting these assumptions, research using the scientific method displays six characteristics which distinguish it from other methods of enquiry, as shown in Box 1.3.

Box 1.3   Characteristics of enquiry by scientific method

1 *It is generated by a question*   We are surrounded by unanswered questions, unresolved problems, with conjecture and unproven beliefs. A questioning mind is the precondition for research. Why, how, when do things happen? What do events mean? What caused them? All these are questions which can generate research activity. Such a question is often referred to as the research problem.

2 *It necessitates clarification of a goal*   Without a clear statement of the objectives and what is intended to be done, the research cannot be successful.

3 *It entails a specific programme of work*   Research needs to be carefully planned in order to achieve its objectives and reach conclusions.

4 *It is aimed at increasing understanding by interpreting facts or ideas and reaching some conclusions about their meaning*   The significance of facts or ideas depends on the way in which the intellect can extract meaning from them.

5 *It requires reasoned argument to support conclusions*   In order to communicate an ordered sequence of ideas, a clear logical argument is required.

6 *It is reiterative in its activities*   Advances in knowledge and interpretations of facts are based on previous knowledge, which, in turn, is expanded by the advances. Then resolution of research problems often gives rise to further problems which need resolving.

In addition, research often:

• divides the principal question or problem into more practicable sub-questions or sub-problems. Problems are often too large or abstract to examine as a whole. Dividing them into component parts (sub-problems) enables them to be practically investigated.

- is tentatively guided by assertions called hypotheses (informed guesses or tentative assertions). Testing these hypotheses provides a direction for exploration.
- requires measurable data in attempting to answer the question which initiated the research.

EXERCISE
1.1

1   Without looking back in the text, can you list five major assumptions which underlie scientific method?

2   Examine the following texts, which were written by researchers to describe their research subjects, and decide whether they contain any of the characteristics of research using scientific method. If you can find them in the texts, summarize in a few words the following:

(a)   the main question or problem
(b)   the main goal or objectives of the research
(c)   how the research work was done
(d)   the main conclusion(s)
(e)   the main argument followed.

Was the text clearly written, making the characteristics (a)–(e) easy to find, or did you have to search carefully to find them amongst all the words? Briefly describe the difficulties, if you experienced any.

Note: references in texts are not included in the reference list at the end of the book.

Text 1 (based on Mikellides, 1990, pp. 3–18)

We need light to see around us and colour to add beauty to our lives. The effect on us of light, however, goes beyond our everyday assumptions and expectations. Rikard Kuller, in his *Annotated Bibliography*, listed 1700 references on the psychophysiological effects of light. In both scientific and aesthetic accounts, colours have been classified according to their purported effects on humans. Hues such as orange, red and yellow are seen to be exciting and stimulating, while blue, turquoise and green are regarded as calming and relaxing.

To counter criticism of these views, Robert Gerard showed in his studies in 1958 that the different effects of blue and red on the organism could be measured by changes in the central and automatic nervous systems. Ali, in 1972, supported these findings by demonstrating differing levels of cortical arousal following the shining of blue and red light directly into the eyes of ten normal subjects for six minutes. A different approach taken by Lars Sivik (1970) demonstrated, using photo-simulation techniques, that chromatic strength rather than hue affects the exciting or calming properties of a colour. Kuller (1972) using full-scale spaces showed that strong and weak colours appeared exciting and calming respectively.

The approaches of these four studies were very different. The first and second used physiological measures using coloured light whilst the other two used semantic differential analysis using pigments as the colour stimulation. The first two showed pure coloured light in a laboratory setting, the second two, colour in the context of indoor and outdoor settings. This study aims to bridge the gap between these sets of experiments. Surface pigments in real environments were used, with long exposure periods, using alpha rhythms recorded on EEG and EKG recordings to assess the level of arousal. The objective of the setting was to make a closer simulation of the real-life experience of the subjects.

Twenty-four subjects were exposed to four conditions in a room-sized environment: a completely red visual field, a completely blue visual field, a visual field with the left part blue and the right part red, and vice versa, each for twenty minutes. The measures of chromatic strength and lightness of the blue and red were identical. The data collected were analysed by means of several analyses of variance.

The most notable result of this study was that the central nervous system showed no significant differences when red and blue spaces were experienced. These results support, by the addition of confirming physiological data, Sivik's and Kuller's findings that, chromatic strength and lightness being controlled, colour hues do not affect excitement. This information will have important implications for design, as it contradicts the guidance given in design manuals.

Text 2 (based on Freese et al., 1999, p. 207)
The lasting influences of a person's position in the order of birth in a family have been the subject of an extended and heated discussion in sociology and other disciplines. In response to Sulloway's (1996) *Born to Rebel: Birth Order, Family Dynamics, and Creative Lives*, there has been an increase in interest in the likely influences of the order of birth on social attitudes. In comparison with the variables of gender, class or race, Sulloway found, through the use of quantitative and historical data, that birth order is a better predictor of social attitudes. His original theory attests that the influence of the order of birth is pervasive across time and society.

This study uses current data to test Sulloway's assertion that adults who were born the first in families are more authoritative and conservative and less subtle than those born later. Taking 24 measures of social attitudes from the General Social Survey (GSS), an examination of cases resulted in no evidence to support these assertions, neither in terms of significant effects nor even in terms of the direction of non-significant coefficients. As a result of further research, it was found that comparable results were obtained using all (202) relevant attitudinal items on the GSS yields.

As a result, it was concluded that variables rejected by Sulloway, such as family size, race, gender and social class, were all more strongly linked to social attitudes than was the order of birth. Therefore it can be inferred that theories relating to the order of birth in families might better be considered more modestly in terms of slight influences in limited areas and in specific societies.

Text 3 (based on Walliman, 1993, p. 5)
While the group self-build housing process is widely regarded as being an effective method of reducing the costs of acquiring accommodation, a review of literature indicated that the self-build option was not generally available to people in Britain who were most likely to be in housing need, i.e. those who had low incomes and low levels of building and managerial skills. Since 1980, this problem has been recognized in several pioneering group self-build housing projects, where innovations aimed at lowering the levels of income and skills required of the self-builders were introduced. However, no systematic analysis of the application and effectiveness of these innovations had been made. Necessary feedback for subsequent projects was therefore lacking.

An examination of the history and of the theoretical debate around self-help and self-build housing found a wide diversity of activities and interpretations and concluded that any analysis of a self-help housing project or movement must embrace an awareness of the context in which it operates and the motives underlying the methods used in order that a valid interpretation of the process and its outcomes can be made.

The context and motives behind recent self-build activities in Britain were investigated, and the analysis of recent innovations in group self-build housing in Britain was structured by the formulation of a general question about the effectiveness of the innovative methods, and of three derived questions which centred on the three fundamental procedures of the self-build process: funding, design and management. As a response to these questions, nine selected recent innovative group self-build projects were studied to provide a detailed comparative analysis of the characteristics of the innovations, and their effectiveness in lowering the income and skill thresholds of the self-build process.

It was concluded that innovations in the self-build process had succeeded in reducing, and in some cases virtually obviating, the levels of income and initial skills required of the self-builders. The procedures of funding, design and management were found to be highly interdependent, and that innovations in funding and design required a specific response in the management procedure in order to make them effective.

Though innovative techniques have enabled the group self-build process to be an effective method of producing social housing, the process was found to be complex and requiring government funding and support to make the projects viable, to protect the self-builders from the full effects of market forces and to guarantee their income levels. Because of the complexity of the process, extensive professional support was required to initiate projects and to guide the self-builders.

From these conclusions, recommendations were made about the sectors in which additional public support is required and how improvements in the availability of information about successful innovations in the group self-build housing process could be made.

Thought   *You will find that this technique of analytical reading is a valuable skill which is worth developing to a high degree. You will have to sift through an enormous quantity of written information in the course of your investigations, so the ability to identify quickly the crucial contents of a text will save you time in judging if it is relevant and of value to your research.*

The interpretivist alternative

Although scientific method is widely used in many forms of research, it does not, and never has, enjoyed total hegemony in all subjects. Some of the world's greatest thinkers have disagreed with the tenets of positivism contained in scientific method. Positivism, a theory whose development was influenced by nineteenth century empiricist thinkers such as Bacon and Hume, holds that every rationally justifiable assertion can be scientifically verified or is capable of logical or mathematical proof. The alternative approach to research is based on the philosophical doctrine of idealism. It maintains that the view of the world that we see around us is the creation of the mind. This does not mean that the world is not real, but rather means that we can only experience it personally through our perceptions which are influenced by our preconceptions and beliefs; we are not neutral, disembodied observers.

The German philosopher Immanuel Kant (1724–1804) even went so far as to claim that the objects of our experience, those things we see, hear and feel, are simply manifestations which have no existence of their own apart from in our thoughts. Although he was at the head of various scientific institutions, Goethe (1749–1832), the German philosopher and writer, shared with Blake (1757–1827), the English artist and poet, the belief that the universe was more like a living organism than a mechanism, and that, however exactly it could be measured, life could not be fully conceived of without 'inner experience'. The Danish philosopher Kierkegaard (1813–1855) rejected the dehumanization of the individual, which he believed resulted from scientific positivism. He regarded the capacity for subjectivity to be of greater value than that of objectivity, and that it could bring an individual nearer to the truth.

Steering a course away from the romanticism of these philosophical idealists, another German philosopher, Wilhelm Dilthey (1833–1911), agreed that although in the physical world we can only study the appearance of a thing rather than the thing itself, we are, because of our own humanity, in a position to know about human consciousness and its roles in society. The purpose here is not to search for causal explanations, but to find understanding. As a method, this presupposes that to gain understanding there must be at least some common ground between the researcher and the people who are being studied.

Max Weber (1864–1920), developing and refining Dilthey's ideas, believed that empathy is not necessary or even possible in some cases, and that it was feasible to understand the intentionality of conduct and to pursue objectivity in terms of cause and effect. He wished to bridge the divide between the traditions of positivism and interpretivism by being concerned to investigate both the meanings and the material conditions of action.

More recently, Thomas Kuhn cast doubt on whether science is capable of living up to its claims of being a purely rational pursuit of knowledge. In his book *The Structure of Scientific Revolutions* (1970) he argued that scientists rarely attempt to test existing knowledge by seeking alternatives to established theories, but prefer to find methods of substantiating existing beliefs. The established customs of science as a profession, he maintained, determine the acceptance of particular scientific theories rather than promoting the disinterested rational methods of enquiry. Just as argued by the French philosopher Foucault, the practice of science is shown to control what is permitted to count as knowledge. Thus there is no progress in science, only changing perspectives.

The basic assumptions of scientific method have been questioned by challenging the nature of facts and their rational foundation. Wittgenstein maintained that all our attempts to understand facts are fundamentally affected by the framework of our particular cultural and social background. Similarly, Quine detected a blurring of the scientific distinction between facts and ideas. It is worth, at this stage, looking back at the assumptions of scientific method mentioned earlier in this chapter, to find out which of them have been challenged. The existence of order, as present in the universe, which can be revealed by scientific study, is questioned. It is more likely that we are imposing our ordered understanding of the universe, rather than discovering an order that is already there. We also have an individual understanding of external reality, opened to our own interpretation and based on our view of the world. This reduces the feasibility of attaining reliability, as personal perceptions cannot be reliably shared. In any intellectual thought, parsimony is regarded as a virtue. Whilst understanding of a situation can lead to greater knowledge, it is not always possible or even desirable to ensure generality.

It hardly needs saying that scientists generally refute this challenge to the impartiality and rigour of scientific enquiry. Take for example the lively public debate about the rational foundation of science that was conducted at the annual meeting of the British Association for the Advancement of Science in September 1994 in Loughborough, UK. The debate – about the relationship between science and the sociology of science – was extraordinarily heated. The question, posed by sociologists, was whether science was a 'social construct', an activity inextricably bound up with human society and therefore subject to the vagaries of the social system, rather than an activity dedicated entirely to a dispassionate search for the truth, eliminating as far as possible all disturbing human influences.

A series of articles and comments by eminent researchers in the *Times Higher Educational Supplement* (30 September 1994) presented opposing views on the issues. Harry Collins, professor of sociology at the University of Bath, defended the assertions made by social scientists, and Peter Atkins, fellow of Lincoln College, Oxford, and lecturer in physical chemistry, replied and rejected their viewpoint. Exercise 1.2 contains summaries of their arguments to support the stances taken on the two sides of the dispute.

Anyone actively involved in serious research, in both natural science and the social sciences and in many other disciplines that cross subject boundaries, should be aware of the debate concerning the 'unbiased purity' of the results of scientific method, and of its effectiveness in the search for 'the truth'.

EXERCISE
1.2

Read the following summaries and:

1 Summarize the four or five main points of each argument. Try to summarize each point in one sentence.
2 Search within the arguments for any agreement with the point made on the opposing side. If you find any, what are they? Do you think that the arguments are part of a dialogue and form a direct response to each other?

3 Explain in two or three paragraphs what conclusions you have drawn from the arguments presented, and state whether you think that they have relevance to your own subject, and if so, how.

Note: references in these summaries are not included in the reference list.

Science is a social construct

The study of the sociology and history of scientific knowledge, which has been continuing for a quarter of a century, has revealed remarkable ambiguities in the results of scientific experiments and unexpected flexibilities in theory. It must be concluded that the progress of science depends on a necessary consensus in a society of what could be counted as believable. This reliance on social acceptability depends on the social context. It therefore follows that science must be seen as 'a social construct'. This issue has only recently become an issue with natural scientists; most have reacted positively to the idea. However, the challenge to the unquestioned authority of science has increased uncertainty amongst scientists, resulting in some violent attacks on the findings of the sociology of science. It is particularly the issue of relativism that provokes lively debate.

In this context, relativism can be explained in the following way. A sociologist must examine the course of a scientific development from the perspectives of the scientists involved and not be unduly influenced by the consequences of the development, e.g. the production of a new scientific proof. For example, the special theory of relativity was said to have been proved by the Michelson–Morley experiment of 1887, which showed that light travelled at the same speed in all directions. This 'proof' might deflect the sociologist from the realization that Michelson was never satisfied with the reliability of his experiment. Additionally, an attempt to repeat the experiment by Miller in 1924 showed significant variations in the speed of light, a finding which resulted in Miller being awarded the physics prize of the American Association for the Advancement of Science in 1925. Despite there being no resolution to the problem up to the 1950s, the belief that the special theory of relativity had been proved was not dislodged. The sociologist or historian must therefore ignore whether the speed of light is constant, and rather find an explanation of why the result of one experiment was believed rather than another. This is methodological relativism.

The attacks levelled by some natural scientists on the sociology and history of scientific knowledge are based, not on a rebuttal of the theories and findings contained in reports, but on the accusation that studies are not serious and are a form of pseudo-science. This can be detected in the journal *Nature*'s satirical attack on Jacques Benveniste's study of the homeopathic potency of water. Similarly, Wolpert, at the Loughborough conference, accused social scientists of being hostile to science, obscurantist, and considering only fringe scientific events and presenting no evidence for their views. These accusations are not justified.

Take, for example, the book *The Golem* by Collins and Pinch, which shows how relativism works in practice – a book that Wolpert has read and reviewed. Eight case studies of outstanding achievements in science are examined, amongst them experiments to do with special and general relativity, the origins of life, and the solar neutrino problem – all carried out by foremost scientists. These were definitely not fringe scientific events. As for obscurantism, the book was hailed by a reviewer in *Nature* for its deft and entertaining writing. The tenor of the book was also sympathetic to scientific endeavour, admiring the expertise and craftsmanship of the scientists. These facts all refute Wolpert's attempt to marginalize the work of writers in the sociology and history of science.

It is in the nature of this sociological and historical approach that the results cannot be 'proven' and are therefore open to dispute. It is right that this should be so. The methodologies have slowly developed over 25 years, and case studies have been gradually collected and studied. This is a slow process as these events cannot be set up in a laboratory like those in natural science, but must be waited for till they occur naturally.

Researchers in this field nearly all admit to be lovers of science. They are looking at science in a new way, one that appreciates the valuable work being done but questions the claims that all uncertainty and doubt are being dispelled. In fact, scientific enquiry is akin to study in the arts and social sciences: exciting, down-to-earth and argumentative rather than conforming to its reputation for being steely, impersonal and machine-like in its precision.

Science is not a social construct

It is the responsibility of science to reveal the truth that lies buried deeply in nature's wondrous complexity. The best way to do this is through the use of scientific method, to inch forward with theoretical development refined and inspired by experimentation. Scientific method is probably the only reliable way forward, though other methods are still being undertaken.

One example is religion, definitely conditioned by social forces through its reliance on meditation, personal revelation and social coercion. The dangers of 'socially constructed' methods of discovery are indicated by its enormous capacity to confuse and total failure to clarify.

The universality of science is one indication of its independence from society. Its substantiated laws and theories apply and are accepted worldwide, unaffected by the local historical, religious, political and social circumstances. There is no evidence that Western science has destroyed alternative methods of scientific enquiry, and those that dispute this are probably aroused either by jealousy or by a wish to impede the progress of science. Some reputed areas of knowledge that conflict with the current paradigms, such as the paranormal, are all based on evidence that cannot be tested by verifiable observations. Their theories cannot be meshed into globally coherent theoretical structures.

A second indication is the fact that science evolves and progresses smoothly, despite the turmoils and revolutions in society. The so-called scientific revolutions, such as the development of relativity and quantum mechanics, can now be seen to be elaborations of classical physics, preserving many of its concepts and procedures. Although theories are refined or rejected during the process, science always progresses and expands its power of explanation through rigorous experimentation and theory building, and not through politicking and social manipulation. The truth is exposed despite surrounding social conditions.

A third indication is the compatibility of scientific knowledge gained from highly disparate sources. Despite the social and intellectual variety of sources, e.g. the study of particles at the CERN laboratories and the monitoring of sea slugs in Peru, the implications of the results never conflict as one would expect them to if science were based on social differences – a social construct.

The fourth indication is science's reliance on mathematics to explain most of the fundamental aspects of nature (e.g. elementary particles, motion, space–time, cosmogenesis), which removes it totally from the social sphere. Mathematics is a totally logical form of expression with an internal consistency unaffected by time and surrounding conditions. So how can knowledge gained in this way be regarded as a social construct?

This independence from social, political, racial and religious influences indicated by science's universal character contradicts the belief that it is a social construct. Any deliberate effort to distort the truth by a powerful social group would soon be exposed, because scientists depend totally on their efforts to uncover the truth, both for their livelihood and professional advancement and perhaps for a share of posterity.

It would be difficult to understand how modern technology, based as it is on the profound postulates of conventional science, would be able to operate if science was a social construct. It is ridiculous to maintain that the development of technology is part of a sinister plot by an exclusive group, even with regard to the emerging industry based on genetic engineering. Science is remarkable for its characteristic of uniting minds across the world, rather than dividing and segregating them as in the social constructs of religion and politics. There are no social barriers to anyone who wants to take part in scientific endeavour, as long as they are willing to conform to the high standards of integrity and the principle of open experimentation that is the ultimate path to greater knowledge.

It seems clear that, if eminent academics disagree on the most fundamental aspects of research, there is little scope for you to discuss these issues at great length in your thesis or research report in order to try to arrive at a definitive answer. It will be necessary to personally decide (and if relevant, explain) your position in the debate, and take your argument from there.

Thought

It would be impossible, within the scope of this book, to investigate in detail all the different approaches used in academic research. As scientific method is used, if only partially, in many forms of modern research, this book sets out to explain the theory and techniques of scientific method, and how it can be applied to various research topics. However, there is also explanation about a range of other research approaches, particularly those that have been developed to produce a more holistic or discursive examination of situations and phenomena, mostly focusing on humans and human activities in society.

While a more detailed examination of forms of enquiry is made in Chapter 5, it is worthwhile at this stage to point out some of the ways of categorizing the different types of approach to systematic research. One way of broadly distinguishing different approaches to research is by looking at the way in which the collected information is appraised, as in Box 1.4.

Box 1.4 Ways to appraise data
1 By counting and assessing numbers: *quantitative research*.   2 By measuring and evaluating qualities: *qualitative research*.

Yet another way is to examine what are the general aims of the research. A popular view is that research is dedicated to increasing knowledge in a particular subject and to systematizing our knowledge of the world. A more dynamic view holds that the role of the researcher is to make new discoveries, to change our perception of the world, and to point to ways of improving life. These two aims are not mutually exclusive. Medawar (1984, p. 40) quotes Bacon as urging a combination of both these approaches.

Types of research can be distinguished by the settings in which they take place – natural or contrived. Natural settings are those where nothing (or as little as possible) of the subject of study is changed by the researcher, in order to gain information about things as they are in their undisturbed state. An example of this is observing the movements of people across an open square. In contrived settings, the researcher determines the surrounding situation in order to control conditions: for example, the movement of people in different arrangements of an exhibition may be studied. There is a range of the extent to which a natural setting can be controlled to produce a contrived setting.

More will be said about different types of research in Chapter 3.

STARTING YOUR OWN RESEARCH

Types of research degree

Although they are all concerned with learning to do research, postgraduate degrees such as taught Masters courses, MPhils and PhDs have somewhat different detailed requirements that relate more to the nature and scope of the research activities than to the methods used.

Taught Masters courses do not require original research to be carried out. Original research means that you will end up by making a contribution to knowledge that is novel and unique, and that creates a step forward in that particular branch of learning. The research element in Masters courses is used to deepen understanding of the taught subject in an individual way by employing some of the methods of research, and as a result providing some interesting insights into the subject. This usually takes the form of having to write a dissertation based on one of the themes of the course. The amount of guidance or instruction will vary depending on the type and subject of the course. Sometimes the research topic will be stipulated, which relieves the student from a lot of soul-searching for a suitable research problem. Even when not stipulated, the choice of a research topic is simplified owing to the focused nature of the course and the usual requirements of relevance to it. As usual in these cases, you should carefully read the instructions relating to the required research element to establish the freedoms and constraints involved.

Master of Philosophy and Doctor of Philosophy are pure research degrees that require you to do individual research – the taught elements being concentrated on research theory and practice rather than the subject of your research. You might have total freedom in the choice of your subject or, if you have been engaged on a funded research project, very little. There is a spectrum of situations between these extremes. It is wise to become aware of the situation in your case so that you can take the appropriate actions.

The Master of Philosophy degree is a comprehensive exercise in all stages of the research process, carried out on an individual basis. It is the individual nature of the exercise that distinguishes it from the taught Masters courses. The research into the subject through literature reviews replaces the taught element, and the students are left individually to identify the research topic. Although the outcome of the research must be authoritative and interesting, it is not expected that a significant and original contribution to knowledge be made.

The Doctor of Philosophy does require this. One of the conditions for awarding the degree is that the research has in some way cast new light onto the subject, by promoting greater understanding, producing significant new information, or formulating new theory. This means that for a time, the burgeoning Doctor will be the world expert on his/her particular chosen topic.

The common element in all of the degrees outlined above is that they are, some more than others, exercises in research. The student will have to demonstrate knowledge of research theory and methods and the ability to apply these in an appropriate and successful manner relevant to the chosen topic. You might consider that the topic itself serves merely as a vehicle in order to make this demonstration possible. That is perhaps too cynical a view. The topic must be the driving force behind the project and, particularly at PhD level, the research must make some contribution to knowledge about the subject. But without a proper understanding of research and its application, this knowledge will not be discovered.

Perhaps you are not doing a research degree at all, but are embarking on a research project as part of your work. Most of the issues that you will face will be similar to those faced by academic researchers. The major differences might be the greater resources available to you, the lack of access to supervision and advice, and the stresses of work in a professional work context. What will be the same, however, is the requirement that the research has clear and achievable goals and is carried out efficiently using the appropriate research methods.

Overview of the research process

Although the process of doing research will be examined in more detail in Chapter 6, it will probably be a help to explain briefly what you are letting yourself into at this early stage! A research project, whatever its size and complexity, consists of defining some kind of a research problem, working out how this problem can be investigated, doing the investigation work, coming to conclusions on the basis of what one has found out, and then reporting the outcome in some form or other to inform others of the work done. The differences between research projects are due to their different scales of time, resources and extent, pioneering qualities, and rigour.

Whatever the research approach, it is worth considering generally what the research process consists of and what are the crucial decision stages and choices that need to be made. Box 1.5 poses four basic questions.

Box 1.5   Basic research questions

The answers to four important questions underpin the framework of any research project:

- What are you going to do?
- Why are you going to do it?
- How are you going to do it?
- When are you going to do it?

The actual doing of the research is subject to the nature of the answers to these questions, and involves the most crucial decision making. Obviously the answers are not simple: this book has been written to help you formulate your own answers in relation to your own research project.

What are you going to do?

The title and aims of the research will succinctly summarize the answer to this question. Obviously, a longer explanation will also be needed to elaborate on the purpose of the research and the outcomes that are being aimed at. Clarity is essential. I well remember my supervisor halting me in full flight, as I gave a convoluted explanation of the need for research efforts in my subject, with the question, 'But what are *you* going to *do*?'

Why are you going to do it?

The answer to this question involves an analysis of the current situation in the area of intended research and an argument to support the reasons why the research is necessary. Problems should be revealed that require a solution. Also important is to explain how the outcomes of the research should provide the solutions to the problems that have been revealed.

How are you going to do it?

Research is a very practical occupation, however much brainwork lies behind it. A plan of action must be laid out that shows how the problems will be investigated, what information will be collected using which methods, and how this information will be analysed in order to come to conclusions. These processes may need special equipment, access to special facilities, consultations with particular people, specialist knowledge about computer programs, and many other practical matters.

When are you going to do it?

Programming your time is essential as time is so limited and the possibilities so huge. The practicality of the project can be demonstrated by a chart showing exactly what will be done when.

As an initial indication before we get into a lot of detail, Diagram 1.1 explains the sequence of activities for a typical research project. This will give you an overview of the major steps in the research process, whatever the size of the project. The size of the project has more influence on the extent of the various stages than on their nature.

The diagram shows a rather linear sequence of tasks, far tidier than anything in reality, which is subject to constant reiteration as knowledge and understanding increase. However, a diagram like this can be used as a basis for a programme of work in the form of a timetable, and the progress of the project can be gauged by comparing the current stage of work with the steps in the process.

If you are doing a dissertation for a taught Masters course, your research probably will be fairly light on the detailed research stages, though an MPhil thesis will require fairly comprehensive data collection and analysis stages. PhDs and most contract research are heavily dependent on the latter stages of the research process to produce new information and valuable insights. Notice how in the latter stages, the requirement for writing up the work becomes important. There is no point in doing research if the results are not recorded, even if only for your own use, though usually many more people will be interested to read about the outcomes, not least your examiner.

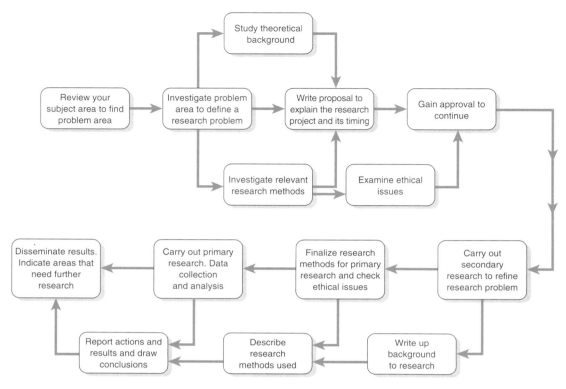

Diagram 1.1 The research process

The research problem

It should be evident from what you have read so far that in order to carry out research, you need to start by identifying a question which demands an answer, or a need which requires a resolution, or a riddle which seeks a solution, which can be developed into a research problem: the heart of the research project.

Students starting their research degree course, and practitioners wishing to become involved in research, tend to come from widely different backgrounds, and are equipped with varied amounts of knowledge and degrees of experience in their chosen field of study. While most are fairly sure of the subject they want to research, many are uncertain of the exact problem they wish to address.

One of the first tasks, therefore, on the way to deciding on the detailed topic of research is to find a question, an unresolved controversy, a gap in knowledge

Figure 1.2 The world is teeming with questions and unresolved problems

or an unrequited need within the chosen subject. This search requires an awareness of current issues in the subject and an inquisitive and questioning mind. Although you will find that the world is teeming with questions and unresolved problems, not every one of these is a suitable subject for research. So what features should you look for which could lead you to a suitable research problem? Box 1.6 lists the most important.

Box 1.6   Features of a suitable research problem

1 *It should be of great interest to you*   You will have to spend many months investigating the problem. A lively interest in the subject will be an invaluable incentive to persevere.
2 *The problem should be significant*   It is not worth time and effort investigating a trivial problem or repeating work which has already been done elsewhere.
3 *It should be delineated*   Consider the time you have to complete the work, and the depth to which the problem will be addressed. You can cover a wide field only superficially, and the more you restrict the field, the more detailed the study can be. You should also consider the cost of necessary travel and other expenses.
4 *You should be able to obtain the information required*   You cannot carry out research if you fail to collect the relevant information needed to tackle your problem, either because you lack access to documents or other sources, and/or because you have not obtained the co-operation of individuals or organizations essential to your research.

(Continued)

---

5 *You should be able to draw conclusions related to the problem*   The point of asking a question is to find an answer. The problem should be one to which the research can offer some solution, or at least the elimination of some false 'solutions'.
6 *You should be able to state the problem clearly and concisely*   A precise, well thought out and fully articulated sentence, understandable by anyone, should normally clearly be able to explain just what the problem is.

It is not easy to decide on and define a research problem, and you will not be expected to do so immediately. The important thing, at this stage, is to know what you are looking for, and to explore your subject for suitable possibilities.

The problem can be generated either by an initiating idea, or by a perceived problem area. For example, investigation of 'rhythmic patterns in settlement planning' is the product of an idea that there are such things as rhythmic patterns in settlement plans, even if no-one had detected them before. This kind of idea will then need to be formulated more precisely in order to develop it into a researchable problem. We are surrounded by problems connected with society, the built environment, education etc., many of which can readily be perceived. Take for example social problems such as poverty, crime, unsuitable housing and uncomfortable workplaces, technical problems such as design deficiencies, organizational problems such as business failures and bureaucratic bungles, and many subjects where there may be a lack of knowledge which prevents improvements being made, for example, the influence of parents on a child's progress at school, the relationship between designers and clients. Obviously, it is not difficult to find problem areas. The difficulty lies in choosing an area which contains possible specific research problems suitable for the subject of a research project or degree.

Some common mistakes

It is worth warning you at this stage of some common mistakes made when a research problem is chosen. These mistakes arise mainly from the failure to grasp the necessity for the *interpretation* of data in the research project. Box 1.7 shows four common mistakes.

1 *Making the choice of a problem an excuse to fill in gaps in your own knowledge*   We all welcome the chance to learn more for ourselves, but the point of research is not just personal enlightenment, but making a contribution to public knowledge. Anyone can find a problem which involves the gathering and duplication

Box 1.7

of information, but it requires an additional effort to find one which requires data to be analysed and conclusions to be drawn which are of wider interest.

2 *Formulating a problem which involves merely a comparison of two or more sets of data*   A comparison of sets of data or records might fill up many pages (e.g. the average age of marriage through the centuries), but without any effort to reveal something new from the information, there is no research activity. The problem should clearly state the objectives behind making the comparison.

3 *Setting a problem in terms of finding the degree of correlation between two sets of data*   Comparing two sets of data to reveal an apparent link between them (e.g. the average age of marriage and the size of families) might be interesting, but the result is only a number, and does not reveal a causal connection. This number, or coefficient of correlation, reveals nothing about the nature of the link, and invites the question – so what?

4 Devising a problem to which the answer can be only yes or no. In order to improve on our knowledge of the world we need to know why things are as they are and how they work. A yes–no solution to a problem skirts the issues by avoiding the search for the reasons why yes or no is the answer, and the implications which the answer has.

Consider the following short sentences claiming to be research problems and decide whether they are researchable, and are a feasible proposition for an individual student, like yourself, to undertake for a research degree or as a research project. Respond first with the answers 'yes', 'no' or 'possibly'. Then, if you think that the research problem is not viable or will present difficulties, briefly give your reasons.

EXERCISE 1.3

1   An enquiry into the history of the building of the Channel Tunnel.
2   A study to compare the results in school history exams for 16-year-olds throughout Europe between 1970 and 1980.
3   The effects of parent unemployment on their children's attitude to schoolwork.
4   The relationship between temperature, humidity and air movement in the cooling effect of sweating on the human skin.
5   The effects of using glass of different thickness and qualities in single, double and triple glazing.
6   What factors must be evaluated and what is their relative importance in constructing a formula for allotting grants to university students in Scotland.
7   An analysis of the influence of Palladio's villa designs on large country houses built in Britain in the eighteenth century.
8   Whether the advantages of foreign borrowing by Third World countries outweigh the disadvantages.
9   The composition of prefabricated elements of buildings in the construction of multi-storey car parks in tight urban situations in large conurbations of the United States of America during the 1970s.

10 A study of how hospital patients' recovery is affected by the colour of their surroundings and of how they react to the effects of different light levels after major operations.

11 An enquiry to identify and evaluate the causes of 'sick building syndrome' in order to indicate possible methods of avoiding the occurrence of this 'syndrome' in new buildings.

12 The impact of local tax and exaction policies on the London commercial office sector.

13 Economic implications of the programme of rental increases and housing sales in China.

14 How the career plans of school leavers compare with their subsequent careers in terms of self-satisfaction and self-adjustment, and what information the analysis of the difference between planned and realized careers provides to assist in career planning.

Thought

As you can see, it requires a good deal of thought and knowledge of your chosen topic of study in order to isolate a suitable research problem. Unless you have come to do your research with a particular detailed problem already identified (probably following on from some previous research which you have done), you will need to narrow down to a specific problem from a wider problem area.

Aids to locating and analysing problems

Booth et al. (1995, p. 36) suggest that the process for focusing on the formulation of your research problem is as shown in Box 1.8.

Box 1.8 How to focus on a research problem

1 Find an interest in a broad subject area (problem area).
2 Narrow the interest to a plausible topic.
3 Question the topic from several points of view.
4 Define a rationale for your project.

---

problem area

Initially, it is useful to define no more than a **problem area**, rather than a specific research problem, within the general body of knowledge which interests you, e.g. housing and homelessness, parks in cities, building regulations and historic conservation. Your aim should be to subsequently narrow down the scope of the idea or problem until it becomes a highly specific research problem. This narrowing process will require a lot of background reading in order to discover what has been written about the subject already, what research has been carried out, where further work needs to be done and where controversial issues still remain.

You should keep in mind three questions when engaged in the preliminary exploratory work. The first is, *what is your motivation for doing the research?* A major motivation should be a curiosity about the research results. Another will undoubtedly be the fulfilment of the requirements of a research degree. Learning about the process of research – practical knowledge which can be used in the future – is also likely to be a motivation. The choice of problem is likely to be influenced by these motivational factors.

The second question is, *what relevant interest, experience or expertise do you bring to bear on the subject?* Obviously, interest in a subject is essential if you are to concentrate happily on it for a year or more. Although experience or expertise in a subject is not a prerequisite to doing research in that field, it does have an effect on the preliminary and information gathering stage of the work, as you will be familiar with the literature and the potential problem areas. However, a 'new light' may be cast on a subject by someone looking at it with 'fresh eyes'.

The third question is, *what are you going to produce?* As a researcher, your priority will be to produce a defendable thesis or useful research report within your time limit. If you are a research student, you should check the requirements of your university or college in the regulations issued about the nature of suitable research topics. (It might be a good idea to do that now. You will find the information in the latest university research degree regulations kept in the library. You should also be issued with your own copy.) If you are doing a dissertation as part of a course, check the course notes for guidance. If you are doing a funded research project, then you will need to know the requirements of the likely funders or of the policy of the organization for which you work.

Figure 1.3 What are you going to produce?

Initial literature review, and defining the problem area
The objective of the initial review of the literature is to discover relevant material published in the chosen field of study and to search for a suitable problem area.

Fox (1969) mentions two kinds of literature which should be reviewed. The first is 'conceptual literature'. This is written by authorities on the subject you have in mind, giving opinions, ideas, theories or experiences, and published in the form of books, articles and papers. The second is 'research literature' which gives accounts and results of research which has been undertaken in the subject, often presented in the form of papers and reports. Chapter 2 in this book tells you how you can effectively carry out this search through the literature.

As every piece of research contributes only a small part to a greater body of knowledge or understanding, researchers must be aware of the context within which their research work is to be carried out. At this stage it is important to get an overview of the subject, rather than knowledge in depth. This will provide you with an understanding of the principal issues and problems or controversies, and the opportunity to select a problem area within a frame of reference. Within this problem area, it is important that you familiarize yourself with those aspects which have already been well established by previous research, and are generally accepted as true. These 'truths' can then be assumed to need no further proof, and the research problem simply uses them. It is not possible for a researcher to question absolutely everything in his/her investigations. Alternatively the research problem can be in the form of a challenge to veracity of one or more of these 'truths'. Advances in wisdom are only made by building on the solid foundations of previous knowledge. Obviously, someone who is already familiar with the subject investigated will tend to be quicker to advance through this stage.

Thought

At this early stage in your research programme you are exploring your subject field only to identify a problem area, and do not need to try to define your research problem in any detail. All the same, I think it is useful to know what the next steps will be so that you can see the direction in which you will be moving. This might well help you to choose a problem area. The knowledge and techniques which you will require for defining your specific research problem in detail are explained in Chapters 2–8 of this book.

Research problem definition

From the interest in the wider issues of the chosen subject, and after the selection of a problem area, the next step is to define the problem more closely so that it becomes a specific **research problem**, with all the characteristics already discussed. This stage requires an enquiring mind, an eye for inconsistencies and inadequacies in current theory, and a measure of imagination. It is often useful in identifying a specific problem to pose a simple question, for example, 'Does the presence of indoor plants affect people's frame of mind?' or 'How can prevention measures reduce vandalism?' or 'Can planning and building regulations prevent the destruction of indigenous architecture?'

research problem

Such a question can provide a starting point for the formulation of a specific research problem, whose conclusion should aim to answer the question. At this stage, the nature of the question will give some indication of the type of research approach (or approaches) which could be appropriate. Will it be a historical study or a descriptive inquiry, an analysis of correlations or an experimental exercise, or a combination of more than one of them? (More about this in Chapter 3.)

Seemingly simple questions are riddled with ambiguities, which must be cleared up by careful definition. For example, in the above questions, what does 'frame of mind' mean, what sort of 'prevention measures' are envisaged, and does the question embrace all types of 'indigenous architecture' everywhere? It is likely that the problem is too broad if you can state it in less than half a dozen words. A few additional questions posed against each word can help to delineate the problem – where, who, what, which, when? Break the problem down into short sentences, not worrying at this stage about the overall length of the problem statement. It is a useful trick to put each sentence on a separate slip of paper, so that they can be put into order in different sequences. When the best logical progression from sentence to sentence is achieved, the statement can be edited into a more elegant form. (Chapter 4 deals in more detail with the techniques of problem statement.)

While developing a specific research problem, keep in mind the skills which you will require to carry out the research posed by the problem. Fox (1969, p. 39) defines five types of skill which are essential: research design, instrument development, data collection, data analysis and research writing.

Designing research can be learned, in consultation with your tutor or supervisor (just wait till Chapters 5 and 6). Instrument development is, however, a highly specialized skill, so it is advisable to formulate the problem so that you can use standardized or previously developed instruments. The skills required by data collection techniques are generally readily acquired (introduced in Chapter 7), though consideration must be given to the extent of data needed. Data analysis does require specialist skills, which can be of a highly sophisticated nature (specialist help is on hand when you get that far). It will definitely be worth your while to consult your tutor or supervisor on the implications for data analysis that the research problem might have. Skills in research writing will be developed in Chapter 8, and by consultation with your tutors or supervisors over the next months (or years). Careful consideration of these points will ensure that the planned research is practicable and has a good chance of success.

The sub-problems

Most research problems are difficult, or even impossible, to solve without breaking them down into smaller problems. The short sentences devised during the problem formulation period can give a clue to the presence of **sub-problems**.   sub-problem
Does one aspect have to be researched before another aspect can be begun? For

example, in one of the research questions asked above, the kinds of prevention measures that can be used against vandalism, how they can be employed and for what types of vandalism they are suitable, will have to be examined. The sub-problems should delineate the scope of the work and, taken together, should define the entire problem to be tackled as summarized in the main problem.

According to Booth et al. (1995, p. 40) you can organize your questions to define the sub-problems by looking at your topic from the four perspectives shown in Box 1.9.

Box 1.9   Questions used to define sub-problems

1   What are the parts of your topic and what larger whole is it a part of?
2   What is its history and what larger history is it a part of?
3   What kind of categories can you find in it, and to what larger categories of things does it belong?
4   What good is it? What can you use it for?

Second review of literature

A more focused review of literature follows the formulation of the research problem. The purpose of this review is to learn about research already carried out into one or more of the aspects of the research problem, as shown in Box 1.10.

Box 1.10   Purposes of a literature review

1   To summarize the results of previous research to form a foundation on which to build your own research.
2   To collect ideas on how to gather data.
3   To investigate methods of data analysis.
4   To study instrumentation which has been used.
5   To assess the success of the various research designs of the studies already undertaken.

A full introduction to the techniques of literature review, information storage and information retrieval is given in Chapter 2.

EXERCISE
1.4

In order to exercise what you have learned about the characteristics of the research problem and how it should be presented, here is part of a research proposal written by a postgraduate research student. It aimed to describe accurately and succinctly the relevant background, the problem to be researched and its importance. Obviously, you are not required at this stage to write anything as detailed as this yourself. The point of this exercise is for you to examine this text to see how a research problem can be extracted out of a context and defined and described in such a way as to convince the reader that the project is both worthwhile and possible to carry out.

After reading the following short research proposal, check the report against the following criteria:

1 Is the research problem clearly stated? What is it? Write it out. If it is not clear, try to detect what it probably is and then summarize it.
2 Does the problem seem to arise naturally from the background information and questions? Summarize the main points of the argument which lead up to the problem. If you have difficulty finding the relevant background information and argument, explain where you see the gaps.
3 Are any sub-problems stated? If so, what are they? Write them out. Do they really form parts of the main problem?
4 Is the proposed research limited in scope? What are the limitations? (It will help you if you think of different aspects of the research, e.g. time, place etc.)
5 Did the researcher state what type of research approach would be used? If so, write a summary of the research activities to be undertaken.
6 Is there any indication of the importance of the study? Describe how, if at all, this is conveyed.
7 Is there any reference to, or discussion of, related literature or studies by other researchers? If so, which?

Research proposal
A study of group-living accommodation for young physically disabled people
The aims of this study are to investigate different forms of group-living accommodation designed for people with physical disabilities; and to evaluate their effectiveness in meeting requirements for independent living, particularly for young severely disabled people.

The ethos behind segregation of disabled people has been that those who are incapable of managing their own lives might reasonably be placed in institutions that can take over those responsibilities. Admission into such institutions has for a long time implied, by circumstance or design, a relinquishment of certain rights, most particularly that of independent living.

As distinctions between those who are dependent on others have become more clear – the poor, sick, old and abandoned – so institutions and buildings, such as workhouses, orphanages and asylums, have evolved to provide for them. Their common ethos was segregation. After World War II, that acceptability of segregated institutions was called into question and alternatives to institutional living were sought for those dependent on others for their care. The response of the caring institutions was to shift away from segregation and towards the integration of people with disabilities into mainstream society. The underlying problem for architects was how buildings would need to change to accommodate this shift. Architects needed to devise a diversified range of buildings that widened the options for independent living for people with differing degrees of disability.

In the 1950s and 1960s new building forms such as sheltered and special needs housing were developed, but these were predominantly for the elderly. For younger disabled people there continued to be few alternatives between admission to an institution or staying at home.

However, by 1970 new concepts were developed; most striking were young disabled units (YDUs) for severely disabled people of working age who had to leave home.

Over 320 YDUs and similar buildings have been built in the last two decades, providing places for 10,500 people. Some are built in the grounds of hospitals and some in the community; they generally accommodate 30 residents with their own bedroom and shared common facilities. Their objective has been to meet requirements for independent living, across the age range of residents, from school leaving age to retirement. However, research on the effectiveness of these schemes is sparse. Investigation so far suggests that their design has been more successful at accommodating the needs of older residents and less successful at accommodating the requirements for independent living of younger disabled people.

The focus of this study will therefore be to investigate the influences on different YDU built forms, and evaluate their effectiveness in meeting the independent-living needs and aspirations of the young people with severe disabilities who live in them.

Indicators of independent living established early in the study will be used to measure the effectiveness of independent living attained in the different building types, all purpose-designed to wheelchair parameters. Data will be collected by undertaking detailed multi-method surveys of different YDU-type group-living schemes. The surveys will include detailed appraisal of plans and measurements of buildings, observation of the building in use and structured interviews with residents across the age range.

The findings of the study are intended to make an original contribution to research in this area, and provide recommendations of practical value for the design of independent-living schemes which set out to optimize the independence of young people with severe physical disabilities.

(Proposal by David Bonnett – who successfully completed his PhD three years later.)

Thought

Are you finding it quicker to analyse a given text now? The example given above is the first part of a research proposal for an MPhil with intention to transfer to a PhD. What has been left out in this example is the detailed methodology, explaining exactly how the research will be carried out. As already mentioned, you are not expected to be able to write anything as detailed as that at this stage. However, after Chapter 8, you should be able to write something comparable and this extract gives you some idea of what you are aiming at. Of course, your subject may be completely different, but the criteria listed above will be the same.

CONCLUSIONS

This chapter has aimed to provide an introduction to what academic research is about, and also to indicate that there is no generally accepted single correct approach to enquiry. It is clear, however, that the principles of scientific method do provide a reliable framework for carrying out an academic research project aimed at achieving a research degree. You will now have a basic idea of the attributes of academic research; you can use them to help you to assess the quality of the background literature you are reading in your subject, as well as to provide you with a starting point for your own thoughts about a possible suitable research approach.

As a principal purpose of a research thesis or dissertation is to provide a vehicle for learning about the theory of research and for correctly putting into practice relevant research techniques, it is generally inappropriate to stray far from the mainstream of research methods. That can come later! However, it may be that you are planning a research project within a specialized field in which you work. You will then need to make yourself familiar with the appropriate approaches and methods relevant to this field.

You are probably still not certain about what exactly you wish to research.   Thought
That is why it is important to explain the nature of a research problem as a first step. Knowing about the attributes of a suitable problem, and keeping them in mind, will help you to explore the literature with more purpose than reading out of general interest. In order to launch you in the direction of problem finding, in the next section you are asked to apply what you have just learned to your own subject.

THE NEXT STEPS: FINDING YOUR RESEARCH PROBLEM AREA

The aims of this section are:

- to review the contents of this chapter in relation to your intended research
- to explore your own subject for problem areas
- to assess the practicality and suitability of possible research into those areas, in order to narrow down your choice and define a research problem
- to decide what further information you require
- to consult and discuss your ideas with others.

Checklist of activities that will progress your research

Step 1: *define research*
Here is my attempt: 'Research is a systematic investigation of a question or resolution of a problem, based on critical analysis of relevant evidence.' It is not just a

matter of collecting facts or shuffling them around. Check that what you are planning to do fulfils this definition. If you find this too constricting, what is your definition and how does it compare with others? Having to define the nature of what you are going do is the best way to understanding it yourself.

Step 2: use your assets to identify problem areas

Your own academic, professional and personal experiences are valuable assets in your research. Make sure you make the best of them. On the basis of what you already know about your subject, and your understanding of the nature of research, examine your field of interest and identify two or three problem areas which might be researchable. Problem areas might be found by detecting systems or organizations which do not seem to perform satisfactorily, either theoretically or practically. Larger scale issues, for example energy conservation related to the environment, might interest you. Have you read of any widely held beliefs in your subject which you think are misleading or quite wrong, or is there a significant lack of information about a topic you consider to be of importance?

When you have selected the problem areas, explore the issues involved by devising a number of questions which highlight the nature of the problem or reveal different aspects of it. This will help to lead you to more specific research problems that could be the basis of your own research project.

Step 3: employ science

Scientific method forms the bedrock of much of our knowledge and understanding. It is based on the concepts of order, external reality, reliability, parsimony and generality. How far do these concepts apply to the information you have found about your own area of interest? Does relevant research display the characteristics of scientific method?

Step 4: seek alternatives

The interpretivist alternative is based on a more relativist and personal view of the world. Investigate whether writers in your subject area take this approach in their investigations. If so, what is the basis of their thinking, 'where are they coming from', what perspectives are they taking? Without knowing this, it is difficult to place their contribution to knowledge into an overall picture. You could map out the different approaches on a diagram to clarify the background information you have collected.

Step 5: be alert

Keep your eyes and ears open for interesting research topics. At the end of virtually all research papers and reports, and even books, there is a section that outlines the need for further research, often quite precisely defined. These could provide you with a good lead to your own research problem.

Step 6: choose a research problem

Consider what further information you might need to obtain to clarify and delineate the problem areas. Do not try to be too specific at first. It is a good idea to make a list of your key interests in your subject, so that you can look at problems which contain some or all of your interests.

Choosing a research problem to tackle for your project is a crucial step that will affect your life for months or even years. Make sure that you are sufficiently fascinated in the issues to motivate you through to the end. Keep the project manageable, however interesting and important the subject is. Do this by limiting it to aspects within your own expertise. Leave the other specialist areas for further research by others.

As a guide to your investigations you may find it useful to answer the following questions in each of your research problems:

1   Has anyone else done research into the same or similar problems?
2   Can you imagine how a methodical and scientific approach could be adopted to research into these particular problems?
3   What issues would need to be explored?
4   How important do you think that research into these problems is?
5   Do you think it might be possible to narrow them down (delineate them) so as to make them a practical subject for your thesis? If so, can you suggest some simple examples?

Step 7: break down the problem

In order to see what might be involved in tackling a research problem, break down the problem into practical components, i.e. sub-problems or sub-questions. Work out what you will actually need to do to answer these. Can you manage to do it in the time allotted? If not, narrow the scope of the problem.

Step 8: reason

Reasoning is an essential ingredient in communication about research. How can you convince anyone of the value of your work if you do not base it on dispassionate argument? Consciously map out the steps in your argument.

Step 9: consult

Consult as many relevant people as possible to discuss your ideas – tutors, experts, fellow students. Mere verbal discussion about ideas is difficult to pin down. In order to communicate your latest ideas as clearly as possible, write them down. This gives the people you consult something concrete to comment on. Keep developing your ideas by redrafting your proposals in response to your discussions.

Step 10: discuss

Prepare a set of notes so that you can discuss these issues with your tutor or supervisor; it is best to give it to him/her to read before your discussion. This is an exploratory exercise, so do not try to formulate your detailed research problem at this stage. This will come later. Having studied this chapter of the book, at least you will know what sort of problems you are looking for!

Consolidation and assessment

Following the above steps should lead to the identification of promising problems and to a preliminary analysis of the issues involved in each. This will help you to define the type of background information which you need to explore and to delineate what issues might be of importance in narrowing down and clarifying a researchable problem to use as a basis for your research.

When you are prepared, you should arrange a tutorial with your tutor or supervisor and hand over your notes for him/her to read. Your tutor or supervisor should discuss with you the potential for research in your suggested problem areas and selection of possible research problems, and will also suggest what you need to do next in your background investigations. You will now be able to demonstrate an understanding of the basic characteristics of academic research, and you may want to discuss with your tutor some of the issues about research raised in this chapter.

Key words

Experience	Parsimony
Reasoning	Generality
Order	Problem area
External reality	Research problem
Reliability	Sub-problem

Further reading

A good place to start is to look at previously completed theses in your subject. This will not provide you with instructions on how to proceed, but will give you plenty of food for thought, and help to stimulate your own critical faculties about the content and quality of the work presented. This will be important when it comes to reviewing your own work later on.

Most books on this subject cover the whole sequence of preparing and writing dissertations and theses, but hardly any actually discuss why you should do a thesis, and what the examiners will be looking for. Despite this it is interesting, if you have time, to compare the advice given at this stage of the process. The approaches vary, depending on the level of dissertation or thesis aimed at, and in some, the specific subject area catered for. Only look at the preliminary advice given in the first sections of the books and scan the contents page to see if there is anything else of interest further on. You can probably do this in the library without even taking the books out on loan.

The following books are aimed at postgraduate research, and selective reading of the preliminary chapters will provide further hints about getting started. Each gives a slightly different view of the issues, so refer to as many as possible. Consult your own library catalogue for these and any similar ones that are available. When you locate them on the shelves, look at the contents list of promising books for relevant chapters.

Blaxter, L., Hughes, C. and Tight, M. (1996) *How to Research*. Buckingham: Open University Press.

The first chapter gives an entertaining review of what research is about.

Murray, R. (2002) *How to Write a Thesis*. Buckingham: Open University Press.

Rudestam, K. E. and Newton, R. (2001) *Surviving Your Dissertation: a Comprehensive Guide to Content and Process*, 2nd edn. Thousand Oaks, CA: Sage.

Glatthorn, A. A. (1998) *Writing the Winning Dissertation: a Step-by-step Guide*. Thousand Oaks, CA: Corwin.

EXERCISE 1.1

1 Assumptions: there is order in the universe; agreement on external reality; human perception and intellect are reliable; simple explanations are better; it is possible to generalize.

2 Examination of texts as follows.

Text 1

(a) The question, though not stated as such, was whether the different techniques used in the described studies had a significant effect on the outcomes.

(b) The main objectives were to bridge this gap in methodology and to get nearer to real-life experiences of the subjects. Also to test the results of the previous experiments by using the latest measuring devices such as EEG.

(c) A brief but clear description of the experiment is given, and the methods of measurement using EEG and EKG recordings are mentioned. The data analysis by analysis of variance is also mentioned.

(d)   The main conclusion demonstrated support for one aspect of the previous research by Sivik and Kuller, made more significant by the use of different measuring techniques and settings.

(e)   The main argument runs like this. There have been studies which show that colour experienced by subjects affects their levels of excitement. The studies were carried out using different experimental techniques and different methods of data collection and analysis, and came to different conclusions. By combining features of the different approaches and getting nearer to a real setting, it is possible to produce results which test the previous results and give useful information for designers.

Text 2

(a)   The problem, though not specifically mentioned as such, is the controversial nature of the claims made by Sulloway about the importance of the order of birth in determining an adult's social attitude.

(b)   The main goal of this research is to test these claims.

(c)   This was done by using information on social attitudes already collected from the General Social Survey, from which, no doubt, the order of birth could also be obtained. No mention is made of the number of cases examined. The correlation between the order of birth and the social attitudes held was then examined.

(d)   These consisted of a rejection of Sulloway's claim that the order of birth was the paramount influence on social attitudes, and that, although this may have an influence, numerous other factors should also be taken into account.

(e)   If Sulloway's claims were to be true, then further research into the subject should produce additional evidence to support them. As this evidence was not forthcoming, his assertions should be either rejected or modified.

Text 3

(a)   The first mention of a problem is that the people in Britain most likely to be in housing need, i.e. those with low incomes and low levels of building and managerial skills, cannot use the group self-build housing process to reduce the costs of acquiring their accommodation. This is not, however, the research problem. It is the lack of systematic analysis and feedback of the application and effectiveness of the innovations aimed at lowering the levels of income and skills required by self-builders which is the problem. Could it be more clearly stated? Probably.

(b)   The main goal or objectives of the research are not clearly spelt out. They can be deduced from the implications of the problem, i.e. to make a systematic analysis of the application and effectiveness of the innovations, but there is no clear statement to this effect.

(c) Much better this time! The third paragraph is all about method, i.e. one general and three derived questions were formulated and a comparative study of nine cases was made to investigate the effectiveness of the three fundamental procedures.

(d) 'It was concluded that' – an obvious way to introduce the conclusions, but simply effective, as shown in paragraph four. Innovations were successful in reducing the necessary levels of income and skills, but the procedures were highly interdependent and required specific management procedure to make them successful. The next paragraph elaborates further.

(e) The main argument seems to go as follows. The cost reductions of the group self-build process have only been made available to those who need economic housing most by innovations which reduce the required levels of income and skills. The effectiveness of innovations needs to be appraised; this can only be usefully carried out with an awareness of their context. By an analysis of the theory of self-build and an investigation of this process in several case studies, conclusions could be drawn about the success of the innovations and the intricacies of the process. This allowed recommendations to be made.

EXERCISE 1.2

1 I have extracted these points which I think are the main ones. What is important is that they follow each other in the form of an argument. You might have picked on other points. If you have, does the argument differ very radically? In the second report, you will notice that the main points are helpfully numbered!

Science is a social construct

The sociology and history of scientific knowledge has shown that the results of scientific experiments are ambiguous, and theories are more flexible than generally believed. Therefore science depends on the consensus within society on what is plausible: hence, science is a 'social construct'.

Because of this new awareness, experienced by most scientists, natural scientists are becoming less secure in their role and feel that the unquestioned authority of science is being undermined.

In his attack on the idea of 'science as a social construct', Wolpert rejected the sociology and history of scientific knowledge because he regarded the justifications for its ideas as outside the body of what is normally considered to be scientific work.

Collins replied that, far from undermining the value of science, researchers in the social aspects of science value its expertise, while removing the false impression of impersonality and precision which is associated with scientific enquiry. Science is a 'warmer' subject than commonly supposed.

Science is not a social construct

Scientific enquiry has proved to be the most powerful and reliable method of getting towards the 'truth' which underlies nature.

Scientific laws and theories are accepted worldwide and transcend sociological differences.

Scientific progress has been built up incrementally and smoothly over time, and independently of the social milieu.

Science is made up of a huge network of ideas from a wide range of sources, which, far from clashing as they would if science was a social construct, slot together in a complementary fashion.

The pre-eminence of mathematics in scientific theories distances science and scientists from any dependence on, or influence by, social forces.

All these observations lead to a rejection of the idea of science as a 'social construct'.

2   Nothing in the second argument agreed with anything in the first. Is this symptomatic of the steely, cold convictions reputed to be the result of scientific knowledge? In the case supporting science as a social construct, the argument seems to be a pleading that the sociology of scientific knowledge is being misunderstood or misconstrued, and that its investigations have been carried out in a genuinely 'scientific' fashion. It does not disagree with the 'correctness' of science, but states that 'correctness' is based as much on agreement within society as on a reflection of the truths of nature.

These two arguments do not engage in a direct discussion, but rather present opposing views. The points made in each argument are not directly confronted by the other. They therefore should be seen as part of a wider debate.

3   There cannot be a model answer for this question, as, of course, any answer will depend on your own views and your subject. However, an important issue is raised, which is of significance whatever the direction of your research.

The evidence given in the first argument about the 'proof' of the special theory of relativity tends to show that scientific work and beliefs, in the short term, are subject to social pressures. However, in the long run, socially accepted 'working' theories must be reliably supported by scientific evidence in order to survive, or eventually be replaced or improved by some other theories, which themselves, though 'socially' regarded as superior, might need to wait some time for substantial proof or replacement. It is unlikely that, through social pressure, a false theory can survive as true for ever. Societies change too much over time to allow this.

The points made in the second argument tend to show that, in the long run, science has been built on firm foundations established through repeated questioning from all sides, regardless of culture and time. Science can therefore be regarded as one of the most powerful 'social unifiers' and a colossal reservoir of human understanding which evolves and improves over time.

Whatever the subject of your research, a distinction should be made between the object of scientific investigation and the scientific knowledge which you will acquire. It is one of the assumptions of scientific method that there is a real world which can be studied (i.e. as the object of scientific investigation), even though we are inextricably entangled in it. How we interpret the knowledge which we derive from these studies must, however, be influenced by the society of which we form a part. 'The knowledge that is constructed is independent of reality but the aim of science is to adequately represent this reality' (Godwin, 1994, p. 18).

EXERCISE 1.3

1   No. Plenty of information may be collected on this subject, but there is no indication of any planned analysis. The sentence needs to continue: 'in order to … '.

2   No. There are two main defects. What will be done with the comparison? No indication is given of why the comparison is made and what is to be learned from it. The scope of the study is enormous. How can ten years of exam information from all the schools in Europe be collected by one person in about six months?

3   Possibly. This is better, but still rather vague. Is this a worldwide study, or will only a sample of families be investigated?

4   Possibly. This has probably already been investigated, and the form of the problem is too simplistic. A short study would probably reveal a set of relevant equations showing the correlation coefficient between the sets of data.

5   No. A seemingly straightforward technical study. But what are the 'effects' which will be studied? They could be on anything – on the environment, on glass production, on individual temperature. More precision about which 'effects' are to be studied is required.

6   Yes. This has the vital ingredients of a researchable problem. You should know by now what the ingredients are!

7   Possibly. Although this has probably been investigated several times over, the feasibility of the research problem depends on the number of large country houses built in Britain in the eighteenth century, or on a selection of representative case studies.

8   No. The solution to the research problem could be a simple yes or no. So what? Advantages to whom? Over what time-span?

9   No. Nicely delineated, but where is the problem? This is pure information collection.

10   Possibly. The difficulty is that this is two problems, involving two areas of study.

11   Possibly. Well formulated, but a large scale undertaking. A lot of research into this subject has already been undertaken, and some aspect which has not yet been investigated or some conflicts in existing research would have to be identified.

12 Possibly. This is too general as it stands. Is this a historical study or is it investigating the current situation? More delineation is needed. Does it require sociological as well as financial data?

13 Possibly. There is no indication of which programme is meant. You would need good Chinese contacts for this one. 'Economic implications', a very general term, could do with some delineation.

14 Yes. Quite usefully formulated.

EXERCISE 1.4

1 Though the research problem is not labelled as such (e.g. this research project addresses the following problem etc.), it is clearly and succinctly stated in the fifth paragraph. The main research problem is the lack of knowledge of the effectiveness of YDUs, particularly in meeting the requirements for independent living of young disabled people. The 'aims of the study' in the first paragraph describe what the researcher aims to do in response to the problem.

2 There is a clear progression from paragraph two, culminating in the problem in paragraph five and a statement of the focus of the study in paragraph six. This is achieved in the following way. The general structure of the argument is based on a historical account of the development of socially provided care for people with disabilities, with particular emphasis on the concepts of segregation and independence. The account shows a progression from provision which segregated disabled people from society to forms of accommodation and care which were intended to allow more integration of residents, culminating in the YDUs. The point is added that, despite a shortage of research, existing evidence shows that the requirements of younger disabled people are not adequately met.

3 The sub-problems are implied rather than stated. It is possible to detect from the text that the researcher has identified two unknowns which require examination in order to investigate the main research problem:

(a) The influences on different YDU built forms. This is rather too general a statement to mean very much. Which influences need to be studied in order to investigate the main problem – economic, political, design, managerial etc.? This vagueness is possibly a result of not defining this aspect as a specific sub-problem.

(b) The way that independent living can be measured (hence the need to establish indicators). This is important to the main problem. Independent living is an abstract concept, and it is not initially obvious how it can be measured.

4 There are many limitations which narrow down the scope of the research, including the following:

(a) Country: implied, but rather surprisingly not stated in the text, limitation of the study to conditions in the UK or probably England.

(b) Time: current, i.e. not a historical study.

(c) People: young physically disabled in YDUs.

(d) Place: YDUs, purpose-designed to wheelchair parameters. Though there are over 320 of these, the study is limited to survey different types or built forms of YDU group-living schemes. This implies that only a sample of the 320 will be surveyed.

(e) Subjects: independent living, aspirations and needs of young people with severe disabilities.

(f) Scope of surveys: detailed multi-method surveys are listed including appraisal of plans, measurement of buildings, observation of buildings in use, structured interviews with residents. Providing a list like this implies that these are the principal survey methods to be used, but does not preclude other types of survey activity, e.g. study of the history of the building, interviews with officials and designers etc.

(g) Criteria: to measure the effectiveness in meeting the independent-living needs and aspirations of young people with severe disabilities. 'Effectiveness' is a very general term, but it is stated in paragraph seven that the study will be limited to the indicators of independent living devised early in the research.

5   By investigating different YDU built forms, a comparative type of research will be carried out. It is pretty obvious that it will be a qualitative rather than a quantitative study. The research will also take place in a natural setting – investigating what the situation is as it exists. There is a specific intention expressed in the last paragraph that the research should increase knowledge of the subject.

6   In the last paragraph, the text stresses the originality of the contribution to research, and the practical value of the recommendations. The importance of the study lies in how it will help to improve the design of independent-living schemes to the benefit of the young disabled occupants.

7   As you see, no-one's particular theory or study is referred to in the text. The main point of the proposal is to stress the point that there is a lack of research in the subject. This paucity is the reason for proposing the study. In the original version of this proposal, each major statement was backed up by a numbered reference to the relevant literature, listed at the end.

2

Information, and How to Deal With It

Written with Bousmaha Baiche

Introduction
Finding the Information
  Sources of Information
  The Internet
  Search Techniques for Online Catalogues, Databases and the Net
Dealing with Information
  Reading
  Note-Taking
Doing a Literature Review
  Critical Reading Skills
  Doing the Review
  Style and Content of the Reivew
Conclusions
The Next Steps: Devising Your Own Information System and Writing Your Literature
  Review
Checklist of Activities That Will Progress Your Research
  Consolidation and Assessment
Key Words
Further Reading
Answers to Exercises

- To explain what is involved in different methods of secondary data collection and to describe different systems of recording the information.
- To help you to develop the skills of reading and note-taking.
- To present efficient techniques of storing and retrieving your own collected information.
- To provide practical advice on how to carry out a literature review.

INTRODUCTION

One of the most important tasks that you have to undertake in the early stages of research is a review of the literature relating to your research problem. Careful consideration at this stage is crucial, as the way you organize your note-taking and information storage will have repercussions in terms of both the management of your time and the quality of your results and written reports in the subsequent stages of the research process.

Because a huge amount of relevant literature may be available, reviewing this literature ought to follow a systematic, meticulously designed process, characterized by perceptive reading and an attention to detail, particularly that which relates to your research problem. Your reading will help you to become aware of how others have dealt with topics in your research subject, and of what knowledge they have acquired, and of how to collect data appropriate to your research problem.

According to Wiersma, in his book *Research Methods in Education* (1986, pp. 47–8), the process should focus on the three questions posed in Box 2.1.

1   *Where is the information to be found?*   The first question deals with specific sources of books, journals and written reports, and reproductions such as microfiche, CD-ROM and the Internet, that can be found in, or obtained through, the library. Looking for the relevant information means using printed reference works, such as bibliographies and indexes, and electronic guides, such as CD-ROM databases and computer-based catalogues. All are very useful means of finding potential data relating to the research problem.

2   *What should be done with the information?*   The second question deals with critical analysis of the literature reviewed, the writing of notes, and the assembly and organization of the relevant data, so that they can be retrieved at later stages of the research process without the need to return to the information sources because of an unanticipated gap in the information assembled.

3   *What use is to be made of the information?*   The third question considers the techniques involved in writing literature reviews, reports, chapters or papers, based on the material accumulated in your database of notes, whereby the information related to the research problem can be put together in a consistent and scholarly way.

This chapter is concerned with the first two of these questions: how to find the information, and how to deal with the information once it has been located. It is concerned with the third question in so far as it gives guidance on how to write a literature review.

FINDING THE INFORMATION

Finding the information involves reviewing the literature relevant to the research problem. This should start at the beginning of the research process and continue throughout the project. Reviewing the literature includes some specific activities that take place in a sequence. Because of the amount of information available, you should follow a systematic process. In addition, it is advisable that, at each stage of the review, you do as complete and as accurate a job as possible. This will minimize the need to go back to the source of the information for a missed detail, which will save you later time and effort. Students, in the last stages of writing their thesis, sometimes spend hours of valuable time frantically trying to retrace the details (e.g. page numbers, author's name or journal title) of an important reference that they had collected a year or two previously.

Reviewing the literature is essential, not only in providing a context for the research subject and specifically limiting and identifying the research problem, but also in providing you with important information for subsequent parts of the research investigation (Wiersma, 1986, p. 48; Leedy, 1989, p. 69).

Sources of information

The university, college or specialist professional library is likely to be the most valuable starting point for seeking information. It provides access to a wide range of material, including books containing background information, reports of research studies, periodicals, technical reports and academic theses, available either in the library itself or from other libraries.

There are different, but similar, systems of cataloguing the contents of libraries in different institutions. Therefore an essential early task is to find and understand the system your library utilizes, and where materials in the library are located. This should be done as soon as possible to allow you to find your way through the shelves and computer terminals of the library to obtain the materials required. Librarians are mobilized at the beginning of each academic year to help you and other new students to understand the way the library works and how to look for required materials. If you are a new student you are strongly advised to attend not only a library tour, usually arranged by the library staff at the beginning of term, but also information sources seminars which are often organized specifically for research students.

There are essentially two main types of information source which you need to be aware of, as shown in Box 2.2.

Box 2.2   Main types of information source

1   *Bibliographic aids and indexes*   These are the indexes, catalogues and other bibliographic tools which enable you to trace the secondary sources you require.
2   *Secondary sources*   These consist of the 'literature' of your subject, i.e. the books, journal articles, reports and papers which you need to find for the information you require for your research.

This chapter concentrates on bibliographic aids and indexes, and describes the various types which you are likely to find useful.

Library catalogues are usually restricted to the bibliographical details of items in the library's collection, and their numbering on the library's shelves. Most library catalogues are now offered on computer, and are often referred to as online public access catalogues (OPACs). There is usually access to document references by author, title and subject, and most libraries operate on a similar basis. However, there may be significant differences. It is important to learn the best way to operate the catalogue, and library staff will be happy to show you. Note that some long established libraries do not list their older books online, so you may need to resort to the card or microfiche index for these.

library catalogue

It is also possible to search the OPACs of other libraries worldwide through the Internet. You may want to do this if there is a library specializing in your subject, e.g. German literature, or if there is a major copyright library which receives copies of all new books published in a particular country, e.g. the British Library.

journal of abstracts

Journals of abstracts appear at regular intervals and commonly comprise catalogues of the bibliographical details (journal title, issue number, date, author/title of article etc.) of journal articles. They are devoted to journals in individual subject areas. Additionally there are publications which catalogue other document types, such as dissertations or conference proceedings. Entries are often arranged in broad subject groups, with a key word index. Some abstract journals cover a broad area, e.g. sociological abstracts; others are more specific, e.g. leisure, recreation and tourism abstracts. They may be limited by language(s) covered, geographical area of publication etc. The main feature of an abstract journal is that it contains summaries of articles, the length of which varies. They may simply indicate what the article is about (indicative abstracts) or may be more detailed, giving the main arguments and conclusions (informative abstracts).

index journal

Index journals are similar to journals of abstracts, but do not contain summaries of articles. They often contain key words as part of the entry, to indicate the content of the article.

bibliographies

Bibliographies, which are lists of references on specific subjects, are often published in response to demand or as the by-product of research. These are often useful to researchers, and can be found via the library catalogue. Additionally you may find the large national bibliographies such as Books in Print (USA), which has a subject arrangement, or the British National Bibliography, useful for tracing details of relevant items.

bibliographic database

Most books and many abstract and index journals are now available in **bibliographic database** form for key word searching. CD-ROM databases are increasingly available in libraries, for use by staff and students. Training in their use is normally given by library staff. Some databases not purchased by the library in CD format can often be searched online for research students by library staff. This can be a relatively expensive service, but the cost may be borne by the library and/or your university or college department. Online searching is usually available at the discretion of the subject librarian. Results of both CD and online searching are normally available in machine-readable format, and can form the basis of a personal reference database.

Directories of organizations, although not bibliographical sources, are nevertheless useful in tracing details of organizations in specific fields, and of key personnel in those fields.

Finally, *people* are also non-bibliographical sources, but frequently can advise on where to look! Librarians are people – use them! In particular, make sure that your subject librarian knows about what subject you are researching.

It is worth noting that bibliographic aids and indexes, even those devoted to a specific subject, are rarely anything like comprehensive. For example, the Architectural Periodicals Index contains references to articles from many, but not all, architectural journals. It is limited to those purchased by its producer, the library of the Royal Institute of British Architects. This means you will need to do an additional organized literature search through the sources most likely to cover your research subject. See whether there are any courses of instruction, organized by your subject librarian, to offer guidance on these.

Obviously, with the range of bibliographic aids and indexes available to you, you are likely to want to see books and articles which are not available in your own university library. The system of *inter-library loans* makes it possible to get hold of most published material, either from libraries in this country or from those abroad. Note that because of the paperwork and postage involved, several weeks can pass before the book, microfiche, journal etc. is delivered to you.

Do not overlook the existence of *specialist libraries*. Many professional bodies, associations and other organizations possess their own collection of specialist literature. A visit to the libraries appropriate to your subject may be essential, as the information contained therein may be unobtainable elsewhere. You can also gain access to other non-specialist but certainly 'special' libraries, such as the Bodleian in Oxford and the British Library in London, as well as the national libraries in other countries, e.g. the Bibliothèque Nationale de France or the Library of Congress in Washington, where valuable historical publications and manuscripts can be found.

Private collections and *historical records*, which are located throughout the country, may be of interest to you, particularly if you are doing historical research.

The internet

With thousands of pages being added every day, the World Wide Web (WWW) is the biggest single source of information in the world. However, the content is of extremely variable quality, and the biggest challenge when using it is to track down good quality material. You can easily waste hours trawling through rubbish in search of the goodies. Careful use of search terms helps to eliminate the trash. Usually, the more precise your search parameters, the more manageable the search results will be. Not all information on the web is free.

You will need browser software in your computer in order to access the web. Most academic and commercial organizations running Microsoft Windows in its various versions will use Microsoft Explorer. Other standard browsers are Netscape Navigator, often used as it is available for PC, Macintosh and Unix platforms, and Mozilla, which is becoming increasingly popular. The main facilities provided by browsers enable you to save a file to disk, to print a file including pictures, to search the text of a file, and to cut and paste sections of the file to other Windows applications.

The strengths of the medium are its international content, its usually good currency and its sheer mass of data. The mass of information can result in many false leads, causing time wasting and frustration, and the authority of the information is often questionable and should be checked with other sources if accuracy is vital. The problems of tracking down relevant and reliable information are partially solved by the use of good search engines (programs which select data in response to key words). Access is convenient from a personal computer, and data can be easily saved and copied (depending on copyright restrictions and the issue of plagiarism). Some information is charged for, but charges are defined before access is gained and therefore costs are controllable.

It is worth knowing, however, the different ways that search engines work, so that you can use them to your best advantage and are aware of their limitations. There are four basic types – free text, index based, multi-search and intelligent agents – as described in Box 2.3.

Box 2.3   Types of search engine

- *Free text*   These search engines automatically 'crawl' the web and make their own database of web pages. These are selections, made at regular intervals, and therefore do not contain all the pages on the web. In response to your search input of one or several words, they produce a list of pages, ranked according to their own parameters, e.g. whether the words appear in the URL, or several times in the text. You will notice that different search engines make completely different selections, so it is worth trying several – AltaVista, HotBot, Infoseek, Google etc.
- *Index-based compilers*   Yes, actual people categorize web pages under a series of subject headings and subheadings. To search these you will need to follow a series of links, starting from the general and working down to the

---

Box 2.3

particular. This is a help to users unsure of using free text searches, but has the disadvantage of being limited by the particular choices made by the compilers, e.g. an American perspective in Yahoo.com based in the USA, which is the biggest of this type. Yahoo has now also created a UK version. Some other index-based compilers are Galaxy, Looksmart, Lycos, Netscape Search.

- *Multi-search engines*   These are actually not search engines as such, but web pages that offer several search engines that you can use simultaneously. Just one input will be searched by all the selected engines. However, as they work in different ways, you might get plenty of hits on one, and none on another. The advantage is that they might offer search engines that you have never heard of before. Examples of these are Dogpile, Metacrawler and Mamma.
- *Intelligent agents*   Unlike normal search engines that start a search from scratch every time you use them, these learn from your choices as you accept or reject the results they offer. Every time you rerun them they automatically refine the search on the basis of your past profile. Although these are still being developed, they promise to be a useful labour-saving device.

Though the searching procedure is relatively simple and easily learned, a familiarity with computer use is required. No special computer equipment is required apart from a modem or connection to a network with access to the Internet. If you are working from home, a subscription to an Internet service provider (ISP) is necessary, many of which now offer a free service. Payment for information is sometimes required, and making payments over the Internet is not always secure. This problem is being overcome by encryption of information. Check before you pay that the payment method is secured.

More data are continuously being posted on the Internet (there are currently over 40 million web pages, with pages being added at the rate of one every four seconds), including research information which is not available elsewhere, e.g. in electronic journals, as well as free factual and bibliographic databases which include abstracts and summaries. You should consult your academic library for information about free access to information services (such as Janet in the UK), which make easy access available to a wide range of databases of journal articles, abstracts, conference literature etc.

There are numerous Internet guides published throughout the world that help you to find useful sites and services (also try your library for lists devoted to subject areas). Some are specifically aimed at students and list useful search engines, sites and databases. Many are written from a US perspective, so if you wish to buy one it is worth looking carefully to select one that has the right information for you. Note that the price level is not always a guide to quality! Beware that these books tend to become rapidly out of date, especially those listing addresses of Internet sites.

Evaluating web sources

Anyone can add pages to the World Wide Web, so how can you judge if the information you have found is reliable? Box 2.4 gives seven different tests you can make to judge the quality of the contents.

Box 2.4   Tests to evaluate websites

- Is the website accurate? Does it say what sources the data are based on? Compare the data with other sources. If they diverge greatly, is there some explanation for this?
- What authority is it based on? Find out who authored the pages – whether they are recognized experts or part of a reputable organization. Check if other publications are cited or if they provide a bibliography of other articles, reports or books. You may need to track down the 'home page' to get to the details. Also see if there is a postal address and phone number to indicate the 'reality' of the organization. Web addresses that end in 'ac' (meaning academic) are likely to be university or college addresses and therefore point to some intellectual credibility – no guarantee of quality but nevertheless a useful indicator.
- Is it biased? Many pressure groups and commercial organizations use the web to promote their ideas and products, and present information in a one-sided way. Can you detect a vested interest in the subject on the part of the author? Find out more about the authors, e.g. does the information about animal experiments come from an antivivisection league, a cosmetics company, or an independent research institute?
- How detailed is the information? Is the information so general that it is of little use, or so detailed and specialized that it is difficult to understand? Investigate whether it is only fragmentary and misses out important issues in the subject, and whether the evidence is backed up by relevant data. There may be useful links to further information, other websites or printed publications.
- Is it out of date? Pages stay on the web until they are removed. Some have obviously been forgotten and are hopelessly out of date. Try to find a date of posting or updating (perhaps on the View/Page Info option on your web browser). Note that some updates might not update all the contents. Check any links provided to see if they work.
- Have you cross-checked? Compare the contents with other sources of information such as books, articles, official statistics and other websites. Does the information tally with or contradict these? If the latter, can you see why?
- Have you tried pre-evaluated 'subject gateways'? The information on these sites has been vetted by experts in the relevant subjects, so can be relied upon to be of high quality. Try BUBL Link (www.bubl.ac.uk/link/).

Search techniques for online catalogues, databases and the net

Here are a few basic hints on how to make effective searches for information. In order to find what you want, it must first be clear what you are looking for.

Searches rely on single words or a combination of several words. Every subject will contain several crucial terms that distinguish it from other subjects, so the trick is to select these. If you are unfamiliar with the subject, look it up in a specialist dictionary or an encyclopedia to see what terms are used so that you can build up your own list of key words. Remember also the use of different words and spellings in different parts of the world, e.g. car/automobile, lift/elevator, pavement/sidewalk, organisation/organization.

Databases usually provide the option of a free text search, or a key word, subject or index search. The former looks for your chosen word(s) in all the text contained in the database, whilst the latter only searches the key words, subject lists or index lists provided by the authors with their books or papers. These lists focus on the subject matter of the publication, and so give a more reliable guide to the contents. Many databases include a thesaurus – a list of indexing terms that will help you to use the standard terms. Sometimes the number of articles to which the term is assigned is given.

It is usually possible to narrow your search by indicating place and time, where these are relevant. The publication date is a basic piece of bibliographic data.

Adding a * to words or parts of words automatically widens the search parameters in the form of wildcards. For example, 'automa*' will find all the words starting with that stem, e.g. automation, automatic, automaton etc. Inserting the * symbol into a word takes care of different spelling versions e.g. 'labo*r' will find labour and labor.

Boolean logic is a fancy word for the technique of using connecting words such as 'and', 'or', and 'not'. These refine the search by defining more closely what you want to include or not. For example:

- Schools and finance: this narrows down your search by only selecting records that contain both terms.
- (Lifts or elevators): this widens your search by selecting records that contain either or both terms. Note that 'or' statements must be in brackets.
- Nurseries and playschools not schools: this eliminates the terms that you do not want to consider. However, be careful that you do not eliminate useful records.

It is best if you keep the search terms simple and search several times using different variations and terms.

The commonest way of searching for information on the web is to use a search service (search engine) such as Lycos, AltaVista, Excite, Infoseek, Google etc. You should carefully read the instructions on the search methods recommended. The commonest way is to use concepts in the form of key words, together with the use of Boolean Logic.

The Internet also provides a simple and cheap (often free) method of communicating throughout the world in the form of e-mail. This can be really useful for making contacts relevant to your research effort.

This is another practical task to practise your use of the Internet, particularly if you are not familiar with it.

1 Open Netscape Navigator, Mozilla or Microsoft Internet Explorer, then select a search service (examples above) and, using Boolean logic, set up a search of concepts related to your research topic. Note the number of sites selected, then try to narrow down the choice if the number is unmanageably large, or widen it if there are none selected, or only very few. Check through the results to see if there is anything potentially useful.
2 Go to your library and look through any Internet guides it might have. Select the one you think will be the most useful. You will then have a wealth of information to follow up in the future! If you cannot find a suitable book or have no easy access to an academic library, try the following sites for more information and training in Internet skills:

http://www.netskills.ac.uk/TONIC
http://www.gateway.lib.ohio-state.edu/tutor/
http://www.december.com/web/text/index.html

Thought   *The best way to learn how to get the most out of the Internet is to use it. Trying things out yourself is the only way to explore what potential this medium has to help you in your project. It is useful, however, to consult a guide that provides more information than I have been able to include here about the features of the web and the tools for exploring it. One guide that I have found useful is Niall Ó Dochartaigh's The Internet Research Handbook: A Practical Guide for Students and Researchers in the Social Sciences (Sage, 2001).*

DEALING WITH INFORMATION

After you locate the references and the data in your literature search, you might wonder what to do with them. In fact, if there are many references, you might get worried and say: 'How am I going to read all these reports?' The first step that you should take is to determine whether the data included in a document, book or other source are appropriate to your research problem or not. If not, the source should be discarded. If you decide that the source contains information relevant to your research problem, then you should follow a systematic and consistent approach to dealing with this information, in order to make it easy to retrieve when you require it.

Although several approaches for storing and retrieving information are suggested, you will have to decide on a system which suits you best, or even develop your own methods. This must work well for you, but it must also conform to the basic guidelines of good practice, which are explained below. Activities relating to dealing with your information include the following.

Reading

Since you are likely to be dealing with masses of written sources, you have to acquire the appropriate technique of reading their contents in a limited time. That means, as Newman (1989, p. 12) puts it, acquiring the technique of learning how to 'tear the heart out of books' or how to 'gut' them efficiently and quickly. This will enable you to work your way through the large masses of information.

According to Fairbairn and Winch (1991, pp. 7–14), reading involves (1) finding meaning in written texts, (2) literal, inferential and evaluative comprehension of texts, and (3) reading in different ways. In addition, Krantz and Kimmelman (1992, pp. 12–105) state that your goals are as in Box 2.5.

Box 2.5   Goals of reading

1 To review the text.
2 To use context clues and a dictionary to understand new words.
3 To identify and mark important ideas in a chapter.
4 To recognize how authors organize and develop ideas.
5 To identify new words and phrases that describe the methods or patterns of organizing and developing ideas.
6 To apply comprehension skills to vocabulary and text material.

Reading text quickly is not easy if you do not have the appropriate technique. Reading systematically to fully understand a textbook demands a lot of effort and may be time-consuming and not really necessary. You can possibly find short cuts to locate the part or passage of the text that interests you and this will enable you to develop ways of using your reading time more effectively. There are, in fact, several available techniques contained in many publications on increasing reading and comprehension speed (Fairbairn and Winch, 1991, pp. 14–21; Krantz and Kimmelman, 1992, pp. 12–103; Freeman and Meed, 1993, p. 41; Smith and Smith, 1994, pp. 53–89; Newman, 1989, pp. 12–14).

Each of the above-mentioned authors suggests techniques of reading, but do not forget that you might develop your own technique of reading that might work better for you in terms of time, effort and comprehension. For example, Freeman and Meed (1993, pp. 31–41) suggest the techniques in Box 2.6.

Figure 2.1 Reading text quickly is not easy if you do not have the appropriate technique

---

Box 2.6   Reading techniques

1   *Skimming*   This involves looking quickly through the book and reading only things like contents, headings, introductions and conclusions. This is a quick and efficient way of familiarizing yourself with a publication and is useful if you wish to check whether a written report is relevant, or wish to find particular information or ideas quickly.

2   *Scanning*   This is a very rapid search for some important point. It may be a page number, a title or a key word. The essential thing is that you deliberately ignore everything except the one item for which you are scanning. You use scanning when you look up a number in the telephone directory.

3   *Reading to understand*   This involves detailed study of a chapter, passage or article in order to absorb all the major facts and ideas. You may read it more than once, and take notes to summarize what you have read.

4   *Word-by-word reading*   Very occasionally, you actually need to read every word extremely carefully; for example, when reading an exam question or following a set of instructions.

5   *Reading for pleasure*   This is the reading you do to relax and enjoy, as with a novel.

Smith and Smith (1994, pp. 54–89), in an alternative approach, suggest some techniques for reading skills which include: (1) efficient scanning with the use of key words and key terms, (2) use of titles to anticipate the contents of a reading passage, and (3) finding out the content of a text by looking at the first sentence of each paragraph.

With respect to an adequate reading speed, Newman (1989, pp. 12–14) argues that reading techniques fall into a basic pattern involving four stages:

Stage 1   Try to gain some quick impression of what the book is about; what question or questions the author is trying to answer; how the book is structured; and whether, in fact, the questions tackled and the answers put forward are relevant to your needs. You can do this by glancing over the cover or jacket, the preface (if any), the list of contents, and the index. Try then to gain an overall impression of the book and its structure.

Stage 2   If you decide that the book is relevant to your research subject, then you must formulate the question or questions that you anticipate will be answered in the book. This enables you to locate the required information and will save you time and effort, as you cannot afford to go on reading aimlessly through the book. In addition, at this stage you must adopt an active and analytical attitude.

Stage 3   After formulating the main question or questions that you anticipate the book will answer, you must review the book to look for answers to your questions. This involves locating the parts of the book where your questions are dealt with. You must then look for the answers or conclusions that the author has drawn, and also at how the author arrived at them. You will also look at arguments and evidence put forward to support the views expressed and you will make an attempt to assess the validity of the evidence and the structure of the argument which utilizes such evidence. There are, however, cases where conclusions are unsupported, arguments or evidence are non-existent, or sometimes there is no conclusion at all.

Stage 4   Supposing that you have extracted the relevant information from the written report, you must now record your data in note form, so that later you can retrieve it and use it easily at the appropriate stage. The different ways of doing this are explained later in this chapter.

Put your reading skills to the test by reading an article in different ways. Select, from the information you have collected about your subject, any article or research paper that you have not yet read but that you think might contain useful information. Now read it in the following ways:

EXERCISE 2.3

1   First skim the text and write down very briefly the main points of the information offered. Remember to first check the contents or abstract, the main headings, and perhaps part of the last paragraph about conclusions. Do not write down more than twenty words, but make sure that they are quite precise and organized in a coherent way so that you will easily understand your notes at a later date.
2   Next, select two main concepts that you are interested in and that seem to be featured prominently in the article (perhaps they are mentioned in the title). Scan the text and note what is written about these two concepts.

3 Now take just one section headed by a subtitle and read it carefully, making detailed notes on all the major issues and facts. You should have about ten short notes to cover the information properly.

4 Finally, read the last paragraph(s) very carefully indeed. What are the main conclusions and why are they important, or perhaps they are not? What effect do they have on your thinking about your subject? You could express this as personal notes to remind you of the significance of this article in some aspect of your work.

5 The other type of reading – reading for pleasure – you can practise without needing it to be the subject of an exercise!

Thought

It is good to be aware of how you are going to read a text before you begin. Your reading method should be decided by the type and detail of information which you require from the text. A conscious decision before reading or scanning can save you much time by avoiding inappropriate techniques, resulting in too much or too little information being extracted.

Note-taking

You should take notes only of the information that you judge relevant to your research subject. It is generally agreed that, except for quotations, when you take notes you should use your own active vocabulary and not the author's. Newman (1989, p. 15) says that it is important to use your active vocabulary in note-taking, because it helps to ensure that you have a reasonably full grasp of the meaning of the information concerned; it might assist in laying down a better memory trace in the brain; and finally, when you come to reread and synthesize the notes, your personal active vocabulary is more easily comprehensible and recognizable.

Reasons for taking notes

You might sometimes wonder why you take notes. Freeman and Meed (1993, p. 43) lay down a number of reasons why. You should remember that note-taking is not restricted to making records from written reports, but may also be applied to lectures, conferences, interviews and so on. Reasons for taking notes include those in Box 2.7.

Box 2.7   Reasons for taking notes

- *To help you remember something*   You can't hope to retain a whole lecture, book or discussion permanently in your memory, so instead you make notes of the most important items and use the notes for revision and reference.

- *To keep a permanent record of something* If you attend a lecture or visit somewhere as part of your course, your notes may be your own record of what took place.
- *To help in your planning*   Notes can be a good way of starting off a project or a piece of writing; you can note down the main things you need to do, the books you need to read, and so on.
- *To reorder material*   Making notes, which can be reshuffled, provides one of the most useful opportunities for rearranging material in whichever form is most convenient to you.
- *To help you understand what you are learning*   Writing things down yourself forces you to think them through properly and is one of the best ways of remembering them.
- *To help you to concentrate*   If you are listening to someone talking, your mind may easily wander; making notes helps to keep you active and involved.
- *To show other people* You may want other learners to benefit from the notes you have made.

When making notes, you will have to make judgements all the time about what information will, or might, be of use to you. These judgements will depend on your own knowledge of your subject and the nature of your research problem. During your investigations, suggests van Dalen (1979, p. 92), you may want to copy many specific facts from references, such as dates, places, names, statistics, formulas and definitions; or summarize arguments, questions, explanations, illustrations or descriptions. In addition you may find it useful to write comments about your reactions to the reference materials and state relationships, conclusions or interpretations that come to mind during the contemplative phases of your work. You may also want to jot down items that require further checking.

When writing a report you may want to draw upon your notes for a variety of reasons, for example, to support a particular position or to illustrate a point of view. You may want to make comparisons, weave a web of logical evidence, or buttress arguments by passages from recognized authorities. A body of notes, collected with discrimination, could provide the building blocks for all of these, assuming that the range of your notes is sufficiently wide. However, a haphazard collection of notes will leave you with an impoverished resource, and may cause your investigation to collapse (1979, pp. 92–3).

Note-taking techniques
Smith and Smith (1994, pp. 93–103) put forward what they call 'golden rules' to help you take successful notes, including those shown in Box 2.8.

1   Clarify your purpose.
2   Write all your notes on the same sized paper or cards.
3   When you begin, set out your notes properly. In making a full bibliographic record of the source of the notes you are writing, include author (or speaker); date of publishing or of event (e.g. lecture, interview); title of book, article, conference, web page, lecture etc.; where published or held; detailed page numbers referring to the individual points, opinions and data which are noted; and usefully, the library catalogue number or other information to enable you to locate the book, article, web page etc. quickly at a later date.
4   Use the title of the chapter or lecture to help you anticipate the main ideas of the text.
5   Keep your own ideas, comments and criticisms separate from those in the text.
6   When you finish, sum up what you have written.

Do not forget that you take notes to help in your writing at a later stage of your research project. To assist this, your notes should be brief and clear; if they are too long, you will find it tedious to go through them, either to search for a specific point, or to refresh your memory. For the same reason they should be easy to read and understand; if you cannot read through them to refresh your memory, they will fail in their purpose. You should organize them to suit the way you learn and your reasons for learning. You will find that if they are not relevant to you, you will never look at them again (Freeman and Meed, 1993, p. 44).

Wiersma (1986, pp. 70–1) argued that, when taking notes on research reports in particular, you should use some form of abstracting which involves a summary in note form, containing the items of information shown in Box 2.9.

Box 2.9   Information required from research reports

- *Bibliography entry*   An accurate and complete bibliographic entry heads the notes.
- *Problem*   This is a statement of the research problem of the report being reviewed; it may include statements of hypotheses.
- *Subjects*   The individuals involved in research studies are often called 'subjects' of the research.
- *Procedures*   This section describes how the research was conducted. It includes such items as the measurements used and the analyses performed. This section may also be called 'methodology'.
- *Results and conclusions*   This section identifies the relevant results and conclusions of the study. A distinction may be made between results and conclusions – results being whatever occurred, such as certain statistics, and conclusions being what the researcher has made of the results. In long reports with many results and conclusions, it is best to number them.

Figure 2.2 There are many different ways of taking notes

For further details on the type of abstract or summary recommended by Wiersma (1986, pp. 70–4), including some samples of abstracts, you may refer to the original.

There are many different ways of taking notes and you have to find a system that works for you. However, there are some important points that you should bear in mind. Never make notes on the text as this would spoil the source (and invoke the rage of the librarian!). Keep your own separate notebook or set of empty cards in an accessible place, for you never know when you want to record something; notes on backs of envelopes *always* get lost.

When you locate a passage which you think is relevant to your research project, read it first and before you take notes so that you can be really selective. The notes, written in your own words, do not have to be in the form of fully articulated sentences, but make them clear enough for you to understand them when you use them at a later stage, when you might have forgotten their context. Carefully copy direct quotations from the text when you think you might wish to use them later, but keep these fairly rare and precisely referenced.

Do be ready to learn from the writing of others on how to improve your own writing. You may come across examples of excellent style in sentence structure, vocabulary or metaphor that can be beneficial for your own writing (Fairbairn and Winch, 1991, pp. 21–2).

Collecting and ordering your notes

There are two basic formats for storing and retrieving notes:

- paper based
- computer based.

The *paper-based format* needs no electronic equipment, though a few accessories make life easier. The principle behind this system is to write your notes on sheets of paper or card, and then order the sheets in such a way that you can find the notes when you need them later. You will need to think of the manner in which you want to accumulate your notes. Many different formats are suggested, but you can design your own setup which might be more suitable for you than another. However, the most important feature is that each card, piece of paper or other form of record must include only *one* idea or *one* fact or *one* item or *one* question. That is because at this stage you do not yet know in which part of the structure of your research project this *one* piece of information will fit, or if it will be used at all.

You can use A4 sheets of paper and store them in ring folders, or alternatively use index cards (the larger sizes are more useful) and store these in boxes designed for the purpose. The idea is to store your notes under certain headings so that you can find what you have collected on those subjects. The headings can be various, depending on your subject and how you will be approaching it. You will have to work out the best method yourself. The kinds of headings commonly used are:

- key words
- author names
- publication titles
- dates (particularly useful in historical studies)
- subjects – or aspects of the main subject.

An effective note-taking system preserves the most significant ideas in a form that facilitates shifting, comparing, grouping and ordering items (Newman, 1989, pp. 15–16; van Dalen, 1979, p. 88). Leedy (1989, pp. 68–70, 131–3) makes useful suggestions on the use of coloured duplicated note cards and bibliography cards, with separate copies filed under different headings, producing parallel files of e.g. author, place, date, subject etc.

This way allows you to find the material whether, for example, you are looking for the writings of a particular author, or information about a particular subject or a particular date. It is best to keep the notes short, that is, concentrated on one topic or aspect of the subject. Start another page or card when the topic of your notes changes. This is because you may want to search out all your notes on one topic, so you can pull out all the pages or cards under that topic heading.

The greatest advantage of this format is that you can make and take your notes anywhere without needing any equipment apart from paper or card and a pen. The main disadvantage is that you will need to rewrite the material from your handwritten notes on the word processor when you use them.

The *computer-based formats* rely on various database programs. These are set up to deal with lots of bits of information so that you can easily store and retrieve them. The most common non-specialist database programs come with standard program packages, such as Microsoft Access. More specialized programs are aimed at exactly this job of notes and referencing. The current main ones are EndNote, ProCite and Citation. Check if they are available on your university or college network. You can even devise a simple system using your normal word processing package.

The basic requirements of the system using a computer format are similar to those of a paper-based one. Notes should be short and on a single topic, they should be thoroughly referenced, and they should be stored under allotted headings. The major advantages of a computer-based system are that you have much more powerful search facilities; your notes are easily retrieved, copied, revised and edited; and you do not need to rewrite your reference information (lots of complicated formatting and punctuation), you can just copy it for lists etc. You can also store all your notes on a compact floppy disk. The main disadvantage is that, in order to avoid copying out, you need to have your own computer with you wherever you need to make the notes – not such a problem if you own a laptop. You will also have to spend time learning how to use the program.

Further information on which applications are suitable and how to use them can probably be obtained from your university computer centre. Standard database programs, such as Microsoft Access, have a limit on the length and format of fields used for storing your information, so do set up a typical record of the notes on one book to see if you can include all the information you want and in the way you want it. It is advisable to use a specialist bibliographic database program if it is available to you.

There are several bits of information that you must record for each and every one of the notes that you take, irrespective of the format you use, as shown in Box 2.10.

Box 2.10   Essential information to record on every note

- The author(s) of the text – surname and first names. Perhaps the name on the book is the editor of the book, who has compiled a series of chapters or papers by various authors. In this case you will also need all name(s) of the author(s) of the relevant text.
- The title of the book – including a subtitle. If it is a journal or newspaper, you will have to record the full name of the journal or newspaper.
- If it is an article or paper in an edited book or journal or newspaper, with different authors for different chapters or papers, then the title of the relevant chapter or paper is also required.
- If it is a website, the URL (web address).

(Continued)

- The date of publication (in a book, look on the reverse of the title page for this).
- The place it was published (ditto).
- The name of the publisher (ditto).
- The page number or numbers where the information you have made notes from appears.
- Also useful is a reference to where you found the information, e.g. which library and the book code number, so that you can easily track it down again.
- You might also use material from lectures or conferences. In this case, give full details including the speaker, title of talk, conference title, venue and date.

This information, attached to every note, will enable you to fully reference it, and to find the original information again if you need to.

Obviously, you can devise your own system that uses the best features of each format. Whichever format you want to use, you must decide exactly how you will do it, and test it out before putting it into general use.

There are several advantages and disadvantages in relying on a computer system compared with using a paper-based system, as indicated in Box 2.11.

Box 2.11   Advantages and disadvantages of using a computer-based note system

The advantages are:

- You need write the notes only once. You can copy the text when you want to use it and edit it without writing it all out again. This promotes accuracy as well as saving time. (There are dangers in using this facility; see the disadvantages to follow.)
- You can easily search through your notes for key words, authors, concepts etc.
- You can repeat bibliographic information for each note at the touch of a button.
- You can link notes to outlines, subjects, authors, dates and other categories of your choice.
- You can keep all your notes on highly portable floppy disks.
- You can easily devise bibliographic lists with the copy facility, so that you need write the bibliographic details only once. This means that you can be sure that the information is correct, however many times you need to copy the references.

The disadvantages are:

- It takes time to learn how to use the database program effectively.
- You need to have frequent (perhaps even constant) access to a computer.

Box 2.11

- You are limited to where you can take notes, i.e. to where you can take or use a computer. Possessing a laptop computer helps in this respect.
- You can be tempted to miss out on valuable redrafting stages as you electronically copy and order your notes for use in essays, papers etc. There is a danger that you may consider the sets of ideas and quotations which you have listed in some sort of order from your notes, and printed out, to be a finished piece of writing. In fact, considerable further effort will be necessary to turn what is basically a list of notes into a clear and concise argument. Having to physically rewrite text always prompts you to think analytically about what you are writing.

Finally, do not forget that *you* should decide which form of note-taking you should adopt and which suits your research project best. Notes are a means to an end, not an end in themselves. However they are recorded and stored, the essential thing is that they are useful and contain the necessary information, and can be traced when required (Wiersma, 1986, p. 74).

This exercise practises some of the skills involved in note-taking which, of course, also involves an analytical approach to both the form and the content of what is read. The text which follows is a description of a large research project conducted by Peter Townsend. Note that this is not a direct account by Peter Townsend of his research work, but an adaptation of a review by J.S. Grant in 1980, describing and commenting on Townsend's survey published in 1979.

EXERCISE 2.4

1 Read through this text quite quickly so that you get an overall understanding of what it is about.
2 You should now have a good understanding of the contents of the article. The next task is to analyse and record what you have read. You should use one of the note-taking techniques (e.g. filing cards, sheets of paper or computer database) which have been described earlier in this chapter. Use the following questions to act as a guide to your note-taking, making a brief note in response to each question.

    Do not forget to put no more than one subject item on each card/sheet/record. Remember to put with each note: the name of the author(s), the date of the publication(s), the source of the information (i.e. title of book, article etc., which can be abbreviated), and the page number(s) where the information appears.

    (a) What were the main aims of this social survey?
    (b) The method of collecting data was by questionnaire, and some interviews. Describe the main features of the questionnaire and any interesting points about how difficulties in collecting the required information were to be overcome.

(c) What were the results of this survey?

(d) What conclusions were drawn in the report?

(e) Poverty means different things to different people. How was poverty defined for this study?

(f) When and where was the research carried out?

(g) Describe the sampling method used.

(h) Poverty is an abstract concept which is difficult to measure. How was the measurement of this concept devised and what crucial point was made about its measurement? How important was this aspect to the value of the results?

Compare your notes with those suggested in the answers to exercises at the end of this chapter.

3 Now you have a comprehensive set of notes on the contents of the article. To retrieve the notes at a later date, it is important that each note is filed under one, or several, key words or subject headings. For this exercise we will use the following key words or subject headings: poverty, definition; poverty, research data; measurement of concepts; sampling; questionnaires; research studies by date; Townsend P.; Grant J. S.

Use the letters (a)–(h) to identify the note prompted by each question, and make a list of the note letters which belong under each heading. Some headings will have several (or even all) of the note letters listed beneath, others might have only one.

A review of Peter Townsend, *Poverty in the United Kingdom*, Penguin, 1979

Based on Grant, J. S. (1980) 'Britain, an impoverished nation?', *International Journal of Income Studies*, Vancouver: Collingdale, pp. 33–8

Aims and background

This large scale social survey research programme had two main aims:

1 to estimate how many people in the UK were living in poverty or near poverty

2 to discover what the features of poverty were and what problems these presented for poor people, in order to help to explain the phenomenon of poverty.

The fieldwork was begun in 1965 and completed in 1969. Ten years were required for analysing the large amount of collected data, after which the book was published in 1979. The research project was made up of four stages:

1 a pilot research focusing on particular minority groups

2 preparation work and piloting for the main survey

3 the main survey work

4 follow-up surveys highlighting areas of poverty in four parliamentary constituencies.

There were several uses for the pilot research carried out between 1965 and 1968. It was used to refine the methods of measuring such variables as unemployment and lack of work, sickness and disability, and living style which included assessing facilities in and around the home. In autumn 1967 a 120-page questionnaire designed for the main survey was submitted to 150 households situated in various locations in London and the surrounding areas. The results of the pilot survey and other previous research showed that, contrary to widely held beliefs, poor families were not a homogeneous group. In fact, there was a wide range of different as well as common problems experienced by families that were fatherless, or were dependent on low incomes, or whose main earner was unemployed, or that were burdened with a chronically sick or disabled adult at home. Within each category there were found to be large differences, for example between separated wives and widows in the category of single mothers.

Fifty-one constituencies in the UK were targeted for the main survey carried out in 1968–9. Altogether 6098 individuals in a total of 2052 households were questioned. In parallel, four local surveys, involving 3950 individuals in 1208 households, were also undertaken in other poor areas.

Definitions of poverty

It was necessary to formulate methods of measurement of poverty before the research could be undertaken. Townsend pointed out three ways that poverty could be defined and measured:

1 by comparing supplementary benefit levels, just as the government had done in its own surveys
2 by comparing the average levels of income of different types of household, and of disposable personal income
3 by identifying and gauging deprivation by the exclusion from a range of activities and customs enjoyed by the majority of the population of the UK.

The third option was preferred by Townsend because he considered it possible to devise a measure which he called a 'deprivation index'. This was a relative and objective measure that established the level of income of different household types below which they were unable to participate in a style of life which was commonly accepted as normal in our society. He devised 60 indices of deprivation which included a wide range of social, household and personal activities and conditions.

Examples of these are: not having had a week's holiday away from home within the last twelve months (53.6% of the population); not having an afternoon or evening out for entertainment in the last two weeks (47.0%); household does not have a refrigerator (45.1%); children did not have a party on their last birthday (56.6%); not having had a cooked meal on one or more days in the last fortnight (7.0%); and household does not have sole use of four amenities, namely indoor toilet, sink with cold water supply, bath or shower, gas or electric cooker (21.4%).

Townsend plotted graphs for the different income levels to show the number of deprivations experienced. He took as the poverty line the level of income, which varied depending on family size, below which the number of deprivations experienced increased disproportionately.

He noted that people were likely to experience some individual deprivations owing to their own cultural or religious preferences. It was the accumulation of deprivations which was the measure for poverty. For example, not having a Sunday joint might not be regarded as a deprivation in a vegetarian family, or not having a week's holiday may be a chosen option. This makes deprivation difficult to detect at the margins. Townsend regarded a score of five or six deprivations to be highly suggestive of poverty and noted that 20% of households scored an average of six or more.

The questionnaire

Trained interviewers conducted the main survey using a 39-page questionnaire. This had nine section headings, revealed as important issues in the pilot survey:

1 housing and living facilities
2 employment
3 occupational facilities and fringe benefits
4 cash income
5 assets and savings
6 health and disabilities
7 social services
8 private income in kind
9 styles of living.

The answers to the questionnaire were intended to give a complete depiction of each individual's resources and lifestyle. Hence, the calculation of earnings included subsidiary forms of income, such as from casual work like gardening and from social security benefits. The difficulty in measuring some of these earnings often required elaborate interviewing and editing procedures.

Obviously, the gathering of reliable information depended largely on the skills of the interviewer. In order to ensure that there was consistency in the interpretation of the questions amongst the numerous interviewers, the research team set up its own interviewing organization. There were 25 main interviewers and several more who worked for part of the project. Where possible, interviewers were involved in the pilot study as well as the main survey. They were given very detailed notes on how to ask each question and record the answer and instructed in detail during lengthy briefing meetings.

Some of the questions on income required the interviewer to have a good knowledge of the monetary value of various services and goods, such as the value of private income from gardening and the value of 'perks' from the workplace. Each answer was recorded in pre-coded boxes next to each question, so the skill of the interviewer was relied upon to code the answer correctly. The coded answers were subsequently fed into a computer for statistical analysis. Despite these careful preparations, it was recognized that the interviewer's approach could significantly influence the results, and that the information it was possible to collect in a survey was also 'structured' by the design of the questionnaire.

Selecting a random sample

It was important to select a representative sample of the population of the country as a whole in order to fulfil the aim of the survey to gain a general picture of the extent and types of poverty in Britain.

A multi-stage stratified technique was used for selecting the sample. Two stages of selection and stratification were employed. Firstly, in order to reduce the need for travelling whilst maintaining a variety of income profiles, areas were selected in the country stratified into high, middle and low income areas. Secondly, the samples of the populations within these areas were further stratified according to age and family size. The representative quality of the sample was then checked by comparing the selected sample with the figures of the population of Britain as a whole as shown in official figures of the Registrar General. A good match was found.

Townsend anticipated that the response level, and therefore the results, might be adversely affected by non-response from the elderly, the incapacitated and families with large children, who might find difficulty in granting an interview. It was just these people who were likely to be poor. In order to avoid weakening the estimates of the incidence of poverty owing to a lack of information about these non-responders, interviewers were instructed to call back and to at least obtain some basic information such as the composition of the household and ages of the members, the social class of the head of the household, whether the accommodation was rented or owner occupied, housing amenities and other matters. Interviewers were asked to fill out special forms, giving the limited information available from the 388 households who refused a full interview.

Despite these fears, the response rate to the questionnaire was high. Almost 76% of households selected gave complete information, and another 6% provided more limited information, giving an overall response rate of 82%.

Results

It was shown by the survey that the problem of poverty in 1968–9 was significantly greater than the figures based on supplementary benefits claimants presented by the Department of Health and Social Security.

Three standards of poverty were employed: the state standard (net disposable income last year of less than 100% of supplementary scale rates plus housing costs); the relative income standard (net disposable income last year less than 50% of mean household income for type); and the deprivation standard (net disposable household income last year less than a level below which deprivation tends to increase disproportionately as income diminishes). Standards were also set for near poverty.

According to the survey, relative poverty was suffered by 25% of households (22.9% of the people surveyed), which represents 12.46 million people. Not all groups of people were at 'high risk'. Those at high risk were described as one-person households, large families, one-parent families, lower class people working in poor conditions, the unemployed, the disabled and old people.

Conclusion

Townsend pointed out that the chief conclusion of the report was that poverty was more extensive than was generally and officially believed. He added that poverty was not only a direct result of severe social inequality, but also an outcome of the actions of the rich to preserve and increase their wealth, and of the power of institutions created by that wealth. Any policies aimed at abolishing or alleviating conditions of poverty must therefore take as a central consideration the manner in which wealth is generated and passed on.

Reference

Townsend, P. (1979) *Poverty in the United Kingdom: a Summary of Household Resources and Standard of Living*. London: Penguin.

Thought

This was a rather long exercise, but it should have given you an idea of what is involved in understanding, analysing and recording a written text. Note-taking is a meticulous process if done correctly. Ideally, if you wanted to keep a collection of notes under each key word or heading, you would need to make multiple copies of many of the notes, or at least work out some system of cross-referencing. This duplication can be avoided if you use a database program, where you can give key words to each note for easy retrieval by key word.

Remember, if you devise and maintain your own efficient system of recording and ordering notes, it will save you hours (possibly days) of time and frustration later in your studies.

Personalized bibliographies

As well as compiling a collection of notes, you will need to make a separate list of all the references which you have used, and of references that you think may be useful – a personalized bibliography. The format of the information in your bibliography must comply with one of the established systems. The 'Harvard system' (author, date) is the one which is used most commonly nowadays, particularly in the sciences and social sciences. Details of the format are discussed in Chapter 9, but you can easily look at the references in this book for a model of how to do it.

Check that you have the information in Box 2.12 for each of your references.

Box 2.12   Checklist of information needed for each reference

1   The author or authors.
2   The date of publication.
3   The title of the book, paper or article, or anything else such as lecture, tape, film etc.
4   If it is a published work, the place of publication and the publisher.
5   If it is a paper in a journal or an article in a newspaper, the title of the journal or newspaper, the volume and issue numbers, the page numbers of the paper or article.
6   If it is a chapter in an edited book, the title of the edited book, the name of the editor, and the page numbers of the chapter.

Don't forget to add any relevant publications, dissertations, reports etc. that you have written in the past.

The traditional way to store these references was on individual cards, but nowadays it is more convenient to keep them on a computer database. This obviates the need to rewrite the references whenever they are needed in a text – a common source of mistakes. A database is also much more convenient for searching by name, subject, key word, or even publisher or date etc. Obviously, you cannot always have a computer with you, so do remember to make a note of the details of interesting books you might come across on the library shelves, and remember to add them to your bibliography later. As noted earlier, there are computer programs which are designed to help you set up your own bibliography and which can instantly convert your lists to any of the common bibliographic formats (e.g. ProCite or EndNote).

It is very easy now to compile huge lists of publications by saving the results of electronic searches in the library onto disk. These lists can be convenient for trawling through at your leisure away from the library, but do be selective and discard inappropriate references. When you compile a bibliography for a paper or a dissertation, make sure that only the relevant references are included, i.e. only the publications referred to in the text. Padding out the list to show how well read you are does not impress the reader!

DOING A LITERATURE REVIEW

The oft-repeated instruction to 'do a literature review' belies some of the complexities of the task. What is a literature review, and why do you need to do one? Look at it this way. When you have finished your thesis and come to some really useful conclusions, will you not want other people interested in your subject to read what you have written? Your thesis should take its place in the collection of other writings, all of which contribute to the sum of knowledge about that subject. So, in order to understand the present 'state of the art' you too need to read what other people have written and make some kind of an assessment of where your research will fit into that body of work.

Swales and Feak (2000, p. 115) explain that literature reviews fall into two basic types: a survey article (an expert's general review of current literature on a particular topic), and a review that forms part of a research paper, proposal, thesis or dissertation. We are obviously concerned with the latter, and in particular with the proposal literature review. This type of review forms an important introduction to the research project and underpins the argument about why the project is worth doing. It therefore forms a distinctly recognizable section near the beginning of the proposal and leads on to the more specific and practical description of the research activities.

Not all of the material you will read will be relevant to your interests, and where it is relevant, not all of the ideas put forward will be agreeable to you. Doing a literature review means not only tracking down all the relevant information but also taking a critical position on the ideas contained therein, and producing an argument that leads to the exposition of the research problem.

Critical reading skills

Critical reading is a skill that needs to be developed. Anyone who has studied their language and its literature and has analysed important literary works will have an idea of some of the issues that need to be investigated. Critical reading of academic texts faces similar challenges, as discussed below.

Firstly, before looking at the different aspects of criticism, what do we actually mean by 'criticism'? Perhaps a better word in this context would be 'analysis', because the point of the exercise is not just to denigrate or find fault with the style of writing or ideas, but to present a critique, a scrutiny, an analysis, or an examination of them. Providing a description is not enough; your task is to give your own personal and professional appraisal of the content and quality of the text in question. In order to be able to do this, you will have to look at the text from different perspectives to reveal a multidimensional view of the work. So, what are these perspectives?

1 *The structure of the argument* You can analyse this by first detecting the conclusion-type words or so-called conclusion indicators (e.g. 'therefore', 'it follows that', 'as a result', 'we can conclude that', and other such similar words and phrases) in order to pinpoint the conclusion(s). The main conclusions should normally appear towards the end of the work, though there may be intermediate conclusions scattered throughout. There are then three aspects that need to be examined:

  (a)   What evidence is given to support the conclusions?
  (b)   Is the evidence credible, i.e. does it come from reliable sources?
  (c)   Is the logic of the argument sound, i.e. what are the steps in the argument that lead from the evidence to the conclusions?

  You need to do this kind of analysis coolly, like a judge appraising the argument of a lawyer making a case. A useful technique is to extract the evidence and conclusions in the form of short phrases, and arrange them in the sequence of the argument. This lets you examine the logic form without being distracted by the surrounding text. This process sounds a lot simpler than it often is – arguments can be quite convoluted or incomplete – but, just like a judge, you should make a note of your summing up of this aspect of your critique. You will see that Chapter 4 goes into much more detail about the characteristics of argument.

2 *The assumptions upon which the writings and arguments are based* All writing is rooted in theory and based on values, and must be appraised in relation to these. Sometimes these are quite clearly stated at the beginning of the text; sometimes they are obscured or not mentioned. You will need to have some knowledge of the different theoretical positions in your subject in

order to be able to detect them and know what they imply. Some common examples of these are: a feminist approach in social science, a Keynesian approach in economics, a modernist approach in architecture, and a Freudian approach in psychology. In each subject there are competing theoretical standpoints with their own values. Only by being aware of these can you make your own considered evaluation of the literature.

3 *The wider context of the work*   Intellectual work is carried out in a complex arena where power, politics, fashion, economics, competing orthodoxies and many other factors play influential roles. These can be determining factors in the formulation of views and need to be exposed in order to understand the forces behind them. For example, the forces behind the industrial revolution were formative in the thinking of the day, just as those of the electronic revolution are today.

4 *Comparison with other work*   There are no absolute values to which you can appeal in order to make assessments. There are no clear rules about what is right and wrong. 'Research writing is a contested terrain, within which alternative views and positions may be taken up' (Blaxter et al., 1996, p. 106). Critical reading can however be used to make comparisons between texts in order to highlight the different approaches, levels of thoroughness, contradictions, strength of arguments, implications of theoretical stances and accepted values, and types of conclusions. This will enable you to group together or divide the various strands in the literature to help you map out the larger picture that forms the background to your project.

Doing the review

The review will need to be carried out in four major directions, not just narrowly confined to your specific subject area. They are shown in Box 2.13, arranged from the general to the particular, their relative importance depending on the nature of your subject.

Box 2.13   Directions of investigation for literary reviews

1 *Research theory and philosophy*   To establish the intellectual context(s) of research related to your subject.
2 *History of developments in your subject*   To trace the background to present thinking.
3 *Latest research and developments in your subject*   To inform about the current issues being investigated and the latest thinking and practice, to discuss the conflicting arguments, and to detect a gap in knowledge.
4 *Research methods*   To explore practical techniques that have been used, particularly those that might be relevant to your project.

You will find that doing the literature review is not a linear process. Reading, writing and reviewing form an iterative process: the more you read and learn, the more you will be able to understand the areas of consensus, conflict and uncertainty. Whilst it is important that you give the impression that you are widely read in the subject, you must be selective in the references you use. You do not have much space to write the review. If the amount of relevant literature is huge, you might have to restrict the scope of your project by narrowing down the issues addressed. It is easy to see that, in many topics, economics, politics, philosophy, social conditions, legislation, governance etc. all play a part. But you cannot cope with all these! Pare your topic down to the core of your interest, and stay as much as possible within your area of expertise. On the other hand, if there seems to be a paucity of literature, this could be because your topic has not been researched much or that you have not spent enough time searching! If there really has not been much research, then you have an excellent reason for doing some.

Literature reviews do not all follow the same structure, so it is difficult to be prescriptive as to the form the review should take. Here is, however, a useful technique that you can use to structure your review in a way that suits your subject and your argument, as used by Swales and Feak (2000, p. 143) in one of their exercises. You will find that it requires several attempts to achieve a sequence that produces a good argument, backed up by relevant literature, which leads logically to the research problem.

1 Select the notes you made from the literature that you think are most relevant to your project. Select only those notes that summarize the positions, ideas or evaluations of the various writers. Also review any comments you have made about the texts when you first read them. This is where brevity in the notes will be seen as a virtue. Alternatively, if the notes are too long, summarize each set of notes into one paragraph that states the essential ingredients. Print these out so that you can scan them easily by eye. You may have perhaps between ten and twenty of these; more than this becomes unmanageable.
2 Number the notes in any order.
3 Draw a sequence of four or five paired boxes in a line. This will help you to map out the review of the literature together with the steps of your argument: one sequence of boxes to outline the steps in your argument, the other paired boxes to list the supporting literature notes at each step (Diagram 2.1).
4 If you already have an idea about it, you might be able to insert the outline of the argument in one line of boxes in the form of a short statement in each box in turn to trace the steps of the argument. If not, leave these blank.

Diagram 2.1 Literature review boxes

5   If you have formulated the argument in this way, insert the numbers of the notes that underpin each step in the adjacent box.

6   If you have not already inserted an argument, insert into the other boxes the numbers of the notes. Group the ones that cover the same topic into the same

boxes and put the groups into a sequence that leads from the general to the particular. For example, you may have notes on general theoretical background to the subject, notes on views about aspects of the subject that raise problems, notes on solutions to those problems, evaluations of the already attempted solutions.

7   Now work out the steps of an argument in the paired boxes.

8   The last box should not have any literature notes numbers, as the last step of the argument is to state the conclusion or, in effect, to state the research problem.

9   Add or subtract paired boxes as required: different arguments have different numbers of steps.

10   Review what you have constructed. Correct, strengthen or alter the sequence and content, or even explore new versions until you are satisfied with the result.

If you are doing a PhD direct, make sure that the review contains some of your own published (or even unpublished) work relevant to the subject. You need to persuade the readers that you already have expertise in the chosen research topic, equivalent to the preparatory MPhil stage of the work.

Style and content of the review

Once you have decided on the content of your review and the sequence required to support your argument, you will have to consider the way that you present the review as a clear introduction to your proposal.

Assume that your reader knows nothing about your subject. University research committees which vet student research proposals at MPhil and PhD levels are made up of academics from a variety of disciplines. Consequently, you will need to start your proposal with a short but clear statement of the focus of the proposed study. This is not part of the literature review, but sets out the subject of study. The review should begin with a general outline of the features of the relevant literature. For example:

> Accounts of polar exploration expeditions are not a new phenomenon. The tendency in early descriptions was to laud the heroism of inspirational figures that had pioneered new routes, such as Cook or Amundsen. The more recent approach has been to analyse the physical and mental achievements of the explorers in relation to human strength and endurance. Most recently, exploration history has been examined in a context of social and political power struggles, technological advances and scientific research.

This gives you a good excuse to introduce literature that supports your introductory statements. You have a choice on how to refer to the literature at different levels of detail. Hyland (1999, p. 350) identified four levels of citation, listed in Box 2.14 in decreasing order of detail (the citations are for illustration only).

Box 2.14   Levels of citations

1   *Block and indented quotations*

Ranger insisted on the need for good quality design:

> Buildings will not function properly if insufficient consideration is given to solve complicated design problems. Poor design results in inconvenient planning, poor quality of spaces, higher maintenance costs and frequent breakdown of services. We owe it to clients to insist on the inclusion of sufficient resources to devote to the design activities in development projects. (2004, p. 36)

2   *Within-sentence quotations*

According to Ranger, 'Buildings will not function properly if insufficient consideration is given to solve complicated design problems' (2004, p. 36).

3   *Paraphrase/summary*

Ranger (2004) argued that neglecting the resolution of design issues results in poor quality buildings.

4   *Generalization (combining several sources)*

There is wide agreement that lack of sufficient time and resources to resolve design problems in buildings results in poor quality developments (Hendry, 1998; Waldren, 1999; Smith, 2002; Ranger, 2004).

You will not have enough space to use block quotations, and only if the quotation is absolutely central to your argument should you use a within-sentence quotation. As the aim of the literature review is to cover a lot of ground, use should be made of the fourth option to combine several sources, leaving the third option for significant views of influential writers.

With regard to the citation system, I recommend method A (numbered) as described in Chapter 9 rather than method B as used in the examples above. This allows you to easily include a lot of references without laborious lists of names.

When making citations, take care to avoid ambiguity. It should be clear whether the author cited actually made the discovery or formulated the idea, commented on it, or compiled information about it. For example:

Much has been written about the effects of poverty (Kraus, 2003).

or:

The relationship between poverty and health has been extensively studied in recent years (Kraus, 2003).

Does this mean that Kraus has written or studied a lot about it himself, or has he made an analysis of the writings, or has he compiled a list of relevant literature? More precision would clear up these ambiguities.

Another issue to watch is the accuracy of your summaries of the ideas and the fairness of the evaluation of the writings of others. You need to make the judgement as to the amount of information given to provide an accurate impression of the original, and to paraphrase it in such a way as not to mislead or misrepresent the work.

Box 2.15 gives a checklist of useful points for you to review the content and form of your literature review, based on a compilation of comments from professors listed by Swales and Feak (2000, p. 149).

Box 2.15   Checklist for your literature review

1   Make sure that your review is not just a list of previous research papers or other literature, devoid of any assessment of their relative importance and their interconnections. Make an overview of the literature to produce a guide to the rich interplay and major steps in the development of research in your subject.

2   Check that the important issues of your research problem are introduced through the analysis of the literature. A simple chronological account of previous research will not give a sufficient thrust to the argument of why your research problem is significant and how it continues the research effort.

3   Ensure that the general theoretical background is intimately connected to your examination of the more detailed writings about ideas and specific research that lead up to your own research project. The theory should help the reader understand the attitudes behind the reviewed literature and your own philosophical stance.

4   Make links across discipline boundaries when doing an interdisciplinary review, rather than keeping each separate and examined in turn. Many research subjects anyway cannot be hermetically sealed within one discipline, so the connections are there to be exposed. You might even be able to suggest some new links that need to be investigated.

5   Ensure that you have included some account of how the previous research was done, so that you have a precedent for your own approach to methodology.

How many references should you have? This depends on the subject, but as the literature review part of a research proposal has to be very short and compact owing to limitation of space, you are unlikely to be able to cite more than 20–30 authors, and 5–10 might even be sufficient in a narrowly defined field. The important thing is to select those that are really significant for your work. As usual, it is a good idea to look at previous proposals in your subject area to see what has been successful before.

CONCLUSIONS

How you take notes and how you organize them *matters*. The quality of your research depends on it. Many sections of your thesis will be directly based on analysis of the information that you have collected over many months from a wide variety of sources. The richer your collection of notes and the better your system of filing and retrieval, the more resources you will have at your disposal for your analytical review.

It is very difficult to change or improve your system at a later date, so time spent now on devising a system which is tailored to your needs is well spent.

THE NEXT STEPS: DEVISING YOUR OWN INFORMATION SYSTEM AND WRITING YOUR LITERATURE REVIEW

The aims of this section are:

- to devise your standardized note-taking, referencing, storage and retrieval system
- to produce a first draft of your literature review.

Checklist of activities that will progress your research

Step 1: use your library
Make the most of your university or college library. Become adept at using all the different information sourcing techniques available. You will need to enrol on training sessions to learn how to do electronic searches and to learn about all the different databases and other sources of information. Find out about web-based information services (e.g. Web of Science, Janet, Copac, Gabriel, Zetoc etc.). You should also be able to get a list of subject related information sources and databases from your subject librarian.

Step 2: get online
You will not always need to go to the library for this information. There are a lot of web-based databases and library catalogues that you can access from a computer

anywhere. You might need to have a password to access some of them: consult your university/college library to obtain these.

Step 3: be alerted

You can sign up for alerts to new information from some database organizations. This saves you constantly making new searches.

Step 4: track forward

Track forward to further sources by consulting citation indexes. In which other works has the paper you are reading been referred to?

Step 5: track back

Also check the references and bibliographies of anything you read for relevant past literature.

Step 6: keep track

The web is a seductive and sometimes frustrating source of information. Avoid getting sidetracked into irrelevant issues and poor quality sites of little academic credibility. It is a good idea to limit the time for each session so you don't get lost. Earmark useful sites to visit in more detail during future sessions.

Step 7: read

Become conscious of the level of reading you need to use in each circumstance. Are you scanning for leads to information or are you actually analysing the text in detail? The type of notes you make will be different in each case.

Step 8: take note

Spend some time analysing your note-taking procedures. Differentiate between making a précis and making a commentary: both are valuable but should not be confused. Also differentiate between opinions, factual information, theory, methods, results, interpretations, examples, as well as sorting into subjects and concepts.

Step 9: get sorted

Your system of recording notes, storing and retrieving them is of vital importance to your project. Now is the time to sort it out! Although I have given a balanced review of paper-based and computer-based systems, I would strongly recommend you using a specialized computer bibliographic database program such as EndNote or ProCite to store your notes. They provide more flexibility and useful compatibility with web as based bibliographic databases.

Using a set of notes which you have made from your reading of your subject literature, decide on the system which you will use to collect, reference, store and retrieve all the information that you will collect over the next year or two (or three or four!).

Think carefully of the conditions under which you will be making your notes or collecting information, e.g. in the university library, at home, in a distant library, at an interview etc. This will affect the medium in which you make your initial notes; it can be cards, paper sheets, photocopies, tape recordings etc. Will you then transcribe all the notes onto one medium, e.g. cards or a computer database, or will you keep them on a range of media? Decide on a standard form of referencing for each snippet of information. Consider how you will cross-reference your notes with your bibliography list. Under how many headings or key words can you organize your information?

Step 10: try it out

How you will be able to retrieve your information will depend on how it is referenced and stored. Try to evolve a system which reduces the amount of rewriting of text and references. This will reduce the amount of errors. Computers can help here.

Whatever system you decide on, check, by making a test on a small sample of your notes, that you can do the following:

(a) trace the exact location of each source from which you made the notes, including where you found it, library sort code if relevant, full publication details, and page number
(b) easily pick out all your notes on a particular subject, concept or keyword
(c) trace all notes on the writings of a particular author
(d) distinguish between quotations, summaries and commentaries.

Step 11: back up!

Make regular copies or backups of your notes in case they get lost or damaged. This is particularly important with electronic media as they are particularly vulnerable.

Step 12: start your literature review

Using the framework of Diagram 2.1, construct the structure for your literature review. Use the notes you have collected so far to back up the steps in your argument. You will probably not be able to complete it at this stage, but you will be able at least to make a start – always the most challenging part of a task! As you read more and develop your ideas, you will easily be able to adjust and add to the boxes until you (and your supervisors) are satisfied that the structure is sound. You can then write it out in full as part of your research proposal.

Consolidation and assessment

When you are prepared, you should arrange a tutorial with your tutor or supervisor. Discuss with him/her your decisions on relevant information sources and search methods.

You should be able to demonstrate to him/her, with actual examples of your notes, how you propose to manage the recording, referencing, storage and retrieval of your collected information.

This exercise should result in you having an appropriately targeted method of information collection, and in the creation of your own well considered system of recording, storing and retrieving information. This will be in place from an early stage in your research programme, in order to enhance your efficiency and result in a significant saving of time later in your studies.

Next, explain how you have structured your literature review with the aid of Diagram 2.1, and run through the argument as you have structured it. You might also be able to provide one or two examples of the notes that you will use to back up the crucial steps of your argument. The main outcome of this discussion should be whether your argument appears to be sound, and whether it reveals a research problem that is researchable in the context of your studies.

Key words

Library catalogue
Journal of abstracts
Index journal
Bibliographies
Bibliographic database

Further reading

I have given a short description of what you may find useful in the following books, starting with searching and reviewing the literature.

Hart, C. (2001) *Doing a Literature Search*. London: Sage.

A whole book providing a guide on how to search the literature in the social sciences.

Hart, C. (1998) *Doing a Literature Review*. London: Sage.

A guide through the multidimensional sea of academic literature with techniques on how to deal with the information when you have found it.

On the Oxford Brookes University library catalogue there were 2350 references to information guides! Many of these were bibliographies devoted to a particular subject; you could search on your university or college catalogue for one relevant to your topic. Here are three examples: the first very general, the next less so, and the third quite narrowly focused.

Hurt, C. D. (1998) *Information Sources in Science and Technology*, 3rd edn. Englewood Cliffs, NJ: Libraries Unlimited.

Amico, E. B. (ed.) (1998) *Reader's Guide to Women's Studies*. London: Fitzroy Dearborn.

English Sports Council (1998) *Women and Sport*. London: English Sports Council.

And here are some of the multitude of books to help you navigate the Internet. Always try to get the latest edition as they get out of date fast! The first one, as the name suggests, is specifically aimed at students and I think is really useful.

Winship, I. and McNab, A. (2002) *The Student's Guide to the Internet*. London: Library Association.

Ackermann, E. (1999) *The Information Specialist's Guide to Searching and Researching on the Internet*. Wilsonville, OR: Franklin, Beedle.

Sherman, C. (2001) *The Invisible Web: Uncovering Information Sources Search Engines Can't See*. Medford, NJ: CyberAge.

Ó Dochartaigh, N. (2001) *The Internet Research Handbook: a Practical Guide for Students and Researchers in the Social Sciences*. London: Sage.

And now, some books about note-taking and organizing your information. Most books about how to do research will have a section on this, but you may want to compare advice and approaches with those given in this chapter. The first two are examples of these.

Blaxter, L., Hughes, C. and Tight, M. (1996). *How to Research*. Buckingham: Open University Press.

Chapter 4 deals with reading and note-taking quite comprehensively, though there is nothing on computer-based bibliographic databases.

Leedy, Paul D. (1989 and later editions) *Practical Research: Planning and design*. New York: Macmillan.

Chapter 4 gives American advice on note-taking and filing, using cards.

Here are some books more narrowly dedicated to taking notes and getting organized. The two Fry books complement each other well.

Krantz, H. and Kimmelman, J. (1992) *Keys to Reading and Study Skills*, 4th edn. Fort Worth, TX: Harcourt Brace Jovanovich.

Fry, Ronald W. (1997) *Take Notes*. London: Kogan Page.

Fry, Ronald W. (2000) *Get Organized*, 2nd edn. Franklin Lakes, NJ: Career Press.

Below is information about bibliographic database programs. Check what is available on your college/university network before you make an expensive decision to buy a program yourself.

EndNote. Institute for Scientific Information. http://www.endnote.com.

ProCite. ISI Research Software. http://www.procite.com/pchome.html.

Citation. Oberon Development Ltd. http://www.citationline.net. Nice website with free download demo version.

If you are interested in speed reading, here are some books. But beware, these skills take time and practice to perfect. Have you really got the time now?

Buzan, Tony (1997) *The Speed Reading Book*, rev. edn. London: BBC.

Scheele, Paul R. (1999) *The Photo Reading Whole Mind System*. Wayzata, MN: Learning Strategies.

Dudley, Geoffrey Arthur (1995) *Rapid Reading: High Speed Way to Increase Your Learning Power*. London: Thorsons.

ANSWERS TO EXERCISES

EXERCISE 2.1

You will progressively develop your skills in tracking down information. The important point is to keep yourself well informed and not to hesitate to explore different sources and techniques of information retrieval.

EXERCISE 2.2

Obviously you can only devote a short time to exploring the resources of the Internet at this stage. You will develop skills the more you use it. Take care that you do not get diverted from the subjects that you are searching information on. Like looking up a word in an encyclopedia, it is very easy to get stuck reading all the other interesting topics on the same page!

EXERCISE 2.3

1   When you reread your notes, now that you have read the article more thoroughly, does your initial summary contain all the essential points in the argument?

2   These notes will probably be rather fragmented, but will contain useful definitions and descriptions. The list form is often a useful way of recording information about concepts.

3   Make sure that your notes are not longer than the original text! Note that the first sentence of a paragraph usually introduces the subject of the paragraph. The following sentences elaborate or explain further. The last sentence might make a conclusion or a bridge to the next paragraph.

4   These last paragraphs often contain the real essence of the article or paper. This is why it is often good to begin reading a long thesis or paper by starting at the end! It is important not just to make notes summarizing the information you collect, but also to consider, as you are reading, the significance it has for your present thinking about your subject.

5   Try a Barbara Cartland novel (she wrote one every two weeks!)

EXERCISE 2.4

1   Having read the text to get an overall idea of the content and structure, you are now in position to make notes.

2   Here are notes that I have made in response to the questions. Compare them with those made by you. The reference appears at the top of each 'card', followed by the note.

(a) Grant, J. S. (1980) 'Britain, an impoverished nation?', *International Journal of Income Studies*, Vancouver: Collingdale, p. 33

on Peter Townsend's survey *Poverty in the United Kingdom*.

The main aims of this social survey were:

- to estimate the numbers in the population living in poverty or on the margins of poverty

- to discover the characteristics and problems relating to those in poverty and thus contributing to the explanation of poverty.

(b) Grant, J. S. (1980) 'Britain, an impoverished nation?', *International Journal of Income Studies*, Vancouver: Collingdale, pp. 35–7

on Peter Townsend's survey *Poverty in the United Kingdom*.

The main survey was conducted using a 39-page questionnaire, administered by trained interviewers. Nine issues were identified as important in the pilot research. These were each accorded a separate section in the questionnaire. The answers given were recorded by the interviewer in the precoded boxes alongside each question. These were later fed into a computer to allow statistical analysis.

Because great detail of each individual's lifestyle and resources was required, e.g. casual sources of earnings, elaborate interview and editing procedures were often required. Good interview skills and consistency of interpretation of answers were crucial. Townsend recognized that the nature of the questions and how they were asked crucially influenced the data obtained.

Non-response was potentially a major problem, distorting the results. Strenuous efforts were made to gain basic information even if the households refused to respond to the questionnaire or interview.

The actual response rate was high, with nearly 76% giving complete information, and a total of 82% giving a complete or partial response.

(c) Grant, J. S. (1980) 'Britain, an impoverished nation?', *International Journal of Income Studies*, Vancouver: Collingdale, p. 38

on Peter Townsend's survey *Poverty in the United Kingdom*.

The results showed that 25% of households (22.9% of the people surveyed), i.e. 12.46 million people in the total population, were affected by relative poverty. The estimation of the problem from this survey was seen to be much greater than the figures provided by the DHSS, which were based on claimants of supplementary benefits.

Seven groups fell into a 'high risk' category:

- one-person households
- large families
- one-parent families
- lower class people working in poor conditions
- unemployed people
- disabled people
- old people.

(d) Grant, J. S. (1980) 'Britain, an impoverished nation?', *International Journal of Income Studies*, Vancouver: Collingdale, p. 38

on Peter Townsend's survey *Poverty in the United Kingdom*.

When the results were compared with government figures, they showed that poverty problems are affecting more individuals than is generally or officially believed. This poverty is caused not only by social inequality but also by the actions of the rich to pre-serve and promote their wealth. Any action taken to alleviate poverty must recognize this.

Comment: since the definition of poverty is essentially subjective, the results of any survey carried out on this subject are open to debate. The validity of the results should be considered in relation to all the ingredients and actions constituting the survey.

(e) Grant, J. S. (1980) 'Britain, an impoverished nation?', *International Journal of Income Studies*, Vancouver: Collingdale, p. 34

on Peter Townsend's survey *Poverty in the United Kingdom*.

Of three poverty definitions mentioned, Townsend chose one which represented an inability of people to partake in a substantial number of commonplace activities enjoyed by the majority of people in the UK.

(f) Grant, J. S. (1980) 'Britain, an impoverished nation?', *International Journal of Income Studies*, Vancouver: Collingdale, p. 33

on Peter Townsend's survey *Poverty in the United Kingdom*.

The pilot research was conducted between 1965 and 1968. The subjects consisted of 150 households scattered in and around London.

The main survey was carried out in 1968–9, in 51 constituencies in the United Kingdom. A total of 2052 households covering 6098 individuals were involved. In parallel, four local surveys were carried out in poor areas covering 1208 households or 3950 individuals.

The book describing the survey and showing the results and conclusions was published in 1979.

(g) Grant, J. S. (1980) 'Britain, an impoverished nation?', *International Journal of Income Studies*, Vancouver: Collingdale, p. 35

on Peter Townsend's survey *Poverty in the United Kingdom*.

A random sample representing the population as a whole was very important in this social survey. A stratified multi-stage technique was adopted, in an attempt to make the sample as representative of the whole country as possible. Areas of the country were first chosen, stratified into high/middle/low income areas. The population of the areas was further stratified according to age and family size.

Representativeness of the sample was checked by comparing it with the population of Britain as a whole from the Registrar General's figures. The sample was found to be very representative.

(h) Grant, J. S. (1980) 'Britain, an impoverished nation?', *International Journal of Income Studies*, Vancouver: Collingdale, pp. 34–5

on Peter Townsend's survey *Poverty in the United Kingdom*.

On the basis of the definition of poverty, 60 indices of deprivation including all areas of personal, household and social life were devised. Graphs were plotted showing the number of deprivations suffered at different income levels. The income level at which the number of deprivations suffered increased disproportionately was taken as the poverty line. The total number of deprivations suffered was the crucial measurement of poverty.

3 These are the notes which should be included under the following headings:

- Poverty, definition: (e), (h).
- Poverty, research data: (c), (d).
- Measurement of concepts: (h).
- Sampling: (g).
- Questionnaires: (b).
- Research studies by date: (f).
- Townsend P.: (a), (b), (c), (d), (e), (f), (g), (h).
- Grant J.S.: (a), (b), (c), (d), (e), (f), (g), (h).

3

Types of Research

Introduction
Concepts and Theory
    Models
    Concepts
    Concept Measurement
    Quantification of Concepts
    Theory
Types Of Research
    Historical
    Comparative
    Descriptive
    Correlation
    Experimental
    Evaluation
    Action
    Ethnogenic
    Feminist
    Cultural
Conclusions
The Next Steps: Which Type of Research for Your Topic?
Checklist of Activities That Will Progress Your Research
    Consolidation and Assessment
Key Words
Further Reading
Answers to Exercises

- **To explore the nature of concepts and how they can be measured.**
- **To investigate the role of theory.**
- **To examine different types of research and their characteristics.**

INTRODUCTION

In your background reading you are sure to have noticed a variety of approaches in the research in your subject area. Obvious differences will have been in the scope of the work undertaken: for example, some studies survey the field in general, while others concentrate on specific cases or detailed aspects of the subject. Other differences between research studies in the levels of abstraction will have been clear. You might have also noticed different stresses put on quantitative or qualitative analysis and the amount of subjectivity inherent in the research. When exploring your subject area for a suitable problem on which to base your research, it must have become obvious to you that different types of problem require different methods to investigate them.

This chapter begins with a brief survey of the main components of enquiry – *concepts and theory*. It aims to clarify the meaning and significance of terms constantly used in research. Using these terms correctly will make it easier for you to communicate on a more technical level when discussing and analysing your research problem. This should help you to define your problem more accurately and help to indicate what research approach will be appropriate. It is worth noting that the precise meaning of many technical terms, such as theory, law and hypothesis, often depends on the context in which they are used and also on the interpretation of their meaning by the writer.

This is followed by an exploration of different *types of research*, categorized by the kind of research methodology used; this is dictated by the type of data to be collected and processed.

The intention of this chapter is to enable you to understand some of the basic choices you have for engaging in different types of research, and to help you understand how the nature of your research problem will influence the type of research you pursue.

CONCEPTS AND THEORY

Models

model   **Model** is a term used to describe the overall framework that we use to look at reality, based on the philosophical stance, e.g. postmodernism, poststructuralism, positivism, empiricism etc. The model tells us what basic elements it contains and describes what reality is really like, and conditions by which we can study it. The ideas derived from particular models are called concepts.

Concepts

concept   **Concepts** are general expressions of a particular phenomenon, e.g. cats, dogs, anger, achievement, alienation, speed, intelligence, socialism. If we examine these examples more closely, it is evident that each is a word which represents an idea. Cohen and Manion express this more accurately: 'a concept is the relationship between the word (or symbol) and an idea or conception' (1994, p. 17). Everybody, everywhere makes use of concepts. Of course, within the same culture, many concepts are commonly shared, such as baby, hate, justice; others, however, are only used and understood by small groups of people, specialists or members of professions, for instance idioglossia, interstitial condensation, anticipatory socialization.

It is through the use of concepts that we are able to impose some sort of coherent meaning on the world: it is through them that we make sense of reality, and perceive order and coherence. We use concepts to communicate our experience of the environment around us. Our perception of our surroundings is therefore highly dependent on the scale of our knowledge and our familiarity with a wide range of concepts. The more we know and use, the more sense we can make of the data we pick up and the more certain we will be of our perception (and cognitive) grasp of whatever is 'out there'. If it is the case that we see and understand the world only through the concepts which are available to us, then it follows that people who have a different repertoire of concepts will be inclined to perceive the 'same' objective reality differently. A lawyer examining a case will utilize a very different range of concepts from, say, the simple and common knowledge notions of the lay person in that context; and a visitor to the modern urban context from a primitive rural culture would be as confused by the hustle and bustle of the modern city as would be the mythical man in the moon (or Indiana Jones for that matter).

According to the model being followed, researchers in natural sciences will try to define the meaning of concepts very precisely. This, in many instances, is possible within the terms of the research. Social scientists, on the other hand, often recognize that the concepts within their model may be based on opinions, emotions, values, traditions, rules etc. and cannot be pinned down in the same way.

The use of concepts on their own in research is limited. If one assumes that the aims of research are to provide a system of classification (a typology), offer explanations, make predictions, and acquire a sense of understanding, then it is evident that it is only the first, providing a typology, which can be achieved using concepts alone. The remaining aims (offering explanations, making predictions, and acquiring a sense of understanding) must be expressed in the form of **statements** – statements **statement** that contain concepts. It follows that, in most research, the meaning and value of concepts cannot be assessed apart from their use in statements. In other words, according to Reynolds, 'the scientific value of concepts can only be judged in terms of the scientific utility of the statement containing them' (1971, p. 45). However, it is possible to evaluate concepts by an assessment of the clarity with which they are described. Clarity can be measured by the degree of agreement about a concept's use and its meaning among the users of the concept.

Concepts, which can perhaps be defined as a unit of understanding, are expressed and communicated through **symbols** in the form of language, spoken or written, **symbol** natural or artificial (such as mathematics). To convey meanings accurately, it is obviously essential that the sender and receiver of the symbols should agree on their meaning.

Symbols, in the form of words in spoken or written language, are normally referred to as **terms**, while the word 'symbol' is generally reserved for a mathe- **term** matical sign, e.g. £, +, %. It is possible to identify two types of terms used in any language, natural or artificial. Firstly, there are *primitive terms*. These cannot be described by using other terms, but rely on a shared agreement as to their meaning. Examples of these are: individual, interact, stone, hope. Secondly, there are *derived terms*. These can be described by the use of primitive terms, for example: group, business organization, curtain wall. Obviously, the meaning of primitive terms is more difficult to convey than that of derived terms, as one can explain them only by indicating examples and non-examples of the term.

Here are some terms, some of them primitive and some derived. State which they are and, if derived, how they can be defined using primitive terms. Here is an example to start with: EXERCISE 3.1

Lecture Derived. Defined using primitive terms (speech, person, front, audience): a speech given by a person in front of an audience.

The terms are:

1 car
2 meeting
3 railway line
4 doctor
5 neighbourhood.

You should observe that either a derived term, or its definition composed of primitive terms, expresses the same concept. The main advantage of the derived term is that its use is more efficient, and requires less effort than a set of words that compose the definition of the derived term.

Confusion can often occur when a term or symbol, however closely defined, is used in a particular context, but has different meanings in other contexts. Take for example the term 'architecture', which has one meaning in the built environment, but represents a completely different concept in the context of information technology. The symbol π will have different meanings for a mathematician and a Greek scholar.

Figure 3.1 Confusion can often occur when a symbol has different meanings in other contexts

This problem in research is common, particularly if the term or symbol is utilized in everyday language for other concepts. Often this added meaning, unintended by the writer, can dramatically change the meaning of a statement. To overcome this problem, researchers often use abstract symbols, invented or seldom-used words, or even Latin or Greek phrases to label a concept. However, such symbols or terms are often criticized for being abstract, sterile or difficult to read. Unfortunately, as long as readers are careless about their understanding of symbols or terms and insist on an 'easy read', there seems to be no simple solution to this problem. Problems of a more serious kind are caused when the writer does not define his/her symbols or terms in the first place.

Another type of definition should be mentioned: dictionary definition. This attempts to describe the concept indicated by the term. You will discover that most dictionary definitions are circular; looking up one word leads to a second which leads to a third which leads back to the first word. This is because the dictionary cannot describe primitive terms by using everyday language. An assumption must be made that the reader understands certain primitive terms. Pictures are often used to help illustrate the terms.

Abstract and concrete concepts

Concepts have characteristics which can be defined as *abstract* and *concrete*. According to Reynolds, abstract concepts are those concepts that are completely independent of a specific time or place. In other words, abstract concepts are not related to any unique spatial (location) or temporal (historical time) setting. They are often developed by and closely associated with particular types of research, e.g. marginality (ethnographic research), rhetorical organization (discourse analysis). If a concept is specific to a particular time or place, then it is considered concrete (Reynolds, 1971, p. 49).

Consider the following concepts and decide whether each is concrete or abstract. If it is concrete, can you describe what it is specific to? Here are two examples:

EXERCISE 3.2

Temperature Abstract.
Temperature of the sun Concrete – specific to location.

The concepts are:

1 three days
2 4 December 1967 to 6 December 1967
3 attitude
4 what Mr Smith thinks of Mr Jones
5 social system
6 the Women's Association
7 group
8 an afternoon in London.

You will notice that in each case of a concrete concept, it is possible to identify the abstract concepts which are contained therein; the concrete concepts are instances of abstract concepts.

Thought

Only one meaning of the word 'abstract' (independence from time and space etc.) has been discussed so far. There is another meaning which relates to the 'depth' of abstraction. Although it may be seen that two 'abstract' concepts are independent from time and space, one concept may nevertheless be more abstract than the other. If one concept is included within the meaning of the other, the second or more general concept is considered the more abstract. Reynolds (1971, p. 50) explains this by the following example. Consider the concept 'sentiment', an emotional disposition directed towards another, and the concept 'liking', a positive feeling for another. The concept 'sentiment' may be considered as including 'liking' along with 'love', 'respect' and 'admiration', but also 'hate', 'loathing' and others. In this example, 'sentiment' is the more abstract concept, for it encompasses the meaning of 'liking'.

When concepts are used in research, it is important that their level of abstraction is appropriate to the type of research undertaken. Concepts can be too abstract or too broad to be useful.

Concept measurement

One of the most important features of a scientific statement in the natural sciences is that it should have relevance to the real world: it should be possible to compare the statement to some phenomenon or phenomena. Normally, this is achieved by identifying palpable events or occurrences which can be perceived to demonstrate instances of the theoretical concepts. This means that it is essential that some of the theoretical concepts relate to sensory impressions in concrete situations. It is not obligatory, however, to be able to measure all of the concepts in a set of statements or theory. After all, it is not possible to actually see an atom or an electron. What can be seen are the effects which can be ascribed to electrons or atoms. Theoretical concepts that cannot be directly measured in a real-life setting are sometimes called 'hypothetical constructs'.

In the social sciences, concept measurement is commonly a difficult issue. It is impossible to be so precise when dealing with matters of belief, customs, behaviour and values. It may be obvious that there are differences in, say, levels of commitment, strength of belief etc. A measurement of these levels will depend on the communication of the person (or persons, institutions etc.) and the perception and personal judgement of the researcher. No simple reading of a thermometer dipped into the hot bathwater here! However, social data can be collected which are amenable to some forms of measurement, for example economic data, population statistics and suchlike.

In order to determine the existence of a theoretical concept in a real-life setting, one must devise special types of definitions to provide the necessary instructions. These types of instructions are called **operational definitions**. Reynolds defined these as in Box 3.1.

operational
definition

Box 3.1   Definition of operational definitions

A set of procedures that describes the activities an observer should perform in order to receive sensory impressions (sounds, visual or tactile impressions etc.) that indicate the existence or degree of existence of a theoretical concept. (Reynolds, 1971, p. 52)

The significant feature of operational definitions is that they are abstract, that is, independent of time and space. This enables them to be used in different real-life situations and at different times.

For example, it may be possible to measure a group of people's individual state of fitness (the overall physical condition of the body) in any of three ways:

1   allow trained observers, e.g. sports teachers or trainers, to indicate their judgement on the basis of a series of performance tests
2   collect measures of physiological activity, such as blood pressure, breathing rate or pulse rate, at rest and during action
3   give the individuals a questionnaire and study the pattern of activities which are regularly undertaken (a 'yes' answer to the question 'do you run more than 5 miles every week?' may be considered as an indicator of greater fitness than 'no').

Each of these procedures can be seen to relate to the theoretical concept of fitness and can be used to measure fitness in different situations. Each gives a description of what needs to be done (without going into technical details) in order to gain a sensory impression related to someone's degree of fitness, i.e. ratings of expert observers, measurements related to physical characteristics, or the individual's responses on a questionnaire.

Consider how measuring a group of individuals' level of fitness in this way is different to assessing how fit they generally feel, i.e. measuring not fitness but the feeling of fitness. The operational definitions would be quite different and relate to more abstract and subjective procedures of a qualitative nature rather than quantitative measurement.

In these cases it is important that the methods of assessment or measurement of these concepts are critically examined from the point of view of reliability. In the above example you could:

1   question the subjects as to what they regarded fitness to be, and how near to that condition they felt they were
2   observe their attitudes towards carrying out physical tasks, such as carrying heavy shopping bags or running for a bus
3   analyse their conversations about the subject of fitness to gauge their attitudes and feelings.

These forms of assessment tend to rely heavily on individual interpretation. So further attention should be given to the issue of the reliability of these measures. Subject error might occur if the subject does not really understand the questions, or subject bias might result if the subject tries falsely to impress the researcher as to how fit he/she feels. Observer error might also occur if the researcher asks or observes some subjects at a particularly stressful time, perhaps after an exceptionally strenuous day at work. Observer bias might result in uneven criteria being used, e.g. the conviction that overweight people must feel unfit.

The relationship between theoretical concepts and the suitability of operational definitions for measuring the existence of the theoretical concept is largely one of judgement. According to Reynolds (1971, p. 55), a single operational definition can be evaluated by two criteria, as in Box 3.2.

Box 3.2   Criteria for evaluating an operational definition

1   Gauge its suitability as a measurement procedure.
2   Assess its relation to a theoretical concept.

---

intersubjectivity

A major test of the suitability of an operational definition as a measurement procedure is that of **intersubjectivity** or inter-observer agreement. If two or more properly trained observers independently follow the procedures specified to measure the same object or phenomenon, will they arrive at the same results? In reality there is seldom a total agreement between observers when they apply the same operational definition to a phenomenon, owing to random errors, errors of measurement and, when dealing with humans, to changes of mind, different moods and many other factors. The issue central to the research effort is whether the degree of agreement which results is sufficient to answer the research question. The level of agreement that is acceptable depends very much on the type of research technique which is used and the situation in which the tests are carried out.

As for the relationship between the operational definition and the theoretical concept, this is not so straightforward to assess. By carefully studying a theoretical concept one can reasonably devise or deduce some of its characteristics which can possibly be measured (features of a person, group, organization, experience etc.) and which can be seen to be directly related to the theoretical concept. This process will always be largely a matter of judgement. The suitability of an operational definition for measuring a theoretical concept can only be assessed by the level of intersubjective agreement which can be attained. It is a sobering fact, when seen from a positivist perspective, that this, the most important step in linking abstract theories to concrete phenomena, relies ultimately on informed judgement.

Use your informed judgement to devise three operational definitions for each of the following theoretical concepts:

1 school
2 fear
3 community
4 condensation
5 hunger
6 magnetism
7 pressure group.

Quantification of concepts

The theoretical concept of 'school building' acts as a label for a particular type of building. There is rarely any need to measure to what degree a building is a school building: either it is or it is not. A concept like 'fear', however, which refers to the characteristics of an object or a phenomenon, can differ in degree, e.g. extreme or mild. There is, therefore, a need to use some method to measure, or quantify, this form of concept. But can it be quantified in the same way as counting the number of sheep in a flock?

The **quantification** of concepts is usually associated with the operational definitions, e.g. measuring attitudes on a scale from −3 to +3, but it can also be applied to theoretical concepts. When applied to operational definitions, the different types of quantification are generally referred to as **levels of measurement**.

In 1946, S. S. Stephens suggested a hierarchy of levels of measurement that has been widely adopted by statisticians and researchers, not only for use in the measurement of concepts and operational definitions, but also for measuring data. His system comprises four levels of measurement, which he calls nominal, ordinal, interval and ratio levels of measurement. Basic to all measurement is the essential nature of the concepts, operational definitions or data, which lend themselves to measurement at one level or another according to their characteristics and the manner in which they are considered and classified for analysis.

The word **nominal** is derived from the Latin word *nomen*, meaning 'name'. Nominal measurement is very basic and unrefined. Its simple function is to divide the data into separate categories that can then be compared with each other. By first giving names to or labelling the parts or states of concepts or by naming discrete units of data, we are then able to measure the concept or data at the simplest level. For example, many theoretical concepts are conceived on a nominal level of quantification. 'Status structure' as a theoretical concept may have only two states: either a group of individuals have one or they do not (such as a collection of people waiting for a bus). Buildings may be classified into many types, e.g. commercial, industrial, educational, religious etc. Many operational definitions

quantification

levels of measurement

nominal level

are on a nominal level, e.g. sex (male or female), marital status (single, married, separated, divorced or widowed). This applies in the same way for some types of data, e.g. dividing a group of children into boys and girls, or into fair-haired, brown-haired or black-haired children, and so on.

In effect, different states of a concept or different categories of data which are quantified at a nominal level can only be labelled, and it is not possible to make statements about the differences between the states or categories, except to say that they are recognized as being different.

We can represent nominal data by certain graphic and statistical devices. Bar graphs, for example, can be appropriately used to represent the comparative measurement of nominal data. By measuring this type of data, using statistical techniques, it is possible to locate the mode, find a percentage relationship of one subgroup to another or of one subgroup to the total group, and compute the chi-square. We will discuss the mode and chi-square later (in Chapter 7); they are mentioned here merely to indicate that nominal data may be processed statistically.

If a concept is considered to have a number of states, or the data have a number of values that can be rank ordered, it is assumed that some meaning is conveyed **ordinal level** by the relative order of the states. The **ordinal** scale implies that an entity being measured is quantified in terms of being more than or less than, or of a greater or lesser order than, a comparative entity, often expressed by the symbols < or >.

For anyone studying at school or at university, the most familiar ordinal measures are the grades which are used to rate academic performance. An A always means more than a B, and a B always means more than a C, but the difference between A and B may not always be the same as the difference between B and C in terms of academic achievement. Similarly, we measure level of education grossly on an ordinal scale by saying individuals are unschooled, or have an elementary school, a secondary school, a college or a university education. Likewise, we measure members of the workforce on an ordinal scale by calling them unskilled, semi-skilled or skilled.

Figure 3.2 For anyone studying at university, the most familiar ordinal measures are the grades which are used to rate academic performance

Most of the theoretical concepts in the social sciences seem to be at an ordinal level of quantification. In summary, 'ordinal level of quantification' applies to concepts that vary in such a way that different states of the concept can be rank ordered with respect to some characteristic.

The ordinal scale of measurement expands the range of statistical techniques that can be applied to data. Using the ordinal scale, we can find the mode and the median, determine the percentage or percentile rank, and test by the chi-square. We can also indicate relationships by means of rank correlation.

The **interval** scale has two essential characteristics: it has equal units of measurement; and its zero point, if present, is arbitrary. Temperature scales are one of the most familiar types of interval scales. In each of the Fahrenheit and Celsius scales, the gradation between each degree is equal to all the others, and the zero point has been established arbitrarily. The Fahrenheit scale clearly shows how arbitrary is the setting of the zero point. At first, the zero point was taken by Gabriel Fahrenheit to be the coldest temperature observed in Iceland. Later he made the lowest temperature obtainable with a mixture of salt and ice, and took this to be 0 degrees. Among the measurements of the whole range of possible temperatures, taking this point was evidently a purely arbitrary decision. It placed the freezing point of water at 32 degrees, and the boiling point at 212 degrees above zero.

interval level

Although equal-interval theoretical concepts like temperature abound in the physical sciences, they are harder to find in the social sciences. Though abstract concepts are rarely inherently interval based, operational measures employed to quantify them often use quantification at an interval level. For example, attitudes are frequently measured on a scale like this:

Unfavourable   −4   −3   −2   −1   0   +1   +2   +3   +4   Favourable

If it is assumed that the difference between +2 and +4 is the same as the difference between say 0 and −2, then this can be seen as an attempt to apply an interval level of quantification to this measurement procedure. This is quite a big assumption to make! The tendency for some social scientists to assume the affirmative is probably because some of the most useful summary measures and statistical tests require quantification on an interval level, e.g. for determining the mode, mean, standard deviation, t-test, F-test and product moment correlation.

Questions are also frequently raised about the unrealistic preciseness of the responses. Are the meanings intended by the researcher's questions equivalent to those understood by the respondent? Is the formulaic choice of answers given compatible with what the respondent wishes to reply? I am sure you remember your reaction to attitude quizzes, where the answer 'it all depends' seems more appropriate to a question than any of the multiple choice answers offered.

The **ratio level** of measurement has a true zero, that is, the point where the measurement is truly equal to nought – the total absence of the quantity being measured. We are all familiar with concepts in physical science which are both theoretically and operationally conceptualized at a ratio level of quantification. Time, distance, velocity (a combination of time and distance), mass and weight are all concepts that have a zero state in an interval scale, both theoretically and operationally. So, there is no ambiguity in the statements 'twice as far', 'twice as fast' and 'twice as heavy'. Compared with this, other statements which use this level of measurement inappropriately are meaningless, e.g. 'twice as clever', 'twice as prejudiced' or 'twice the prestige', since there is no way of knowing where zero clever, zero prejudice or zero prestige are.

A characteristic difference between the ratio scale and all other scales is that the ratio scale can express values in terms of multiples of fractional parts, and the ratios are true ratios. A metre rule can do that: a metre is a multiple (by 100) of a centimetre distance, a millimetre is a tenth (a fractional part) of a centimetre. The ratios are 1:100 and 1:10. Of all levels of measurement, the ratio scale is amenable to the greatest range of statistical tests. It can be used for determining the geometric mean, the harmonic mean, the percentage variation and all other statistical determinations.

In summary, perhaps Senders has encapsulated this discussion in the simple test for various kinds of concept and data measurement given in Box 3.3.

Box 3.3 Simple tests for levels of measurement

If you can say that:

- one object is different from another, you have a *nominal scale*;
- one object is bigger, better or more of anything than another, you have an *ordinal scale*;
- one object is so many units (degrees, inches) more than another, you have an *interval scale*;
- one object is so many times as big or bright or tall or heavy as another, you have a *ratio scale*. (Senders, 1958, p. 51)

EXERCISE 3.4

What level of quantification is appropriate for the following concepts and operational measures:

1   reading interest: poetry, fiction, biography
2   sex: girls, boys
3   voltage: 25 V, 75 V, 2000 V
4   intelligence quotient (IQ): 90, 102, 125, 130

5   exam grade: C–, C+, B, B+, A
6   comfort level: very uncomfortable, uncomfortable, comfortable, very comfortable
7   atmospheric pressure: 0.5 bar, 1.3 bar, 2.7 bar, 10 bar
8   wealth: destitute, poor, middle income, high income, wealthy
9   annual income: less than £1000, £1000–£4999, £5000–£9999, £10,000 and over
10   annual income: £3000, £7300, £9000, £17,000
11   dew point (point at which condensation occurs): 2 °C, 12 °C, 17 °C, 24 °C
12   titles: baronet, knight, duke, earl, viscount, lord
13   trades: plumber, electrician, mason, carpenter
14   playbricks: red cube, yellow pyramid, red cylinder, blue sphere, yellow cube, red sphere?

It will be seen that one of the principal advantages of using quantification is that it permits the formulation of more precise statements regarding the degree of association, or correlation, between two or more concepts. (This will be treated in more detail in Chapters 5 and 6.) Exploration of the relationships between concepts is often one of the important activities in research. Different levels of quantification can be used to categorize the different types of relationship between concepts. A nominal level of association is equivalent to the statement that two concepts are or are not related. An ordinal level of association is equivalent to the statement that concepts are positively, not or negatively correlated.

When data are analysed, such statements of association are generally related to operational definitions. Levels of quantification, if correctly applied, are particularly useful when discussing the interrelations among more than two variables.

Thought

We have discussed at some length the nature and characteristics of concepts, and how they can be measured. In your research, you will be using many concepts and probably measuring some of them too. However, what will certainly be of most interest to you, and to everyone else, is not just the meaning of the concepts, or their measurement, but the nature and extent of the relationships between them, which if explained will lead towards a greater understanding of the subject under scrutiny. This is where theory is important.

Theory

Cohen and Manion (1994) maintained that, for professional scientists, science is seen as a way of comprehending the world; as a means of explanation and understanding, of prediction and control. For them, the ultimate aim of science is **theory**.   theory
Theories are expressed in the form of statements, i.e. theoretical statements.

Kerlinger (1970) defined theory as 'a set of interrelated constructs (concepts), definitions and propositions that presents a systematic view of phenomena by specifying relations among variables, with a purpose of explaining and predicting phenomena'. Theory effectively combines diverse and isolated pieces of empirical data to create an intelligible conceptual model which is capable of being more generally applied. Mouly (1978) expressed it like this: 'if nothing else, a theory is a convenience – a necessity, really – organizing a whole slough of unsorted facts, laws, concepts, constructs, principles, into a meaningful and manageable form. It constitutes an attempt to make sense out of what we know concerning a given phenomenon.'

Additionally, however, theory provides a useful platform from which to launch a quest for information and discoveries, and an impetus for research. New hypotheses can be suggested and new questions revealed. Theory formulation leads to the identification of important areas which require further research, points out where information is missing, and makes it possible for a researcher to propose the existence of hitherto unidentified phenomena.

Figure 3.3 Theory formulation makes it possible for a researcher to propose the existence of hitherto unidentified phenomena

Theory varies greatly in status and quality, depending on the type of discipline or subject area considered. In well established natural sciences, for example in chemistry, theories tend to be highly developed and refined, while in other fields, for example in the social sciences, they tend to be relatively undeveloped, less widely accepted and of more uneven quality. This is due to the pioneering quality of much theoretical work carried out in comparatively new disciplines. In the social sciences, Silverman (1998, p. 103) sees theories as living entities, developed and modified by good research. However, because they instruct us to look at phenomena in particular ways, theories, and the concepts on which they are based, are self-confirming, meaning that they can never be disproved, as in natural science, but only found to be more or less useful. The nature of a theory is therefore strongly influenced by the level of maturity of the particular specialization. The early stages of a science must be dominated by empirical work, that is, the accumulation and classification of data. Only as a discipline matures can an adequate body of theory be developed.

What criteria are there for judging the quality of a theory? Mouly identified, from a positivistic point of view, what he thought were the main characteristics of a good theory, as shown in Box 3.4.

Box 3.4   Main characteristics of a good theory

1   A theoretical system must permit deductions that can be tested empirically; that is, it must provide the means for its confirmation or rejection. One can test the validity of a theory only through the validity of the propositions (hypotheses) that can be derived from it. If repeated attempts to disconfirm its various hypotheses fail, then greater confidence can be placed in its validity. This can go on indefinitely, until possibly some hypothesis proves untenable. This would constitute indirect evidence of the inadequacy of the theory and could lead to its rejection (or more commonly to its replacement by a more adequate theory that can incorporate the exception).

2   Theory must be compatible with both the observation and previously validated theories. It must be grounded in empirical data that have been verified and must rest on sound postulates and hypotheses. The better the theory, the more adequately it can explain the phenomenon under consideration, and the more fact it can incorporate into a meaningful structure of ever-greater generalizibility.

3   Theories must be stated in simple terms; that theory is best that explains the most in the simplest way. This is the law of parsimony. A theory must explain the data adequately and yet must not be so comprehensive as to be unwieldy. On the other hand, it must not overlook the variables simply because they are difficult to explain. (Mouly in Cohen and Manion, 1994, pp. 15–16)

This sounds all very well for the natural sciences, but some of these conditions cannot be achieved in the social sciences. In point 2, it may be impossible to ground the theory on empirical data that have been verified in the sense of measurement and repeated observations. Following this, it may be difficult therefore to objectively test the validity of its various hypotheses as demanded in point 1.

What is important to stress, though, is the relationship between developing theory and previously validated theory as mentioned in point 2. The theoretical background to one's enquiries will determine how one looks at the world. As Quine (1969) argued, our experience of the world of facts does not impose any single theory on us. Theories are underdetermined by facts, and our factual knowledge of the external world is capable of supporting many different interpretations of it. The answer to the question 'what exists?' can only receive the answer 'what exists is what theory posits'. Since there are different theories, these will posit different things. There will always be more than one logically equivalent theory consistent with the evidence we have. This is not because the evidence may be insufficient, but because the same facts can be accommodated in different ways by alterations in the configuration of the theory (Hughes and Sharrock, 1997, pp. 88–91).

One philosopher of science expressed it this way: 'it is generally agreed … that the idea of a descriptive vocabulary which is applicable to observations, but which is entirely innocent of theoretical influences, is unrealizable' (Harré, 1972, p. 25). Therefore, without a theory, one could argue that phenomena cannot be understood, and research cannot be carried out without a theoretical underpinning: 'models, concepts and theories are self-confirming in the sense that they instruct us to look at phenomena in particular ways. This means that they can never be disproved but only found to be more or less useful' (Silverman, 1998, p. 103).

It follows then that all theories must, by their very nature, be provisional. However sophisticated and elegant a theory is, it cannot be all-encompassing or final. The fact that it is a theory, an abstraction from real life, means that it must always be subject to possible change or development, and in extreme cases, even replacement.

Figure 3.4   All theories must, by definition, be provisional

Reynolds (1971, Chapter 5) claimed that scientific knowledge is basically a collection of abstract theoretical statements. He identified three different conceptions of how sets of statements should be organized in order to constitute a 'theory'. The first, which plays a very important part in science, is the view that knowledge is essentially a set of laws – statements that can be considered, for the time being anyway, to be the 'real truth'. The second conception of what constitutes a theory is axiomatic in form, i.e. based on self-evident truths. The third, referred to as the causal process form, sees theory as made up of an inter-related set of definitions and statements. The following summary of his descriptions of these theoretical forms will indicate some of their main characteristics.

The firm foundations upon which most scientific enquiry is based is usually expressed as a law or a system of laws. Basically, a law is a statement that describes a relationship in which scientists have so much confidence that they consider it an absolute 'truth'. An example of one of these is the law of gravity. Most statements that are called laws contain concepts that can be measured or identified in concrete settings, and many scientists insist that they should define an associational or, better still, a causal relationship between concepts. A theory can thus comprise a set of separate, though interrelated, laws. The usefulness of a **set of laws theory** for achieving the goals of science can be judged by testing to what extent the theory can be used to classify and organize the components of the phenomenon under study, whether it can provide logical explanations and reliable predictions.

set of laws theory

The main disadvantage of this concept of theory is that, despite achieving most of the basic goals of science, it cannot lead to a 'sense of understanding' of the phenomena. 'Why?' and 'how?' are questions not considered in laws.

Another concept of theory is **axiomatic theory**. This type of theory comprises an initial set of statements (axioms or self-evident truths), each independent of the others (they say different things), and from which it is possible to logically derive all the other statements (propositions) of the theory. Unlike the set of laws type of theory, the initial statements (axioms) are not required to be 'laws', fully supported by empirical evidence. In fact, in the most familiar form of axiomatic theory, Pythagorean geometry, the axioms are abstract and independent of the 'real world'.

axiomatic theory

As with the set of laws form of theory, the axiomatic form can be used to classify and organize phenomena and to logically derive explanations and predictions. Similarly, it also fails to provide a means of gaining a 'sense of understanding' of the phenomena, unless the statements are put in a causal process form.

Unlike the previous two concepts of theory, the **causal process theory** is designed to promote an understanding of the events studied. It consists of an interrelated set of definitions and statements which not only define the theory, but describe when and where the causal processes are expected to occur, and explain the causal processes or causal mechanisms by identifying the effect of the independent variables on the dependent variables. All the statements are regarded as of equal importance, unlike in the axiomatic form in which there are two categories of statement (axioms and propositions), and they are expressed as a causal sequence. In this form, as in the axiomatic form, unmeasurable concepts are allowed and limits must be drawn on the scope of application to which the theory will be relevant.

causal process theory

The causal process concept of theory shares with the other two types the ability to classify and organize phenomena and logically to derive explanations and predictions. Its additional strength is that it promotes understanding of how and why events occur as they do. One main advantage of the causal process form is that it seems to be derived naturally from common methods of analysing and developing ideas, particularly in the social sciences, by asking how and why things occur.

I will add one more concept of theory which has a direct bearing on the social sciences. The problem of establishing 'facts' within the studies of humanity and society makes the positivist approach to theory, based on delineated observable and often measurable phenomena, difficult to follow. If the idea that observation is an entirely theoretically neutral affair is challenged, then it follows that the observer is a component in the construction of knowledge.

> On this view, scientific theories become like inventions actively engaged in creating a reality, not passively awaiting their substantiation by the facts of the external world. (Hughes, 1990, p. 64)

conceptual scheme theory

As experimentation to 'falsify' social 'facts' is not possible in order to challenge social theories, such theories are better seen as **conceptual schemes** designating, or even prescribing, what constitute the characteristics of these facts. Theories provide the impetus for research as 'living entities'.

Thought

A lot has been said in the previous paragraphs about theoretical statements. It will be useful at this stage to introduce a list of terms used for theoretical statements which will provide a kind of hierarchy, with at the lowest extreme those statements which are conjectural and untested, and at the highest extreme those statements which are generally recognized to be true.

In the early stages of a research project, tentative theoretical statements are often made which are products of the research problem. Preliminary investigation into the problem might suggest reasons behind it, or relationships between factors creating or influencing it. Sometimes, especially in the social sciences, owing to the qualitative nature of the data, it is not possible to formulate a theoretical statement which can be rigorously tested, in the sense that clear evidence for support or rejection will result. Nonetheless, a statement can indicate a clear direction and scope for the research work needing to be carried out. In this case, theoretical statements can be formulated as **research questions** or **propositions**.

research question proposition

If, however, the reasons or relationships are expressed in a theoretical statement which has not yet been tested against data collected in a concrete situation, but which it *is* possible to test, the statement is called a **hypothesis**. The source

hypothesis

of the hypothesis may be a variation of a law or a development of axiomatic theory, or may be initiated by a scientist's informed guess or intuition; but its essential feature is that it can be compared with experimental or observational data collected in the real world. It should be possible to devise tests for the hypothesis which will provide clear evidence to support it, or lead to its rejection.

If research reveals a similar pattern of events in a number of empirical studies, the pattern is often summarized as an **empirical generalization** – a generalization based on several empirical studies. Obviously, because they summarize patterns in empirical research, all the concepts in an empirical generalization must be directly measurable.

empirical generalization

Scientists' confidence in **laws** is considerably greater than it is in empirical generalizations. As already noted, laws are statements that describe relationships. They are so well supported by evidence, and confidence in their reliability is so strong, that they are considered to express the 'truth' in the cases to which they apply.

law

Paradigm is a term used not to describe a particular type of theoretical statement, but rather to indicate the overall effect of the acceptance of a particular general theoretical approach, often expressed as a law or a theory (e.g. Newton's laws of mechanics and of gravitation, Einstein's theory of relativity), and the influence it has on the scientists' view of the world. Kuhn used the term 'paradigm' for scientific achievements which shared two essential characteristics, as in Box 3.5.

paradigm

Box 3.5   Essential characteristics of a paradigm

A paradigm is:

1 ... sufficiently unprecedented to attract an enduring group of adherents away from competing modes of scientific activity ...
2 ... sufficiently open-ended to leave all sorts of problems for the redefined group of practitioners to resolve. (Kuhn, 1970, p. 10)

As a result, actual scientific practice, following from the acceptance of these scientific laws and theories, including application and instrumentation, provides models from which spring particular coherent traditions of scientific research. The basic innovative work has been completed, and there is a consensus among the scientific body that these theories represent a firm foundation for further investigation. This 'normal' scientific work is concerned with research which searches for evidence in the real world for the workings of the theory, enumerates and measures the theory more precisely, and explores the validity of the theory in related fields.

A summary of this discussion is given in Box 3.6.

Box 3.6 Statements, hypotheses, empirical generalizations, laws and paradigms

- At its most tentative, a *theoretical statement* can be formulated as a research question or proposition in order to direct the research efforts.
- If there is as yet no empirical evidence for or against a theoretical statement, but it can be tested empirically, it is called a *hypothesis*.
- If there is moderate support, it is called an *empirical generalization*.
- If the support is overwhelming, it is called a *law*. Be warned that since scientists have different standards for evaluating theoretical statements, one person's law may be another person's hypothesis.
- When a system of laws is commonly accepted, it leads to a sanctioning of particular ways of thinking and methods of investigation: this is called a *paradigm*.

TYPES OF RESEARCH

The different kinds of questions which instigate research require approaches to research which are distinguished by their theoretical background and methodologies. A brief summary of various types of research will illustrate the possibilities for your research efforts.

Several major types of research can be identified, as in Box 3.7. Writers differ in how they distinguish between them, and some catalogue many more than those listed.

Box 3.7 Major types of research

1 Historical.
2 Comparative.
3 Descriptive.
4 Correlation.
5 Experimental.
6 Evaluation.
7 Action.
8 Ethnogenic.
9 Feminist.
10 Cultural.

I will use these types as convenient overall headings and include under them a variety of approaches which share some common features.

Historical

Historical research has been defined as the systematic and objective location, evaluation and synthesis of evidence in order to establish facts and draw conclusions about past events (Borg, 1963).

It involves exploring the meaning and relationship of events, and as its resource it uses primary historical data in the form of historic artefacts, records and writings. It attempts to find out what happened in the past and to reveal reasons for why and how things happened. The value of historical research has been categorized by Hill and Kerber (1967) as in Box 3.8.

Box 3.8   Values of historical research

- It enables solutions to contemporary problems to be sought in the past.
- It throws light on present and future trends.
- It stresses the relative importance and the effects of the interactions that are found within all cultures.
- It allows for the revaluation of data supporting selected hypotheses, theories and generalizations that are presently held about the past.

Historical evidence, consisting of primary historical data, must be scrutinized from two points of view. The first is to ascertain whether the artefact or document to be studied is genuine. There have been many mistakes made in the past, either through a lack of analytical rigour by over-enthusiastic researchers, or through fraud. (You might remember the Piltdown Skull, fraudulent skull bones which researchers long believed to be the 'missing link' in human history.) The second is to examine, in written evidence in the form of historic documents etc., the authenticity of the contents. What is the meaning of what is written, and how accurate is it? For example, many authentic medieval texts are known to be wildly inaccurate and vague in their descriptions of events.

Figure 3.5   The first is to ascertain whether the artefact to be studied is genuine

According to Gottschalk (1951) there are four aspects of historical research which determine the scope of a study, as shown in Box 3.9.

Box 3.9 Aspects of historical research that determine scope

1   Where the events take place.
2   Which people are involved.
3   When the events occurred.
4   What kind of human activity was involved.

The degree to which an aspect is studied can be varied, i.e. the number of human activities examined can be increased or decreased, the time-span covered can be extended or contracted etc. It must be remembered that the mere collection of historic facts, or the setting up of chronologies of events, does not constitute research. Although these are a necessary part of historical research, an interpretation of the meanings and an assessment of the significance of the events are required.

Historic research is not based purely on scientific method. For instance, the data used are seldom based on direct observation or experimentation. But it should share many of the disciplines of scientific method, such as objectivity and the desire to minimize bias and distortion, the use of scientific techniques such as chemical and radioactive analysis, and statistics. The problem for historians tends to be the paucity of information, while scientists are often overwhelmed by it!

All research students, whatever their chosen field of study, have to undertake a review of the literature. This is a study of what has been done and written in the past, and so the principles of historical research can be seen to be of direct relevance to this part of their work.

Comparative

Comparative research is often used together with historical research. Researchers compare people's experience of different societies, either between times in the past or in parallel situations in the present. These studies can be on the macro level, e.g. studying the role of revolutions in class struggle, or on the micro level, e.g. individual experiences in different types of marriage.

It is often easier to understand phenomena when they are compared with similar phenomena from another time or place. Culture and society rely heavily on what has gone before and often use references from the past to justify the present. The constitution, the tax system, social mores are all rooted in their own histories. Similarly, place also determines that phenomena develop differently.

The study and comparison of differences help to reveal the origins and development of social phenomena, locating them in a certain time and place, and thus defeating claims that they are universal and atemporal.

> Many social theories are presented as if the generalizations that they embody are valid for all times and places, when in fact they were arrived at on the basis of limited contemporary Western experience. (Llobera, 1998, p. 74)

We can also learn by making comparisons both with the past and with experiences elsewhere. It would be foolish for politicians to introduce, say, sweeping changes to the electoral system, without carefully studying the effects of such changes in the past and in other situations.

Experimental research (described below), where the researcher can artificially control causal factors, is not really possible in social research. However, the idea is put forward that history and comparison can often supply the researcher with what is a natural experiment. According to Mill's method of agreement (one of his five 'methods of experimental enquiry' devised in the nineteenth century), 'If two or more instances of the phenomenon under investigation have only one circumstance in common, the circumstances in which alone all the instances agree is the cause (or effect) of the given phenomenon' (1973, p. 390). Using this test it is possible to compare the suggested causes of several instances of a phenomenon (e.g. an industrial strike) and eliminate those that are not present in all instances as being non-essential to the occurrence of the phenomenon. For example, reasons for striking could be trade union power struggles, poor working conditions, resistance to change, low pay, unfair labour relations etc. If, say, one cause only is present in all cases, e.g. unfair labour relations, then one could conclude that this is likely to be the determining cause. One could then check to see if a situation where unfair labour relations did not result in a strike could be found. If not, then this would support the foregoing conclusion.

This kind of comparative exercise to explore and test causal factors is an emblem of good research of this type, and helps to overcome the fact that the researcher has no control over the available variables.

Descriptive

Instead of examining record or artefacts, descriptive research relies on observation as a means of collecting data. It attempts to examine situations in order to establish what is the norm, i.e. what can be predicted to happen again under the same circumstances.

'Observation' can take many forms. Depending on the type of information sought, people can be interviewed, questionnaires distributed, visual records made, even sounds and smells recorded. The important point is that the observations are written down or recorded in some way, in order that they can be subsequently analysed. It is important that the data so collected are organized and presented in a clear and systematic way, so that the analysis can result in valid and accurate conclusions.

The scale of the research is influenced by two major factors, identified in Box 3.10.

Box 3.10   Influence on scale of descriptive research

1   The level of complexity of the survey.
2   The scope of the survey.

For example, seeking relationships between specific events inevitably requires a more complex survey technique than aiming merely to describe the nature of existing conditions. Likewise, surveying a large number of cases over a wide area will require greater resources than a small, local survey.

In order both to save on unnecessary work and to give accurate information on the subject of your research, the sample of people or events surveyed (technically called the population) must be carefully chosen and delineated. To do this, it is necessary to be aware of the precise subject focus of the research so that specific objectives can be formulated.

As descriptive research depends on human observations and responses, there is a danger that distortion of the data can occur. This can be caused, among other ways, by inadvertently including biased questions in questionnaires or interviews, or through selective observation of events. Although bias cannot be wholly eliminated, an awareness of its existence and likely extent is essential.

Correlation

The information sought in correlation research is expressed not in the form of artefacts, words or observations, but in numbers. While historical and descriptive approaches are predominantly forms of qualitative research, analytical survey or correlation research is principally quantitative. 'Correlation' is another word to describe the measure of association or the relationships between two phenomena.

In order to find meaning in the numerical data, the techniques of statistics are used. What kind of statistical tests are used to analyse the data depends very much on the nature of the data.

This form of quantitative research can be broadly classified into two types of studies, as shown in Box 3.11.

Box 3.11   Types of quantitative studies

1   Relational studies.
2   Prediction studies.

The first is an investigation of possible relationships between phenomena to establish if a correlation exists and, if so, its extent. This exploratory form of research is carried out particularly where little or no previous work has been done, and its outcomes can form the basis for further investigations.

Prediction studies tend to be carried out in research areas where correlations are already known. This knowledge is used to predict possible future behaviour or events, on the basis that if there has been a strong relationship between two or more characteristics or events in the past, then these should exist in similar circumstances in the future, leading to predictable outcomes.

In order to produce statistically significant results, quantitative research demands data from a large number of cases. Greater numbers of cases tend to produce more reliable results; 20–30 is considered to be about the minimum, though this depends on the type of statistical test applied. The data, whatever their original character, must be converted into numbers.

One of the advantages of correlation research is that it allows for the measurement of a number of characteristics (technically called variables) and their relationships simultaneously. Particularly in social science, many variables contribute to a particular outcome (e.g. satisfaction with housing depends on many factors). Another advantage is that, unlike other research approaches, it produces a measure of the *amount* of relationship between the variables being studied. It also, when used in prediction studies, gives an estimation of the probable accuracy of the predictions made. One limitation to what can be learned from correlation research is that, while the association of variables can be established, the cause and effect relationships are not revealed.

Experimental

Experimental research differs from the other research approaches noted above through its greater control over the objects of its study. The researcher strives to isolate and control every relevant condition which determines the events investigated, so as to observe the effects when the conditions are manipulated. Chemical experiments in a laboratory represent one of the purest forms of this research type.

At its simplest, an experiment involves making a change in the value of one variable – called the independent variable – and observing the effect of that change on another variable – called the dependent variable. (Cohen and Manion, 1994, p. 164)

Thus, the most important characteristic of the experimental approach is that it deals with the phenomenon of 'cause and effect'.

However, the actual experiment is only a part of the research process. There are several planned stages in experimental research. When the researcher has established that the study is amenable to experimental methods, a prediction (technically called a hypothesis) of the likely cause and effect patterns of the phenomenon has to be made. This allows decisions to be made as to what variables are to be tested and how they are to be controlled and measured. This stage, called the design of the experiment, must also include the choice of relevant types of test and methods of analysing the results of the experiments (usually by statistical analysis). Pre-tests are then usually carried out to detect any problems in the experimental procedure.

Only after this is the experiment proper carried out. The procedures decided upon must be rigorously adhered to and the observations meticulously recorded and checked. Following the successful completion of the experiment, the important task – the whole point of the research exercise – is to process and analyse the data and to formulate an interpretation of the experimental findings.

Figure 3.6 Not all experimental research has to, or even can, take place in a laboratory

Not all experimental research has to, or even can, take place in a laboratory. The experimental methods used must take account of how much it is possible to control the variables. Writers of textbooks on research have classified experimental designs in different ways. Campbell and Stanley (1966) make their categorization into four classes, as in Box 3.12.

1 Pre-experimental.
2 True experimental.
3 Quasi-experimental.
4 Correlation and *ex post facto*.

Pre-experimental designs are unreliable and primitive experimental methods in which assumptions are made despite the lack of essential control of variables. An example of this is the supposition that, faced with the same stimulus, all samples will behave identically to the one tested, despite possible differences between the samples.

True experimental designs are those which rigorously check the identical nature of the groups before testing the influence of a variable on a sample of them in controlled circumstances. Parallel tests are made on identical samples (control samples) which are not subjected to the variable.

In quasi-experimental designs, not all of the conditions of true experimental design can be fulfilled. The nature of the shortcomings is however recognized, and steps are taken to minimize them or predict a level of reliability of the results. The most common case is when a group is tested for the influence of a variable and compared with a non-identical group with known differences (control group) which has not been subjected to the variable. Another, in the absence of a control group, is repeated testing over time of one group, with and without the variable (i.e. the same group acts as its own control at different times).

Correlation design looks for cause and effect relationships between two sets of data, while *ex post facto* designs turn experimentation into reverse, and attempt to interpret the nature of the cause of a phenomenon by the observed effects. Both of these forms of research result in conclusions which are difficult to prove and they rely heavily on logic and inference.

Evaluation

This is a descriptive type of research specifically designed to deal with complex social issues. It aims to move beyond 'just getting the facts' in order to make sense of the myriad human, political, social, cultural and contextual elements involved. The latest form of this type of research, named by Guba and Lincoln as fourth-generation evaluation, has, according to them, six properties, as in Box 3.13.

Box 3.13 Properties of evaluation research

1 The evaluation outcomes are not intended to represent 'the way things really are, or how they work', but present the meaningful constructions which the individual actors or groups of actors create in order to make sense of the situations in which they find themselves.

2 In representing these constructions, it is recognized that they are shaped to a large extent by the values held by the constructors. This is a very important consideration in a value-pluralistic society, where groups rarely share a common value system.

3 These constructions are seen to be inextricably linked to the particular physical, psychological, social and cultural contexts within which they are formed and to which they refer. These surrounding conditions, however, are themselves dependent on the constructions of the actors which endow them with parameters, features and limits.

4 It is recognized that the evaluation of these constructions is highly dependent on the involvement and viewpoint of the evaluators in the situation studied.

5 This type of research stresses that evaluation should be action oriented, define a course which can be practically followed, and stimulate the carrying out of its recommendations. This usually requires a stage of negotiation with all the interested parties.

6 Due regard should be given to the dignity, integrity and privacy of those involved at any level, and those who are drawn into the evaluation should be welcomed as equal partners in every aspect of design, implementation, interpretation and resulting action. (Guba and Lincoln, 1989, pp. 8–11)

There are a range of different approaches or evaluation models. Two of them are systems analysis and responsive evaluation.

Systems analysis is a holistic type of research, which reverses the three-stage order of thinking which is typical of scientific enquiry, i.e. breaking the problem or phenomenon to be investigated down into researchable parts, then separately evaluating the parts, and finally aggregating these evaluations into an explanation of the whole. In systems analysis, there are also three stages, but they start from appraising the whole, as in Box 3.14.

Box 3.14 Stages of systems analysis

1 Identifying an encompassing whole (system) of which the phenomenon or problem is a part.
2 Evaluating the behaviour or properties of the encompassing whole.
3 Explaining the behaviour or properties of the phenomenon or problem in terms of its roles or functions within the encompassing whole.

Systems analysis lends itself to creating understanding in complicated situations, particularly those involving people and organizations; such problems are often referred to as 'messes' because of their indeterminate nature and large number of interconnected variables. Modelling and diagramming are two of the principal techniques used to describe systems.

In the responsive evaluation model a series of investigative steps is undertaken in order to evaluate how responsive a programme is (e.g. an advertising campaign, a new degree course or an experimental traffic scheme) to all those taking part in it. Typical steps are shown in Box 3.15.

Box 3.15   Steps in responsive evaluation

- *Data collection*   Identifying issues from the people directly involved in the programme; identifying further issues from the programme documents; observing how the programme is actually working.
- *Evaluation*   The design of an evaluation based on the data collected and reporting findings.
- *Suggesting changes*   Informing the participants of the findings in ways specifically designed for each type of audience.

A common purpose of evaluation research is to examine programmes or the working of projects from the point of view of levels of awareness, costs and benefits, cost-effectiveness, attainment of objectives and quality assurance. The results are generally used to prescribe changes to improve and develop the situation, but in some cases might be limited to descriptions giving a better understanding of the programme (Robson, 1993, pp. 170–9).

Action

This can be seen as related to experimental research, though it is carried out in the real world rather than in the context of a closed experimental system. A basic definition of this type of research is: 'a small scale intervention in the functioning of the real world and a close examination of the effects of such an intervention' (Cohen and Manion, 1994, p. 186).

Its main characteristic is that it is essentially an 'on the spot' procedure, principally designed to deal with a specific problem evident in a particular situation. No attempt is made to separate a particular feature of the problem from its context in order to study it in isolation. Constant monitoring and evaluation are carried out, and the conclusions from the findings are applied immediately, and further monitored. Action research depends mainly on observation and behavioural data. As a practical form of research, aimed at a specific problem and situation and with little or no control over independent variables, it cannot fulfil the scientific requirement for generalizability. In this sense, despite its exploratory nature, it is the antithesis of experimental research.

Ethnogenic

In this approach, the researcher is interested in how the subjects of the research theorize about their own behaviour rather than imposing a theory from outside. The test of success is that the subjects themselves recognize the description of familiar features of their culture. As a process of studying human behaviour, according to Goetz and LeCompte (1984), the ethnogenic approach has three characteristic features: it aims to represent a view of the world as it is structured by the participants under observation by eliciting phenomenological data; it takes place in the undisturbed natural settings of the subjects; and it attempts to represent the totality of the social, cultural and economic situation, regarding the context to be equally important as the action (Uzzell, 1995, pp. 304–5).

This is a difficult form of research for several reasons. As so much of culture is hidden and rarely made explicit, the data being sought by the researcher need to be pursued by delving deep into the language and behaviour of the subjects of the study, and of the surrounding conditions in which they live. There is an ever-present danger that the cultural background and assumptions of the researcher will unduly influence the interpretations and descriptions made on the basis of the data collected. In addition to this, there can be confusions produced by the use of language and the different meanings which may be given to words by the respondents and researcher.

The accounts of events in the past can never capture the infinite contents of history. Historical knowledge, however well authenticated, is always subject to the biases and memory of its chronicler. It is also very difficult for one living in the twenty-first century to understand a world outside the framework of contemporary beliefs, values and attitudes.

Apart from these problems of interpretation of data, there is the fact that when working in a naturalistic setting, with social groups engaged in everyday activities, it is impossible to repeat the situation in order to verify the research. Social reality is not stable: a thing never 'is', as it is always changing into something else. It is therefore of great importance that multi-method and confirmatory data sources are used to capture the moment.

Feminist

Feminist research is a particular model of social research which involves theory and analysis that highlight the differences between men's and women's lives. It claims that researchers who ignore these differences have invalid knowledge, as non-feminist paradigms usually ignore the partiality of researchers' ideas about the social world. Value neutrality is impossible as no researcher practises research outside his or her system of values and no methods of social science can guarantee that knowledge is originated independently of values.

No specific methods are seen to be particularly feminist, but the methodology used is informed by theories of gender relations. However, feminist research is undertaken with a political commitment to the identification and transformation of gender relations. This tends to reveal that this form of research is not uniquely political, but rather exposes all methods of social research to be political.

Cultural

Many of the prevailing theoretical debates (e.g. postmodernism, poststructuralism) are concerned with the subjects of language and cultural interpretation, with the result that these issues have frequently become central to sociological studies. The need has therefore arisen for methodologies that allow analysis of cultural texts to be compared, replicated, disproved and generalized. From the late 1950s, language has been analysed from several basic viewpoints: the structural properties of language (notably Chomsky, Sacks, Schegloff), language as an action in its contextual environment (notably Wittgenstein, Austin and Searle) and sociolinguistics and the 'ethnography of speaking' (Hymes, Bernstein, Labov and many others).

However, the meaning of the term 'cultural texts' has been broadened from that of purely literary works to that of the many manifestations of cultural exchange, be they formal such as opera, TV news programmes, cocktail parties etc., or informal such as how people dress or converse. The main criterion for cultural texts is that one should be able to 'read' some meanings into the phenomena. Texts can therefore include tactile, visual and aural aspects, even smells and tastes. Three approaches to the consistent interpretation of cultural texts can be mentioned here briefly: content analysis, semiotics and discourse analysis.

Content analysis was developed from the mid 1900s chiefly in America, and is a rather positivistic attempt to apply order to the subjective domain of cultural meaning. A quantitative approach is taken by counting the frequency of phenomena within a case in order to gauge its importance in comparison with other cases. As a simple example, in a study of racial equality, one could compare the frequency of the appearance of black people in television advertisements in various European countries. Much importance is given to careful sampling and rigorous categorization and coding in order to achieve a level of objectivity, reliability and generalizability and the development of theories.

Semiotics takes an almost opposite approach by attempting to gain a deep understanding of meanings by the interpretation of single elements of text rather than to generalize through a quantitative assessment of components. The approach is derived from the linguistic studies of Saussure, in which he saw meanings being derived from their place in a system of signs. Words are only meaningful in their relationship with other words, e.g. we only know the meaning of 'horse' if we can compare it with different animals with different features.

This approach was further developed by Barthes and others to extend the analysis of linguistic-based signs to more general sign systems in any sets of objects:

> semiotics as a method focuses our attention on to the task of tracing the meanings of things back through the systems and codes through which they have meaning and make meaning. (Slater, 1995, p. 240)

Hence the meanings of a red traffic light can be seen as embedded in the system of traffic laws, colour psychology, codes of conduct and convention etc. (which could explain why in China a red traffic light means 'go'). A strong distinction is therefore made between denotation (what we perceive) and connotation (what we read into) when analysing a sign.

Discourse analysis studies the way that people communicate with each other through language within a social setting. Language is not seen as a neutral medium for transmitting information; it is bedded in our social situation and helps to create and recreate it. Language shapes our perception of the world, our attitudes and identities. While a study of communication can be simply broken down into four elements (sender, message code, receiver and channel), or alternatively into a set of signs with both syntactical (i.e. orderly or systematic) organization and semantic (i.e. meaningful and significant) relationships, such simplistic analysis does not reflect the power of discourse.

It is the triangular relationship between discourse, cognition and society which provides the focus for this form of analysis (van Dijk, 1994, p. 122). Two central themes can be identified: the interpretive context in which the discourse is set, and the rhetorical organization of the discourse. The former concentrates on analysing the social context, for example the power relations between the speakers (perhaps due to age or seniority) or the type of occasion where the discourse takes place (at a private meeting or a party). The latter investigates the style and scheme of the argument in the discourse, for example a sermon will aim to convince the listener in a very different way to a lawyer's presentation in court.

Poststructuralist social theory, and particularly the work of the French theorist Michel Foucault, has been influential in the development of this analytical approach to language. According to Foucault, discourses are 'practices that systematically form the objects of which they speak' (1972, p. 43). He could thus demonstrate how discourse is used to make social regulation and control appear natural.

Space does not allow the description of other types of research. Different disciplines, such as philosophy, theology, metaphysics, have types of research which are specifically suited to their purposes, but are beyond the scope of this book. It is important to point out that the above types of research are not generally mutually exclusive in a research project. More than one of these approaches may be relevantly used in order to achieve the outcomes aimed at in the research.

After reading each of the following five sample research proposals, answer, in one or two sentences, these questions for each proposal. The detailed description of the methods to be used has been omitted from the proposals, so you will have to read them carefully to ascertain which types of research are likely to be applied.

1   Does the proposal mention any theory which is relevant to the research? If so, what is it?
2   Which are the principal theoretical concepts which form the basis for the research?
3   Which concepts will be measured? Are any operational definitions mentioned? What sort of scales of measurement, if any, are mentioned or implied?
4   Is the approach more factual or theoretical in its investigations?
5   What *type* of research does this proposal indicate needs to be undertaken? (Perhaps there is more than one type of research which will need to be carried out.)

Note: references in these proposals are not included in the reference list.

Sample proposal 1

Disability and dementia: a study of empowerment

(Ruth Bartlett, School of Social Sciences and Law, Oxford Brookes University)

The aim of the investigation is to explore the relevance of the social model of disability in relation to older people with dementia living in supported accommodation.

The objectives are to:

1   examine the concept of empowerment with regard to older people with dementia living in a residential setting or sheltered housing scheme
2   develop a tool which allows for the evaluation of empowering practices
3   investigate the extent to which exclusion from decision-making episodes is a feature of the care context rather than an individual's cognitive impairment
4   identify the disabling social barriers that occur in respect of an older person with dementia living in supported accommodation.

The purpose of the research is to test the social model of disability in relation to older people with dementia living in residential care. In particular, it will explore the extent to which older people with dementia are systematically excluded from decision-making episodes. These range from key life-changing decisions such as where to live, to low level daily decisions such as what time to get up – decisions that are often made by carers for a person with dementia. As Parker and Penhale explain: 'The views of people with dementia are often overlooked, ignored, or assumed not to exist.' This study marks the gradual shift away from the medicalized view of dementia to one that regards the whole person and not simply the disease.

The literature critique involves reviewing two key bodies of work: disability theory and dementia care developments. The worldview of disability is changing from one that considers disability in terms of an individual's medical problem to one that holds that it is society that actually oppresses and disables people. Over the past few decades the disability movement has consistently demanded that we focus on the barriers that exist in society for people with disabilities rather than a person's individual impairment. In the late 1980s the social model of disability finally reached the shores of dementia discourse to bring about a new culture of dementia care, a culture that also urges us to think of an individual's health problems in terms of a social disability. As Tom Kitwood, a leading advocate in dementia care, explains: dementing illnesses should be seen, primarily, as forms of disability. How a person is affected depends crucially on the quality of care. Furthermore, this new culture is interested not only in developing care practices that are person-centred but also in designing research projects that aim to identify high standards of care.

Disability theory provides a model for carrying out research with people with disabilities. A clear distinction is made between participatory and emancipatory research. The former means that the disabled are involved and the latter that disabled people control and organize the research. Certainly for many theorists the only means to empower (and by that they mean transform the lives of) disabled people is to adopt an emancipatory approach to disability research: 'empowerment is not the gift of the powerful ... empowerment is something that people do for themselves collectively ... disabled people have decided to empower themselves'. This is an interesting global view of disabled people: have *all* disabled people really decided to empower themselves, and indeed can they so decide? This highlights one of the areas which prove problematic when disability theory is applied to people with dementia: that is, the extent to which observations made by disability theorists are applicable to people with dementia. For example, one of the main tenets is that 'Disability is caused not by the functional, physical or psychological limitations of impairment but by the failure of society to remove its disabling barriers and social restrictions.' The model does tend to negate not only disabilities caused by mental health problems but also subjective accounts of what it means to be disabled. Indeed, disability theory is commonly criticized for this reason. The tension within the disability movement is around the concept of empowerment. Whereas, for some, empowerment and inclusion for people with disabilities can only be achieved collectively through the raising of political consciousness, others perceive a less radical route to empowerment.

A focus on the subjective experience of empowerment is arguably the most appropriate and useful model to underpin research with people with dementia. This is because not only is it the least explored, but also the real issues 'may rest not so much on having more power but feeling more powerful'. In this sense, to be dismissive of, to ignore or to deride a person with dementia is considered as disabling as the illness. A subjective discourse also allows consideration of how for some individuals being able to feel in control demands some measure of self-confidence and self-esteem. Furthermore, others report individual and generational differences in the desire for control: 'Among the elderly, especially women, it is usually seen as desirable to be humble and self-sacrificing, not to fight for power.' The point is that older people with dementia living in residential care are not a homogeneous group with a shared desire for more control. Any attempt to promote empowering practices, or to operationalize this concept, must take into account individual differences such as social class, culture, education and family patterns.

The social model of disability also highlights the way in which people with mental and physical impairments are routinely disabled by individual reactions and societal attitudes. For example, a person with dementia may be labelled as presenting with 'challenging behaviour', such as wandering, whereas the activity could be viewed as a valid form of self-defence, rationally deployed by people with dementia when faced with a difficult social situation. Further evidence of disability theory influencing sociological discourse can be found in work of Nancy Harding. This author describes how dementia was scientifically constructed in the 1970s primarily to raise funds and awareness: as a result, 'senility became not a natural process of ageing, it became a disease, with a name and specific chemistry'. Moreover, she goes on to suggest that 'confused, dependent, uncooperative may be symptoms not of physical or mental incapacity, but of resistance to oppression through an assertion of individuality'.

Other dimensions of disability theory which can be critiqued, or put to the test, include the contention that the 'caring culture' can have a negative impact on an individual's autonomy. For instance, the view that disabled people confront two main stereotypes – one of being dependent and grateful, the other of being demanding and undeserving – seems particularly pertinent when you consider older people with dementia living in residential care. However, for a less dichotomous view of the influence of caring practices on a person's sense of self-control one may turn to dependency theory. The two most useful models here are 'learned helplessness' and 'selective optimization with compensation'. Although Baltes's work is with older people who are not cognitively impaired, her research could inform this study as she focuses on the *positive* aspects of dependency and also our *internal* decision-making processes. Baltes's argument is that dependency in old age is largely due to society's negative attitude towards older people: '[Dependency] is more a self-fulfilling prophecy than a reflection of the true competence of the elderly.' Moreover, Baltes suggests that older people have an 'energy reserve' which they choose whether or not to dip into: 'The elderly are making decisions concerning priority and energy investment.' It will be interesting to see to what extent this model fits with older people with dementia.

The project will use qualitative methods including focus groups, semi-structured interviews, participant observation and documentary analysis to meet the research objectives. The first stage of the study will be undertaken in three different settings: sheltered housing, residential and/or nursing homes and a day centre. Anchor Trust has already given permission for a large part of the research to be carried out in their facilities. A day centre will be accessed through a charitable organization such as the Alzheimer's Disease Society. All participants will be over 65 years. The aim will be to involve equal numbers of men and women who also reflect differences in socio-economic groups, severity of dementia and length of time in the care setting. For comparison purposes the sample will also involve people without a diagnosis of dementia. The fieldwork will involve two distinct phases as follows.

Phase 1: charting disabling social barriers (MPhil component)

Phase 1 will involve the organization of focus groups and individual interviews. Focus groups will take place in each of the three study sites. For the sheltered housing scheme and day centre the focus groups will comprise between four and eight service users without dementia. In the residential sites separate focus groups will comprise similar numbers of formal and informal carers. Potential strategies and questions to guide the focus groups have been developed. There will be semi-structured interviews with four people without a diagnosis of dementia in each of the study sites. Identification of participants will be achieved in co-operation with the care managers. A brief interview schedule has been devised but the approach to the interviews will be open to ensure that the participant's own perspective is the focus of research. The data gained from phase 1 will be transcribed and analysed using Ethnograph. The aim of the analysis at this stage will be to identify the decisions and opportunities that older people and their carers consider important and the barriers which people consider exist which prevent them from participating in them fully. This will form the basis of a framework to structure phase 2.

Phase 2: disabling social barriers in practice (PhD component)

Using the framework for decisions that older people are likely to face and the barriers that may exist to participating in these decisions, as established in phase 1, I will then undertake case studies in two of the study sites to identify how people with dementia experience these barriers to empowerment. Six participants from two of the study sites will be selected, providing a total of twelve case studies (six residents living in a sheltered housing scheme and six living in a residential or nursing home). The case studies will involve interviewing residents with dementia, informal carers, key workers, participant observation and document analysis. The assessment tool BASOLL will also be administered to key workers to observe different perceptions about a resident's ability. The researcher will adopt a combined ethnographic and phenomenological approach during fieldwork and give considerable thought to the applicability of scientific concepts such as 'reliability' during the data analysis stages.

Sample proposal 2

An examination of the importance of socializing for the long term commitment to physical activity

(Mark Austin, School of Social Sciences and Law, Oxford Brookes University)

There are two main aims of the investigation:

1 to explore how long term sporting behaviour is influenced by the type and quality of inter-relationships that are created within the sports club environment
2 to identify, through comparing and contrasting different types of sport, those socially constructed factors that best facilitate the long term adoption of physical activity into the lifestyle.

The dissertation for my master's degree in the sociology of sport (1996) investigated the variations in participation rates in sports and physical activities with respect to the lifecycle. The study found that the desirability and feasibility of participating in sport or a physical activity are subject to a range of socially constructed factors, the most influential of which are: the support of significant others, preconceptions about age-appropriate activities, class and gender. The research was centred on a questionnaire-based survey of 309 individuals. The questionnaire was primarily designed to provide both a quantitative study of sports participation patterns and an analysis of perceived motivators and inhibitors to sports participation. Though the results of the survey showed that a strong consensus exists that both adults and children should do more sport (especially amongst the female population), there is a decrease in peer support with increasing age of participant.

Of the initial motivators to participate in sport, the survey found most important to be the maintenance of health and fitness. This link between exercise and improved health is almost universally accepted. Jones (1994) finds that young people define health in terms of fitness and strength whilst older people define good health in terms of mobility and ability to function (both of which are firmly linked to physical capability). Similarly the 'Active for Life' campaign run by the Health Education Authority emphasizes the need to incorporate some form of regular physical activity into the modern lifestyle in order to improve the health of the nation. Though taking part in sport or physical activity is regarded as being beneficial for a range of reasons, my survey results show that there is a general decrease in the amount of sporting activity undertaken with increasing age of participant. Similarly Minten and Roberts (1989) report a steady decline in participation rates in Great Britain, from 58% of 16- to 19-year-olds down to 17% of over 65-year-olds taking part in sport. However, increasing age in and of itself is not a barrier to sports participation; for instance Clark (1986), in her exploration of the world of the ageing athlete, biographies numerous elderly athletes who are extremely competent at their sport. Though deteriorating health is seen as a factor that inhibits participation in sport, it alone cannot explain the decrease in participation rates. Furthermore, this factor is in general confined to the very elderly.

There is therefore a discordance between the opinion that exercise is good for you and the long term adoption of physically oriented activity into the lifestyle. Further, the results from my study show that over 89% of the adult population believe that, in general, adults should take part in more sport, and over 80% of the population believe that you are never too old to take part in less active sports such as swimming. Mihalik, O'Leary, McGuire and Dottavio (1989) attribute such variations in sporting behaviour across the lifecycle to 'adjustments of lifestyle'; similarly Rudman (1989) notes that participation is primarily affected by 'social factors'. For example, one socially constructed factor is that of conforming to 'age-appropriate behaviour', and the results of my survey show that ageing results in a cumulative peer pressure to forgo participation in sport. The most important of such inhibiting factors are lack of time, pressures of work and family commitments, whilst physical constraints such as cost and access to facilities rate least.

Taking into account the various 'inhibiting factors', and given that it is desirable for the populace to embrace physical activity as a lifelong pursuit, the question arises as to how the relationship between participant and sport can be reoriented so as to minimize the observed decrease in activity with increasing age. Though my initial observations were primarily directed towards quantifying the main sociological causes of the variations of sports participation rates across the lifecycle, long term participation was seen to be strongly linked to both the support of significant others and the development of social relationships with other participants. Similarly Wankel (1985), in his study of male commitment to a fitness programme, also identifies the importance of socializing for long term commitment to sport.

The development of social relationships with other participants is achieved mainly through membership of a sports club, and for a sports club to be successful it requires a stable body of committed participants. This may be in the form of short term participation with a high turnover (for example, children's gymnastics), or a core of long term dedicated athletes (as is the case for masters weightlifting). In reality most sports clubs consist of a mixture of short, medium and long term participants, with each group having its own characteristic wants and needs. The structure of a sports club, in terms of organization, is usually maintained through the dedication of 'long term' core members, who are in turn supported both physically and financially by short and medium term transient members.

Sports clubs are not egalitarian institutions but are hierarchical; for example, team positions are allocated by club captains, and in golf clubs membership is often governed by rules formulated by a committee (elected or otherwise). How members relate within a sports club is dependent both upon the overall character of the club, and upon the relative location of members within the club. For example, a national league hockey club is markedly different in character to a swimming club for pensioners, and relationships between team members are different compared to those between player and coach. Interrelationships between club members are further complicated by differential allocation of power to club members. Positions of authority – club chair, secretary and captains etc. – attract a degree of power commensurate with their responsibilities, and these positions are usually held (and often cherished) by well established club members. Possession of physical capacity, however, is a commodity that often attracts a disproportionate amount of power. For example, club rules strictly administered to lesser athletes may be 'bent' to maintain the favour of a needed star player. In this respect a second pecking order related to sporting competence often coexists with the formalized hierarchy of club structure.

The complex nature of the interrelationships developed within sports clubs necessitates an in-depth qualitative approach to research. In order to achieve this end I propose to develop my research through the use of focus groups, the members of which will be stratified through the use of preliminary questionnaires. Initially basic categorization such as age and sex will be used to define a focus group, though I hope to refine group selection with increasing knowledge of the functioning of sports clubs. Each focus group will be investigated through the use of semi-structured group interviews, the results of which will be transcribed through the use of analogue tape recordings. Through the additional interviewing of individuals within focus groups, I shall be able to further define the nature of both individual interrelationships and group interrelations within the sports club. As this method of inquiry is very qualitative in nature and apt to provide a large quantity of material, I am currently investigating the possibility of using a computer package such as NUDIST to aid my analysis of the results.

As mentioned above, the nature of a sports club varies markedly according to the type of sport it pursues. Analysis restricted to any one sports club is therefore limited in worth when addressing the broader problem of general sports participation rates. It is therefore proposed to research clubs representing the following five sports:

- *Golf:* owing to its broad range of age groups, lack of need for fitness, high socio-economic catchment.
- *Hockey:* owing to its emphasis on the team, the need for fitness, prominence of mixed gender teams, and broad socio-economic catchment.

- *Running:* owing to its emphasis on the individual, low cost, and broad age range of participants.
- *Bowls:* owing to its lack of physical emphasis, and prominence of elderly participants.
- *Weightlifting:* owing to the success of its masters, poor image, Cinderella status, poor socializing and personal knowledge of the sport.

An additional advantage of selecting these five sports is that they each have a representative club situated within the Headington area of Oxford, some of which have already expressed an interest in co-operating with my research. Such close proximity of clubs also helps to minimize any effects due to differences in socio-economic environments.

By undertaking a comparative analysis of these sports and their contrasting participation patterns (established through a quantitative survey of membership records) I intend to identify what, if any, key factors exist that help facilitate the long term adoption of sport into the lifestyle.

Sample proposal 3

Platonic geometry in plans of medieval abbeys and cathedrals

(Nigel Hiscock, School of Architecture, Oxford Brookes University)

This study aims to test the hypothesis that a degree of correlation exists between the geometry of Platonic figures and drawings of plans of medieval abbeys and cathedrals, and to determine a historical explanation for such use of geometry.

Numerous theories have been advanced suggesting possible design methods underlying medieval church architecture. Many have been linked with metaphysical beliefs which the proposed systems are presumed to be expressing, commonly in the layout of plans. Such systems are usually geometrically based, involving one or two of the figures normally associated with Platonic geometry, and typically centre on the twelfth century.

A common objection to these theories alleges a lack of evidence of any connection between the holding of such beliefs and their expression through the use of geometry in architectural design, such as:

1 the transmission of such ideas by the schoolmen to builders, or
2 the actual use of geometry as proposed from known working methods of masons and architects.

Instead, it is commonly suggested that geometry provided no more than a practical working method for masons.

This study, therefore, undertakes to:

1 re-examine the historical context for evidence of beliefs held, including attitudes towards architecture, and the building methods used
2 test the geometry against drawings of a wide sample of plans.

A study of the literature reveals a growing polarity between:

1 design theories derived from geometric exercises applied to architectural drawings, which have been criticized for an inadequate foundation in history, and
2 conclusions based solely on documentary research, which either ignore the evidence of the architecture or insist upon an exclusively practical interpretation of the use of geometry for which evidence does exist.

Given this divergence, it was considered necessary to re-examine primary sources in translation, allowing the authors to speak for themselves, rather than attempt to weigh subsequent interpretations of their writings by others. Regarding the architectural evidence, in order to test the geometric hypothesis, a set of criteria has to be developed for evaluating each case. This is designed to reflect known or likely working practices of architects and the existence of known architectural groupings among the examples selected.

The likely outcomes are the discovery of a high degree of correlation between the geometry and the plans in examples dated from a particular period early in the middle ages. A historical explanation for the use of such geometry is anticipated, together with a further explanation for its apparent presence from the particular period in question. A review of the documentary sources concerned with medieval architectural practice is expected to reveal possible internal evidence for the use of geometry as hypothesized, which has previously been overlooked.

Sample proposal 4

Middle management and the special educational needs co-ordinator (SENCO): a postmodernist study of management in practice

(Suanne Gibson, School of Education, Oxford Brookes University)

The aims of the investigation in the MPhil phase are:

1 to define the managerial roles of the special educational needs co-ordinator (SENCO)
2 to assess the present nature of management of SEN policy in schools; the focus will be upon assessing the traditional modernist approach of management models
3 to design a framework for practice for the management of school-based SEN policy taken from a postmodern perspective.

The aim in the PhD phase will be:

1 to contribute to the knowledge base of middle management in schools in England within the context of the postmodernist debate.

The present emphasis on inclusive education has emerged following developments in informed government policy, local education authority (LEA) provision, school provision and resource allocation for special educational needs (SEN). This series of developments began with the Warnock Report (1978) noting that 20% of all pupils have some form of SEN. A decade later the Education Reform Act (1988) presented the principle that was to drive SEN practice; this focused on all pupils participating as fully as possible in the National Curriculum. The subsequent Department for Education circular (DfE, 1994) provided the framework for SEN and multi-agency support in schools commonly known as the Code of Practice (CoP). The CoP was a watershed, a bringing together of previous legislation and practice associated with SEN in schools. Thus SEN policy in schools is a statutory issue. The 1997 Education Act and the 1998 Green Paper, *Excellence for all Children: Meeting SEN*, have added a further legislative base for meeting *where possible* inclusive education.

Central to this is the relationship between policy, procedures and practice. Increasing weight of SEN demands issued from the government has increased pressure on middle management teams and practitioners in schools.

Thompson, Head of the Policy Unit for the Association of Teachers and Lecturers, stated in response to the Teacher Training Agency (TTA) draft National Standards for SENCOs that:

> The introduction of the SEN CoP has led to the evolution of a job unique in schools – that of the SENCO. The implications of the SEN CoP and the SENCO role were not adequately thought through before the imposition of the Code … There seems to be a danger in these standards that there is, in Michael Fullan's terms, 'pressure' but without support. In our view the TTA should be unequivocal in that its focus is not assessment but development. (1997, p. 2)

Tarr and Thomas's study of school SEN policies revealed that 93% of schools had a SEN policy and:

> only one-quarter of these policies mention the strategic management of SEN provision, only one-third mention allocation of resources and only a very small minority are specific on this, only one-third mention means to integration, only one-third gave details on how parents should complain or how that complaint would be handled. (1996, p. 6)

Following Tarr and Thomas this research will focus on the implementation of the management of SEN policy. In recognizing the middle management role of the SENCO, the TTA states:

> The standards set for meeting the needs of SEN pupils are essentially standards for the school as a whole and, therefore, the management and organisation of SEN provision is ultimately the responsibility of the head teacher and governing body. (1998, p. 3)

In practice the situation is complex, as Tarr and Thomas indicated:

> The great majority of policies gave no information at all on budgets for SEN. While SENCOs in our subsequent interviews expressed no particular concern over their own schools' allocation of resources to SEN, the lack of specificity concerning resource allocation in policies raises the possibility that accountability for the use of these resources will be lacking. (1996, p. 6)

This leads to inevitable questions such as the following. What is the role of the SENCO? What are the managerial aspects to his/her role? How is s/he to effectively combine all roles – manager, teacher, team member, team leader and communicator? How are SENCOs presently meeting the challenges posed by changing government policy in the SEN sector? Is there an alternative to the functionalist model of school management? If so, what is it, and how can it be put into practice?

Sample proposal 5
Auditorium acoustics modelling based on non-linear realizations

(Lawdy Wong, School of Architecture, Oxford Brookes University)

Before the twentieth century, many auditoria were designed with a small knowledge of acoustic theory. Most designers of these halls used information from other halls on which to base their designs. This resulted in a vast number of auditoria with variable acoustics all over the world.

At the end of the nineteenth century, attempts were made by Professor W. Sabine to study room acoustics and behaviour scientifically. It was established that reverberation time was the main acoustic criterion used for designing and assessing an auditorium. However, in the latter half of the twentieth century, more complex criteria such as early decay time, intimacy, spatial impression, lateral fraction and interaural coherence were used to explain perceived differences in auditoria. These new criteria may help to explain particular acoustic conditions but they are of little value in early design stages because very detailed data, which are not always available, are required for their calculation.

Acoustic scaled model experiments with actual sounds emitted are often used in early design stages of an auditorium. However, in practice, it is not always easy to match the acoustic characteristics of the materials of the scaled model, e.g. furnishings, seating, wall and ceiling surfaces, with the actual materials. Furthermore, the reliability of the scaled model is highly dependent on the accuracy of its construction, making any modifications extremely time-consuming.

Since the development of digital computers, computer simulation, by which it is possible to observe and predict sound propagation, becomes an effective tool for designing. The most common techniques used are the image source method and the ray tracing method owing to their established algorithms and the convenience of being able to calculate macroscopic sound fields of basic room configurations even with personal computers. However, both methods are based on an assumption that the angle of incidence of sound to a surface, like light, is the same as that of its reflection, as with reflection at an infinitely large rigid plane. Consequently, the validity of both methods is limited to medium and high frequency ranges where wavelengths are relatively short compared with the dimensions of the reflection plane in the room. They produce conspicuous errors when dealing with multiple reflections among boundaries of a room, especially at low frequencies. Therefore, it is difficult to use these methods to provide highly accurate prediction of a sound field covering the entire audio frequency range.

Over the past ten years, the exciting development and the increasing acceptance of the theories of non-linear, fractal and chaotic phenomena have made more and more impact in many fields of science. It is evident that period-doubling bifurcations and strange attractors are common phenomena for a large class of previously unreasonable and unsolvable non-linear dynamical systems.

The earliest acoustic chaos was observed by Esche in 1952. A tank of liquid is irradiated with sound and a hydrophone in the liquid picks up the sound transmitted. The outcome is peculiar in that when a single frequency f_0 is radiated at high enough intensity, not only are the harmonics of nf_0 received but also a subharmonic $1/2f_0$ and its harmonics $nf_0/2$; in addition, $1/3f_0$ and its harmonics as well as $1/4f_0$ and its harmonics are observed clearly in the power spectrum of the recorded signal. His seminal work has initiated much subsequent work in the search for an explanation.

Similar subharmonic bifurcation phenomena have also been observed by Lauterborn and Cramer, again in liquid. They have devised an interesting technique of compressing and presenting the spectral data called a spectral bifurcation diagram, where the amplitudes of the spectral lines are encoded on the grey scale and the succession of frequency spectra is plotted against the driving sound pressure amplitude. Acoustic chaos is not only limited to liquid. Kitano, Yabusaki and Ogawa have demonstrated period bifurcations in air using a simple acoustic system composed of a microphone, a non-linear circuit, an amplifier and a loudspeaker.

The proposed research programme is an attempt to further investigate the non-linear and chaotic properties of sound in an auditorium and to utilize the observations and knowledge gained from the rapidly expanding field of chaos theory as the key consideration of auditoria acoustics modelling. It will overcome the shortcomings of the established image source and ray tracing techniques to give a more precise physical interpretation and prediction of auditorium acoustics.

You might have experienced some difficulty pinpointing a number of the required features in the above texts because they were not explicitly mentioned. It should have become clear, however, that in a research project these factors are always present though they may not be acknowledged or even implied. When writing a description of your own research project you should be aware of, and describe, the theoretical context of your projected work and be able to demonstrate that some form of measurement can be applied to the concepts used.

Thought

CONCLUSIONS

It is clear that there are many different types of research. These derive from the nature of the problem, the concepts and theories involved and also from the type of data to be collected and the methods used in the analysis. You will need to look carefully at the background to your research and the objectives you have set in order to determine the appropriate type or types of research that will provide the basis for your project.

THE NEXT STEPS: WHICH TYPE OF RESEARCH FOR YOUR TOPIC?

The aims of this section are:

- to examine the important concepts which are used in your subject, and the appropriate dimensions and indicators
- to investigate which relevant existing theories, hypotheses or arguments are related to your problem field
- to determine the appropriate type of research approach for your topic
- to explore the type of appropriate research activities for your data collection and processing.

Checklist of activities that will progress your research

Step 1: list concepts
Concepts are the foundations of thinking and communication. List and define the main concepts in your area of study. The most important of these should appear in your thesis title, though you might list several more.

Step 2: make statements
You can devise statements using these concepts to describe the focus of your study.

Step 3: operationalize
Abstract concepts are useful to express complex phenomena and ideas. However, they are difficult to study without defining operational definitions for them. Do this for the main concepts that you will be investigating in order to give you an indication of what sort of data you will need to collect and analyse. This will give you an indication of the likely scale of your project. At this stage you can reduce the scope of the research if it looks like becoming too much to manage, or goes outside your fields of expertise.

Step 4: quantify
The possible levels of quantification for the different concepts will determine the appropriate types of analysis. Check these for your main concepts, keeping in mind their operational definitions. This will indicate what analytical methods might be suitable.

Step 5: theorize
Your background reading should have given you a good indication of the theory surrounding your chosen topic. Briefly describe the most important laws, theories and hypotheses relevant to your subject area, and their relationship to your research problem.

There might be arguments about what theory is relevant or most helpful in finding solutions to the problems you have identified. Trace the theoretical strands in what you have read, and investigate any controversies, and ask yourself where you stand in the debate. This will be an essential aspect of the discussion of the background to your study when you write your research proposal.

Step 6: categorize

Look at your area of study and, using what you know about the various research approaches, select those most appropriate. Be prepared to discuss why.

It might be obvious which category of research your work will fall into, but it is also likely that sections of your research will be of different types. This is no bad thing, as looking at a problem from different perspectives provides a more holistic view. Consider, in the light of your investigations in response to the above points, what types of research you will be doing.

Step 7: check the scope

The types of research will indicate the appropriate research methodology to use. You can now trace out the sort of research activities you will have to undertake. This will help to answer the question, 'What will I actually do in my project?' Try not to become too detailed at this stage, but get a feel for the likely scale of the work needed (i.e. don't devise the questions to a questionnaire, but do consider which and how many people you might need to question, what sort of topics you need to cover, how you might analyse the results). Again, this exercise will give you an indication of the likely scale of the work so you can check as to its practicability.

Step 8: redraft

You should now be in a position to explain the main concepts that lie at the foundation of your research, where they came from in your background reading, how they form your research problem and how they will be investigated. You will be able to define the type(s) of research that you are proposing, the general nature of your methodology and the expected scope of the project.

Draw up another draft (or the first one if you have not got that far yet) of your proposal. Try to incorporate all the results of your investigations so far in a logical sequence. You should explain the main issues and theories surrounding your subject and show how your research project emerges from these. The best way is to demonstrate that there is a gap in knowledge that you can help to fill; or that there is a theory or belief that you disagree with and wish to contest; or that there is a debate in which you want to participate, to add something new or to find a new synthesis. Once you have explained this, you can then describe the main concepts that are important in your investigations, the type of research these investigations will fall into, and the sort of research methods that will be appropriate.

Consolidation and assessment

When you are prepared, arrange a tutorial with your tutor or supervisor. Explain the main concepts that underpin your area of study and how these are used to describe the focus of your study. Demonstrate an understanding of the relevant theories and concepts etc. and how they relate to the subject and problem which you have chosen.

Discuss how the main concepts can be investigated through their operational definitions. Give some indication of the dimensions and indicators which could be used to examine and measure the concepts. Explain how this will affect the nature of your research work. This is to do with practical matters, so try to bring the discussion down to what you will actually be doing to research these concepts. Do this by explaining the relevance of your proposed research approach(es) and the type of research activities which are associated with them.

Although you are likely to be still at a very exploratory stage in your research, this exercise should encourage you to consciously examine the sorts of issues and terminology which feature in your chosen field of study. Knowledge about these is often taken for granted by specialists in the field, because they are so much a part of their everyday thinking. You should therefore acquire a good understanding of the concepts and theories etc. which feature as a main part of your subject.

Knowledge about different types of research will put your own research efforts into context, within the range of options open to you. You will appreciate that the type(s) of research you undertake will have an important influence on the research activities that you will need to pursue.

Key words

Model	Ratio level
Concept	Theory
Statement	Set of laws theory
Symbol	Axiomatic theory
Term	Causal process theory
Operational definition	Conceptual scheme theory
Intersubjectivity	Research question
Quantification	Proposition
Levels of measurement	Hypothesis
Nominal level	Empirical generalization
Ordinal level	Law
Interval level	Paradigm

Further reading

The foundation stones of research, i.e. concepts and theories, are discussed in much more detail in specialized books on the philosophy of research. Of those cited in this chapter, I can recommend the following if you want to delve further into this aspect:

Reynolds, P. D. (1971) *A Primer in Theory Construction.* Indianapolis: Bobbs-Merrill.

See Chapters 3 and 5 initially. The rest makes for stimulating reading too.

Cohen, L. and Manion, L. (1994) *Research Methods in Education.* London: Routledge.

Read the introductions to Chapters 2–9 for succinct summaries. Delve deeper if you find you need to know more.

For a really comprehensive examination of contemporary and traditional varieties of qualitative research practices, have a look at:

Seale, C., Gobo, G., Gubrium, J. and Silverman, D. (eds) (2004) *Qualitative Research Practice.* London: Sage.

And another clear introduction to different types of research, for which see the chapter headings:

Payne, G. and Payne, J. (2004) *Key Concepts in Social Research.* London: Sage.

And to show that you can mix and match types of research, see:

Thomas, R. (2003) *Blending Qualitative and Quantitative Research Methods in Theses and Dissertations.* London: Corwin/Sage.

EXERCISE 3.1

1   Primitive.

2   Derived. Made up of primitive symbols (people, gather together, close proximity, same, time, particular purpose): a number of people gathered together in close proximity at the same time for a particular purpose.

3   Primitive.

4   Primitive.

5   Derived. Made up of primitive symbols (section, city, connected together, physical, conceptual, links, set apart): a section of a city which is connected together with physical and conceptual links which set it apart from the other sections of the city.

ANSWERS TO
EXERCISES

Observe that some primitive symbols are abstract, i.e. not just a label for an object or a thing. You probably have used some primitive symbols different from those which are chosen here to define the derived symbols. This effectively demonstrates that, in order to agree on the definition of a derived symbol, we must also agree on its meaning!

EXERCISE 3.2

1   Abstract.

2   Concrete – specific to time.

3   Abstract.

4   Concrete – specific to person.

5   Abstract, if the two words are taken to mean a complete concept; or, if the words are separated, the concept could be argued to be concrete, in that the system is specific to type, i.e. social type.

6   The same can be said for this concept as for 5, except that the capital letters indicate that this is a complete term, and not a description of an association.

7   Abstract.

8   Concrete – specific to time of the day and place.

EXERCISE 3.3

1   (a)   Observation of the features of a building: does it have classrooms, assembly hall, teachers' room, playing fields etc.?

     (b)   Observation of the activities held in the building: does teaching take place in groups, are people (perhaps children) grouped according to age or ability, is there an organized daily routine, including, for example, gymnastic exercises, music activities etc.?

     (c)   Communication with members of the organization and other associated people, i.e. teachers, pupils, parents, authorities: do they believe that this is a school?

2   (a)   Observation by qualified people of the behaviour of the subject (person perhaps) to detect symptoms of fear, e.g. urge to run away, frozen on the spot, hair standing on end, pallid, ashen expression, shortness of breath, dilated pupils etc.

     (b)   The use of sensory equipment to measure the subjects' heartbeat, brain activity, sweat production, temperature etc. Some agreement must exist beforehand about the medical signs of fear in a subject.

     (c)   If human, questioning the subject about their feelings of fear.

3   (a)   Comments of people that they perceive social connections within a group, with the exclusion of others regarded as not members of the group.

(b) Observations of communal activities, street parties, friendly relationships etc.

(c) The presence of communal organizations such as societies, mutual help groups etc.

4 (a) Observation of water forming on a surface, e.g. mist on a bathroom mirror.

(b) By calculations involving relative humidity and changing temperature in a given situation.

(c) By moisture meters placed in areas prone to condensation.

5 (a) Recording the diet of the subject over a period of time, and comparing it with data about nutritional needs.

(b) Medical examination of the subject over time, recording bowel movements, muscle wastage, fat content etc.

(c) Asking the subjects what they understand by hunger and how they feel in relation to that understanding.

6 (a) Observation of the movement of a compass needle.

(b) Pattern produced by iron filings on a sheet of paper around a magnet.

(c) Measurement of magnetic current detected by a magnetometer.

7 (a) Observation of concerted activities of a group of people who agree to promote a particular course of action in others.

(b) Records of meetings or communications between individuals indicating that a group has formed to support a particular cause actively.

(c) Asking people in power about the nature of the groups that have made representations to them on particular issues.

EXERCISE 3.4

1 Nominal.

2 Nominal.

3 Ratio.

4 Interval. Note that although these are also numbers, 0 has no meaning in this context, i.e. no-one has an IQ of 0 – they would probably be dead if they had!

5 Ordinal, though they are often thought of as interval when regarded as being equally spaced out along the line of achievement.

6 Ordinal.

7 Ratio (0.0 bar would be a vacuum). The measurement takes its values from 1.0 bar being approximately atmospheric pressure at sea level.

8   Ordinal.

9   Ordinal.

10 Ratio.

11 Interval (0 °C has no particular significance in this context).

12 Ordinal.

13 Nominal.

14 Cannot all be quantified in entirety. One could quantify all nominally by colour or by shape, but not both together. One could quantify some (while rejecting others) by, say, colours of cube or shapes in red.

EXERCISE 3.5

Sample proposal 1

1   Disability theory is important in this research, equated with the worldview of disability which has changed from considering disability in terms of medical problems to considering it in terms of the oppressive and disabling effects of society. Dependency theory, in relation to Baltes's work, is also seen as useful.

2   Numerous theoretical concepts are features of this research. Disability, dementia and empowerment are all in the title, and of obviously crucial importance. Exclusion, decision-making episodes, both appear in the objectives. Other relevant concepts picked from the text are dependence, societal attitudes, learned helplessness and selective optimization with compensation.

3   The extent to which older people with dementia are systematically excluded from decision-making episodes will be explored. How this extent will be measured is not specifically mentioned, but the qualitative approach rather excludes a quantitative analysis. The assessment tool BASOLL, which measures different perceptions about a resident's ability, will also be used. One would have to look up the reference to learn how this was done.

4   This research is heavily reliant on a theoretical approach, but is concerned with a very practical problem. This is a good example of how theory can be harnessed to investigate ways of making life better in certain situations.

5   The main type of research indicated here is evaluation research, in combination with a cultural research approach to examine attitudes and power relations.

Sample proposal 2

1   There seems to be no established theoretical precedent to this subject, indicating that it is an area which is under-theorized. This study will attempt to develop a theory.

2   Again, the title is a good place to look for important theoretical concepts. Socializing and long term commitment are two, while physical activity is more a practical than a theoretical concept! Several other concepts important to the study can be mentioned. Sporting behaviour and socially constructed factors appear in the aims, while initial motivators and inhibiting factors seem to be crucial elements of the study.

3   Contrasting participation patterns will be measured, the operational definition being based on membership records. The quantitative survey mentioned could involve simple numbers (ratio) and also nominal measurements, e.g. types of sport and sex of participants; and perhaps ordinal too, e.g. age groups of participants.

4   Despite the very practical nature of the subject of sport, this research is aimed at developing a theoretical explanation of long term sporting behaviour.

5   This is a comparative study, comparing the situations in clubs dedicated to different sports. Within each case a combination of descriptive and evaluation types of research will be pursued. From the comparisons, the researcher hopes to identify some common themes which could form the basis of a theory about socializing and commitment to sport.

Sample proposal 3

1   There is mention of 'numerous theories', though none by name. The main features of the theories are very briefly described.

2   As in the previous text, there are numerous important theoretical concepts which form a basis for the research. Platonic geometry is probably the central concept. Others which could be mentioned are: design methods, metaphysical beliefs, historical context, attitudes towards architecture, building methods, design theories, foundation in history etc.

3   It is clear that several theoretical concepts will have to be measured in the proposed research, such as attitudes towards architecture, building methods and geometry, working practices of architects and architectural groupings. No operational definitions are mentioned, although it is stated that 'in order to test the geometric hypothesis, a set of criteria has to be developed for evaluating each case'. This certainly implies that operational definitions will be developed. The development of another operational definition is hinted at in the statement that the study undertakes to 'test the geometry against drawings of a wide sample of plans'. No scales of measurement are mentioned. Nominal and ordinal scales are those most likely to be used when comparing the outcomes of geometrical studies. The geometrical studies themselves will have to be carried out on a ratio scale of measurement.

4   There seem to be plenty of theories about design methods underlying medieval church architecture. The problem is, which ones can be verified? This study is conceived to find out facts which may underpin or reject the theories.

5   There is obviously a strong historical element to this research. All the evidence will be of a historical nature. There is also a strong qualitative element, involving the examination of drawings and buildings in relation to geometric parameters.

Sample proposal 4

1   There is no specific naming of particular theories as such, though one could pick the term 'inclusive education' as a theory with important repercussions for this research. Two theoretical positions are mentioned: 'traditional modernist approach' and 'postmodern perspective'.

2   There is a range of theoretical concepts contained in this proposal. The title is full of them: special educational needs, postmodernist study, and management in practice. Other important ones are policy, procedures and practice, and later, resource allocation and accountability.

3   There do not seem to be any measurable concepts in this proposal. The stress is more on assessment, design and practice (of management). However, there is mention of standards set for meeting the needs of SEN pupils. These could possibly be used as a form of measurement to test management effectiveness. No operational definitions are specifically mentioned. No scales of measurement are mentioned.

4   Any practical outcomes of this enquiry will be firmly based on a theoretical approach, within the context of postmodernist debate.

5   The main type of research will be evaluative. There could also be elements of historical and descriptive research in order to get relevant data, and systems analysis could well be carried out to explore the management structure and the roles of the SENCO within it.

Sample proposal 5

1   Acoustic theory is the obvious relevant theory, as is chaos theory which is mentioned further on.

2   Numerous theoretical concepts are referred to. Some of the important ones are: reverberation time, decay time, intimacy, spatial impression, lateral fraction, interaural coherence, sound propagation, period-doubling bifurcations and strange attractors. However, those central to this research are in the title: the theoretical concepts of auditorium acoustics and of non-linear realizations.

3   The main aim of this research is to measure auditorium acoustics, particularly by modelling. Operational definitions are not presented in any complete form. The indication is that the auditoria acoustic model will investigate non-linear and chaotic properties of sound by detecting subharmonic bifurcation phenomena in the frequency spectrum. Measurements will be of amplitudes of spectral lines, driving sound pressure amplitude, and the presence of harmonics. It is not spelled out exactly what form these measurements take, but presumably they will be ratio measurements, with a meaningful zero.

4   This is a theoretical investigation, which attempts to use an existing theory of chaos to predict factual information of intrinsic value.

5   It is not clear what type of research is going to be undertaken in this project. No doubt, some experimental work must be done to test whether the model bears any relation to reality. Descriptive research might be a part of the work, as evaluation of the quality of auditoria acoustics is highly subjective. The mass of information gained from the modelling will probably require correlative studies to be undertaken to test or establish relationships between variables. All this is conjecture, as no hint is given of research methodology.

4

Nature and Use of Argument

Introduction
Language
   Three Uses of Language
   Statements: Existent and Relational
Argument
   Deductive and Inductive Arguments
   Logic in Argument
   Fallacies in Argument
   Classification and Analogy in Argument
Conclusions
The Next Steps: What Argument Will You Pursue?
Checklist of Activities That Will Progress Your Research
Consolidation and Assessment
Key Words
Further Reading
Answers to Exercises

- To examine the nature of argument, its uses and abuses.
- To sharpen analytical skills during reading and discussion.
- To analyse the components of argument.
- To develop skills in constructing your own arguments.

INTRODUCTION

The medium of words, spoken or written, is by far the most common method of communication among humans. Most of the problems we face are expressed in words and the information we use to combat these problems comes to us in words, mostly through the mass media. Most of our thinking is done in words. It is only when we express an idea in a sentence that we can appreciate what it actually is, how it can connect with other ideas, whether it is true or has a value when compared with other ideas.

We cannot develop critical skills unless we have developed a skill in handling language: investigating and defining meanings, appreciating the effects of grammatical forms, and understanding the thread of an argument through an extended piece of text.

Argument lies at the heart of research. Doing a literature review is a large exercise in analytical reading. All the books, articles, websites etc. that you read will contain arguments in order to try to convince you, the reader, of the truth of the message or information imparted. Not all of these arguments will be sufficiently rigorous to justify the claims made, and it is up to you to detect the shortcomings and inconsistencies.

LANGUAGE

We often fail to appreciate the complexity and subtlety of the many uses of language. Here, as in many other situations, there is danger in our tendency to oversimplify.

Three uses of language

Copi (1982, pp. 69–72) suggested that some order can be imposed on the staggering variety of language uses by dividing them into three very general categories, as in Box 4.1. He admitted that the threefold division of the functions of language presented here is a simplification, perhaps an oversimplification, but it has been found useful by many writers on logic and language.

Box 4.1 Types of language

1 Informative.
2 Expressive.
3 Directive.

---

informative

The first of these three uses of language is to communicate information. Normally this is done by devising propositions and then maintaining or refuting them, or presenting an argument about them. Here language is used to function in an **informative** way. This is not to say that the information is true or that the arguments are valid; misinformation is also included in this category. The function of informative discourse is to describe the world and to reason about it.

expressive

The two other basic uses, or functions, of language are referred to by Copi as expressive and directive. While science can be seen to use language in an overtly informative mode, poetry tends to exploit the **expressive** possibilities of language to the full. Take for example the following lines from Burns:

> O, my Luve's like a red, red rose
>   That's newly sprung in June:
> O, my Luve's like the melodie
>   That's sweetly play'd in tune!

In these lines, Burns certainly has not aimed to increase our factual or theoretical knowledge about roses, music or even about his 'Luve'. Instead, he intended to inspire in the reader the kind of emotions and feelings which he ardently felt, and used language in its expressive function to do this. Emotive language of other, baser kinds can be included in this category, including many kinds of political haranguing and 'soft sales talk'.

Language serves the **directive** function when it is used for the purposes of causing (or preventing) overt action. The most obvious examples of directive discourse are commands and requests. When a soldier is told to fire his gun, there is no informative or emotional content in the command. The form of language is directed at getting results. Even asking a question can be regarded as directive discourse: it is directed at getting an answer! Copi pointed out that even a curt command can be transformed into a question or request by a suitable change in the inflection of the voice or facial expression, or the simple addition of the word 'please'.

In this chapter we are primarily concerned with examining the characteristics of the *informative* function of language, of informative discourse. In order to inform, it is necessary to assert a statement in such a manner as to evince or invite belief in it. However, before we go further, it is necessary to investigate what statements are.

Statements: existent and relational

According to Reynolds (1977, pp. 67–76), statements can be classified into two groups: those that state that a concept exists, and those that describe a relationship between two concepts.

Existence statements state that a concept exists, and provide a typology or a description. Existence statements claim that instances of concept exist in the real world. For example, here are some statements that make existence claims:

> That object is a cow.
> That cow is brown and black.
> That object is a human.
> That human has a high level of intelligence.
> That (event) is a traffic jam.

Each of these statements follows the same basic pattern: it provides a concept, identifies it by a term, and applies it to a thing or an event. The above are examples of existence statements in their simplest form. They can, however, be more complicated without losing their basic form. For example:

If

(a) there are 40 or more individuals in group X
(b) each individual plays an orchestral musical instrument, and
(c) each individual co-operates in X to perform pieces from the symphonic repertoire

then the group X is a symphony orchestra.

Existence statements can be 'right' or 'wrong' depending on the circumstances. Take for example the rather abstract statement 'It is 5 o'clock here.' This can be seen to be correct anywhere once a day. If, however, we state in a more concrete fashion that 'It is 5 o'clock on 15 November in London', this can only be correct once and in one place. It can thus be seen that the level of abstraction of a statement has a powerful influence on its potential for correctness, i.e. the more abstract a statement, the more capacity it has to be right, and conversely, the more concrete a statement, the more capacity it has for being wrong.

relational statements **Relational statements** impart information about a relationship between two concepts. By referring to the instance of one concept, they state that another concept exists and is linked to the first. For example:

If a person is an acrobat, then he will be agile.

Relational statements form the bedrock of scientific knowledge. Existence statements can only provide a typology or a classification of objects or phenomena by applying definitions to the world around us; we must rely on relational statements to explain, predict and provide us with a sense of understanding of our surroundings.

Figure 4.1 Relational statements form the bedrock of scientific knowledge

There are two broad classifications of relational statements. The first describes an association between two concepts, and the second describes a causal relationship between two concepts. The above relational statement can be taken as an example of an associational statement:

If a person is an acrobat, then he will be agile.

By slightly changing the wording of this sentence we can transform it into a causal statement:

Becoming an acrobat will make a person be more agile.

That is, becoming an acrobat will cause that person to be more agile.

With **associational statements**, when measures of association at the interval or ratio level of quantification are used, the word 'correlation' is often employed to refer to the *degree* of association.

associational statements

There are three types of correlation between two concepts:

- *positive*, e.g. strong people are muscular (and vice versa), i.e. high value in one concept associated with high value in second concept, or low value associated with low value
- *negative*, e.g. grass at low altitudes grows longer, i.e. low value in one concept associated with high value in second concept
- *none*, e.g. men and women have equal rights in a democracy, i.e. no information about associated high or low values in either concept.

The degree of association is often measurable and is usually expressed by +1.0 as maximum positive correlation, 0.0 as no correlation and −1.0 as maximum negative correlation.

In **causal statements**, which describe what is sometimes called a 'cause and effect' relationship, the concept or variable that is the cause is referred to as the 'independent variable' (because it varies independently), and the variable that is affected is referred to as the 'dependent variable' (because it is dependent on the independent variable). An example is 'smoking a lot makes one ill', where 'smoking a lot' is the independent variable and 'ill' is the dependent variable.

causal statements

It may be possible to examine causality between two or more concepts if quantification is possible. Three ways of measuring the variation of the dependent variable should be considered:

- the *direct* variation effect of each variable
- the *interaction* of the variations of variables
- variations caused by *mistakes* and errors of measurements.

Causal statements can be deterministic, meaning that under certain conditions an event will inevitably follow, e.g. 'if you drop an apple, it will fall'. However, it is not always possible to be so certain of an outcome, so a probabilistic statement might be more suitable, e.g. 'if parents are intelligent, their children are likely to be intelligent too'. A quantification of the order of probability may be possible, e.g. 'with a probability of 0.7'.

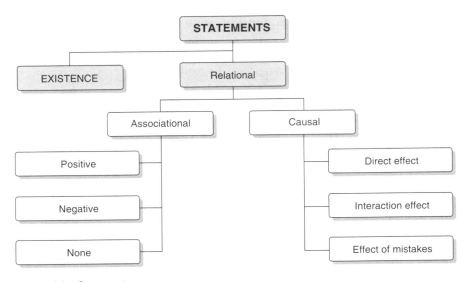

Diagram 4.1   Statements

The classification of statements described is summarized in Diagram 4.1. Statements can be made on three **levels of abstraction**:

1   *Theoretical statements* These are abstract statements which are based on theoretical concepts, e.g. 'bodily comfort depends on environmental conditions'.
2   *Operational statements* These are less abstract in that they are based on the definitions of theoretical concepts which are capable of measurement, e.g. 'the rate of heartbeat relates to the surrounding still air temperature and the level of activity'.
3   *Concrete statements* These are based on specific findings, i.e. the measurements themselves, e.g. 'the heart beats at 102 beats per minute at a surrounding air temperature of 32 degrees Celsius at an energy consumption level of 42 kilocalories per hour'.

Statements on their own provide information on discrete units. When they are strung together to form a larger structure, they are often referred to as a **discourse**. There are many different forms of discourse, depending on the use to which language is put – informative, expressive or directive (i.e. the different uses of language described earlier).

In this chapter, as we are concerned with the informative use of language in which statements are used to make assertions about the world, we should examine what Beardsley refers to as **assertive discourse** (see Beardsley, 1975, pp. 11–27, for a more detailed account of the qualities of discourse and argument). This type of discourse consists of, or contains, assertive statements. These are the discourses that invite us to approach them from a logical point of view.

Beardsley went on to make a further distinction which divided the class of assertive discourses into two subclasses – arguments and expositions. While he admitted that this distinction was not perfectly sharp, he maintained that it could be made sufficiently clear, and that it was logically fundamental. In this section we will only investigate the qualities of the former, i.e. arguments.

In some assertive discourses, statements are not merely presented for our information (or misinformation, as the case may be); they are connected in a specific logical way. Some of the statements are offered as reasons for others. This kind of discourse is termed an **argument**. It is a discourse that not only makes assertions but also asserts that some of those assertions are reasons for others.

argument

In the case of ordinary speech the term 'argument' is often used when referring to a dispute, or a situation in which people who hold different views on some controversial subject try to bring the other person around to their way of thinking. But as a technical term in logic, argument is a special kind of discourse, in which a claim is made that one or more particular statements should be accepted as true, or probably true, on the grounds that certain other statements are true. Put another way: by the process of reasoning, using the operation of logic, a conclusion is inferred from the statements given. An argument can be seen as the verbal record of this reasoning. You can check for the minimal ingredients of an argument using Box 4.2.

Box 4.2   Minimal ingredients of an argument

1 At least one statement that is reasoned for (this is the *conclusion* of the argument).
2 At least one statement that is alleged to support it (this is the *premise* of the argument).
3 Some signal or suggestion that an argument is under way (where this is a word or phrase, we shall call it the *logical indicator*).

There is a great variety of English expressions, some rather roundabout, which can serve as logical indicators, so you have to be on the lookout for them. Beardsley (1975, p. 14) has given a useful list of the commonest ones. He suggested that each of the words or phrases in Box 4.3 usually shows that the statement that follows is a conclusion. Such expressions are called *conclusion indicators*.

Box 4.3   Conclusion indicators

therefore ...
hence ...
thus ...
so ...
implies that ...
entails that ...
which shows that ...
proves that ...
indicates that ...
consequently ...
allows us to conclude that ...
we may deduce that ...
points to the conclusion that ...
suggests very strongly that ...
leads me to believe that ...
bears out my point that ...
from which follows that ... .

Each of the words or phrases in Box 4.4 usually shows that the statement that follows is a reason. Such expressions are called *premise indicators*.

Box 4.4   Premise indicators

for ...
since ...
because ...
for the reason that ...
in view of the fact that ...
on the correct supposition that ...
assuming, as we may, that ...
may be inferred from the fact that ...
may be deduced from ...
as shown by ...
as indicated by ...
as is substantiated by ... .

Even with the use of this list of logical indicators, it is sometimes difficult to determine whether a discourse is an argument: there are cases, especially in a complex piece of text, when it is impossible to be sure whether the minimal ingredients of an argument are indeed present. Usually, the presence of a logical indicator is quite decisive – but even here it is vital to establish that the logical indicator is being used in a logical sense, rather than in some other sense.

EXERCISE
4.1

Can you recognize an argument when you see one?

Which of the following sentences are statements and which are arguments? If statements, of what kind are they, and if associational, what type of correlation do they state? If arguments, what are the premise or premises, the conclusion, and the logical indicators (premise and conclusion indicators) in each?

1 Since Parliament increased the amount of taxation on petrol, the amount of traffic on the roads has decreased appreciably.
2 The criminal is not to blame for what he did. His sense of social responsibility was diminished by a deprived upbringing.
3 If it is true that the outcome of the vote was the result of bribes, then the election should be held again.
4 Why do I insist that London is still the best place in the world to live? Look at the unequalled variety of drama, music, art and educational opportunity there.
5 The train drivers have gone on strike because the railway company is not offering them a sufficient pay rise.
6 An informal atmosphere in the office environment is associated with low stress levels in the workforce.
7 The railway company could not be offering a sufficient pay rise to the train drivers, as they are threatening to go on strike.
8 In Western wedding celebrations the age of the couple and the extent of the wedding celebrations are associated; the greater the age of the couple, the smaller the celebrations tend to be, while the greater celebrations are enjoyed by the younger couples.
9 I do not regard Parliament as trustworthy, my reason being that its members have misled us too often.
10 The ban on fishing lobsters has been continued, so it follows that lobsters will soon be unobtainable.
11 Cod will soon be scarce. Halibut will be scarce too.

ARGUMENT

Argument is one of the basic elements in research. The quality of the argument used in

- the introduction of the research problem
- the examination and analysis of the problem
- the presentation of the findings
- the analysis and conclusions

strongly determines the quality of the overall research project. It is important for researchers, therefore, to have a clear understanding of the various types of argument, the ingredients of sound argument and of the logic contained therein, and the pitfalls which may be encountered by the unwary.

In the following, we will concern ourselves, therefore, primarily with the analysis of arguments, with their logical soundness or unsoundness, i.e. whether their reasoning is good, or how good it is. It can be said that when the reasoning is very good, an argument can be tantamount to a proof. It is not possible, however, to achieve this high standard in all circumstances. On a practical level, we must often deal with important issues at a lower level of reasoning. In this situation it is essential to be able to estimate the level of soundness of the arguments.

Figure 4.2   The simplest kind of argument consists of just one premise and conclusion

Once we have recognized the existence of an argument, the next step is to examine what it is arguing for, and how the argument is built up. The first thing to establish is what is the point of the argument, that is, the conclusion. Unless the argument goes in a circle, there will be at least one assertion (perhaps more) that is supported by reasoning, but is not itself used in the reasoning to support other assertions. This assertion is the argument's final conclusion. If there are several such assertions then the argument has several conclusions. The second thing to observe is that there will be at least one assertion that is made which is not based on reasoning and is not itself a conclusion from any other assertions. Such an assertion is a premise in an argument and provides a foundation on which the argument rests.

The simplest kind of argument consists of just one premise and a conclusion that is claimed to follow from it, or to be implied by it. An example in which each is stated in a separate sentence is the following:

The most prominent political issues are those about which the press writes the most. Therefore journalists have a great influence in the selection of political issues around which public debate revolves.

Copi gives a slightly more complicated example, in which the single premise and the conclusion are contained in the same sentence:

In proportion as the capital of the country is diminished, its production will be necessarily diminished; and, therefore, if the same unproductive expenditure on the part of the people and of the government continues, with a constantly diminishing annual production, the resources of the people and the state will fall away with increasing rapidity, and distress and ruin will follow. (1982, p. 7)

Other arguments may offer several premises in support of their conclusions. For clarity, the premises are sometimes listed and numbered, or, as in the following argument, appended with letters of the alphabet. Note that in this argument, the conclusion is stated first:

To say that statements about consciousness are statements about brain processes is manifestly false. This is shown (a) by the fact that you can describe your sensations and mental imagery without knowing anything about your brain processes or even that such things exist, (b) by the fact that statements about one's consciousness and statements about one's brain processes are verified in entirely different ways, and (c) by the fact that there is nothing self-contradictory about the statement 'X has a pain but there is nothing going on in his brain'. (1982, p. 7)

When analysing an argument, it is the logical indicators that we must look to first for clues to the logical structure. You will find that the main problem in formulating an argument is making the elements of verbal texture – the syntax, the order of words and topics, the connectives – clearly reveal the logical relationships of the argument. Beardsley (1975, p. 19) suggested that there were two fundamental rules to keep in mind, as in Box 4.5.

Box 4.5   Rules for logical statements

1   *The rule of grouping*   As far as possible, reasons for the same conclusion should be kept together, and their similar logical status called to the reader's attention.
2   *The rule of direction*   When there is a series of assertions, each being a reason for the next one, the argument should move in a single direction, so that the order of the words helps to remind us of the order of the thought.

What is the conclusion of the following arguments? If the conclusion is not explicitly stated, put it in your own words.

1   We must accept that the chemist made a mistake in giving Mrs Smith a bottle of tranquil-lizing pills instead of the contraceptive pills which she requested. But how can she claim damages against him, when any inconveniences she suffered are far outweighed by the birth of a fine, healthy eighth child?

2   People are always complaining about the amount of traffic in cities. They do not realize what enormous costs would be involved in reducing traffic. We would need to introduce barriers to through traffic, build ring roads, improve public transport, restrict deliveries to shops, build new car parks, and employ an army of traffic wardens to enforce the new legislation. The price of everything would go up to cover the expense of reducing urban traffic.

3   Bicycles make far less noise than cars; they produce no carbon monoxide; they can eas-ily get through city traffic without violating traffic regulations; they can be parked any-where; they are just as fast as cars in congested city centres; they require no petrol; and they carry as many passengers (namely, one) as most commuter cars. Even if they have disadvantages, these facts ought to persuade the authorities to provide more special facil-ities and designated routes for the cyclist in town centres.

4   In the long run the greatest medical danger lies in reducing infant mortality amongst poor people. Saving the lives of an increasing number of babies will cause the population of the underprivileged to expand so quickly that widespread hunger and overcrowding are bound to result.

5   It is difficult to disagree with the opinions of environmental experts that, because of the dif-ficulty of disposing of radioactive waste, the dangers of transporting the waste, and the prob-lems of processing radioactive substances, nuclear power is not the answer to our energy problems; it is to be noted that even politicians are beginning to take note of these views.

Thought

It is worth noting in the above arguments how the rules of grouping and direction, if followed, are a great help in making the argument readily understandable and easy to read. When working out an argument yourself, ideas never come in an orderly fashion. Flashes of insight, repetitive mulling over the ingredients of the argument, and constant shuffling of its components, belong to the developmental process of an argument. However, when the time comes to communicate it to others, it is well worth spending the time to organize its presentation in the simplest and most lucid way possible.

Deductive and inductive arguments

Arguments are traditionally divided into two different types, deductive and inductive. Although in every argument there is the claim that its premises provide some grounds for the truth of its conclusion, only a *deductive* argument involves the claim that its premises provide *conclusive* grounds. We use the technical terms 'valid' and 'invalid' in place of 'correct' and 'incorrect'.

A deductive argument is said to be *valid* when its premises, if true, do provide conclusive grounds for its conclusion; and, the other way round, when premises and conclusions are logically related in such a way that it follows that the premises could not possibly be true if the conclusion was not true.

In order to discriminate between valid or invalid deductive arguments, we can apply the rules of deductive logic to clarify the nature of the relation between premises and conclusion. Deductive argument must be either valid or invalid. Determining whether it is one or the other may be easy in short, succinct arguments, but often presents more of a problem when the argument is extended and complex. A more detailed discussion of logic in deductive arguments appears a little later in this chapter.

In comparison to a deductive argument, an *inductive* argument contains the claim that its premises only provide *some* support for the conclusion, rather than furnishing conclusive grounds for its truth. This results in the fact that inductive arguments can be neither 'valid' nor 'invalid' in the 'black and white' sense used for deductive arguments. They can, however, be evaluated on the strength of the support they provide for their conclusions by their premises. The stronger the support, the more likely that the conclusions will tend to be true.

Deductive and inductive arguments can be seen as seeking the truth from opposite directions. Through deductive argument we infer the particular from the general, while through inductive argument we infer general truths from the particular. This is illustrated more easily by quoting a well known classical example of deductive argument:

> All humans are mortal.
> Socrates is human.
> Therefore Socrates is mortal.

The particular conclusion (Socrates is mortal) is inferred (validly) from premises, the first of which (all humans are mortal) is a general or universal proposition.

Compare this with another classical illustration of inductive argument:

> Socrates is human and is mortal.
> Xanthippe is human and is mortal.
> Sappho is human and is mortal.
> Therefore probably all humans are mortal.

Here, a general or universal conclusion (probably all humans are mortal) is inferred from premises all of which are particular propositions (e.g. Sappho is human and mortal). Note the important reservation about the strength of proof of the argument – 'probably'. While this is a simply explained method of distinguishing between deduction and induction, it is not adequate in all cases.

A better and more universally applicable method of distinguishing between deductive and inductive arguments is as follows. If we take a valid deductive argument, we find that its conclusion follows unequivocally from its premises regardless of what may be added. From the two premises 'all humans are mortal' and 'Socrates is human', the conclusion 'Socrates is mortal' follows necessarily, no matter what else may be true. The argument remains valid no matter what additional premises may be added to the original pair. We can add all kinds of information about Socrates, or any other subject for that matter, e.g. that Socrates is old, or that the sky is blue: the enlarged set of premises will not affect the validity of the argument because the conclusion still follows strictly from the two original premises. If the argument is valid, nothing can make it *more* valid: by adding more premises we cannot enhance its logic or validity.

But for inductive arguments, this is not the case. Consider the following inductive argument:

> Most rich people drive large cars.
> John Smith drives a large car.
> Therefore John Smith is probably rich.

This is a pretty good inductive argument: if its premises are true, its conclusion is more likely true than false. However, by adding new premises to the original pair we can either strengthen or weaken the resulting argument. On the one hand, for example, we may enlarge the premises by adding:

> John Smith belongs to the Millionaires' Club.
> Only rich people can belong to the Millionaires' Club.

The conclusion is then strongly reinforced, i.e. the additional premises add to the likelihood that the conclusion is true. On the other hand, we may enlarge the original set of premises by adding the following additional premises instead:

> John Smith has filed for bankruptcy.
> Bankrupt people suffer from a shortage of money.

Then the original conclusion which maintains that John Smith is rich would have to be drastically revised. We would deduce just the opposite! (For a more extended discussion see Copi, 1982, pp. 51–4.)

Using the above tests, determine which of the following arguments are deductive and which are inductive.

1 I read about a boy who played professional soccer from the age of 16. He must have been a good junior player.
2 The car was priced at £5000, and I paid £500 in deposit; according to my calculation I still owe £4500.
3 The Minister of Industry looked pale as he emerged from the meeting with the General Workers' Union; it looks as if they gave him an ultimatum.
4 She will probably die soon; she is definitely getting weaker all the time.
5 There are traces of non-permitted chemicals in his blood; he has obviously been taking stimulants.
6 A car is a vehicle, so a car's wheel is a vehicle's wheel.
7 There are more people in the world than there are hairs on any one person's head; it follows that there must be at least two people with the same number of hairs on their heads.
8 Reptiles are cold blooded; so lizards must be cold blooded.
9 This vase is ancient, has been found in a tomb by the Nile, is covered in hieroglyphics; it must be an Ancient Egyptian artefact.
10 The referee said he infringed the rules; so he did infringe the rules.

Logic in argument

We have mentioned before that we should be able to detect a correct logical structure in an argument to determine whether the argument is valid or invalid. So what are the characteristics of logic, which governs the structure of argument?

Hodges (1977, p. 13) defined logic as the study of consistent sets of beliefs. He added that some people preferred to define logic as the study of the validity or the correctness of arguments. That there is no conflict in these views can be demonstrated in the following discussion.

The principal concern of the discipline of logic is **consistency**. However, there are many types of consistency, and logic is concerned only with one of them – the *compatibility of beliefs*. This is very different to the type of consistency that a man displays if he supports the same football team throughout his life, or when a racehorse wins every race he runs. The type of consistency we will be considering is not to do with loyalty, faithfulness or maintenance of standards, but is rather to do with how a set of beliefs can be shown to be consistent with each other. Hodges sums it up in this way:

consistency

> a set of beliefs is called consistent if these beliefs could all be true together in some possible situation. The set of beliefs is called inconsistent if there is no possible situation in which all the beliefs are true. (1977, p. 13)

A good way to test whether you can distinguish between a consistent and an inconsistent set of beliefs is to try the next exercise.

EXERCISE
4.4

Which of the following sets of beliefs do you think are consistent?

1   I've never sat on a horse in my life. But if I mounted one now, it would only take me two minutes to become an expert horseman and be able to win a show jumping competition.
2   I knew I would never get ill. But somehow I just caught a disease.
3   There is no financial crisis in Britain today – it is just a rumour that is put about by politicians who want to increase taxation in order to pay for the rapidly increasing national debt.
4   Peter joined the sports club three years ago, and has become its most generous member. Last year he paid for the travel expenses of all the teams.
5   So many people travel abroad for their holidays. The English seaside resorts are not as popular as before.
6   I think that killing animals is immoral and should be stopped. We should therefore not export live animals for slaughter.

When we were discussing the difference between deductive and inductive arguments, we briefly mentioned the difference between the concepts of validity and truth. These concepts, logical truth and validity, have been two of the most important notions in the history of reason, so we will examine them more closely. In fact, the elements of these notions must be clearly understood before there can be any worthwhile discussion of the processes of argument.

You can find two major types of true statements in discourse. One kind is empirical, which means to say, derived from experience. This is the type of statement that people make every day when they say that something is true or that it is a fact. This kind of true statement is also at the basis of all scientific observations and historical assertions, for example, 'the bat is a type of flying rodent', 'steam is emitted when water is boiled', and 'Henry VIII had six wives'. However, in this section we will consider the other type of true statement in more detail. This second type is based on **logical truth**.

logical truth

Logically true statements can be subdivided into three varieties. The first type is called *trivial*, because the truth revealed is so obvious that nothing new is learned from it: for example, 'Today is Sunday, therefore it is not Saturday', or 'If she is a daughter, then she must be a female.' These are known as tautologies: it is manifest that these 'truths' are an inherent part of the semantics of language, and do not really increase our knowledge about the terms. However, in more complicated or abstract statements, they might in fact be very useful in making evident relations between words which were not previously obvious.

In arithmetic, statements are made about the relationships between numbers and arithmetic concepts. These mathematical propositions define the rules of arithmetic and are said to be *true by necessity*. For example, it would be difficult to imagine that 2 + 2 did not equal 4, and it would be senseless to assert otherwise.

Figure 4.3 True by necessity

There is a third variety of true statements which logicians frequently speak of, namely those *true by definition*. There are all sorts of definitions, but it is not the truth of the definitions that the logicians have in mind. In argument, a special definition of a term is often introduced, which may or may not conform very closely to ordinary usage. This is done, among other reasons, to control the ambiguity of ordinary usage. Clearly, it is meaningless here to ask if the definition is true. Like any other kinds of logical truth, definitional truth is innocent of any factual substance.

It must be remembered that logic is concerned not with the truth or falsity of premises or conclusions, but rather with the correctness of arguments. Therefore we do not say that inductive arguments are true, incorrect or untrue; we say that they contain valid deductions, correct inductions or, at the other extreme, assorted fallacies.

It follows, therefore, that the **validity** of deductive arguments is determined by their logical form, not by the content of the statements which they comprise. As mentioned previously, when the premise or premises of such an argument are related to the conclusion in such a way that the conclusion must be true if the premises are true, then the argument is said to be valid. Any argument where this is not the case is called invalid (i.e. if there is any possibility that the premises could be true and the conclusion false). See Salmon (1984, pp. 19–20) for a more detailed explanation.

validity

Salmon points out that each of the following three combinations is possible for valid deductive arguments:

1 *True premises and a true conclusion*   For example:

    All diamonds are hard.   True
    Some diamonds are gems.   True
    Therefore some gems are hard.   True

2 *Some or all premises false and a true conclusion*   For example:

    All cats have wings.   False
    All birds are cats.   False
    Therefore all birds have wings   True

3 *Some or all premises false and a false conclusion*   For example:

    All cats have wings.   False
    All dogs are cats.   False
    Therefore all dogs have wings.   False

Although some of the premises in the above arguments are false, if they were true the conclusions would have to be true. However, this cannot work the other way round: a deductive argument cannot be valid if it has true premises but a false conclusion.

It might be easy in simple sentences like the above to distinguish between valid and invalid arguments, as the premises are short and unambiguous and the construction of the arguments is simple. But how can we analyse more complex deductive arguments in order to demonstrate whether they are valid or **Venn diagram** invalid? The **Venn diagram** provides us with a clear and untechnical method of checking the validity of deductive arguments. An argument is made up of a series of statements, and the Venn diagram is based on a number of overlapping circles which represent classes in each statement. Take for example this simple statement:

Some engineers are females.

A circle representing the class of engineers is drawn, and another circle to the right, overlapping the first, representing the class of females is then drawn (Diagram 4.2). The overlapping area of the circles represents the engineers who are females. This area that represents the statement is shaded in. The other areas represent on the right those engineers who are not females, and on the left those females who are not engineers.

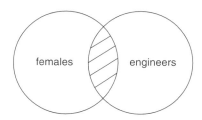

Diagram 4.2 Venn diagram: some engineers are females

This pair of overlapping circles is the standard form of Venn diagram for a statement. Using this format of two overlapping circles enables you to identify the classes of the three areas for the statement, and identify the one which represents the statement. There are four basic forms of expression for statements using quantifiers (e.g. all, some):

All X are Y.
Some X are Y.
No X are Y.
Some X are not Y.

The basic overlapping Venn diagram can illustrate all of these. In order to denote those areas which are impossible according to the statement, simply cross them out. For example, Diagram 4.3 shows the Venn diagram for the statement:

No spiders are insects.

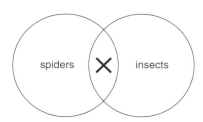

Diagram 4.3 Venn diagram: no spiders are insects

Make a Venn diagram for the following statements, crossing out the impossible areas:

1 All men are human.
2 Some apples are green.
3 No whales are fishes.
4 Some cats are not long-haired.

EXERCISE 4.5

Arguments that contain three categorical statements, called syllogisms, can also be represented in Venn diagrams, this time involving three overlapping circles, which create seven areas, or eight if you count the surrounding area outside all the circles (Diagram 4.4).

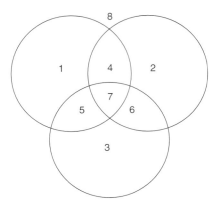

Diagram 4.4   Venn diagram: syllogisms

The diagram can be used to test the validity of arguments. This is how it works. Take this simple argument:

> All elephants are animals.
> Some elephants have tusks.
> Therefore some animals have tusks.

We represent the class of animals, the class of elephants and the class of tusks as interlocking circles as in the above example, and cross out the impossible areas according to the statements in the first two lines. If the area represented by the concluding statement is not crossed out, the argument is valid (Diagram 4.5). The shaded area represents the animals that have tusks and are elephants.

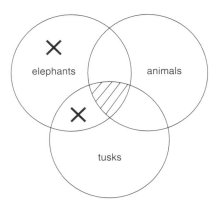

Diagram 4.5   Venn diagram: some animals have tusks

Let us try another:

> Some philosophers are mathematicians.
> All scientists are mathematicians.
> Therefore all scientists are philosophers.

Using the method as in the previous argument, you will find that the concluding statement fits in the area of overlap of the philosopher and scientist circles. However, as all scientists are mathematicians, the part of the scientists' circle not overlapped by the mathematicians' circle has been crossed out as impossible. A part of the remaining area of the scientists' circle lies outside the philosopher circle, so only some and not all scientists are philosophers. The argument is invalid (Diagram 4.6).

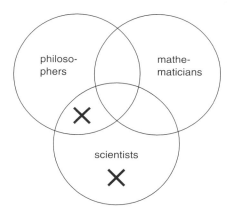

Diagram 4.6   Venn diagram: all scientists are philosophers

Here are some more arguments to test using Venn diagrams. Draw the diagrams using the standard three overlapping circles format, cross out the impossible areas and test the concluding statement. Which arguments are invalid and which are valid?

EXERCISE 4.6

1   Some people with high earnings are clever investors.
    All lawyers have high earnings.
    Therefore some clever investors are lawyers.

2   All gangsters are unsocial.
    All gangsters are resourceful.
    Therefore all resourceful people are unsocial.

3   No lawyers are criminals.
    John is not a lawyer.
    Therefore John is a criminal.

4　All chickens are birds.
　　No snakes are chickens.
　　Therefore no snakes are birds.

5　All researchers are clever.
　　Some students are researchers.
　　Therefore some students are clever.

6　All businessmen wear suits.
　　No tramps are businessmen.
　　Therefore no tramps wear suits.

7　All dogs are mammals.
　　All mammals have warm blood.
　　Therefore all dogs have warm blood.

Thought

Arguments are not often stated quite so succinctly in books or research papers, so it is usually necessary to read the text very carefully to distil the argument down to a series of simple statements. Determine first if the argument is inductive or deductive. If it is deductive, and there is any doubt about the validity of the argument, you can devise your own Venn diagram, or even series of Venn diagrams, to test out the overlaps in the statements and determine where the invalidity occurs. This provides you with a very powerful source of criticism!

Fallacies in argument

Logic is the protection against trickery and sloppy thinking. Logic deals with arguments which are based on reason. Mistakes are possible and even frequent in applying forms of logical argument. These mistakes are termed fallacies. However, not all mistakes in argument are genuine mistakes; there are innumerable examples of the calculated use of quasi-reasoning in order to convince or convert the unwary.

The recognition of fallacies is not new, many of them having been noted as early as Aristotle. You can probably devise an argument yourself which is entirely logical, whose validity is clearly demonstrated by the conclusion being derived from its premises, and which carefully follows all the rules of syllogism, but which is based on premises that are phoney, tricks and delusions. There are brilliant deceptions for getting people to accept all sorts of false premises as true, and these tricks of argument are so common that even when people realize that they are being hoodwinked they tend to let it pass.

Fearnside and Holther (1959, p. 2) maintained that arguments are a highly complicated human activity and cannot be successfully studied in a sort of vacuum, as if the language uttered and answered itself. There is no simple connection between the presentation of an argument on the one side, and the acceptance of it on the other. Even the most exotic television commercial usually contains some kind of argument, some assertion of reasons and drawing of conclusions, e.g. 'you must buy this because it's so romantic'. Even when you read books on logic you find that the arguments are seldom spelled out fully, except in the examples. After all, one can take for granted that people will recognize the unstated premise in this type of argument: 'This man cannot be a trapeze artist because he is unable to stand heights.' The argument runs:

> Trapeze artists must be able to stand heights. (unstated)
> This man is unable to stand heights.
> Therefore, this man is not a trapeze artist.

The word 'fallacy' is often used in two ways: sometimes it is used to describe any kind of attitude that is fraudulent or deceitful, and at other times it is used, in a narrower sense, to indicate a defective manner of reasoning or a wily or cunning form of persuasion. In the following analysis of fallacies, it is the second meaning which is taken, i.e. where an argument purports to abide by the rules of sound argument but in fact fails to do so.

Pirie (1985, p. 183) suggested that there are five broad categories into which fallacies fall. The most important division is between the formal fallacies and the informal ones, although there are important distinctions between the various types of informal fallacy.

Formal fallacies have some error in the structure of the logic. Although they often resemble valid forms of argument, the logical route only takes us from A to B by way of disjointed or missing paths. In brief, the fallacy occurs because the chain of reasoning itself is defective. **formal fallacies**

Informal fallacies, on the other hand, often use valid reasoning on terms which are not of sufficient quality to merit such treatment. They can be linguistic, and allow ambiguities of language to admit error, and leave out something needed to sustain the argument; permit irrelevant factors to weigh on the conclusion; or allow unwarranted presumptions to alter the conclusion which is reached. **informal fallacies**

There are five categories of fallacy, as in Box 4.6.

Box 4.6   Categories of fallacy
1   Formal.
2   Informal, linguistic.
3   Informal, relevance omission.
4   Informal, relevance intrusion.
5   Informal, relevance presumption.

It is not possible in this book to discuss all the different types of fallacy, so some of those which are considered to have the greatest relevance to academic research work have been selected here. Most types of fallacy have been given titles or technical names and are well known to logicians. It is not necessary that you remember the names, though it will impress people if you point out the shortcomings in their arguments by quoting the type of fallacy by its name! The following exercise tests your ability to spot the types of fallacy according to the above five categories. The technical name of each is given in the answers.

EXERCISE 4.7

Each of the following texts contains a fallacy. Can you spot what it is, and fit it into one of the above categories, and explain the nature of the fallacy? When you look up the answers, the category and technical name will be given, and you can check to see if you discerned the characteristics of the various types of fallacy.

1   If I dance too much, I'll be tired. Since I have not danced too much, I will not be tired.
2   The duchess has a fine ship, but she has barnacles on her bottom.
3   The ship of government, like any other ship, works best when there is a strong captain in charge of it. This is why government by dictatorship is more effective.
4   Look, you're a lecturer. Your university decided to increase your working hours because they knew it will be good for lecturers. It must therefore be good for you.
5   Talk of the Loch Ness monster is nonsense. We know that it does not exist because every single attempt to find it has failed utterly.
6   I'm not going to get a job. There will be all that extra responsibility, not to mention the loss of my freedom. Think of the costs of travelling to work and buying suitable clothing. Then there are the increased worries about status.
7   All musicians are really sensitive people. It happens that some really sensitive people are not properly appreciated. So some musicians are not properly appreciated.
8   The small, domesticated carnivorous quadruped positioned itself in sedentary mode in superior relationship to the coarse-textured rush-woven horizontal surface fabric.
9   If the Americans wanted good trade relations, they would encourage the production of specialist goods in other countries. Since they do support this type of production, we know that they want good trade relations.
10 I don't think we should employ Mr Smith. I am told that he is a poor golf player. Careless people are bad at golf, so I don't think it is a good omen.

Thought

Obviously, it is important to recognize fallacies when you read or listen to people's arguments. It is just as important to avoid fallacies in your own writing (or to use them to best effect if you intend to deceive!). The above examples are only a small selection of types of fallacy: whole books are written on the subject, so if you would like to read more about fallacy in all its guises, I can recommend the books by Pirie (1985) as a light-hearted account (from which I adapted some of the above examples), and Fearnside and Holther (1959) for a more serious and technical approach.

Classification and analogy in argument

The idea of class plays a very fundamental role in much of our thinking, deductive and inductive. From our discussion of the rules of logic, and particularly when we analysed the validity of deductive arguments using Venn diagrams, we could see how:

- One class may be part of another.
- Classes may or may not overlap (that is, have members in common).
- Valid conclusions can be drawn about the relationship between two classes from the knowledge about the way each is related to a third class.
- Under certain conditions we may legitimately infer something about a class from one of its subclasses.

There are other important ways of thinking about class and making classifications which we will consider next.

There are two ways of forming a **class**: by collection or by division. By *collection* we class things which share a common property (or properties), e.g. 'having four legs'. Through *division*, we can further divide this collection into subclasses, e.g. 'brown quadrupeds', 'red quadrupeds', 'grey quadrupeds' etc. Division not only creates new classes out of an old one, but also relates the new classes to the old one, i.e. they are *subordinated* to it.

class

Division is only one way of relating classes to each other. We can also relate classes to each other by subsumption and by co-ordination.

Subsumption goes in the opposite direction from division. We start with a class, say a discarded tin can, and ask: of what larger class shall we consider this to be a subclass? We have various alternatives to choose from: metal objects, refuse, used packaging, cylindrical objects etc.

When we divide a class into subclasses, the subclasses between themselves have parallel status: they are *co-ordinate classes*. When we subsume one class under another, the subsumed class is at least implicitly contrasted with the other subclasses that could also be subsumed co-ordinately with it. Take, for example, the simple divisions in Diagram 4.7. The classes subsumed under 'male', i.e. 'postman' and 'policeman', can be contrasted with those subsumed under 'female', i.e. 'air hostess' and 'businesswoman'.

The diagram represents a *classification*. The classes named in the diagram are called *categories*, which are ordered in various levels, or *ranks*, from the most

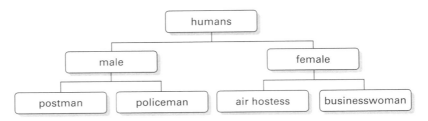

Diagram 4.7   Classification tree

general to the most specific. Within each rank, the co-ordinate categories are distinguished by reference to a particular property, which is the basis of division, i.e. in the diagram at the first rank the basis of division is sex, at the second rank the basis of division is profession.

The rule that guards against confusion is this: in each rank the categories are to be distinguished according to only one basis of division. A classification that violates the single-basis rule commits the *fallacy of cross-ranking*. For example, in 'men; women and children' the second category really involves two ranks lumped together. The fallacy might not be so easy to detect as in this example.

Other serious faults can be found in classifications. Sometimes the categories in a given rank will fail to be exclusive of each other, so that the same thing belongs in both of two or more overlapping categories, e.g. if the third-rank categories in Diagram 4.7 had been, say, engineer, designer, lecturer, architect (which could be either men or women). Sometimes a given rank will fail to be exhaustive, so that we find that we have no category for some of the things we want to classify, e.g. what happens if one of the females we want to classify using Diagram 4.7 is neither an air hostess nor a businesswoman?

EXERCISE 4.8

Test your skill in recognizing which of the following class divisions: (a) are technically correct; (b) use more than one basis of division; (c) produce overlapping categories; (d) leave gaps?

1   Books: softback books and hardback books.
2   Bread rolls: soft bread rolls and hard bread rolls.
3   Pies: one-crust pies, two-crust pies, mud pies.
4   School buildings: primary school buildings and secondary school buildings.
5   Prime ministers: distinguished prime ministers, mundane prime ministers, insignificant prime ministers.
6   Days: sunny days, rainy days, foggy days, cold days, snowy days.
7   Pens: fountain pens, ball-point pens, felt-tip pens.
8   Sources of energy: atomic fusion or fission, fossil fuels, water.
9   Planets: those which orbit between earth and sun and those which orbit beyond the earth.
10   Cars: diesel cars, petrol cars, four-door cars, electric cars, two-door cars.

There are many ways of classifying objects and events. Depending on the situation, one way may be more useful or revealing than another. As our knowledge of a class increases we may repeatedly revise our classification scheme in order to add new categories or to reject some bases of division in favour of others. It is well worth asking oneself before setting up a classification: what purpose will the classification serve, and what relevant new information will the classification provide?

Sometimes it is very useful to compare two things of widely different categories. We call this activity drawing an **analogy**. This type of comparison can enable us to see an object or an idea in a new light, and hint at new hypotheses or generalizations that we otherwise might not have contemplated. Analogies are widely used in inductive argument, and this is how they work.

analogy

When we compare objects of two categories, we can sometimes observe that objects of one category are similar in certain respects to objects of the other category. If we know that objects of the first category have certain other characteristics, but do not know whether these are present in the second category, we could conclude by analogy that, since objects of the two categories are alike in some respects, they are alike in other respects as well. Therefore, objects of the second category also have the additional characteristics observed in the first category.

The carrying out of medical experiments on animals is a common manifestation of this argument, where it is claimed that similarities between animals and humans will allow the effects of drugs on humans to be predicted by their effect on animals. Researchers do not claim that animals are identical to humans (they could be put into the same class if they were), but hold that the differences, for the purposes of the tests, are not significant.

Figure 4.4 Analogical arguments may be strong or weak

Like other kinds of inductive arguments, analogical arguments may be strong or weak. The strength of an analogy depends principally upon the similarities between the two types of objects being compared. Any two kinds of objects can be similar in many ways and dissimilar in many others. Salmon pointed out that:

> The crucial question for analogical arguments is this: are the objects which are being compared similar in ways that are relevant to the argument ... The more relevant similarities that are present, the stronger the argument, and vice versa. (1984, p. 108)

It is not always easy, in a particular situation, to determine precisely what should be regarded as relevant or irrelevant for similarities or differences between objects of the classes. The question which must be posed is: what kinds of similarities or differences are likely to have a significant effect on the outcome of the phenomenon being investigated? For example, when testing drugs on rabbits, the fact that humans do not have long ears is unlikely to be a relevant difference. The fact that both are mammals will be a relevant similarity.

Analogical arguments appear not only in scientific discourse. They are commonly used in philosophical literature (e.g. in Plato's *Republic*, where he compares the state and the individual). It must be remembered that in dealing with an argument from analogy, as with other forms of inductive argument, there is no way of proving that the argument is correct in all instances, or even exactly to what extent it is reliable.

EXERCISE 4.9

Here are three different texts which rely heavily on analogy for their reasoning. (a) List the assumptions which are made in each argument. (b) Describe briefly what each aims to prove. (c) What shortcomings do you detect in the relevance of the analogies?

Text 1

The 'balanced aquarium' is a well known concept amongst environmentalists. It is an aquarium sealed with a glass cover. Within it is a closed cycle, so without food being added and without being cleaned it maintains itself for years. Plants capture sunlight and produce energy-rich food; a few snails graze on the rich bacteria flora which develops in the sand. But only two tiny fish can be supported in an aquarium of about five gallons of water. If more fish are added, the cycle falls into a spiral of irreversible decay. The plants die, causing the water to become foul, after which the bacteria take over in massive numbers until their food, too, is used up. Our earth is that aquarium. We have too many fish in the tank, there is too much waste being produced, and only the bacteria will reap a brief benefit if we don't act quickly.

Text 2

I speak in my role as the President of the National Funeral Directors' Association, against the regrettable but increasingly common funeral practice of cremations. I totally agree with our Chairman of the Board of Directors who stated last month that in his opinion, 'a funeral without a body is like a baptism without a baby, a birthday celebration without the birthday child or a wedding without a bride'.

Text 3

The security of a nation is comparable to the health of an individual. Admittedly, what counts as good health may be different in an athlete or an expectant mother, this depending on the adopted lifestyle (just as what counts as national security depends on the nation's lifestyle); nevertheless there are standards in both cases. Health and security are essential for the success of any organization, of whatever kind; and the greater the aspirations – in the individual, to succeed in great tasks; and in the nation, to meet vital challenges and provide leadership among other nations – the greater the need for sturdy health. A person who has due regard for his health, who consults his doctor for a check-up at regular intervals, takes regular exercise etc., is not regarded as a hypochondriac, but is praised for taking due care of his life. Similarly, the administration's measures to protect national security against external and internal perils should not be condemned. Quite the opposite: we should favour strong policies to protect the state against violations of secrecy (such as the unauthorized publication of the *Pentagon Papers*), to enhance its security classifications (the present system of 'top secret' classifications is not enough), and to use every means necessary (whether secret surveillance, phone-tapping, bugging, burglary etc.) to pursue those whose words or actions can be regarded to be potentially threatening to national security.

CONCLUSIONS

In the course of your research project and later in your career, you will need to do a lot of communicating, particularly in writing, but also verbally. A sound technique in argument will therefore be a valuable asset to enable you to put your points across strongly and effectively. You will also be in a good position to analyse the work of others, to test the validity of their arguments, and to avoid the pitfalls presented by fallacies. In the next section, an initial attempt at compiling a sound argument on the basis of your thoughts about your research subject will enable you to practise the previously explained elements of discourse.

THE NEXT STEPS: WHAT ARGUMENT WILL YOU PURSUE?

The aims of this section are:

- to apply your knowledge of argument in the analysis of the writings of others
- to practise the virtues of sound argument within your field of research
- to analyse the components of argument which you use and to test the validity of your argument.

Checklist of activities that will progress your research

Step 1: look at statements
During your literature review you will come across many statements that make assertions about the concepts you are interested in. Are you sure what these statements imply and are they backed up by any evidence? Do they merely state that something exists, or do they assert that there is a relation between things. If so, what is the type of relationship – associational or causal? The nature of these statements in relation to your research problem will have significant implications for the type of research that you will need to carry out.

Step 2: identify arguments
Look out for premise and conclusion indicators when you are doing your background reading. These will help you to identify the arguments being made. You can perhaps then distil the arguments into a few words, cutting out all the 'padding' in order to come to their essence. This will help you to categorize the different strands of thinking in a subject, particularly important when doing your literature review.

Step 3: analyse arguments
In order to 'cut out the padding' you need to identify the premises and conclusions to an argument. This will not be as easy as analysing three-line syllogisms as there will probably be several more premises and possibly more than one conclusion. You could try producing a Venn diagram, or if that is too difficult, at least a logical thread to the argument with a series of premises and a conclusion.

Step 4: detect fallacies
Doing this kind of analysis should quickly reveal arguments without substance or those based on a fallacy. The important thing is to exercise your critical faculties. The fact that the article or book has been published does not mean that it is right! Do not be afraid to challenge what you think is wrong and analyse what you think is right.

Step 5: identify fallacies
Fallacies come in many forms, some more obvious than others. The whole point of some is to deceive, so they are by their nature difficult to spot. Whilst most academic writing aims to be based on good logical argument, strong convictions underlie many approaches, particularly in the human sciences. This may lead to arguments based on selective evidence or a blinkered view of the world. A good understanding of the genealogy of ideas will provide you with a better understanding of 'where the writer has come from'. The scope and depth of your background reading will help here. Have you encountered any arguments in your subject

relevant to your problem area with which you disagree, or which you think are invalid or fallacious? If so, give an account of these.

Step 6: select analogies?

Analogies are useful but sometimes dangerous ways of making assumptions. While there are plenty of very complex discussions about the use of analogy in philosophical texts, here are a couple of simple ways to check that the analogies you use are not wildly irrelevant. Firstly, do not choose examples from very different contexts. The similarities are bound to be rarer. Secondly, do not select elements to compare within the examples that are subject to very different circumstances. The circumstances are what determine the outcomes, so these are bound to be very different.

Step 7: outline your own argument

Outline in a series of short sentences three or four arguments which could be a framework for your research into your chosen problem. Use concepts used or developed in relation to your own work as a basis for statements that are combined to create your arguments. Make sure that your arguments reach conclusions.

You are not expected at this stage to provide the definitive argument which will be the basis of your research work! Use this opportunity to explore the possible approaches from several angles. Use your knowledge of the subject to frame arguments: even simple syllogisms will do to start. You can subsequently develop them into more complex arguments.

Step 8: check your arguments

Check that your arguments are logical, consistent and valid. What kind of statements have you used, and at what level of abstraction are they? Make a list of the premises on which you based your argument. Try to construct at least one plausible deductive and inductive argument, and one which makes use of analogy. Beware of fallacies, or, if you want to, try to introduce one (temporarily) to see if you can get away with it!

Consolidation and assessment

When you are prepared, you should arrange a tutorial with your tutor or supervisor. Present your arguments and try to demonstrate not only their formal qualities, but also their value as a basis for research into your subject.

This should lead to a discussion on the suitability and potential of your proposed arguments, and the implications they will have on the form of your research activities.

A discussion on the arguments which you have found presented in the literature on your subject, and with which you disagree, will also help to direct your future research strategy, and the possible form of your counter-arguments.

Further reading

You can quickly get into deep water on the subject of thinking and argument. I would recommend Brink-Budgen to start with, and perhaps follow up the references in there if you want to find out more on specific issues. The others I have listed need a bit more persistence, and will be useful if you have a special interest in these subjects.

Brink-Budgen, R. (2000) *Critical Thinking for Students: Learn the Skills of Critical Assessment and Effective Argument*, 3rd edn. Oxford: How To Books.

Pearson, R. A. (1993) *Academic Vocabulary and Argument: an Introductory Guide*. Sheffield: PAVIC, Sheffield Hallam University.

Kuhn, D. (1991) *The Skills of Argument*. Cambridge: Cambridge University Press.

If you really want to get into more depth about logic and argument, these are reasonably approachable books, listed in order of easiest first.

Salmon, W. C. (1984) *Logic*, 3rd edn. Englewood Cliffs, NJ: Prentice-Hall.

Gensler, H. J. (1989) *Logic: Analyzing and Appraising Arguments*. London: Prentice-Hall.

Fisher, A. (1998) *The Logic of Real Arguments*. Cambridge: Cambridge University Press.

These are three books about fallacy that might interest you; see the comments I have made for more guidance.

Pirie, M. (1985) *The Book of the Fallacy: a Training Manual of Intellectual Subversives.* London: Routledge and Kegan Paul.

Well written and entertaining.

Fearnside, W. W. and Holther, W. B. (1959) *Fallacy.* Englewood Cliffs, NJ: Prentice-Hall.

A more serious, academic approach.

Thouless, R. H. (1974) *Straight and Crooked Thinking*, rev. edn. London: Pan.

Old, but still entertaining and thought provoking.

Worth a look for aspects of writing:

Taylor, G. (1989) *The Student's Writing Guide for the Arts and Social Sciences.* Cambridge: Cambridge University Press.

EXERCISE 4.1

1 Argument. Premise: increased taxation on petrol. Conclusion: less traffic on the roads. Premise indicator: 'since'.

2 Argument. Premise: diminished social responsibility of criminal through deprived upbringing. Conclusion: criminal is not to blame. No logical indicators present, but premise indicator 'because' is implied.

3 Statement – relational.

4 This could be seen as an associational statement, with positive correlation inferred. It could also be read as an argument if we take the premise indicator 'look at' to mean 'because of'. Premise: unequalled variety of drama etc. in London. Conclusion: my thinking that London is the best place in the world. The question invites you to seek a premise for the conclusion.

5 Argument. Premise: insufficient pay rise offer. Conclusion: train drivers going on strike. Premise indicator: 'because'.

6 Statement – obviously associational.

7 Argument. Premise: strike threat. Conclusion: insufficient pay rise offer. Premise indicator: 'as' (indicated by the fact that).

8 Statement – associational with negative correlation.

9 Argument. Premise: Members of Parliament have misled us too often. Conclusion: I distrust Parliament. Premise indicator: 'my reason being'.

10 Argument. Premise: continued price freeze. Conclusion: lobsters will soon be scarce. Conclusion indicator: 'so it follows that'.

11 Existence statements. There is no link indicated between the two statements.

EXERCISE 4.2

1 Giving birth to a healthy baby, whatever the circumstances, outweighs all possible disadvantages.

2 The price of everything would go up, to cover the cost of reducing traffic.

3 The facts listed should persuade authorities to provide more facilities for cyclists.

4 The greatest medical danger lies in reducing the infant mortality rate amongst poor people.

5 It is difficult to disagree with the opinions of environmental experts that nuclear power is not the answer to our energy problems.

EXERCISE 4.3

1 Inductive.

2 Deductive.

3 Inductive.

4 Inductive.

5 Deductive.

6 Deductive.

7 Deductive.

8 Deductive.

9 Inductive.

10 Inductive.

EXERCISE 4.4

1 Inconsistent. Expertise in anything takes more than two minutes!

2 Inconsistent. My knowledge was obviously insufficient.

3 Inconsistent. The rapidly increasing national debt could be a strong sign of a financial crisis.

4 Consistent.

5 Consistent.

6 Consistent. I probably want many other practices to stop too.

1   Diagram 4.8.

2   Diagram 4.9.

3   Diagram 4.10.

4   Diagram 4.11.

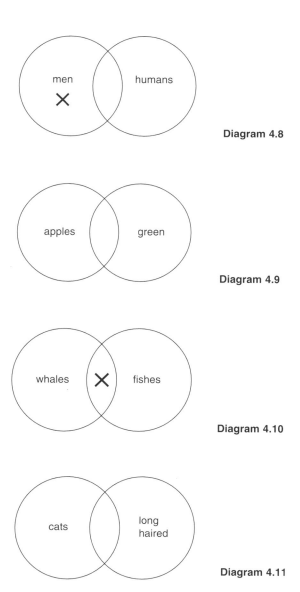

Diagram 4.8

Diagram 4.9

Diagram 4.10

Diagram 4.11

EXERCISE 4.6

1   Diagram 4.12.

2   Diagram 4.13.

3   Diagram 4.14.

4   Diagram 4.15.

5   Diagram 4.16.

6   Diagram 4.17.

7   Diagram 4.18.

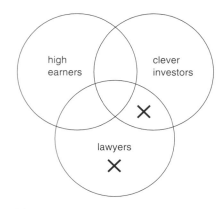

Diagram 4.12

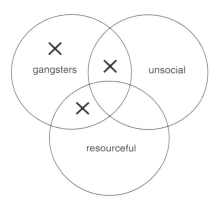

Diagram 4.13

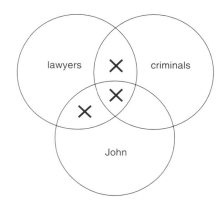

Diagram 4.14

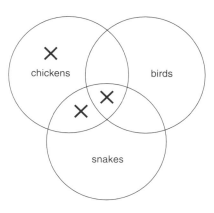

Diagram 4.15

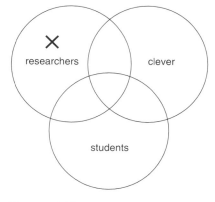

Diagram 4.16

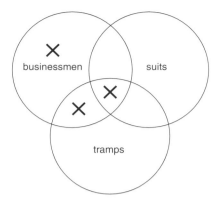

Diagram 4.17

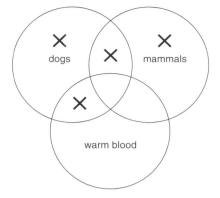

Diagram 4.18

EXERCISE 4.7

1   Formal. Denying the antecedent. This is a result of the writer not really caring if his/her brain is going backwards or forwards. He/she does not recognize that the same result can be produced by different causes.

2   Informal (linguistic). Amphiboly. This is the fallacy of careless grammatical construction which causes an ambiguity of meaning.

3   Informal (relevance presumption). Analogical fallacy. Analogies are often a useful way of describing unfamiliar concepts by talking about them in terms of which the audience already has experience. The fallacy comes in assuming that further similarities, other than those already identified, inevitably occur. None of the false analogies likening the state to a ship ever seem to say much about its cabins, air-conditioning system or boiler capacity!

4   Another example of informal (relevance presumption). Dicto simpliciter. This is the fallacy of sweeping generalization. It ignores the fact that applying a broad general rule to an individual case overlooks the special features which might make the case exceptional.

5   Informal (relevance intrusion). Argumentum ad ignorantium. Just because we lack knowledge about something, it is a fallacy to infer that the opposite is the case, e.g. in this case that it does not exist.

6   Informal (relevance omission). One-sided assessment. This fallacy is committed when only one side of the situation is considered. A balanced view is usually required in order to make an informed decision.

7   Formal. Undistributed middle. A test with the Venn diagram will show you the shortcomings of this argument. The middle term 'really sensitive people' in this example does not cover the whole of its class at least once, so there is a fallacy in the argument (i.e. in this example the middle term never once refers to all really sensitive people).

8   Informal (relevance intrusion). Blinding with science. Pseudo-scientific jargon can be used to try to impress people with your superior knowledge. 'The cat sat on the mat' is a simple way of translating the 'gobbledegook'.

9   Formal. Affirming the consequent. In an 'if … then' construction, the 'if' part is the antecedent, and the 'then' part is the consequent. It is all right to affirm the antecedent in order to prove the consequent, but not vice versa. Affirming the consequent is fallacious because an event can be produced by different causes.

10 Informal (omission). Concealed quantification. When statements are made about a class, sometimes they are about all of the members of it, sometimes about some of them. This fallacy occurs when ambiguity of expression permits a misunderstanding of the quantity which is spoken of (i.e. in this case is it all or some careless people who are bad at golf?).

EXERCISE 4.8

1   Correct.

2   Correct, unless there are finer divisions, e.g. slightly hard, slightly soft etc.

3   More than one basis of division. How many crusts has a mud pie?

4   Correct, unless you feel you should add nursery school buildings.

5   Correct, though there might be some considerable dispute as to the precision of the categories.

6   Overlapping categories; cold days could be also sunny etc.

7   Correct, unless you can think of any other basic pen types. If so, then the classification is with gaps.

8   Gaps left: what about wind, waves, solar etc.?

9   Correct, if you are only talking about planets circling our sun.

10 More than one basis of division. The two types of division also overlap.

EXERCISE 4.9

TEXT 1

(a) Assumptions: our world is a closed system like a 'balanced aquarium'. Also, that the earth's atmosphere and biosphere behave in essentially the same way as a small, enclosed, aquarium of water.

(b) Aims to prove: that too many people on the world will produce too much waste, upsetting the existing delicate balance which maintains life.

(c) The main shortcoming of the analogy is that fish have no way of controlling or processing their waste products, unlike humans (however negligent they may be in doing so), and that the earth is far more complex than a simple aquarium.

TEXT 2

(a) Assumptions: family celebrations are all fundamentally the same, and they require the focus of the celebration to be present.

(b) Aims to prove: that cremations are an inadequate type of funeral.

(c) The shortcoming of the analogy is that whereas, in all the other family celebrations, the focus of the celebration is alive and actively takes part, at a funeral he/she is dead and cannot take an active role. This makes the role played by the deceased in a funeral very different.

TEXT 3

(a) Assumptions: that the health of an individual shares many attributes with the security of a nation. Also, that individual health and national security are subject to certain norms. Both good health and good security are essential for success in any under-taking. Active concern for both health and security is not a sign of weakness but a commendable virtue.

(b) Aims to prove: that in order to be an effective nation, every effort must be made to increase national security.

(c) There are several shortcomings in the relevance of this analogy. Firstly, health and security are two completely different concepts and require totally different techniques to promote them. Secondly, what an individual might be willing to suffer to promote his/her own health is not comparable to what society might be willing to tolerate for the sake of national security. Additionally, the measures it is suggested should be undertaken to promote national security have no parallel with measures taken to promote individual health.

5
More about the Nature of Research

Introduction: The Debate about the Nature of Knowledge and the
    Philosophy of Research
Positivism and Scientific Enquiry
    Pure Induction
    Deduction and the Principle of Falsification
    The Hypothetico-Deductive Method
The Debate about the Structure of Science and the Nature of Knowledge
Positivism and Interpretivism in Social Research
    The Positivist Approach
    The Interpretivist Approach
    The Reconciliatory Approach
Hypotheses: Do You Need Them?
    A Closer Look at Hypotheses and their Formulation
    Operationalizing Hypotheses
    Alternatives to Hypotheses
Conclusions
The Next Steps: Philosophy in the Research Project
Checklist of Activities That Will Progress Your Research
    Consolidation and Assessment
Key words
Further Reading
Answers to Exercises

To provide an introduction to questions about the process of research in order to make you think about what form of enquiry you will use to research into your own problem. This is done by:

- exploring some aspects of the philosophy of research and the debate about the nature of knowledge
- explaining in more detail the forms and characteristics of scientific method
- exploring alternative approaches to research
- examining the nature of hypotheses and their roles in research, and discussing possible alternatives to using hypotheses.

INTRODUCTION: THE DEBATE ABOUT THE NATURE OF KNOWLEDGE AND THE PHILOSOPHY OF RESEARCH

The first chapter of this book contained a brief description of 'scientific method', together with a short review of the debate surrounding research in which the positivist approach was challenged. In this chapter, the underlying philosophies in this debate are considered in more detail. To begin with, the positivist attributes of scientific enquiry are scrutinized to reveal some of its strengths and limitations. The radical questioning of the mainstream assumptions of scientific method, made in the 1960s by relativists and proponents of anti-method, are then discussed. This is followed by a brief examination of the interpretivist epistemology, explaining the drift of the arguments against positivism and the alternative approaches suggested.

It is since the latter part of the nineteenth century that philosophical alternatives to positivism have been developed. However, although the study of human individuals and society can be seen as being quite different from the study of organic and inorganic matter, owing to the ability of humans to think, decide and give meanings to the world around them, some social scientists advocated a natural scientific approach in their investigations, investigating what they called 'social facts'. This approach was fundamentally questioned by maintaining that it is the meaningfulness of the subject matter that is paramount. This 'interpretivist' approach sees social reality characterized by intersubjectivity and common meanings which need to be interpreted and understood. A middle way, using aspects of both philosophical standpoints, has also been promulgated. According to this approach, social life should be studied from both a positivist and an interpretivist viewpoint, and one should verify subjective interpretations by comparison with the actual course of events.

It has often been said that a study of the philosophy of the natural or human sciences is irrelevant to researchers. As a commentary on how theory after theory is erected, only to be torn down by the subsequent one, it has little bearing on the day-to-day practice of research, and only causes confusion. So why do I think that it is necessary to know something about philosophy as a background to research? Because everyone is a philosopher – everyone has a concept of the world.

> The alternative to philosophy is not no philosophy but bad philosophy. The 'unphilosophical' person has an unconscious philosophy, which they apply in their practice – whether of science or politics or daily life. (Collier, 1994, p. 16)

Philosophy works by making arguments explicit. A sensitivity towards philosophical issues is needed to enable you to evaluate research critically. It is necessary to discern the underlying, and perhaps contentious, assumptions upon which research reports are based even when these are not explicit, and thus to be able to judge the appropriateness of the methods that have been employed and the validity of the conclusions reached. Consequently, you will also have to consider these aspects in regard to your own research work.

> All philosophical positions and their attendant methodologies, explicitly or implicitly, hold a view about social reality. This view, in turn, will determine what can be regarded as legitimate knowledge. Thus the ontological shapes the epistemological. (Williams and May, 1996, p. 69)

Some simple examples will help to clarify this. Suppose you have been asked to carry out some research about children's playgrounds in the city. You could collect very different types of data to analyse. For example, you could look at official statistics about how many playgrounds there are in relationship to population figures, their sizes, facilities and locations, records of vandalism and child crime. Or you could arrange interviews with children and parents to find out what they felt about different playgrounds. You could also observe the playgrounds from above and plot children's playing patterns in the form of geometrical shapes; or you could observe from nearby and record how the children used each piece of equipment. You could also make measurements of how much force is exerted by children playing on the equipment, test its strength and measure rates of corrosion, in order to ensure that it is safely built. Each of these approaches involves basic theoretical as well as methodological decisions.

So, for example, if you wanted to establish correlations between 'social facts', you would favour collecting official statistics. However, if you were concerned with finding 'social meanings', then interview studies would be more appropriate. If you were more interested in theories of interactionism or ethnomethodology, you would make a close observation of what people did, either as a whole or in detail. Finally, if you were interested in the technical performance of play equipment, then tests and experiments according to scientific method would produce the relevant answers.

Accordingly, you will have to decide which philosophical standpoint(s) to adopt when carrying out your research. This is not to say that any approach is better or more true than the other. Your research approach will depend on the characteristics of your research problem and your own convictions about the nature of research. The decision will help you to determine the nature of your enquiry, the choice of appropriate research methods, and the characteristics of the outcomes that you can expect.

A particularly important aspect of a project is how you formulate your research problem in such a way that indicates how the research can be carried out. As is explained later in this chapter, research in the natural sciences commonly uses the standard method of focusing the research which entails setting up a hypothesis which can then be tested, from which useful conclusions can be drawn. In the social sciences, it is usually not possible to be precise enough, or to find sufficiently precisely measurable variables, to fulfil the strict criteria of a scientific hypothesis. In these cases, there are more appropriate statements or expressions which can be used as the focus of the research, and these are discussed towards the end of this chapter.

In the final section of the chapter, you are asked to question how the various philosophical approaches might influence the formulation of your own research project.

POSITIVISM AND SCIENTIFIC ENQUIRY

Before looking into the debate surrounding scientific enquiry, it is worth considering what comprises the conventional image of science based on a positivist position. Hacking created a list of nine points, which I reproduce in full in Box 5.1. Although not all are held by any single philosopher or scientist, they present a useful summary of a widespread popular conception of science.

1   *Realism*. Science is an attempt to find out about one real world. Truths about the world are true regardless of what people think, and there is a unique best description of any chosen aspect of the world.

2   *Demarcation.* There is a pretty sharp distinction between scientific theories and other kinds of beliefs.

3   Science is *cumulative*. Although false starts are common enough, science by and large builds on what is already known. Even Einstein's theories are a development from Newton's.

4   *Observation–theory distinction.* There is a fairly sharp contrast between reports of observations and statements of theory.

5   *Foundations.* Observation and experiment provide foundations for and justification of hypotheses and theories.

6   Theories have a *deductive structure* and tests of theories proceed by deducing observation reports from theoretical hypotheses.

7   Scientific concepts are rather *precise*, and the terms used in science have fixed meanings.

8   There is a *context of justification* and a *context of discovery*. We should distinguish (a) the psychological or social circumstances in which a discovery is made from (b) the logical basis for accepting the facts that have apparently been discovered.

9   *The unity of science.* There should be just one science about the one real world. Less measurable sciences are *reducible* to more measurable ones. Sociology is reducible to psychology, psychology to biology, biology to chemistry, and chemistry to physics. (Hacking, 1981, pp. 1–2)

Although scientific enquiry has been carried out in a variety of ways through the centuries, it is possible to detect two approaches representing the extremes of method – induction and deduction. At one extreme, induction aims to establish theories purely on the basis of observations, while, at the other, deduction aims to devise theories by intellectual means and then to test them through observation. The hypothetico-deductive method, a relative newcomer to scientific thought, is a combination of both of these approaches.

Pure induction

induction   The earliest and, even now, the commonest popular form of scientific activity is that of **induction**. Every day, our experiences lead us to make conclusions, from which we tend to generalize. There are, however, certain shortcomings in this form of scientific process. Consider Bertrand Russell's somewhat gruesome story of the inductivist turkey.

This turkey found that, on the first morning in the turkey farm, he was fed at 9.00 a.m. However, being a good inductivist, he did not jump to conclusions. Patiently, he waited many days, observing that he was fed every day at 9.00 a.m., whether the sun shone or it rained, in windy weather and in calm. Eventually, his careful list of observation statements led him to conclude that 'I am always fed at 9.00 a.m.' On Christmas Eve his inductive inference with true premises was shown to have led him to a patently false conclusion, for on that day at 9.00 a.m., instead of being fed, his throat was cut.

This can be seen as an example of naive inductivism. Despite the obvious short-comings of this method of scientific enquiry, the development of this approach in the seventeenth century by such scientists as Galileo and Newton heralded the scientific revolution. The philosopher Francis Bacon summed this up by maintaining that in order to understand nature, one should consult nature, and not the writings of ancient philosophers such as Aristotle, or the Bible.

Many scientific advances have been achieved through inductive reasoning, through the formulation of generalizations and laws derived inductively from experience and observation. However, three conditions must be satisfied for such generalizations to be considered legitimate by inductivists, as in Box 5.2.

Box 5.2   Conditions for inductive reasoning

1   There must be a large number of observation statements.
2   The observations must be repeated under a large range of circumstances and conditions.
3   No observation statement must contradict the derived generalization.

In order to utilize conclusions drawn from inductive enquiry, predictions are made from the derived generalizations or laws, using logic and valid deductive reasoning, e.g. the next eclipse of the sun can be predicted from the laws of astronomy. Despite laws like these having been and still being useful, induction's merit was disputed as long ago as the mid eighteenth century by Hume. He demonstrated that the argument used to justify induction was circular, using induction to defend induction. Consider the following argument:

The principle of induction worked successfully on occasion x_1.
The principle of induction worked successfully on occasion x_2 etc.
The principle of induction always works.

The concluding universal statement is inferred from the repeated successful applications of the principle of induction, and is therefore an inductive argument. This has traditionally been called the 'problem of induction'.

Two further serious problems for the naive inductivist remain. The first is how large the number of observation statements must be; and the second is how large a range of circumstances and conditions must they be repeated under in order that true conclusions can be reached.

It would be a brave (or perhaps foolhardy) person who would put his/her hand into the fire more than once in order to establish that fire burns. On the other hand, it would be rash to assert that smoking causes lung cancer on the evidence of only one case of a heavy smoker dying of the disease. It seems clear that the appropriate number of observational statements required in order to come to a conclusion by induction depends very much on the particular observations made.

The number of circumstances and conditions under which observations of a particular phenomenon are made can be infinitely large. Obviously, some choice must be made in order to reject superfluous variations. But how is it possible to select which of the circumstances and conditions are pertinent to render an inductive inference legitimate? To make valid decisions requires some theoretical knowledge of the situation, that is, theory prior to observation – the naive inductivist's anathema!

EXERCISE
5.1

From your understanding of the preceding sections, briefly answer these questions.

1 Do we still commonly use pure induction as an everyday method of coming to a useful generalization? If so, how might one use this way of thought to come to generalizations about where the cornflakes packets could be found in your local supermarket? Explain the logical steps you use to justify your generalization.

2 Without looking back in the text, can you list what three conditions must be satisfied in order that inductivists will consider your conclusions to be valid? Check that you have fulfilled these three conditions in your answer to question 1.

3 What three serious problems face the naive inductivist when defending his/her position? How have you tackled these problems in your answer to question 1?

The doubts cast on the reliability of conclusions drawn from induction, and the difficulty in fulfilling the conditions required to lead to proof, have led to a partial retreat in the claims of the naive inductivist. While it is no longer claimed that 100% certainty can be achieved in generalizations made through induction, it is held that repeated observations of a phenomenon under a variety of conditions can lead to a conclusion which asserts the probability of the conclusion. The greater the number of observations under the greater the number of conditions, the more likely is the probability of the truth of the generalization. An even more limited approach leads to narrowing the predictions from those of general statements to those of particular cases; for example, engineering science can predict that a particular ship of a certain design will withstand expected sea conditions and not sink, but not that all ships are safe under any conditions. However, the basic circular problem of induction remains.

Briefly, there are responses to the problems of induction. Here are three:

1 The sceptical response made by Hume was: given that science is based on induction, which cannot be justified by appeal to logic or experience, acceptance of laws and theories is little more than a psychological habit acquired as a result of repeated observations.
2 The reasonableness of induction: as all knowledge must be based on observation, induction therefore is an 'obvious' method of reaching conclusions from observations.
3 Induction is non-scientific. Science is not based on induction, and therefore induction does not need to be scientific. This was said by Karl Popper, of whom more later.

Deduction and the principle of falsification

The opposite to the 'research then theory' approach, typified by induction, is the 'theory then research' approach, using **deduction**. Research is guided in this case by the theory which precedes it. Theories are speculative answers to perceived problems, and are tested by observation and experiment. Whilst it is possible to confirm the possible truth of a theory through observations which support it, theory can be falsified and totally rejected by making observations which are inconsistent with its statement. In this way, science is seen to proceed by trial and error: when one theory is rejected, another is proposed and tested, and thus the fittest theory survives. While it may not be possible to prove that a particular theory is true, it can be shown to be the best available for the present, and better than any which preceded it.

    The logical justification for this form of scientific enquiry is simply this: while any number of observations cannot establish the truth of a theory, one observation conflicting with the theory statement is sufficient to prove its falsity. Take for example the theory that 'all swans are white'. Whilst a million sightings of white swans cannot prove the truth of the theory, only one sighting of a non-white swan will be sufficient to reject it. Therein lies the strength of this form of approach.

    In order for a theory to be tested, it must be expressed as a statement called a **hypothesis**. The essential nature of a hypothesis is that it must be falsifiable. This means that it must be logically possible to make true observational statements which conflict with the hypothesis, and thus can falsify it.

deduction

hypothesis

Here are a number of statements. Examine each one and decide which ones are falsifiable, and are therefore possible to use as hypotheses, and which not. If not, can you say why not?

1 It always rains on Saturdays.
2 All squares have four sides of equal length.

EXERCISE
5.2

3   Heavy objects thrown from a height fall earthwards.
4   Water boils when heated to 100 degrees Celsius.
5   Either it is raining or it is not raining.
6   A beam bends when it is loaded.
7   Profits can be made in business enterprises.
8   All circles are round.
9   All round objects are circles.
10 An object is either still or moving.

Thought

These are very simple examples of statements, and it is easy to decide if they are hypotheses or not. In practical, and even more in theoretical, research it is generally more difficult to decide on the truth of hypotheses, as it is often not obvious how they can be tested. It is up to the researcher to demonstrate how effective tests can be formulated in order to attempt to falsify the hypothesis.

falsification

More about statements and hypotheses is given later in this chapter. Before that, we will look further into aspects of **falsification** and matters which arise.

It is widely accepted that science progresses by highlighting and investigating problems. It might be maintained, however, that theories which respond to these problems are devised only as a result of observation, and are therefore inherently inductive. We can show by example that this need not be the case. Observations often simply highlight problems in the explanatory power of existing theories, and therefore give rise to speculative alternative theories, expressed as hypotheses. For example, during the Black Death, when many people were dying of the

Figure 5.1 Observations often simply highlight problems in existing theories

plague, the theory that the plague was spread by odours in the air emanating from the sick and dying was questioned when people who had not been in the presence of afflicted people became ill. Alternative causes of the spread of the disease were sought. A speculation that there was some connection between the omnipresence of flea infested rats and the spread of the disease led to a new theory. The previous theory was rejected.

The hypothetico-deductive method

The process of falsification can lead to a less devastating result than an outright rejection of a theory, requiring a completely new start. Popper maintained that much progress in science has been promoted by the modification and increase in sophistication of current theories. Take, for example, this very simplified illustration.

> A theory states that water always boils at 100 degrees Celsius. It was observed that water boiled at a lower temperature than 100 degrees Celsius at high altitude. This presented a problem, and gave rise to the speculation that differences in air pressure due to altitude might have an influence on the boiling point of water, a factor not considered in the basic theory. The influence of altitude was added to the theory, which now read: 'water boils at 100 degrees Celsius at sea level'. The basic theory is not totally rejected but is refined in the alternative theory.

In this case, the new theory is more precise, and therefore more falsifiable than the original one, and therefore is to be preferred. It is in this way that the sophisticated falsificationist sees the steady progress of science occurring, through the development of progressively more refined and falsifiable theories.

Progress in scientific thought of a much more dramatic nature is gained, on the one hand, by highly conjectural predictions which turn out to be supported by observation, and on the other, by seemingly obvious and unadventurous conjectures being falsified. This approach is commonly known as the **hypothetico-deductive method** and is generally synonymous with the **scientific method**.

A simple summary of the steps in scientific method is given in Box 5.3.

hypothetico-deductive method

scientific method

Box 5.3   Steps in scientific method

1   Identification or clarification of problems.
2   Formulation of tentative solutions or hypotheses.
3   Practical or theoretical testing of solutions or hypotheses.
4   Elimination or adjustment of unsuccessful solutions.

More will be said about the nature and types of hypotheses later in this chapter, which will help you to formulate your own hypotheses in relation to your own research if this approach is appropriate.

There are, however, theoretical limitations to the power of falsification. The most serious is that observation statements are theory-dependent and fallible. While theories can logically be falsified by true observation statements which contradict them, there is no proof that the observation statement is true. One need only call to mind that before Copernicus, the interpretation of observation of the movement of the sun, stars and planets around the earth resulted in the rejection of any theory that stated that the earth was not the centre of the universe. If all observation statements are fallible, then two serious consequences can be imagined. Either a sound theory can be wrongly rejected by a false observation statement, or a false theory is not challenged because a true observation statement is rejected as faulty. Hence:

> Conclusive falsifications are ruled out by the lack of a perfectly secure observational base on which they depend. (Chalmers, 1982, p. 60)

Additional problems are posed by the complexity of testing theories in real life. Realistic scientific theories consist of a complex of statements, each of which relies on assumptions based on previous theories. The methods of testing are likewise based on assumptions and influenced by surrounding conditions. If the predictions of the theory are not borne out in the results of the tests, it could be the underlying premises which are at fault rather than the theory itself.

There are many examples in the history of science where radical theories which had been falsified by current evidence, and according to the falsificationists should have been rejected, were conserved for many years until advances in other areas of science overturned the evidence. Examples of theories which survived in this way are Newton's gravitational theory, Bohr's theory of the atom, Maxwell's kinetic theory of gases, and Copernicus's theory of the solar system. Such valuable theories would have been rejected prematurely if the falsificationist approach had been slavishly followed.

Thought   *It has probably become quite evident to you that, despite its shortcomings, you use inductive reasoning every day quite successfully without even thinking about it, and also that a huge amount of successful scientific research has been carried out using the hypothetico-deductive method. However, there is a wider debate about scientific enquiry which examines the relationships between science and the nature of knowledge.*

THE DEBATE ABOUT THE STRUCTURE OF SCIENCE AND THE NATURE OF KNOWLEDGE

Not everyone agrees that knowledge, even scientific knowledge, is as firmly based on the relationship between reality, verifiable facts and theoretical statements as is commonly accepted. The activities which surround scientific research are much more complicated than the simplistic examples and models used to illustrate the approaches to scientific enquiry. The study of the history of science has shown that merely studying the relationships between theories and individual observation statements, or series of observation statements, does not take into account the complexity of major scientific theories, and the often slow and tortuous development before they reached their precise form.

In order to explore some major and different views on the nature of scientific enquiry, we can compare the critical rationalist approach as put forward by Popper with the relativist approach of Kuhn, and finally with the 'anti-method' stance taken by Feyerabend. These three major approaches to scientific enquiry indicate that there is debate about the issues of theory evaluation and theory selection, and about ways of demarcating science from non-science.

The **critical rationalist** approach, usually associated with Popper and discussed at some length above, maintains that rival theories can be judged against specific, unchanging, universal criteria, which are divorced from or set beyond the influences of time or society. This insistence on universal criteria leads the rationalist to believe that the better the theory performs against these criteria, the closer it is to a universal 'truth'.

critical rationalism

The distinction between science and non-science is easily drawn. If the theory cannot be assessed in terms of universal criteria, then it is not scientific. For example, astrology is rejected by an inductivist rationalist, as it cannot be supported by facts gained by observation. Likewise, the unfalsifiability of Marxist theory causes a rationalist to reject this theory as unscientific. Truth, which is undeniably a value worth striving for, is regarded as the most important goal of science, and can be approached only through rational means.

Opposed to the belief that certain universal rules based on rational criteria can be applied to judge the quality of theories, the stance of **relativism** implies that judgement is principally dependent on the values of the individuals or society and the perspectives from which they make their judgement. No universal criteria can be 'rationally' applied, and an understanding of decisions made by individuals or organizations can only be gained through a knowledge of the historical, psychological and social backgrounds of the participants.

relativism

As a result of his study of the history of science, Kuhn presented in his book *The Structure of Scientific Revolutions* (1970) a concept of science which had profound implications for the understanding of its nature and development.

The fundamental difference of Kuhn's image of science from Hacking's (1981) is not so much a direct opposition to all of Hacking's nine specific points given in Box 5.1, but a challenge to the ahistoric image and a demonstration that the contents of a science and its methods of reasoning are essentially connected to its historical development. This brings his interpretations in conflict, to a greater or lesser extent, with all nine points. A brief summary of Kuhn's image of science demonstrates the differences in his point of view from Hacking.

Figure 5.2   Scientific progress is not a smooth and steady process

Kuhn claimed that a study of the history of scientific development reveals that scientific progress is not a smooth and steady process. Once a branch of science has established itself as an entity, e.g. as physics, biology or astronomy, then development is characterized by a cycle: normal science, leading to crisis, then revolution, which is then resolved in a new normal science. Knowledge has therefore a historical perspective: what is regarded as true at one time can be radically changed or even reversed at a later date.

Normal science is the period in which the established and generally accepted body of knowledge in the discipline is extended and improved, using established and successful techniques. During this time there tends to be a conservative approach, aiming at refining and clarifying concepts and theories. Kuhn distinguished between two characteristics of normal science: the generally accepted body of knowledge and the belief in methodology, which he collectively called a **paradigm**. The former is a set of shared values, which depicts precepts and generalizations shared by specialists; the latter is the measure of achievement, which represents the established methods and techniques of problem solving which is used as a model for those working in the field. Normal scientific activity is carried on within the terms of the paradigm.

paradigm

When, as a result of this scientific activity, evidence mounts that anomalies cannot be solved within the terms of the paradigm, uncertainty sets in as the precepts of the paradigm are brought into question, and new ways of looking at phenomena are explored. This crisis provokes a revolution in ways of thinking and results in a new paradigm being evolved. The new paradigm is generally incommensurable with the old. The concepts in the new paradigm may be different or have completely different meanings and entirely different problems might be addressed. This also means that methods of testing will be quite dissimilar to those under the old paradigm.

> For Popper scientific change is rational or at least rationally reconstructible and falls within the realm of the *logic of discovery*. For Kuhn scientific change – from one 'paradigm' to another – is a mystical conversion which is not and cannot be governed by rules of reason and which falls totally within the realm of *(social) psychology of discovery*. Scientific change is a kind of religious change. (Lakatos, 1970, p. 93)

Science is therefore non-cumulative because the shift from one paradigm to another involves the jettisoning of much information and of no longer valid questions. The often sudden switch when a new paradigm becomes established creates a new way of looking at that branch of science, or even the whole world, e.g. the mechanistic world, the world of relativity, or even more recently the quantum world (Kuhn, 1970).

As a demonstration of this radical switch in features of two successive paradigms, compare the lists of features of Newtonian and quantum physics in Box 5.4, as drawn up by Danah Zohar in a lecture she gave in April 1995 at Oxford Brookes University (see also Zohar and Marshall, 1993).

Box 5.4   Comparison between Newtonian and quantum research

Newtonian	*Quantum*
Determinist	Indeterminate
Certainty	Uncertainty
Continuous (linear)	Discontinuous (non-linear)
Reductionist (non-creative)	Emergent (creative)
Atomistic (isolated)	Holistic (contextual)
Causal	Acausal (non-local)
Hierarchical	Non-hierarchical
Either/or	Both/and
Actuality	Potentiality
Subject/object split	Observer participancy
Non-evolutionary	Evolutionary

But can the scientific view be taken as the only path to knowledge? Feyerabend warned about the dangers of all ideologies, scientific included. Why science? Surely it is generally accepted that science has always been in the forefront of the fight against authoritarianism and superstition, has liberated our intellectual thinking, and has provided us with the means to combat ancient and rigid forms of thought? Do not science and enlightenment go hand in hand? Were Kropotkin, Ibsen, Lévi-Strauss, Marx and Engels all wrong when they rejected traditional institutions and forms of belief, while embracing scientific thinking? 'To these questions my answer is a firm *Yes and No*', wrote Feyerabend (1981, p. 156)! He went on to explain his answer, making the following points:

- Any ideology which makes people question inherited beliefs and challenge accepted truths contributes to the liberation of people, and is therefore welcome. Science in the seventeenth and eighteenth centuries was indeed such an ideology.
- It does not follow that science has remained thus. On the contrary, science has become as rigid and oppressive as the ideologies that it once fought. At school and in universities, scientific 'facts' are taught just like religious 'facts' were taught in the past. Criticism is suppressed.
- By the claim that science is above criticism because it has discovered the 'truth', freedom of thought is inhibited.

It is generally claimed that science holds such an important position in our society because, firstly, science has discovered the proper method for achieving results, and secondly, the method has been proved to be effective by the mass of results which it has produced.

Feyerabend challenged these claims. Scientific method no longer exists, he claimed. The shortcomings of the inductionist method have long been revealed by Hume. Popper and Mill attempted to overcome this methodological problem in different ways. They both agreed that theories cannot be proved, and that their quality cannot be judged except in comparison with other theories. The chosen theory might be deficient in many ways, but as long as it is better than rival theories, then it will take precedence. The alternative rejected theories are not eliminated, as they provide a standard against which the accepted theory is judged, and highlight the content of the preferred views.

Knowledge so conceived is an ocean of alternatives channelled and subdivided by an ocean of standards. It forces our mind to make imaginative choices and thus makes it grow. It makes our mind capable of choosing, imagining, criticising. (1981, p. 159)

Even so, Popper's criteria are clear, unambiguous and precisely formulated. Theories are either falsifiable or not falsifiable. Theories which are not falsifiable have no place in science, and are eliminated. However, Feyerabend claimed that these criteria applied resolutely would eliminate science without replacing it by anything comparable; for theories, particularly when new and revolutionary, are never formulated to reveal how they could be falsified, and anyway contain numerous formal flaws and contradictions. Popperian criteria are therefore useless as an aid to science!

Figure 5.3 Theories, particularly when new and revolutionary, always contain numerous flaws and contradictions

Feyerabend regarded Kuhn's ideas as interesting, but hopelessly vague, and defied anyone to prove that there ever was a period of 'normal science' in history. He went on to contend that science does not deserve a special position because of its results; many other activities regarded as being quite unscientific also produce results. For example, oriental medicine and telepathy are phenomena which are known to produce results, unexplained by scientific theories. They are dismissed because ideological pressures make us listen to science to the exclusion of everything else. Only when a phenomenon can be explained in purely scientific terms is it accepted. But, maintained Feyerabend, history shows that advances in knowledge have rarely relied purely on scientific foundations. Copernicus relied on the ideas of a crazy Pythagorean, Philalaos, when he introduced a new view of the universe; and when the Chinese communists insisted that traditional medicine replaced Western medicine in universities and hospitals, Chinese medical science advanced and Western science learned from it. One must therefore conclude that there is no argument which could support the exceptional role which science plays today in society. Feyerabend concluded that:

Science is just one of the many ideologies that propel society and it should be treated as such ... It is an intellectual discipline that can be examined and criticised by anyone who is interested … Ideologies are marvellous when used in the company of other ideologies. They become boring and doctrinaire as soon as their merits lead to the removal of their opponents. (1981, pp. 162–3)

POSITIVISM AND INTERPRETIVISM IN SOCIAL RESEARCH

For many researchers in the social sciences who follow an interpretive approach, the philosophical debates about the nature of scientific method are of little relevance. They are much more concerned with grasping 'meanings' and understanding complexes of meanings as opposed to discovering 'truths' or approximations to them.

The approaches to scientific knowledge and research so far discussed are those generally based on the natural sciences. The types of research problems investigated in the field of social sciences and the arts are extraordinarily varied and do not all fall comfortably within the parameters of natural science. They extend from the analysis of precise problems, amenable to investigation using 'traditional' scientific method within a well established paradigm, to explorative situations where the variables are unknown and theoretical bases are yet to be formulated, to highly value- and meaning-laden sociological studies for which the latest interpretive and literary analytical methods are appropriate.

It is not surprising that the various alternatives to the positivist approach do not have the authority and precision once possessed by scientific method. Although some of these alternatives have been a long standing counterweight to positivism, some are more recent products of the challenges to positivism outlined above. A common feature is the rejection of a purely objective view of society and the belief that knowledge is itself a social phenomenon. Despite this, social scientists believe that theoretical views of society are still possible, as opposed to only practical ones.

The biggest challenge faced by the social sciences is that the researcher him/herself is part of a society and a culture and cannot be a 'neutral observer'. Moreover, the subjects of study also have a voice and can express their individuality. Thus, 'all knowledge of cultural reality, as may be seen, is always knowledge from particular points of view' (Weber, 1949, p. 81). It is not possible to stand back and take a neutral point of view of any aspect of society.

The difficulty for the social scientist is to come to terms with the fact that their subject-matter and those who study it live in a world constructed through meanings. (Hughes, 1990, p. 137)

How social scientists have grappled with this fact is best explained by briefly describing the different stances taken by some of the leading exponents of developments in this field. Durkheim advocated a natural scientific approach in his work, investigating what he called 'social facts' – the positivist approach. Husserl, Schutz and members of the Chicago School saw the meaningfulness of the subject matter as paramount – the interpretivist approach. Weber believed that both a positivist and an interpretivist viewpoint is required, verifying subjective interpretations with the actual course of events – the reconciliatory approach. By adopting a systematic perspective, Bhaskar revealed the relationships between the natural and social sciences as one of stratification. This could be used as the basis for a strong argument to defuse the 'either/or' confrontation between positivists and interpretivists.

The positivist approach

Social science, understood here as the study of human society in the widest sense, is a rich source of research problems. This important, and sometimes controversial, branch of science was, according to Beck (1979), first defined and named by Auguste Comte, the nineteenth century French philosopher. Comte maintained that society could be analysed empirically just like other subjects of scientific inquiry, and social laws and theories could be established on the basis of psychology and biology. He based his approach on the belief that all genuine knowledge is based on information gained by experience through the senses, and can only be developed through further observation and experiment. He turned his back on pure reason, seeing it as a means of speculation and metaphysical exploration.

Hence, the positivist social scientist believes that the methodological procedures of natural science may appropriately be applied to the social sciences, and its results can be expressed as laws or empirical generalizations similar to those developed for the natural sciences. Social scientists can thereby achieve a clear, well founded analysis and interpretation of social phenomena, based on testable and verifiable data.

Durkheim is famous for his enquiries into the division of labour, suicide, religion and education, as well as for his philosophical discussions on the nature of sociology. Unlike Marx, who tended to define the moral and social aspects of humanity in terms of material forces, Durkheim argued that society develops its own system of phenomena that produce collectively shared norms and beliefs. These 'social facts' as he called them, e.g. economic organizations, laws, customs, criminality etc., exist in their own right, are external to us and are resistant to our will and constrain our behaviour.

In order to carry out their task, which is summarized in Box 5.5, the social scientist must reject all popular conceptions of the processes in society and look at the social world as if for the first time. Having 'discovered' and defined social facts using scientific observation techniques, the social scientist should seek their causes amongst other social facts rather than in other scientific domains such as biology or psychology. By thus maintaining sociology as an autonomous discipline, the social scientist may use the knowledge gained to understand the origins of, and possibly suggest the cures for, various forms of social ills.

In summary, this approach looks at society as the focus for research, and through understanding its internal laws and establishing relevant facts, we can in turn understand how and why individuals behave as they do. However, not all philosophers agreed that human society was amenable to such a disembodied analysis.

The interpretivist approach

From the second half of the twentieth century, some of the most prominent intellectuals refuted the claim that scientific method could adequately provide a real understanding of the complex interrelationships in society and between individuals. From what can be collectively called the viewpoint of **interpretivism**, the principal objections were that positivist social science presented a misleading picture of the individual in society by ignoring the unique personal theoretical

interpretivism

Figure 5.4   The researcher is not observing phenomena from outside the system, but is inextricably bound into the human situation which he/she is studying

stances upon which each person bases his/her actions. Also, unlike the natural sciences, the researcher is not observing phenomena from outside the system, but is inextricably bound into the human situation which he/she is studying. In addition, by concentrating on the search for constants in human behaviour, the researcher highlights the repetitive, predictable and invariant aspects of society and ignores what is subjective, individual and creative.

According to Cohen and Manion (1994, p. 29) there are three main schools of thought represented by opponents of positivism in the social sciences: phenomenology as developed by Husserl and Schutz, ethnomethodology pioneered by Garfinkel, and symbolic interactionism practised by members of the Chicago School. They all reject the assertion that human behaviour can be codified in laws by identifying underlying regularities, and that society can be studied from a detached, objective and impartial viewpoint by the researcher.

In order to compare the alternative bases for interpreting social reality, Cohen and Manion (1994, pp. 10–11) produced a useful table which they had adapted from Barr Greenfield (1975), and which is reproduced as Box 5.6.

Box 5.6   Comparison between objectivist and interpretivist approaches

Dimensions of comparisons	Objectivist	Interpretivist
Philosophical basis	Realism: the world exists and is knowable as it really is. Organizations are real entities with a life of their own	Idealism: the world exists but different people construe it in very different ways. Organizations are invented social reality
The role of social science	Discovering the universal laws of society and human conduct within it	Discovering how different people interpret the world in which they live
Basic units of social reality	The collectivity: society or organizations	Individuals acting singly or together
Methods of understanding	Identifying conditions or relationships which permit the collectivity to exist. Conceiving what these conditions and relationships are	Interpretation of the subjective meanings which individuals place upon their action. Discovering the subjective rules for such action
Theory	A rational edifice built by scientists to explain human behaviour	Sets of meanings which people use to make sense of their world and behaviour within it

(Continued)

Box 5.6

Dimensions of comparisons	Objectivist	Interpretivist
Research	Experimental or quasi-experimental validation of theory	The search for meaningful relationships and the discovery of their consequences for action
Methodology	Abstraction of reality, especially through mathematical models and quantitative analysis	The representation of reality for purposes of comparison. Analysis of language and meaning
Society	Ordered. Governed by a uniform set of values and made possible only by these values	Conflicted. Governed by the values of people with access to power
Organizations	Goal oriented. Independent of people. Instruments of order in society serving both the society and the individual	Dependent upon people and their goals. Instruments of power which some people control and can use to attain ends which seem good to them
Organizational pathologies	Organizations get out of kilter with social values and individual needs	Given diverse human ends, there is always conflict among people acting to pursue them
Prescriptions for change	Change the structure of the organization to meet social values and individual needs	Find out what values are embodied in organizational action and whose they are. Change the people or change their values if you can

Source: Cohen and Manion, 1994, pp. 10–11

The implication of the interpretivist approach to research is that the observers or 'interpreters' cannot be seen as disembodied from the context of their investigations. They bring, perforce, their own meaning and understanding to the investigation, and must recognize and acknowledge the perspective from which they make their observations. There is a strong recognition of the fact that attempts to find understanding in research are mediated by our own historical and cultural milieu.

In contrast to the positivistic approach, we must look at the individuals in society, to understand their values and actions, in order that we may understand the structures and workings of social systems.

The reconciliatory approach

Weber disagreed with the pure interpretivists, maintaining that it is necessary to verify the results of subjective interpretive investigation by comparing them with the concrete course of events. He makes a distinction between what one can perceive as facts, i.e. those things that are, and what one can perceive as values, i.e. those things that may, or may not, be desirable. A differentiation must be maintained between facts and values because they are distinct kinds of phenomena. However, in order to understand society, we have to take account of both of these elements.

How can this be done? Weber maintained that in order to describe social practices adequately we must understand what meanings the practices have for the participants themselves. This requires an understanding of the values involved, but without taking sides or making value judgements. This understanding (often referred to as *verstehen*) is the subject matter of social science. It is then possible to investigate the social practices rationally through an assessment of the internal logic of the situation. In this way, one can make a meaningful formulation of the elements, causes and effects within complex social situations, taking into account the values inherent in them.

It can be argued that it is impossible for the social scientist to take this detached view of values, as he/she is a member of society and culture, motivated by personal presuppositions and beliefs. Weber admits:

> There is no absolutely 'objective' analysis of culture … or of 'social phenomena' independent of special and 'one-sided' viewpoints … All knowledge of cultural reality, as may be seen, is always knowledge from particular points of view. (1949, pp. 72–81)

Accordingly, any analysis of social phenomena is based on a 'view from somewhere'. This is inescapable and even to be desired. In order to make a scientific valuation of a social phenomenon, Weber made the following distinctions. There are those things that have cultural significance for the researcher that are reflected in the concepts used and the values incorporated in the research: these are the 'givens' at the outset of the research project. And then there is the researcher's responsibility to determine the facts in a value-free manner once the topic and framework for the analysis have been formulated: this is the 'scientific' element of the work.

In addition to this dual procedure Weber also offered another approach to understanding 'messy' social phenomena. He formulated a procedure which logically constructed rational, simplified models of social forms generated from one or two central values. These were called 'ideal types'. For example, the model of an ideal bureaucracy would be based solely on the principles of rational and calculative efficiency. Obviously, no such bureaucracy actually exists, but by comparing the ideal with the existing cases, one can begin to isolate those factors that give each bureaucracy its individual character.

This conciliatory approach, then, promotes a reciprocal movement between the study of the individual, his/her beliefs and values, and the study of structures of society, in order to check the results of the one against the other.

The philosopher Roy Bhaskar has provided an alternative to the dichotomous argument of positivism versus interpretivism by taking a more inclusive and systematic view of the relationships between the natural and social sciences. His approach, known as **critical realism**, sees nature as stratified, with each layer using the previous one as a foundation and a basis for greater complexity. Thus physics is more basic than chemistry, which in its turn is more basic than biology, which is more basic than the human sciences (Diagram 5.1). The relationships between these domains, from the more basic to the more complex, are inclusive one-way relationships – the more complex emerging from the more basic. Thus, all humans are composed of chemical substances but not all chemical substances are human. This means that humans are governed by chemical, physical and biological laws. However, whilst a human being is not able to go against the chemical, physical and biological laws, he/she can do all sorts of things that the chemicals of which he/she is made could not do if they were following only their specific chemical laws rather than the biological laws that govern organisms, or the social 'laws' which govern society. Hence, the study of humans cannot be reduced to the study of their biological, physical and chemical properties (Collier, 1994, pp. 107–9). Note how this challenges point 9 on Hacking's list of the popular conceptions of science given in Box 5.1.

critical realism

Human

Biological

Chemical

Physical

Diagram 5.1 The stratification of knowledge

The complexities of the upper strata of this stratified world obviously present problems when one wants to study them scientifically. Whilst the stratified world is an open system, it is easier to isolate phenomena in the lower strata, e.g. to isolate a chemical process that occurs within an organic process. However, it is not possible to isolate an organic process from the effects of chemical processes, since it has its origin in them. Thus the higher up the hierarchy we go, the more difficult it is to isolate phenomena.

Bhaskar also has a profoundly integrationist view of the relationship between the individual and society, called by him the transformation model of social activity. Rather than, on the one hand, studying society to understand individual actions, or on the other, studying individuals to understand the structures of society, or somewhere in between, checking the results of one study against that of the other, Bhaskar argues that the reciprocal interaction between individuals and society effects a transformation in both. Individuals and societies are mutually interdependent: individual actions (praxis) are influenced by the society (structure) in which they are carried out, but these actions in turn influence this same society (transformation).

Collier (1994, p. 146) cites language as a good example of this. We must learn the rules (structure) of a language before we can communicate with it. We then use the language (praxis) to communicate, without consciously thinking of the rules or wanting to change them. But the existence of the language depends on our using it. And through our use of it, we often change the rules without necessarily intending to do so (transformation). You only have to read a Victorian novel to see how much the rules of English have changed through the years.

Hence, although we can conceptually distinguish between individuals and society, the way they mutually act upon one another makes them separable only by analysis.

> Society is both the ever present *condition* (material cause) and the continually reproduced *outcome* of human agency. And praxis is both ... conscious *production* and (normally unconscious) *reproduction* of the conditions of ... society. One could refer to the former as the *duality of structure*, and the latter as the *duality of praxis*. (Bhaskar, 1989, pp. 34–5)

This interrelational view of society and the individual, and the philosophy of 'stratification and emergence', have been widely influential in the human and borderline natural/human sciences. Researchers in the fields of sociology, economics, psychoanalysis, linguistics, history, geography, biology, ecology and feminist theory have put the ideas of critical realism to good use.

1   From what you have read above, and any further reading you have done, summarize, in one or two sentences for each, the essential points put forward by Popper, Kuhn and Feyerabend in their arguments about the nature of scientific enquiry.

2   Of these writers, who do you think might take opposite views with regard to interpretivism as a valid approach to the gaining of knowledge and understanding? Give reasons why you think so.

3   In the description of a research project given in the following text, which aspects do you think demand a positivist or an interpretivist approach? Answer by considering and commenting on each of the four action points (a)–(d) given in the text. You might find it useful to refer to the comparative list given in Box 5.6 as a guide to your answer. Is it necessary to combine the two approaches in this one research project or do you regard them to be mutually exclusive?

Text

This study investigates the relationship between drawings and product design. Interest by designers in how drawings may influence the design of products has led to diverse ideas about how this may occur. Though a number of authors have identified isolated instances where such influences occur, there has been no overall investigation of the implications of drawing in product design. To research this relationship, it is necessary to:

(a)   investigate the relationship of drawings to communication and the process of abstraction

(b)   assess how coded information is perceived in drawings as percepts, and how convincing these percepts may be

(c)   research how drawings and the forms they assume may influence design as a method of wider communication

(d)   empirically assess, through interviews with designers and delineators, the extent of influence that certain types of drawings may have upon their designs.

The study provides a comprehensive overview of the communications aspects of drawings and how these may influence product design. It demonstrates that specific drawing types may influence design through the internal dialogue a designer may have with him/herself while designing, and through the force such drawings may have in communicating the design intentions of one designer to another and, in particular, the recollection of drawing images while a designer is conjecturing during the design process.

Thought

In order to relate this rather wide ranging discussion of the nature of knowledge to your own research work, it is a good idea to examine the objectives of your research in relation to the various philosophical standpoints described above. This will help to clarify which type of strategy might be suitable for your research. Will a positivist approach be appropriate, using induction, deduction and/or hypothetico-deductive methods? Or is your investigation more suited to an interpretivist approach? Perhaps a combination of the two approaches would be the most productive. These decisions will affect the way in which you express your research problem, discussed below, and the methods by which you will search for answers, discussed in Chapter 7.

HYPOTHESES: DO YOU NEED THEM?

The foundation of the hypothetico-deductive approach is the hypothesis, so it is important to know what makes good hypotheses and how they can be formulated. You might find, after you understand what exactly a hypothesis is, that it is not appropriate in your research topic to use one (or several): it might not be possible to summarize your research problem so succinctly. There are less precise methods of expressing the research problem in a researchable form, so these are described subsequently.

Hypotheses are nothing unusual; we make them all the time. They are hunches or reasonable guesses made in the form of statements about a cause or situation. If something happens in our everyday life, we tend to suggest a reason for its occurrence by making rational guesses. For example, if the car does not start in the morning, we might hypothesize that the petrol tank was empty, or that the battery was flat. For each hypothesis, a particular action taken could support or reject it. If the petrol gauge indicated 'full', then the hypothesis of an empty petrol tank could be rejected, and so on. When a particular hypothesis is found to be supported, we have got a good chance that we can take the right action to remedy the situation. If, for example, we hypothesized that a wire to the starter motor had become loose, and then find such a loose wire, fixing the wire back might result in the car starting again. If this was not the result, further hypotheses would be needed to suggest additional faults. Although these examples may seem banal, many of the greatest discoveries in science were based on hypotheses: Newton's theory of gravity, Einstein's general theory of relativity and a host of others.

In your research, you will encounter hypotheses in your background reading, sometimes overt and clearly stated, and at other times, in less scholarly documents, hidden in the text or only hinted at. If you use one in your own research study, a hypothesis should arise naturally from the research problem, and should appear to the reader to be reasonable and sound. There are two grounds on which a hypothesis may be justified: logical and empirical. Logical justification is developed from arguments based on concepts and theories and premises relating directly to the research problem; empirical justification is based on reference to other research found in the literature.

A closer look at hypotheses and their formulation

There are important qualities of hypotheses which distinguish them from other forms of statement. According to Kerlinger (1970), these are as shown in Box 5.7.

Hypotheses:

1 are assertions (not suggestions)
2 are limited in scope
3 are statements about the relationships between certain variables
4 contain clear implications for testing the relationships
5 are compatible with current knowledge
6 are expressed as economically as possible using correct terminology.

A good hypothesis is a very useful aid to organizing the research effort. It specifically limits the enquiry to the interaction of certain variables; it suggests the methods appropriate for collecting, analysing and interpreting the data; and the resultant confirmation or rejection of the hypothesis through empirical or experimental testing gives a clear indication of the extent of knowledge gained.

A hypothesis, as described above, is tested in order to provide evidence to support, or to reject, the existence of the stated relationships between the variables. Another type of hypothesis, called a *null hypothesis*, starts with an assumption that the relationships do exist, and maintains that the assumptions are correct if they are not refuted by the results of the tests. A null hypothesis should fulfil two criteria. Firstly, there must be sufficient justification for the statement to be used as a starting point of the examination (it would be pointless to make a wild guess of an assertion and then easily reject it, or maintain it must be true if it is not rejected). Secondly, the hypothesis must be sufficiently specific and complete in order to be able to make a prediction of the probable outcomes of the tests. Note that null hypotheses always take the form of statistical predictions (see Chapter 7).

A comparison of examples of these two types of hypotheses will demonstrate the difference:

Hypothesis   Rich people tend to spend more money than poor people.

While much evidence might be collected to support or refute this hypothesis, it is not sufficiently precise to use as a null hypothesis, as no prediction is made about the exact expected outcomes of the observations.

Null hypothesis   On any flip of a fair coin, the probability of getting heads is equal to that of getting tails.

The prediction of a 50/50 outcome of the results of flipping the coin gives a precise and specific test. Any significant deviation from this would lead to a rejection of the hypothesis. Note that there is a lot of confidence in the hypothesis before data are collected to test it.

It is often appropriate to balance an *alternative hypothesis* against a null hypothesis. If the null hypothesis is rejected, then the logical alternative is the alternative hypothesis. The alternative hypothesis is not specific and is not directly tested. An example will illustrate this:

Null hypothesis   People with twice the national average annual personal income have twice the national average annual personal spending.

Alternative hypothesis   People with twice the national average annual personal income do not have twice the national average personal spending.

Formulating hypotheses

Hypotheses can be very varied in nature, ranging from concrete to abstract and from narrow to wide in scope, range and inclusiveness. In order to formulate a useful researchable hypothesis, one needs to have a thorough knowledge of the background to the subject and the nature of the problem or issue which is being addressed. The hypothesis is developed from the result of a successive division and delineation of the problem, and provides a focus around which the research will be carried out.

Researchers work on two levels of reality, the operational level and the conceptual level. On the operational level, they work with events in observable terms, involving the reality necessary to carry out the research. On a conceptual level, events are defined in terms of underlying communality with other events on a more abstract level. Researchers move from single specific instances to general ones and thereby gain an understanding of how phenomena operate and variables interrelate, and vice versa to test whether the conceptual generalizations can be supported in fact.

The formulation of the hypothesis is usually made on a conceptual level, in order to enable the results of the research to be generalized beyond the specific conditions of the particular study. This widens the applicability of the research.

Figure 5.5   Researchers work on two levels of reality

An example will help to clarify this point:

> Three primary schools A, B and C are to be examined as to the success of their
> courses.

At the most specific conceptual level, the research could just compare the academic outcomes of the courses and conclude which was the most successful, A, B or C, and which the least. However, this information will not be of any general relevance. It would be more useful to examine the courses to see if they had any difference in approach in order to determine why they might be more or less successful.

At a more general conceptual level, it was found that they used different teaching techniques: A used an individual approach, B used a combination of individual and class group approaches, and C used a class group approach. Results of the research might now be generalized to courses in other primary schools, on the basis of their teaching approaches.

The research problem could be conceptualized even further, extending its possible applicability. The study could concentrate on establishing whether the individual approach which featured a flexible structure in teaching was more or less successful than the tightly structured teaching approach used in a full classroom group. The results of this research could be of value in assessing educational approaches in general.

The wording of the hypothesis should reflect one of these conceptual levels.

Operationalizing hypotheses

It is one of the fundamental criteria of a hypothesis that it is testable. However, a hypothesis formulated on a conceptual level cannot be directly tested; it is too abstract. It is therefore necessary to convert it to an operational level. This is called operationalization. It consists of reversing the conceptualization process described above.

Often, the first step is to break down the main hypothesis into two or more sub-hypotheses. These represent components or aspects of the main hypothesis and together should add up to its totality.

The operationalization of the sub-hypotheses follows four steps in the progression from the most abstract to the most concrete expressions by defining concepts, indicators, variables and values.

- *Concepts*   The building blocks of the hypothesis which are usually abstract and cannot be directly measured.
- *Indicators*   Phenomena which point to the existence of the concepts.
- *Variables*   The components of the indicators which can be measured.
- *Values*   The actual units or methods of measurement of the variables.

Note that each concept may have several indicators, each indicator several variables, and each variable several values. To clarify these terms, consider this operationalization which gives only one example of each expression:

Concept: poverty.
Indicator: poor living conditions.
Variable: provision of sanitary facilities.
Values: numbers of people per bathroom, WC.

Each sub-hypothesis will intimate a different method of testing and therefore implies different research methods that might be appropriate. The various research methods for collecting and analysing data are explained in some detail in Chapter 7.

The following report is based on an article in *The Sunday Times* written by Professor Hans Eysenck, which challenges the widely accepted general hypothesis that smoking is bad for your health. Read it carefully and answer the questions that follow, particularly using the knowledge you have gained from this section of the chapter.

EXERCISE
5.4

Smoking is OK, despite the claims of medical experts

Don't give up smoking – giving up may damage your health. This message was the result of a recently conducted research project carried out by the Australian government. A surprising outcome? No, it stands to logic.

It was found in the survey that more illness was suffered by ex-smokers than by continuing smokers and never-smokers. Actually, it was continuing smokers that were ill the least, though never-smokers fared almost as well. Researchers discovered that those who had given up smoking suffered more 'recent and long-term conditions combined' than the other two groups.

Various illnesses featured differently. Smokers and ex-smokers suffered more frequently from bronchitis and emphysema than never-smokers. However, hypertension, high cholesterol and long term conditions were reported by fewer smokers than by ex- and never-smokers. Small variations were also reported due to age, sex, living situations and other factors. Despite this, the main finding was that 'smokers were, if anything, healthier than never-smokers'. This was despite the fact that smokers tended to be amongst the poorest employed and educated in society, where the poorest health would also be expected.

What does the survey say about passive smoking? 'Only slight differences between children living in households with or without smokers in the likelihood of children experiencing recent and/or long term conditions' were noted. Taking into account the fact that unemployed and poorly educated people tend to smoke more and their children always have worse health records, these conclusions undermine the widely held belief that passive smoking has bad effects on health.

Have our beliefs about smoking been wrong all this time? To begin with, remember that many statisticians and medical experts have challenged the reported claims that hundreds of thousands of deaths are directly attributable to smoking. That heavy smoking is bad for you is not doubted, nor is the fact that smoking increases the risk of suffering from disorders such as cancer and heart disease. However, a causal link between smoking and ill-health is difficult to establish, as it is only one among hundreds of other risk factors. As only one out of ten smokers dies of lung cancer, smoking cannot be regarded as a sufficient cause of death. Similarly, as one out of ten people who do die of lung cancer is not a smoker, smoking cannot be a necessary cause.

So, how can causality be established? If giving up smoking prevented cancer and heart diseases, as is often asserted, then we should have a solid piece of proof. Regrettably there has been no clinical study that has substantiated this assertion, or even established that giving up smoking is good for your health. Some researchers claim that earlier estimated deaths amongst smokers as compared with non-smokers are due to their smoking habits. However, these guesstimates are of questionable value and vary widely amongst experts. They are all based on a very obvious misconception. Whilst they argue that the practice of smoking is a major cause of earlier death, they ignore the fact that smoking is powerfully associated with other risk factors, such as drinking heavily, poor diet, low socio-economic status and many others. It is often the same person who drinks heavily, survives on junk food, lives in poor conditions and smokes heavily. It is well known that cumulative risk factors have the effect of multiplying rather than simply adding to the risk. This greatly complicates the researchers' calculations.

One could easily maintain that smoking is by far the most influential of these risk factors, and therefore of by far the greatest importance. However, consider the following research results about stress, and in particular about stress prone personalities. In the mid 1940s, Caroline Thomas at Johns Hopkins University monitored 1300 healthy medical students, and continued to follow them up over the next 30 years. She discovered that people who habitually stifled their feelings were 16 times more likely to develop cancer than more outgoing types. Compare this with the estimates that smokers were only 2.5 times more likely to die from cancer and only twice as likely to die from heart disease as non-smokers. Claims are made that mortality from heart disease is also strongly affected by personality type.

It is obvious that there is still a lively debate about the effects of smoking. We should therefore demand reliable evidence before we accept a politically correct orthodoxy. The Australian study demonstrates the need to look at the issue from other perspectives. Obviously, smoking is not good for your health, but is it such a lethal habit as is often portrayed? It is one of many risk factors; we should neither under- nor over-estimate its importance. The factors of stress may possibly be of greater importance, and can probably be controlled more easily than smoking. Perhaps some of the millions of pounds spent on research into smoking could more usefully be spent on research into the effects of stress.

Questions

1 What hypothesis does the writer of this article put forward as an alternative to the commonly accepted hypothesis that 'smoking is bad for your health'?

2 Summarize the main conclusions from research projects put forward to support this hypothesis.

3 What argument is given to falsify the hypothesis 'smoking is bad for your health'? Does the argument rely on induction or deduction?

4   Do you detect any clash between objectivist and interpretivist approaches to the issues of smoking and health in this article? If so, give examples of the two approaches and describe how they clash.

5   What points are raised about the operationalization of the hypothesis 'smoking is bad for your health'?

6   Do the assertions in this article challenge the paradigm within which the hypothesis 'smoking is bad for your health' was formulated? If so, how?

Although the term 'hypothesis' is used with many different meanings in everyday and even academic situations, it is advisable to use it in your research only in its strictest scientific sense. This will avoid you being criticized for sloppy, imprecise use of terminology. If your research problem does not lend itself to being formulated in a hypothesis, do not worry: there are plenty of alternatives, many of which involve a completely different research approach to that of the hypothetico-deductive method.

Thought

Alternatives to hypotheses

It is not appropriate to use the hypothetico-deductive method, or even the scientific method, in every research study. Research into society, design, history, philosophy and many other subjects usually cannot provide the full criteria for the formulation of hypotheses and their testing, and it is inappropriate to try to fit such research into this method. What are the alternatives?

In all research projects, on whatever subject, there is a need to clearly define and delineate the research problem. Its nature will suggest appropriate forms for its investigation. Here are several forms in which the research problem can be expressed to indicate the method of investigation.

Question or questions

The method of investigating the problem may be expressed through asking a question or a series of questions, the answers to which require scrutiny of the problem from one or more directions. An example is given in Box 5.8.

Obviously, the question or questions should be derived directly from the research problem, give a clear indication of the subject to be investigated, and imply the methods which will be used. Often the form of the questions can be similar to that of hypotheses: a main question is divided into sub-questions which explore aspects of the main question.

Four broad, interrelated research questions are raised about the representation of contemporary art in the media and about the agenda for public debate which this implies:

1 What are the characteristics of the overall representation of contemporary art issues in the media?
2 What agenda for contemporary art does this imply, and how does this relate to broad values of contemporary art and media?
3 How does this representation differ in coverage presented in different types of media, e.g. television?
4 What role is played by specialist journalists, and specifically art correspondents, in shaping this representation?

Propositions

Focusing a research study on a proposition, rather than on a hypothesis, allows the study to concentrate on particular relationships between events, without having to comply with the rigorous characteristics required of hypotheses. Consider the example in Box 5.9.

In a study on public sector housing for young single people, the main research problem was formulated as three interrelated propositions:

1 Specifically designed public sector housing provided for young single people to rent has been, and continues to be, designed according to the recommendations and standards in the design guidance for young persons' housing.
2 The relevant design guidance is not based on accurate perceptions of the characteristics of young single people.

From these two propositions the third one should follow:

3 There is a mismatch between the specifically designed public sector housing provided for single young people and their accommodation requirements.

Statement of intent to critically investigate and evaluate

Not all research needs to answer a question or to test a hypothesis. Especially at Masters degree level or in smaller studies, a more exploratory approach may be used. The subject and scope of the exploration can be expressed in a statement of intent. Again, this must be derived from the research problem, imply a method of approach and indicate the outcome. Examples of this form of research definition are shown in Box 5.10.

Box 5.10   Research statements: four different examples

The intention of this study is to identify the main aspects of recent developments in government organization and procedures for local taxation in Britain and Iraq, then to assess the extent to which, or whether, features of the British organization and implementation of local taxation can be adopted to improve the system of the administration of local taxation in Iraq.

This study examines the problems in career development of women lawyers in the British legal establishment. It focuses on the identification of specific barriers (established conventions, prejudices, procedures, career paths) and explores the effectiveness of specific initiatives that have been aimed at breaking down these barriers.

In this study it is intended to consider whether relevant British standards for food safety as applied to hotels and restaurants could be transferred to hotels and restaurants in Algeria.

This thesis provides a reassessment of John Thompson's early career and travels up to late 1861. It aims to show the musical foundation of Thompson's career and analyse his early compositions in order to provide a basis for a more objective reassessment of his music.

Definition of research objectives

When a research problem has been identified, in order to indicate what measures will be taken to investigate the problem or provide means of overcoming it, it is necessary to formulate a definition of the research objectives. This should be accompanied by some indication of how the research objectives will be achieved. An example is given in Box 5.11.

Box 5.11   Research objectives: example

It is proposed to provide an adequate assessment of the relationship between the design of security systems in computer networks and the resulting restrictions on the wide accessibility of these systems to the general public. The research problem previously highlighted a lack of such methods of assessment. To overcome this problem it is necessary to:

(Continued)

---

1   *Propose a method of measurement by which the extent of incorporation of security systems can be assessed*   This will enable an objective comparison to be made between alternative design proposals in terms of the extent of incorporation of security features. There is a need to identify and categorize the main security systems advocated in past studies of publicly accessible computer networks in order to establish the general applicability of the methods of measurement proposed.

2   *Propose a method of measurement by which the extent of public accessibility to computer networks can be assessed*   This will enable an objective comparison to be made between computer networks in terms of the extent of their accessibility in use. In order to arrive at a method of measurement, a more comprehensive interpretation of accessibility needs to be developed so that the measures proposed will not be confined to any one particular computer system type.

3   *Assess the extent of accessibility achieved after the incorporation of security systems, by a study of actual computer networks in use*   To achieve this a number of publicly accessible networks need to be examined.

CONCLUSIONS

Any discussion of the issues which surround the nature of scientific enquiry and the acquisition of knowledge must necessarily be very brief to fit the scale of this introductory book. Acknowledging the fact that research can concern itself with a huge range of subjects and disciplines, I have attempted to cover the relevant major perspectives which, I hope, will raise questions about your own research approach, whatever your type of research problem.

The debate about knowledge and how we acquire it is a continuous one, and one which is at the centre of any research effort. I believe it is important, throughout your research project, and probably in your subsequent career too, to gain a deepening awareness of what this involves and how such factors can affect, not only our attitude to life, but also our everyday actions.

THE NEXT STEPS: PHILOSOPHY IN THE RESEARCH PROJECT

This chapter has presented a necessarily brief résumé of a range of philosophical underpinnings to research. The intention in this section is to examine your own research problem area in order to discover which of the philosophical positions discussed earlier have a relevance to the type of approach which you intend to take and whether they have influenced your thinking. The nature of your problem will certainly have a major influence on which type of research strategy might be appropriate. The awareness of your own personal attitude towards the problem, the level at which you wish to investigate it, and the perspectives from which you will approach it, will all help to determine the characteristics of your future work.

The aims of this section are:

- to examine your research problem or problem area to investigate what role the various epistemologies will play in your research strategy
- to explore your own attitudes to your problem, the perspectives from which you will view it, and the level at which you intend to examine it
- to inspect whether the hypothetico-deductive method is suitable for your research project, and if not, to discuss alternative approaches which might be appropriate in the carrying out of your research
- to formulate an appropriate research strategy, and explore suitable styles of expressing the problem.

Checklist of activities that will progress your research

Step 1: examine positions
Whatever you read will be based on some kind of philosophical position. Try to categorize this for each of the books, papers and other material you read. Becoming aware of these will help you to understand the arguments being made and guide you to formulating your own philosophical approach.

Step 2: how scientific are you?
How much do you think your research will conform to Hacking's list of features of scientific enquiry (Box 5.1)? Questioning yourself on how you envisage the development of your project will highlight your own assumptions about the nature and process of research.

Think carefully about how closely your proposed research project fits into the various philosophical approaches. Are the assumptions of scientific method acceptable in your research approach, or is a more relativist basis appropriate? Some of the questions you will have to ask are:

- Is your problem about objects or about people, or the relationships between the two?
- Can it be analysed and explained in terms of forces or inner physical processes, or rather in terms of meanings and subjective forces?

- Are notions of causation an important aspect, or are you seeking to find explanations in order to reach an understanding of a situation?
- Will knowledge be gained through impartial observation and/or experimentation, or will you have to immerse yourself in the situation and make subjective interpretations or value-laden observations?

Based on the conclusions you have reached from these questions, which type(s) of approach do you regard as appropriate for your research project? Discuss the reasons for your decisions in the light of what you have read about the issues surrounding the nature of knowledge and the approaches to research. What questions are raised about the potential value of your research which will need to be further investigated?

Step 3: induction or deduction?

Depending on your subject and on your own position in the debate about research, will your main argument be based on inductive or deductive reasoning, or will you take the hypothetico-deductive approach? In much qualitative social science research, concepts and theories are developed on the basis of observations and consultations – a classic inductive mode of operation. In economics, commerce, marketing, and many other applied subjects, there is plenty of scope for a deductive approach, e.g. do Keynesian theories really work? The natural sciences and many disciplines based on scientific method commonly use hypothetico-deductive reasoning. The way you tackle your research problem and the kind of research methods you use will be intimately connected to your method of thinking. Make sure you are clear about it.

Step 4: 'bedding in' your approach

What I mean by 'bedding in' is that you provide a context for your theoretical approach by referring to sources and ways of thinking that support it. It must be obvious to you by now that you are carrying forward, or challenging, the work of others. Your work will belong to a stream of thought, a tradition or a particular perspective. The results of your literature review will enable you to trace this through by making reference to those before you, and to their way of thinking. Your proposal will need to briefly refer to these in the background section.

Step 5: how will you pose your research problem?

This chapter gives you a variety of ways to present the issue you want to investigate. Depending on the type of problem you are tackling, you may want to present it as a hypothesis for testing, a question to be answered, a proposition to be investigated, or a statement of intent. Decide how your problem is best posed, taking into account the way you will want to investigate it. Remember that, although often used in a loose way, a hypothesis should be tested to see if it can be supported or falsified – scientifically a rather rigid process.

Formulate the main hypothesis, question or proposition, and then develop the sub-hypotheses, sub-problems or sub-propositions as necessary to render the research task less abstract. If you are still unsure about your direction, you can do this in an exploratory fashion, with as many reasonable alternatives as you can devise. Differentiate between theoretical and operational levels of expression.

Then, devise an argument to explain your choice of presentation(s) of the research problem, so that you can justify it if asked. This will entail a discussion of the alternatives mentioned above.

Step 6: operationalize your hypothesis or other statement of the research problem

Consider how each hypothesis, question, proposition etc. might be operationalized and tested or explored. What sort of indicators and variables are likely to be involved? What sort of information will you require and what will you need to establish to produce the required research results? Don't at this stage worry about the precise methods of how you will collect the information or how you will analyse it. Do consider, however, whether the information is available and possible to get hold of.

Explore how alternative types of research approach and the way you formulate the hypotheses, propositions, questions etc. will affect the nature of the conclusions that you will be able to make.

Step 7: define your research aims and objectives

Research problems are often posed in quite abstract terms that do not indicate how they can be investigated practically. Even if they are not so abstract, it is impossible to be precise about how you will go about doing the research in such a compact piece of text. Now that you have explored in step 6 some of the implications of your research problem and the information and practical tasks you might need to under-take, it is time to take stock of the scale of your research project.

Expand your problem to formulate a series of research aims or objectives. These should take into account the complexity of the main problem, and the steps needed to investigate the various aspects contained within it, and relate to the sub-hypotheses or sub-problems. You will be able to check at this point whether the research aims are practical, or are too ambitious for the time and resources available. If the latter, now is a good time to narrow down the research problem by limiting the aims, which will mean revising the statement of the problem in step 5.

Consolidation and assessment

Arrange a meeting with one of your tutors or your supervisor and explain to him/her the results of your thinking which have been prompted by the above tasks. You should be able to demonstrate that you have grasped the significance of the issues surrounding the activities of research and the nature of knowledge, and how these issues are relevant to your own research project.

Do this by discussing the opportunities and dangers inherent in the various possible research approaches and how they might relate to your research problem. Indicate the appropriateness of the use of hypotheses, questions, propositions etc. in your research, and the significance of the choice. Relate the levels of abstraction of the statements or questions to their universality and operationality. Discuss the concepts used and their indicators and variables.

The outcome of the discussion should help you to assess the intellectual rigour on which your research project is based, and prepare you to investigate appropriate options for research design and to explore the question of quality in research. These subjects will be covered in the next chapter.

Key words

Induction	Critical rationalism
Deduction	Relativism
Hypothesis	Paradigm
Falsification	Interpretivism
Hypothetico-deductive method	Critical realism
Scientific method	

Further reading

You can go into much greater detail about the philosophy of knowledge and research if you want to, but I suspect that you will not have enough time to delve too deeply, unless your research topic focuses on some of these issues. However, it is advisable to have a good general knowledge of the debate about the philosophy of scientific knowledge and its detractors, in order to place your research within the philosophical context. When compiling this chapter, I found the following books useful and well worth a browse. The titles give an indication of the subject tackled. I have put the more approachable ones first.

Two good introductory books to start with:

Thompson, M. (1995) *Philosophy*. London: Hodder (Teach Yourself).

This is a simple introduction to philosophy which explains the main terminology and outlines the principal streams of thought.

Couvalis, G. (1997) *The Philosophy of Science: Science and Objectivity*. London: Sage.

A clear, non-technical introduction to the philosophy of science from the nineteenth century to the present.

The following concentrate on scientific approaches and dilemmas. The first four are general discussions about the nature of science, whilst the remainder are important texts that have greatly influenced the debate about science.

Chalmers, A. (1982) *What Is This Thing Called Science?*, 2nd edn. Milton Keynes: Open University Press.

Chalmers, A. (1990) *Science and Its Fabrication*. Milton Keynes: Open University Press.

Medawar, P. B. (1986) *The Limits of Science*. London Methuen.

Trusted, J. (1979) *The Logic of Scientific Inference*. London: Macmillan.

Briggs, J. and Peat, F. (1984) *Looking Glass Universe: the Emerging Science of Wholeness*. London: Fontana.

Bohm, D. and Peat, F. (1987) *Science, Order and Creativity*. London: Routledge.

Magee, B. (1974) *Popper*. London: Woburn.

Medawar, P. B. (1969) *Induction and Intuition in Scientific Thought*. London: Methuen.

Feyerabend, P. (1977) *Against Method*. London: New Left Books.

Hacking, I. (ed.) (1981) *Scientific Revolutions*. Oxford: Oxford University Press.

See pp. 60–79, 'The corroboration of theories' by H. Putnam; and pp. 157–67, 'How to defend society against science' by P. Feyerabend.

Kuhn, T. S. (1970) *The Structure of Scientific Revolutions*, 2nd edn. Chicago: University of Chicago Press.

Lakatos, I. and Musgrave, A. (eds) (1970) *Criticism and the Growth of Knowledge*. Cambridge: Cambridge University Press.

See pp. 91–196, 'Methodology of scientific research programmes' by I. Lakatos.

This one is about bridging between 'hard' natural science and the 'softer' social sciences:

Collier, A. (1994) *Critical Realism: an Introduction to Roy Bhaskar's Philosophy*. London: Verso.

And the following look at the foundations of the social sciences:

Best, S. (2002) *The Beginners Guide to Social Theory*. London: Sage.

Beck, R. N. (1979) *Handbook to Social Philosophy*. New York: Macmillan.

Seale, C. (2004) *Researching Society and Culture*, 2nd edn. London: Sage.

See particularly Part 1.

Zohar, D. and Marshall, I. (1993) *The Quantum Society*. London: Bloomsbury.

Kerlinger, F. N. (1979) *Foundations of Behavioural Research*. New York: Holt, Reinhart and Winston.

Skinner, Q. (ed.) (1990) *The Return of Grand Theory in the Human Sciences*. Cambridge: Cambridge University Press.

ANSWERS TO
EXERCISES

EXERCISE 5.1

1   Yes, we use induction a lot of the time, without even thinking much about it. In the super-market, the most common way to look for items is to go to the place where they have been on the shelves in previous visits. The logic of the argument goes like this:

Every time in the past that I have visited this supermarket, which has been on numerous occasions, at different times of the day, during daylight and in darkness, on different days in the week, in good weather and in bad, I have observed that the cornflakes were on the shelf half-way down the third aisle. I conclude therefore that if I go today to the shelf half-way down the third aisle, I will find the cornflakes displayed there. Furthermore, I conclude that the cornflakes are always to be found there.

2 (a) There must be a large number of observation statements.

   (b) The observations must be repeated under a large range of circumstances and conditions.

   (c) No observation statement must contradict the derived generalization.

   My answer above goes some way to fulfil the three conditions:

   (a) I have visited the supermarket on numerous occasions.

   (b) The circumstances were varied.

   (c) I did not make any observation statements which contradicted the derived generalization, for example that in supermarkets they tend to reorganize the positions of goods on the shelves on a random basis.

3 (a) The argument used to justify induction is circular: it uses induction to defend induction.

   (b) How many observational statements are sufficient in order to come to a conclusion?

   (c) Under how many sets of conditions must the observations be made in order to substantiate the theory?

   There is not much that one can do to overcome the first problem in this answer!

   The number of observational statements necessary to correctly conclude in the general statement in my answer to question 1. does not need to be numerous if it is known that the shelves are not reorganized; in fact a single observation would be enough. However, if, through repeated observations, it was evident that the goods are changed around on the shelves, the validity of the conclusion will depend on the relationship between the regularity of the changes and the regularity of the observations. The more frequent or haphazard the changes, the more frequent must be the observations to achieve some measure of reliability. If the changes are observed to be regular, e.g. once a week on Mondays, then one observation per week after the changes have been made would be sufficient.

   With regard to the sets of conditions, the position of the cornflakes is not likely to change with the weather or from one time of the day to another, so it should not be necessary to check during different weather conditions or morning, afternoon and evening after this likelihood had been established.

EXERCISE 5.2

1 You only have to observe for one sunny Saturday to falsify this one, so it can be used as a hypothesis.

2   This statement cannot be falsified. A square can only be called thus if it has got four sides of equal length. This is an axiomatic statement.

3   It might be difficult to falsify, but in theory it should be possible, e.g. if you are in orbit around the earth, i.e. at a very great height, a thrown object might 'fall' away from the earth! This is an obvious but still valid hypothesis.

4   This is a hypothesis which is capable of being readily falsified, and subsequently refined by a few experiments.

5   This statement excludes the possibility of being falsified because it covers all possible states, and is therefore not a hypothesis.

6   Even if the deflection, or lack of it, cannot be seen, it can be accurately measured. This is a hypothesis.

7   This statement would be difficult to falsify. Even if you only knew about business enterprises which made losses, it would not rule out the possibility that profits could be made. It really begs the question of the meaning of the concept 'business enterprise', which is, after all, a system aimed at making profits, amongst other things. For these reasons, this statement should not be called a hypothesis.

8   An axiomatic statement again, and not a hypothesis.

9   This is more like it. I can think of many round objects which are not circles. It is falsifiable, and therefore a hypothesis.

10   Again, all possibilities are covered by this statement regarding objects and motion. It cannot be falsified.

EXERCISE 5.3

1   This is rather a difficult question to answer, in view of the number of lengthy books that each of these writers has written about the nature of scientific enquiry! However, from the very short summary given in the section, you should be able to extract some of the main views which were described. How do your answers compare with these?

- Popper maintained that scientific progress was a rational process. Although scientific theories were not provable, they must be falsifiable, and the only criterion to judge a theory was by comparison with others, the better theory taking precedence over others.

- Kuhn disagreed that the progress of science was smooth, and maintained that periodic and radical reassessments were made of scientific understanding when persistent findings incompatible with accepted knowledge resulted in a new paradigm being formulated, radically different from the old.

- Feyerabend challenged the position of scientific enquiry as the only reliable method of advancing knowledge by producing useful results. If judged on results, many other disciplines which were regarded as 'unscientific' also successfully produced useful results, despite them not being able to be explained by scientific theories.

2   Probably Popper and Feyerabend might have opposing views about the value of interpretivism as a valid approach to gaining and analysing knowledge. Popper would question whether the theories put forward as a result of the interpretivist approach were falsifiable; or, if so, whether the tests were repeatable. After all, the subjective element will be different in every case, leading inevitably to different results. Feyerabend, following from his refutation of scientific method as the only valid ideology, would probably welcome interpretivism as a valuable additional approach in order to gain knowledge, especially if it was shown to produce useful results.

3   The central issue of this research project is to explore the relationship between drawings and product design. It is possible to perceive that both the objectivist and interpretivist approaches could lead to useful insights into aspects of this relationship.

   (a)   This is an abstract and theoretical relationship which could be investigated without reference to individual subjective attitudes and social reality.

   (b)   The mention of 'how coded information is perceived' indicates that a subjective element is certain to be present. How and what percepts are formed by interpreting coded information on drawings must be, at least partly, influenced by individual background and experience. This will be a qualitative appraisal using descriptive methods of analysis.

   (c)   This aspect of the study does not mention people, but concentrates on the relationships between two concepts, i.e. the forms of drawings and design as a method of communication. A positivist approach seems to be the most appropriate in this case, though the concepts will be difficult to measure.

   (d)   Here, people will be asked about drawings and in what way they influence design. There is obviously room here for an interpretivist approach to the research, though the wording 'empirically assess' makes one suspect that the researcher intends to make a rational assessment based on observation from a neutral standpoint. Isn't this just what Weber was advocating? Firstly to critically assess the value-laden situation, and then to see what actual effects this has on outcomes.

It is probably difficult to combine the two approaches in one study, unless the intention is to provide two completely different perspectives of the research problem, or the research problem divides itself into very different sub-problems each of which demands a different approach. In this project, the two aspects of drawing, i.e. communication and influence on design, might be considered sufficiently diverse.

EXERCISE 5.4

1   The hypothesis is stated at the very beginning of the article: 'Giving up smoking is bad for your health.'

2   The main support for this hypothesis is based on two statistical findings of a research project recently conducted by the Australian government. They are:

- Smokers, together with non-smokers, suffered less illness than ex-smokers.

- Smokers were, if anything, healthier than non-smokers, despite them being found to be amongst those at the lowest level of employment and education.

    The results of a 1946 research project, which concluded that the emotional disposition of individuals is a more important factor in cancer development than their smoking habits, is also mentioned, but this does nothing to support the hypothesis.

3   The results of the Australian research project and Caroline Thomas's 1946 project, summarized in answer 2, are used in the deductive argument to falsify the hypothesis. However, the main thrust of the argument points out that there is a *lack of proof* that smoking causes cancer and coronary heart disease. Statistical records of lung cancer and smoking prove that smoking heavily can be neither a *sufficient* nor a *necessary* cause of lung cancer. If smoking was a sufficient cause, the act of smoking would be sufficient to lead inevitably to lung cancer. If smoking was a necessary cause, people who died of lung cancer must necessarily have been smokers at some time in order to catch the disease. Nor can it be demonstrated in clinical studies that giving up smoking has beneficial effects on health. Even instances of ill-health in children, reputed to be caused by passive smoking, are more likely to be the result of their socio-economic situation. The simplistic assumptions made by researchers who compare the number of deaths of smokers and non-smokers are also questioned.

4   Not really! The arguments are all based on an objectivist approach. There is no attempt to argue about or integrate individual subjective meanings of the concepts of smoking and health, or about the values attributed to smoking. What the article does argue for is a widening of the range of factors which should be considered when researching the relationship between smoking and health. However, as it suggests that stress and personality may be more important factors affecting health, one might presuppose that these factors may be studied using an interpretivist approach.

5   The principal points are that smoking is likely to be only one of many factors which are a risk to people's health, and that the risk factors do not act independently but act synergistically. This is bound to make testing this hypothesis very complicated. It will be necessary to examine the relationships between smoking, socio-economic status, diet, drinking habits, genetic predisposition, personality, stress and other factors, and their combined effect on health, in order to come to conclusions about how important a factor smoking itself is in causing disease.

6 The short answer to this is no. Although the article questions the data, methodology and conclusions used to support the hypothesis, and suggests that smoking is only one, and perhaps only a minor, factor in causing illness, it does not challenge the meanings of the concepts and the shared values of researchers who are working on this subject. It is more concerned with refining the hypothesis, i.e. smoking is only one of the factors which are bad for your health.

6

Research Quality and Planning

Introduction
Good Research
  Objectives of Research
  Desirable Characteristics of Research Findings
  The Research Process
  The Nature and Role of Data
  Quantitative and Qualitative Data
Planning a Research Project
  Choosing a Research Strategy
  Planning Research Projects
Conclusions
The Next Steps: Plan Your Own Research Project
Checklist of Activities That Will Progress Your Research
  Consolidation and Assessment
Key Words
Further Reading
Answers to Exercises

- To clarify the objectives of research.
- To identify the desirable characteristics of the research findings.
- To explain the processes of research.
- To examine the role and nature of data.
- To describe the differences between quantitative and qualitative research.
- To explain how to plan the research project.

INTRODUCTION

This chapter introduces a general review of research as an activity, and explores what makes it a valuable enterprise. It also focuses on how different types of data have a formative influence on the research process, and on the ethical factors which have to be considered when collecting and analysing the data and presenting the results. An introduction is made to the overall planning of a research project, prompting you to consider how your own project might be developed.

GOOD RESEARCH

After working through the previous chapters, you should by now have a clear idea of the problem area which you will be exploring, and a fairly clear idea of the specific research problem that you want to address, and you should have considered the ways in which the problem might be expressed. The identification of the problem is, of course, only the starting point of a research project. However, it should provide valuable pointers to what might be the objectives of the research activities.

Problems invariably raise questions, and questions beg for answers. It is in this search for answers that you will discover, and be able to formulate, the objectives of the research. It is worth checking at this stage what the desirable objectives of research are, and that you clearly understand what characteristics of the likely findings will be of real value, and thus provide a good reason for doing the research.

Objectives of research

Research can have several legitimate objectives, either singly or in combination. The main, overriding objective must be that of gaining useful or interesting knowledge. Reynolds (1977, pp. 4–11) listed five things which he believed most people expected scientific knowledge to provide. These, together with one that I have added myself, can conveniently be used as the basis for a list of the possible objectives of research, as in Box 6.1.

Box 6.1 Objectives of research

- Categorization.
- Explanation.
- Prediction.
- Creating understanding.
- Providing potential for control.
- Evaluation.

---

categorization   **Categorization** involves forming a typology of objects, events or concepts. This can be useful in explaining what 'things' belong together and how. One of the main problems is to decide on the most useful methods of categorization, depending on the reasons for attempting the categorization in the first place. Following from this is the problem of determining what criteria to use to judge the usefulness of the categorization. Two obvious criteria are mentioned by Reynolds: that of exhaustiveness, by which all items should be able to be placed into a category, without any being left out; and that of mutual exclusiveness, by which each item should, without question, be appropriately placed into only one category. Finally, it should be noted that the typologies must be consistent with the concepts used in the theoretical background to the study.

There are many events and issues which we do not fully, or even partly, understand. The objective of providing an **explanation** of particular phenomena has been a common one in many forms of research.

explanation

On the basis of an explanation of a phenomenon it is often possible to make a **prediction** of future events related to it. In the natural sciences these predictions are often made in the form of abstract statements, for example given $C_1, C_2, \ldots , C_n$, if X, then Y. More readily understood are predictions made in text form, for example: if a person disagrees with a friend about his attitude toward an object, then a state of psychological tension is produced.

prediction

Whilst explanation and prediction can reveal the inner workings of phenomenas, i.e. what happens and when, they do not always provide a **sense of understanding** of phenomena – how or why they happen. A complete explanation of a phenomenon will require a wider study of the processes which surround the phenomenon and influence it or cause it to happen.

sense of understanding

A good level of understanding of a phenomenon might lead to the possibility of finding a way to **control** it. Obviously, not all phenomena lend themselves to this: for example, it is difficult to imagine how the disciplines of astronomy or geology could include an element of control. But all of technology is dependent on the ability to control the behaviour, movement or stability of things. Even in society there are many attempts, often based on scientific principles, to control events such as crime, poverty, the economy etc., though the record of success is more limited than in the natural sciences, and perhaps there are cases of attempting the impossible. The problem is that such attempts cannot be truly scientific as the variables cannot all be controlled, nor can one be certain that all relevant variables have been considered. The crucial issue in control is to understand how certain variables affect one another, and then be able to change the variables in such a way as to produce predictable results.

control

Evaluation is making judgements about the quality of objects or events. Quality can be measured either in an absolute sense or on a comparative basis. To be useful, the methods of evaluation must be relevant to the context and intentions of the research. For example, level of income is a relevant variable in the evaluation of wealth, while degree of marital fidelity is not. Evaluation goes beyond measurement, as it implies allotting values to objects or events. It is the context of the research which will help to establish the types of values which should be used.

evaluation

Desirable characteristics of research findings

There is an untold mass of information in the world. By doing research, you will be adding to this plethora of information. What is it that will make your efforts worthwhile? What should the characteristics of your findings be to make your contribution valuable? Reynolds (1977) identified four desirable characteristics of scientific knowledge which we can use as a good guide and as a basis for discussion, as shown in Box 6.2.

Box 6.2 Desirable characteristics of scientific knowledge

- Abstractness.
- Intersubjectivity (meaning).
- Intersubjectivity (logical rigour).
- Empirical relevance.

The common thread between these is that the findings should be relevant to a wider sphere than the specific cases in your research, and that they should be based on a research process that is both accessible to and understandable by others. It is worth considering these characteristics in more detail.

abstractness

The characteristic of **abstractness** is independence from a specific time and place. Research findings are useful if they can be applied in other situations, and can lead to the development of general theories. To discover the causes of a particular phenomenon which occurred in a particular time at a particular place is of little general value if the knowledge gained is not relevant to any other phenomena at different times and in different places. There are two reasons for this.

Firstly, no future predictions about future events can be made using this knowledge, as the phenomenon can only be seen as a unique historical event. As seen above, one of the important objectives of research is to provide predictions about the future. Resulting from this lack of predictability is the inability to affect any control over similar future events.

Secondly, by being restricted to a phenomenon in a particular place, it will be impossible to generalize from the results of this discovery to events which happen elsewhere.

There are cases where the study of a particular event is both useful and unavoidable, for instance in historical and ethnographic research. Historians are unlikely to feel competent to make predictions of future events (e.g. election results) on the basis of historical studies. The main aim of this kind of research is to analyse, explain and gain a sense of understanding. With a better understanding of a social phenomenon, interventions to alleviate problems are likely to be more effective and have more predictable outcomes. Similarly, in investigations following an accident, the findings aim to explain events, understand their causes and invite predictions: for example, a railway signalling fault discovered in an enquiry may cause more accidents if it is not rectified.

intersubjectivity

Intersubjectivity may be understood in two senses. Firstly, to ensure that everyone has the same understanding of words and events, there must be agreement as to the meaning of concepts used in statements. This intersubjectivity of meaning, i.e. agreement between people about meaning, is attained by precise definition of concepts. Secondly, any statement describes the relationship of at least two concepts. Often, many connected statements are used in a research project to make predictions, or to explain a theory. To avoid ambiguity and disagreement about the appropriate combination of statements to use, logical systems have been evolved such as mathematics, statistics, symbolic logic etc. These are used to promote intersubjectivity, i.e. agreement about use, at a logical level.

> If scientists cannot agree on the predictions derived from combinations of statements, then there can be no agreement as to the usefulness of the statements for predicting or explaining phenomena. (Reynolds, 1977, p. 17)

Most of science and all technology is based on empirical foundations, i.e. built on, or guided by, the results of observation and experimentation. The basic purpose of a scientific theory is to explain what causes an event or why one event is associated with another. The basis for these explanations is the recorded measurements made by the researcher of the events. **Empirical relevance** is a measure of the correspondence between a particular theory and what is taken to be objective empirical data, which enable other scientists to verify the results of the research for themselves. The greater the relevance of the empirical data, the more confidence can be put in the veracity of the theory.

empirical relevance

The research process

Whichever type of research you choose, it will be useful to understand something of the process of research. This can help you to form a framework for your activities.

Figure 6.1 Sitting down to writing a 30,000 to 60,000 word thesis is no simple task

Sitting down to writing a 30,000 to 60,000 word thesis is no simple task. The research on which it is based does not develop in a linear fashion, any more than does the writing of the report itself. So how does one go about doing research? You will have undoubtedly noticed by now that the acquisition of knowledge and the questioning of what to do with it is a complex process. From the numerous books on research methods, three interpretations of how the activities of research interweave with each other have been selected, each viewing the process at a different level of detail.

A simple summary of the relationships between five main elements of the research process can be mapped (Diagram 6.1). This compact diagram stresses the circularity of the process and the central role of research theory. Is it clear to you how progress is achieved, and at which point you can enter the system? One should point out that this diagram makes research look a very tidy and logical process, but in reality you may find that it involves guesses, intuition and intellectual cul-de-sacs.

Diagram 6.1 The research process

A spiral diagram developed from that of Leedy (1989, p. 9) illustrates even more strongly the cyclical nature of the research process (Diagram 6.2). The numbering of the segments clearly indicates where you get on board. Notice how each turn through the spiral repeats the basic process. The knowledge gained and questions raised at each turn provide the basis for the next cycle.

To view research this way is to invest it with a dynamic quality that is its true nature – a far cry from the conventional view, which sees research as a one-time act – static,

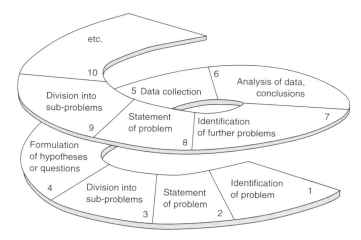

Diagram 6.2 The research process (Leedy, 1989, p. 9)

self-contained, and an end in itself … Every researcher soon learns that genuine research creates more problems than it resolves. Such is the nature of the discovery of truth. (1989, p. 9)

The diagram developed from that of Newman (1989) concentrates on the first stages in the process. It shows a clear direction in sequence of time, and displays how the process involves successive widening and narrowing of knowledge bands (Diagram 6.3). As each level of knowledge is achieved, the subject area is narrowed down to become more specific, followed by subsequent widening of knowledge as that specific area is researched in detail. This sequence of moving into more specific, yet more widely researched subject areas could be extended right through the project, culminating in the specifically narrow conclusions and finally widening out into recommendations which are of more general significance.

Sketch the continuation of Diagram 6.3, using the following stages:

- definition of problem area
- research into area
- definition of research problem
- investigation into relevant concepts, theories and research methods
- research proposal
- data gathering and analysis
- findings and conclusions
- recommendations.

Show what gets rejected every time that the subject is narrowed down.

EXERCISE 6.1

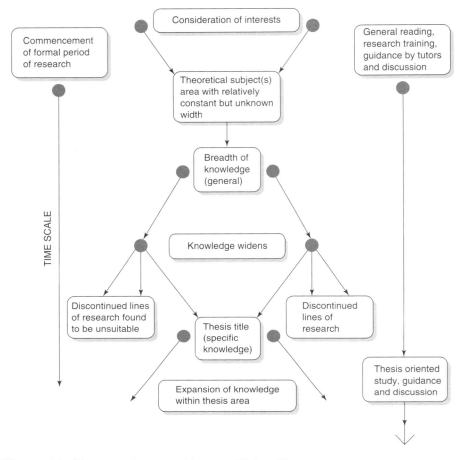

Diagram 6.3   The research process (Newman, 1989, p. 28)

Thought

To be able to design and plan your own research project, you will have to use your understanding of the process of research. The steps to take in planning the project will be explained later in this chapter. But first the nature of the major raw material of research, the data, is examined, and the two principal ways of dealing with data are discussed.

The nature and role of data

Information, in the form of 'facts', is one of the essential raw materials of scientific research. These facts, called data, are the means by which a researcher understands the phenomenon of the world around him/her. However, data can never be reality itself, but are a representation of reality. Whether this representation of reality represents 'the truth' is a matter of philosophical debate, as we have seen in the preceding parts of this book.

If data are understood to be the same as facts, they tend to acquire an air of solidity and permanence. Facts are seen to be akin to the truth, and therefore stable and unalterable. However, data are not like that at all. They are not only elusive, but ephemeral. Observations recorded one day may be different to those made on the next, owing to different conditions of the observer, the observed and their surroundings.

For example, a daily survey of people's voting intentions in a forthcoming general election will produce different results daily, even if exactly the same people are asked, because some change their minds because of what they have heard or seen in the interim period. If the same number of people is asked in a similar sample, a different result can also be expected. Anyway, how can you tell whether they are even telling the truth about their intentions?

Data, therefore, only provide a fleeting and partial glimpse of events, opinions, beliefs or conditions. What may be an accurate and valuable observation today, might be irrelevant and incorrect tomorrow. Data are not only ephemeral but corruptible. Whilst primary data, that is data observed, experienced or recorded closest to the event, are the nearest one can get to the truth, distortions inevitably occur as the proximity to the event decreases. For example, you have a more approximate and less complete knowledge of a football match if you read the newspaper report the following day than if you were at the match and had seen it yourself. Not only is the information less abundant, but it is coloured by the commentator's interpretation of the facts. This is the feature of secondary data.

Other problems which move data away from the truth are the problems associated with recording events. Factors like the accuracy and sensitivity of instrumentation, the exactness of memory, language and descriptive skills, powers of observation, and the differing assumptions and perceptions of observers, all affect the reliability and precision of the data.

Harold Pinter, the English playwright, described the situation as in Box 6.3.

It is therefore a rash researcher who insists on the infallibility of his or her data, and of the findings derived from them. A measure of humility in the belief of the accuracy of knowledge, and also practical considerations which surround the research process, dictate that the outcomes of research tend to be couched in 'soft' statements, such as 'it seems that', 'it is likely that', 'one is led to believe that' etc. This does not mean, however, that progress towards useful 'truths' cannot be achieved.

Apart from any other consideration, we are faced with the immense difficulty, if not impossibility, of verifying the past. I don't mean merely years ago, but yesterday, this morning. What took place, what was the nature of what took place, what happened? If one can speak of the difficulty of knowing what in fact took place yesterday, one can I think treat the present in the same way. What's happening now? We won't know until tomorrow or in six months' time, and we won't know then, we'll have forgotten, or our imagination will have attributed quite false characteristics to today. A moment is sucked away and distorted, often even at the time of its birth. We will all interpret a common experience quite differently, though we prefer to subscribe to the view that there's a shared common ground all right, but that it's more like a quicksand. Because 'reality' is quite a strong firm word we tend to think, or to hope, that the state to which it refers is equally firm, settled and unequivocal. It doesn't seem to be, and in my opinion, it's not worse or better for that. (Pinter, 1998, p. 21)

Sources of primary and secondary data

Commonly, writers about research make a distinction between primary and secondary data. The distinction between these is based on the sources from which the data are derived, i.e. from primary and secondary sources.

primary sources

Primary sources are those from which the researcher can gain data by direct, detached observation or measurement of phenomena in the real world, undisturbed by any intermediary interpreter. It is a matter of philosophical debate as to what extent the detachment and undisturbed state are possible or even desirable. Indeed, in some research, a high degree of involvement is a prerequisite for the successful collection and analysis of data. In every case, though, the researcher is answerable for the reliability and authenticity of his/her sources, and should be able to argue in defence of the quality of the sources. Almost all serious research, particularly that based on a scientific approach, is underpinned by data from primary sources. Data from primary sources can be in the inanimate form of instrumental readings, results of counting and measuring, physical artefacts etc., or in the animate form such as reports of direct observations of events or conditions, or recordings of experiences by those involved. For example, the minutes of a meeting can be regarded as primary data, recording what actually happened during the meeting. It is in order to check on their reliability that the first action at a meeting of an official organization is to ask whether or not the minutes of the preceding meeting are, in the opinion of those present, a true record of what happened.

secondary sources

Where data have been subjected to interpretation they are referred to as coming from **secondary sources**. The most common form of secondary source is writings in books, newspaper reports, articles and other publications. Secondary sources cannot be described as original and do not have a direct physical relationship to the event being studied, either because of the presence of intermediaries or because of the period of time between the recording and the event. It is often pointed out that secondary sources of data are usually of limited value because of errors that result when information is passed on from one person to another. However, they can be valuable in their own right in providing a partial commentary on the events by revealing the different viewpoints and cultural/social background of the sources.

Secondary sources are invaluable in the early stages of research, when you are exploring a subject and seeking problem areas. It is difficult to see how anyone

Figure 6.2 Secondary sources of data are usually of limited value because of errors that result when information is passed on from one person to another

could dive straight into effective research using only primary data sources and ignoring the theoretical or empirical work of others in the same or similar area of study. It has often been observed that great insights can be made into a subject by people who come to it from another discipline, because they are able to review the situation free from the assumptions and theoretical blinkers which surround the experts. That does not mean, however, that they have not acquired a knowledge of the subject through secondary sources, for how otherwise could they know what the problems were? There are types of research where secondary sources often provide an important part of the data. Historical research is one, where ancient texts and commentaries sometimes provide the only record of past events, or reveal the interpretations of the events made by figures of the past.

Whichever type of source you are using, a judgement must still be made as to its reliability. While data from primary sources tend to be more reliable because of their immediacy, they are not guaranteed free from distortion, which may be due to the instrumentation, or the personality and background of the observer. An assessment of the reliability of data from secondary sources must be regarded as an essential part of the conditions for their use in research. If you do not question it, your tutor and examiner certainly will!

Another distinction which can be made between sources of different types, particularly relevant to historical sources of data, is that of records which have been preserved with the conscious intent of transmitting information, and those which have been preserved without any specific intent of this kind. Examples of the former are official records, personal records such as diaries etc., oral and pictorial records, some published materials such as books, newspapers, journals which concentrate on imparting information etc., and some mechanical and electronic recordings. Examples of the latter are physical remains such as buildings, fossils, furniture and equipment etc., and other types of written published and unpublished materials aimed more at immediate or contemporary use.

Which data should be used?

We are surrounded by data. Data can be irrelevant, imprecise and even defective, and a wrong choice of the data on which the research is based has serious effects on the validity of the conclusions. So how do we choose which data are both useful and admissible to use for a particular research project?

Figure 6.3 We are surrounded by data

The answer lies in the precision of the definition of the research proposal. Most types of research planned to be undertaken are designed to be repeatable, and as exactly as possible. This requires that their conditions are precisely defined and delineated. The precision of the description of the research activities will determine which data are required, and hence also which are not. For example, a study of the structural performance of warehouse roofs excludes data on other building types, and other types of performance, such as thermal or weathering, and also data about other parts of the warehouses, such as floors. Even in cases where the investigations are not repeatable, as is the case in some social research, the data collected must be directly relevant to the aims of the study. However, in exploratory research, it cannot be known what information is relevant or not, as the theoretical framework of the research on which this judgement is based is yet to be evolved.

The criteria for admissibility of data can be determined by a host of factors, such as time, place, type, element, limits, range etc. Obviously, greater exactness in the criteria is possible in the pure science subjects where conditions are more closely controllable than in the social sciences. However, the greatest exactness obtainable under the conditions of the research proposal should be aimed at in order to maximize the reliability of the results. Also, the criteria for the admissibility of data must be defined at the outset of the research, as any later adjustments or alterations to them would alter the type of data allowed and pervert the validity of the outcomes.

Define the conditions in as many ways as you think is appropriate in each of the following research topics, and define the criteria of admissibility for data on each definition. Devise extra definitions if there are not sufficient in the title.

EXERCISE 6.2

The following is an example:

Hunger amongst young homeless people in London.

Hunger Definition: less than 1500 calories per day. Admissibility of data: measurement of daily calorie intake of cases calculated by lists of food consumed, compiled by daily interview with cases.

Homeless Definition: living on the streets for at least one month. Admissibility of data: homeless people's estimate of time lived on streets, and residential records of cases.

Amongst people in London Sample criteria.

People Definition: male and female. Admissibility of data: gender of cases, male and female categories.

Young Definition: less than 30 years old. Admissibility of data: age admitted by cases in years.

In London Definition: central London boroughs. Admissibility of data: all above data limited to relevant cases in specified areas of London.

The research topics are:

1   Factors which determine the temperature at which water boils.
2   The effect of sunlight on plant growth.
3   The levels of employment in rural areas in Britain.

Thought

Again, this exercise only scratches the surface, compared with the detail required in a substantial piece of research. It does hint at some of the main factors that need to be considered when deciding what type of data is required. You have probably also noticed that devising precise definitions and strict criteria for admissibility of data provides helpful guidelines as to where and how the data can be collected.

Quantitative and qualitative data

The type of data you find depends very much on the type of data you are look-ing for and also on the method you use to collect them. The preceding discussion about data emphasized the need for a clear definition of the research objectives and a clear definition of the conditions and admissibility of data. The type of data collected partly determines the methods used to analyse them in order to develop an answer to the research problem. But, conversely, it is also the type of research approach which you adopt that determines the nature of the data that you con-sider to be of value. The two major types of research approach are thus also labelled quantitative and qualitative.

Quantitative and qualitative research are said to be two diametrically opposed research approaches. They differ not only in the nature of the data sought and the subsequent methods of data analysis, but also in their philosophical rationale.

What are the characteristics of quantitative and qualitative research? For example, in sociology:

> Quantitative research is typically taken to be exemplified by the social survey and by experimental investigations. Qualitative research tends to be associated with participant observation and unstructured, in-depth interviewing. (Bryman, 1988, p. 1)

Until the mid 1970s the tendency was to associate valid research almost exclu-sively with scientific method, and with the collection and analysis of measurable data, the attributes of quantitative research:

> To do any research we must be able to measure the concepts we wish to study. (Kidder and Judd, 1986, p. 40)

Qualitative approaches were given scant attention because of their inability to conform to the conditions demanded of scientific method, and tended to be regarded as rather marginal in the researcher's repertoire of data collection techniques. There was a clear distinction between quantitative and qualitative research, and qualitative data and the results of qualitative analysis were regarded as limited, unreliable and lacking in solidity. This judgement relied principally on judgements of the technical adequacy of the techniques used.

It was particularly in the field of sociology, with its focus of research on the complexities of people and the society they live in, that the appropriateness of scientific method, developed for the study of natural sciences, was questioned. Research methods were required which could reveal and investigate the unique complexities and ambiguities of human subjects and their interaction in society without imposing on them an inappropriate conceptual framework.

Increasingly, the terms 'quantitative research' and 'qualitative research' came to signify much more than ways of gathering data; they came to denote divergent assumptions about the nature and purposes of research in the social sciences. (Bryman, 1988, p. 3)

Qualitative research developed significant differences in its assumptions and principles from those of quantitative research. This inevitably resulted in the two approaches tending to operate with divergent tenets about the nature of knowledge, particularly that of the social world, and about how knowledge could legitimately be produced. Intellectual positions in qualitative research evolved, the main ones being phenomenology, symbolic interactionism, Max Weber's idea of *verstehen*, naturalism and ethogenics.

These all stress the importance of contextual and holistic understanding, with an emphasis on description, and a commitment to 'seeing through the eyes' of the people being studied. The fear that the researcher may fail to do justice to the subject's orientation to the world led to the tendency for conceptual and theoretical reasoning to be left aside, or used only in the final stages of the research enterprise.

Bryman (1988, p. 94) presented a useful comparison of the contrasting features of quantitative and qualitative research. Whilst qualitative research is used to construe the attitudes, beliefs and motivations within a subject, it can also perform a preparatory role in quantitative research. The researcher doing qualitative research will attempt to obtain an inside view of the phenomenon, getting as close as possible to the subject of the research in order to collect resonant, fertile data to enable the development of a social construct through the dynamic process of research. The quantitative researcher, on the other hand, chooses to remain distant as an outsider, collecting hard and reliable data, as reality is considered to be exoteric and static. The qualitative approach tends to be unstructured, allowing concepts and theories to emerge, while the quantitative approach begins with concepts and theories and tests them in a rigorous, structured fashion with the result that they are either supported, amended or rejected.

Consider the following list of titles of research projects and decide which projects are likely to be quantitative or qualitative in nature, and which might be a combination of both.

1 The effects of poverty on lifespan in nineteenth century Britain.
2 Archaeology and tourism in the Middle East.
3 Architecture and the corporate image of international companies.
4 Housing supply in Russia during the communist period.
5 Design for disaster: a history of rapid response to housing need.
6 Thermal insulation in traditional housing construction in Northern Europe.
7 A comparative study of urban growth in developing countries 1920–80.
8 Water resistance of new synthetic paints.
9 Small hospital design for rural areas.
10 Trends in productivity on large building sites.

Thought

Qualitative research is a rapidly developing discipline, and the subject of lively debate. You might remember the two views argued in Chapter 1, in which a sociologist challenged the reliability of scientific method, claiming that human involvement in any activity, however controlled, is subject to qualitative influences, while the scientist supported the robustness of scientific method as a proven way of understanding the workings of the world.

PLANNING A RESEARCH PROJECT

The purpose of the research plan is to take the initial research problem and decide how it will be researched. A clearly defined and expressed research problem is one important prerequisite for evolving a research plan. Important facts to be considered when designing the project are: available time, financial resources, facilities, availability of data, possible methods of analysis, and your own developing skills as a researcher.

Remember that you do not have a team of researchers to support you, and that you have only a few weeks to complete a dissertation, about one year to complete an MPhil or about three years to complete a PhD. All other research projects are similarly limited in their time frame. There will be some hard choices to make; however fascinating your subject and however important the expected outcomes, it is essential to limit the area of your investigation and keep it within manageable proportions. Keep in mind that working towards a research degree is also a training exercise to develop research skills, and your thesis will finally demonstrate that you have acquired them sufficiently.

Choosing a research strategy

What sort of research will you pursue? It is worth remembering the different overall aims that could be at the centre of your project. Phillips and Pugh (1994, pp. 49–52) identified three basic aims of research, as shown in Box 6.4 and discussed in the following.

Box 6.4 Basic aims of research

- Exploration.
- Testing out.
- Problem solving.

Exploration

This kind of research delves into the unknown, tackling new problem issues or topics. As little or no previous research has been done on those topics, it will be impossible to delineate precisely the scope of the research or to predict its outcomes. Because it will be in a relatively unexplored domain, a necessary part of the research is to explore what existing theories, concepts and methodologies might be used or adapted, or failing those, to devise new ones. It pushes out the boundaries of knowledge in the anticipation that the outcomes will be of value.

Testing out

A common feature of such research is that it makes generalizations from specific instances. But how far are the generalizations valid? Testing out research explores the validity of the generalizations in other circumstances, and tries to define their limits. This basic scientific activity leads to the refinement of theories. There are a host of opportunities in this approach: testing the generalizations in different locations, under different social or physical conditions, in different contexts etc.

Problem solving

This type of research identifies a 'real-life problem'. Its aim is to find possible solutions to the problem by using techniques of systematic appraisal and analysis. As 'real-life problems' tend to be complex, the study might involve several disciplines and a variety of methods, requiring a great deal of background knowledge. Although it is possible to pursue this kind of research on a theoretical level, commonly practical benefits flow from it. However, solutions are unlikely to be obvious and clear-cut.

Figure 6.4 Problem solving type of research identifies a 'real-life problem'

Which type of research lends itself best to gaining a research degree? Phillips and Pugh (1994) pragmatically suggest that the safest option, with the fewest unknown factors, is to be recommended. Testing out research, based on known theories and established methods of testing, avoids the unpredictability (though it might miss out on the excitement) of the other two research approaches. It is probably better to keep your feet on the bottom until you are able to swim! You will still have to introduce some new insights or methods into the subject to make the research worthwhile (rather than just replication), and it can be argued that this mainstream type of research will usefully produce more readily publishable and quotable results than the other two types.

There are greater risks and unknowns in the exploratory and problem solving approaches. They undoubtedly require more expertise and experience on the part of the researcher and demand the enthusiastic support of the supervisor. In such innovative and original research, it is more difficult to achieve the authority in the subject required for it to be publishable, which might, in turn, impede a career in research.

Thought *You should now also remind yourself of the different types of research explained in Chapter 3, and of your thinking about your own research interest which you considered in that chapter. Reflect on how the above types of research might be considered to be appropriate for your own work.*

Planning research projects

Any research project requires planning so that the researcher's time is used efficiently in pursuance of the research objectives. Much effort can be wasted and frustration incurred by haphazard reading and collecting of notes and references, sundry information and opinions. This form of activity might be 'very interesting', but leads in no particular direction and hence does nothing to advance the progress of the research.

> Research planning and architectural planning have much in common. Each requires a conceptualisation of the overall organisation and a detail plan before work on the project can begin. For successful completion, a building requires plans that are clearly conceived and accurately drawn. A research project should be no less totally visualised and precisely detailed. (Leedy, 1989, p. 79)

Bearing in mind what you have learned in previous chapters about how knowledge is gained, through inductive logic and deductive reasoning, interpretation and understanding, and their combination in scientific enquiry, historical or social research, what sort of format should your research project take?

According to Leedy (1989, p. 81), all research has a basic format. Whatever subjects or disciplines are its focus, they all share the need of a central research problem, a search for and collation of data, appropriate methods of analysis and the formulation of substantiated conclusions. This is not to say that the methodology will be similar in all disciplines. On the contrary, much of the planning of research projects is taken up with deciding on the most appropriate techniques for data collection and analysis. The underlying dynamics of the process also include the features of the researcher, such as motivation, experience and skills; aspects of the research situation, such as cost, time, facilities, situation etc.; and the needs and demands of the respondents or others co-operating in the research.

Boxes 6.5, 6.6 and 6.7 give three examples of research plans, two for PhD theses and the third for a funded research programme. Note that references in these plans are not included in the reference list.

Box 6.5   Example research plan 1

OXFORD CITY PRIMARY CARE GROUP: A CASE STUDY OF INTERAGENCY COLLABORATION

Promoting independence in older people

For this part of the study, fracture of the neck of the femur (hip fracture) will be used as a tracer condition. Care provision for this group potentially involves the whole system of health and social care, including prevention (accident reduction), trauma, rehabilitation, primary care, continuing community care, social services, the voluntary sector, carers, day centres, residential care etc. If the PCG is to have an impact on interagency collaboration, it should be apparent in the treatment of this care group.

(Continued)

Box 6.5

The study will seek to identify the impact of the PCG on interagency collaboration from the perspectives both of those at management level and of service users. Semi-structured interviews will be conducted with a purposive sample of representatives at middle management and operational levels of the agencies involved. A SWOT (strengths, weaknesses, opportunities and threats) framework will be used. A sampling frame is being composed by asking senior people in relevant agencies to identify who in their organization would be the most appropriate person to interview in terms of their proximity to interfaces with other agencies. These will be followed by semi-structured interviews to explore the experiences of people who have returned home following a hip fracture and the experiences of their carers. This will provide contextual data to corroborate (or not) the accounts of the 'professionals'. The methodological approach is to investigate the perceptions of professionals and users, including comparing expectations with actuality one year on, rather than measuring impacts directly. Service users and their carers will be accessed through the A&E department at the John Radcliffe Hospital. Medical Ethics Board approval will be sought. Fieldwork will be carried out at two time points: at time 1 (April–June 2000) and at time 2 (April–June 2001).

Evaluation of the PCG's Substance Misuse Services

This project is a PCG initiative that addresses one of its five stated priorities: tackling the city's drug and alcohol problems. The PCG has put in post a Development Officer, Oxford Community Substance Misuse Services, for a year from January 2000 with a budget of £100,000 to develop the initiative. The criteria measured in the present study will be largely the objectives of the initiative, and will therefore be specified in consultation with its steering group.

As with the previous part of the study, semi-structured interviews with a purposive sample of key informers at management and practitioner levels of the relevant agencies will be conducted. A SWOT framework will be used. Service users will also be interviewed to assess the impact of the PCG initiative on their experiences of care. They will be accessed through the street drug agency, Libra. Using the agency's director as a 'gatekeeper', clients will be invited to take part in the study on a voluntary basis. The approval of the Medical Ethics Board will be required. Fieldwork will be carried out at two time points: at time 1 (April–June 2000) and at time 2 (April–June 2001).

Monitoring structural change

The third element of the study will investigate the PCG's impact on partnership working and monitor structural change in the PCG in three ways: through interviews, postal surveys and document analysis. Preliminary analysis of the interviews will inform the construction of two postal questionnaires. Comparisons will be made with the findings of the National Tracking Project which is carrying out a national survey of a 15% sample of PCGs, part of which will be looking particularly at the development of partnerships with local authorities. A theme of particular interest will be the impact of the introduction of the PCG on former fundholding GPs.

Box 6.5

1   *Interviews* Each 6 months (June and November) interviews will be carried out with key informers at the interfaces between agencies. A SWOT framework and/or Stephen Peckham's (1999) separation–integration interview schedule will be used. Interviewees representing constituents of as many agencies as possible will be interviewed.

2   *Postal questionnaires* The first questionnaire will be sent only to ex-fundholders, and will aim to establish the prevalence of the experiences expressed in the interviews with fundholders. The design of the second questionnaire will be informed by the preliminary analysis of all the interviews, and will be sent to each practice in Oxford. Support from the PCG will be provided to encourage the return of questionnaires.

3   *Document analysis* Ongoing analysis of PCG documents will be carried out. These documents will include the agendas and minutes of board meetings, subgroup meetings (Health Improvement Plan Group, Communications and Public Involvement Group, Mental Health Working Group, Clinical Governance) and other meetings, consultation exercises etc.

The collection of baseline data during the first round of fieldwork will constitute the MPhil stage of the study, while the PhD stage will comprise the collection of data a year on and the analysis of how the PCG has impacted on interagency collaboration during its first period of activity.

(Alison Chisholm, Oxford Brookes University)

Box 6.6   Example research plan 2

FACTORS AFFECTING THE TEACHING AND LEARNING OF ENERGY IN SCIENCE AT KEY STAGE 3

Proposed plan

Stage 1   Survey to find out about approaches to teaching energy at KS3. The focus will be curriculum organization, resources used and teachers' subject specialization. This will be done initially with a semi-structured questionnaire aimed at heads of science. It is hoped to quickly follow this up with a short informal interview asking about opinions of the teaching of energy and the possibility for further research with science teachers in the schools. It is aimed initially to contact a random sample of 100 secondary schools from a selection of rural and urban settings over several shire counties and metropolitan districts. This stage will be done as an initial contacting exercise and ice-breaker which will accumulate a useful base of information on how energy is taught in schools. A semi-structured questionnaire is appropriate as the information asked for is fairly superficial and organizational and not of an emotive, sensitive nature. Existing contacts in the School of Education will be used initially. Data will be analysed using a spreadsheet, e.g. Excel.

(Continued)

Box 6.6

Stage 2   Upon securing contact with some volunteer teachers, this stage will be a short exercise with the aim of working with teachers to elicit and prioritize factors they feel important, in their experience, in effecting conceptual understanding. Elicitation will be done through a concept mapping exercise. Ranking and prioritizing will be done through a response scale to gauge actual perceived importance, triangulated with a prioritizing grid to gauge relative importance. This stage will be done to gain a slightly deeper insight into teaching practice within the curriculum framework established in stage 1; to further working relationships with schools; and to get to know teachers and open up the possibility for in-depth case study work, thus providing a start for an action-research-based methodology by encouraging reflection in teachers and the researcher. It is aimed to work with twenty teachers. Data will be analysed with a spreadsheet by triangulating ranked and prioritized factors. The resulting individual 'picture' of factors important to each teacher is intended to provide useful material for reflection on conceptual understanding. 'Pictures' for all the teachers as a group may be examined for evidence of correlation. It is intended to pilot this stage with a group of PGCE students in order to refine the method of concept mapping and facilitate reflection and also gain 35 further useful contacts.

Stage 3   Case studies working with eight–ten teachers and their pupils. The aim will be to assess the effectiveness of teaching energy under particular sets of identified and reflected-upon grounded factors, as elicited, ranked and prioritized in stage 2. This will be done by working with teachers and their pupils from year 7, 8 or 9 classes, closely following a sequence of lessons on energy, or an energy related topic. Effectiveness will be assessed from the point of pupils' *a priori* and *a posteriori* conceptual understandings. This will be done by first negotiating a set of criteria for pupils' expected outcomes for the sequence of lessons. These will contain elements of the school's scheme of work and hence National Curriculum references. Also, the expected level of understanding of the energy concept will be clearly predefined, such as in the model provided. However, it is anticipated that, given the complex nature of the energy concept coupled with the recent shift in its description, some teachers may need to challenge their existing ideas about energy before the teaching sequence begins. Hence it would be favourable to interview teachers in-depth to elicit any misconceptions and provide means for INSET (using methods and materials from the PSTS project). Pupils will be tested on their understandings of energy before and after the lessons using structured and open-ended questions. A sample will be interviewed in-depth to elicit richer meanings for their conceptions. Answers to test questions and interview transcripts will be coded according to various descriptions of the energy concept. Overall, factors to be reflected on and critically examined may include curriculum organization, teachers' subject specialization and subject knowledge, effectiveness of constructivist teaching and learning, and recognition of the shift in the description of the energy concept in school science.

Box 6.6

In summary, the sequence for each case study, after securing contact through stage 2, may include:

- interview the teacher on their understanding of energy using the 'interviews about instances and events' techniques
- test pupils and interview a sample on their preconceptions of energy
- provide opportunity for INSET (if necessary) to the teacher on the energy concept
- reflect on and redesign elements of the teaching sequence taking account of the above (constructivist principle)
- participant observation of sequence of lessons, taking field notes, coding for reporting, reflecting
- test pupils at the end, reinterview a sample
- dissemination, reflection on whole process
- possibly retest pupils at a later date to test for consolidation of conceptual understanding (constructivist principle).

Methodology

It is this researcher's position that this broad and mixed methodology is appropriate in addressing the aims set out for this study. A mixture of qualitative and quantitative methods will be used. Stages 1 and 2 are felt to be necessary prerequisites for stage 3, not only in the information they will yield but, importantly, in the personal realm. The whole design has Kelly's personal construct theory in mind, in particular the 'subsuming of personal construing systems' and sensitivity to 'core constructs'. On initial contact with schools, the aim is to ask only superficial questions about curriculum organization. Then, only when sufficient rapport and trust have been built up with teachers, will it be considered appropriate to probe with deeper questions. For example, the issue of teachers' subject knowledge may arise in stage 3 which, as mentioned, may be a sensitive area for secondary school science teachers. This is especially so when considering the position of a university researcher, not in the current position of teaching, coming in to work with teachers to critically examine practice.

Stage 3 has been designed on action research and constructivist principles. This researcher feels that AR is a good methodology for such in-depth educational research because of practitioner involvement and empowerment in the research process, the grounded nature of the knowledge and the practical value of the research generated. Also, because of the self-reflective process, it encourages the potential for a positive change in practice. Constructivism is felt to be an appropriate pedagogy on grounds of its weighting in current literature, as reported.

View to a PhD

It is intended that this study will contribute to the knowledge base of improving the teaching and learning of the energy concept in science at KS3: in particular, by

(Continued)

Box 6.6

highlighting, critically assessing and reporting on factors crystallized from the research process that are believed to be important in effecting the conceptual understanding of energy. This study will also demonstrate a mixed methodology, drawing on Kelly's theory of personal constructs, action research, constructivism, and qualitative and quantitative methods. This may have the potential for extension into KS4, FE or other subject areas where conceptual understanding is an issue.

Time frame for study

Year 1	Term 1	literature survey
	Term 2	design study, fine detail
	Term 3	contacting, stage 1, pilot stage 2, PGCE students
Year 2	Term 1	main study
	Term 2	main study
	Term 3	stages 1, 2 and 3
Year 3	Term 1	stages 1, 2 and 3
	Term 2	write up
	Term 3	write up

(Robert Illes, Oxford Brookes University)

Box 6.7   Example research plan 3

INITIAL STUDY FOR THE PRODUCTION OF A DATABASE OF CURRENT AND COMPLETED RESEARCH IN FACILITIES MANAGEMENT FOR THE USE OF MANAGERS, DESIGNERS AND RESEARCHERS WORKING IN NHS ESTATES

Objectives and methodology

1 Determination of necessary range and scope of the database subjects, present search methods, preferences and requirements. Method: structured personal and telephone interviews with a small selection (approximately twenty) of managers working in relevant fields on NHS projects. Result: formulation of database 'brief'.
2 Exploration of existing data sources which are being and can be used to locate the research. Method: library searches, telephone and written enquiries to professional and research centres. Result: list of existing databases and sources of research activity information.
3 Investigation of nature of access to these data sources, costs of access, copyright situation with regard to use of data, likely copyright costs. Method: written and telephonic communication with producers and managers of data sources.

Box 6.7

Result: detailed information of availability and costs of collection of data on research activities.

4   Inquiry into suitable vehicles for the database, e.g. CD-ROM, Internet, intranet etc., including review of search engines to enable easy access to database by NHS staff and others working on NHS projects, including estimation of cost implications. Method: sourcing of specialist literature on the subject, consultation with practitioners in the field. Result: list of options with considered advantages/disadvantages and relative estimated costs.

5   Survey of suitable database computer programs, including design features, formats, search methods, print options, updating characteristics and likely costs. Method: collection of available program specifications, scrutiny of program reviews in computer press, consultations with database designers and managers in university and professional fields. Result: draft report on comparative features, suitability and costs of available programs.

6   Review of possible methods of management, maintenance, quality control and periodical updating of database, ownership and licensing options, and relative costs. Method: estimation of requirements depending on system, then consultations with NHS Estates strategic managers on funding and staffing options within the NHS organization and/or use of outside consultants. Indicative cost quotations from consultants. Result: list of possible options and costs with discussion of implications.

7   Production of draft discussion paper together with feedback questionnaire seeking informed opinion from executives and managers. Submission to NHS Estates executive and peer review. Method: preparation of paper containing collation of information gained in stages 1–6, together with a list of options and reasoned recommendations made on the basis of the available information, expert and managerial views recorded during consultations, policy and viability judgements by NHS Estates executives. Questionnaire formulation on the basis of options suggested. Also, recommendations on dissemination of discussion paper. Circulation to selected NHS managers and peer researchers for comments. Corrections and adjustments to discussion paper as a result of review. Result: an approved discussion paper ready for dissemination.

8   Production and dissemination of discussion paper with attached questionnaire. Method: copying and postal dissemination. Result: facilities managers in the NHS informed of options and asked for opinions.

9   Evaluation of questionnaire responses. Method: simple statistical evaluation of questionnaire returns (using SPSS) to analyse and summarize responses to options and recommendations. Summarization of any additional suggestions and comments obtained. Result: summary of feedback from profession.

10 Production of report with recommendations and possibly a proposal based on this for the production and management of a research database. Method: writing of report based on discussion paper and responses to it. Result: a well

(Continued)

informed report aimed at policy and decision makers in NHS Estates on the options, likely costs and acceptability of a database of current and completed research in facilities and estate management. This could form the basis for a proposal for the production and maintenance of such a database.

Project milestones

The plan of work will be carried out in three stages:

1   Formulation of design 'brief' for database and collection and assessment of information (eight weeks).
2   Writing of discussion paper and consultation (five weeks).
3   Analysis of questionnaire returns and production of report with recommendations (six weeks).

The detailed tasks are scheduled in the project plan (not shown here). The milestones for reporting results are: end of collection and assessment of information (25 January 1999), dissemination of discussion paper draft (15 February 1999) and submission of the final report (29 March 1999).

   The information gathering, consultations and evaluations will be carried out by Nicholas Walliman with the occasional assistance (advice) of other members of the team. A casual clerical assistant will be employed sporadically at appropriate times to help in the organization of the data and writing up.

Methods for disseminating and implementing research to the NHS

A discussion paper will be produced which sets out an evaluation of the advantages, options and costs of setting up and maintaining a research database. This will be disseminated to all relevant managers and executives within the Health Service. The paper will include a feedback questionnaire which, when returned, will be evaluated, and a report will be published which makes specific recommendations. This report will be sent to policy and decision makers in NHS Estates and to all the managers and executives on the previous list.

   If the recommendations support the creation of a research database or some alternative to it, these will form the basis of a proposal for the next stages in the production of a system for improving access to the latest research information relevant to facilities management in the NHS, which will be submitted to the appropriate department of the NHS Estates Agency.

(Nicholas Walliman, Oxford Brookes University)

Phillips and Pugh (1994, p. 52) maintained that doing research is a craft skill, in which the basic educational process is that of learning by doing. After you have decided on an overall plan for your project and on your research approach, you should carefully consider how you can acquire the skills required to carry out each of the 'craft' elements. This takes time, and should be included as an element in each phase of the work. You should also consider that some practice is required before you use the skill in your project, giving you the opportunity to gain some feedback and giving you greater confidence when you use it 'for serious'.

Think about your own research topic, and the skills which you will need to develop to carry it out. Then:

EXERCISE
6.4

1   Analyse the examples of plans of work in Boxes 6.5, 6.6 and 6.7 to detect the steps taken to achieve the research aims. Compare the types of approach, and consider what you can learn from them related to your own project. Obviously the subject will be different, but you will see how the main stages of data collection, analysis and making conclusions are a common feature.
2   Make a list of the likely skills that you will need to learn and practise before you can carry out the various stages in your research plan.

CONCLUSIONS

One of the main features of research is the amount of criticism and evaluation to which it is liable to be subjected. Whatever you do, and however you do it, requires to be justified.

This chapter has presented a general overview of some of the principal theoretical and practical issues in research, and a description of some of the main decisions one has to make when planning a research project.

THE NEXT STEPS: PLAN YOUR OWN RESEARCH PROJECT

By now you should have a good general idea of the sort of research that you want to undertake. You will have delineated a problem and considered how you might appropriately investigate it in the coming months. The intention of this section is to give you the opportunity to consciously formulate the objectives of your research and then devise a framework for your research project. You can then make a systematic check to see whether it complies with the criteria for 'good research' described earlier in this chapter.

This is bound to raise a lot of issues and questions, many of which you will not be able to resolve yet. During the tutorial, you will be able to discuss how you have come to your conclusions, and to outline the issues that you think are important but you have not resolved. This provides a good opportunity to work out, with the help of your tutor, a set of priorities for further investigation and clarification.

The aims of this section are:

- to check on the objectives of the research
- to design the basic framework for your research project
- to anticipate the quality of the research findings
- to decide on the type of data required.

Checklist of activities that will progress your research

Step 1: check out the objectives of your research

Are they to categorize, to evaluate, to explain, to predict, to create understanding or to provide potential for control? It could be that your objectives fall into more than one of these categories. What is it that you want to subject to these objectives? Once you are fairly clear about this you will probably be able to explain the objectives in just a few sentences.

Step 2: how abstract (or generalizable) will your research be?

In other words, to what extent will the lessons learned be relevant to understanding or prediction or even control in other situations at other times? If it is only to a limited extent or not at all, how important will the findings be that explain the particular situation in respect to other knowledge (e.g. filling a gap in history or archaeology)?

Step 3: use of terminology

Terminology is often very subject specific: the same words can mean quite different things in different contexts. Be careful to define the concepts (i.e. terms) used in your research. You may have to discuss at some length the different words used for concepts if there is ambiguity in the background research material. This is not uncommon, and you will have to make a choice of which ones to adopt. One step further than this: examine how these concepts are used in important statements about the subject. Are these based on a common form of reasoning that can be understood and accepted by anyone?

Step 4: your argument

In order for an argument to convince, it is almost essential to have evidence to support it. I say almost, because other factors can be used to persuade, e.g. guile, emotions, trickery etc. In scientific research and particularly technology, empirical evidence is prized for its robustness in underpinning arguments. In the social sciences and humanities, evidence of different and more insubstantial kinds is often used. Thoughts, memories, customs, even dreams may be used to support a theory. What sort of evidence will you look for to support your arguments? Will there possibly be any dispute about the solidity of the evidence? What precedents are there for basing arguments in your subject on the type of evidence that you will seek?

Step 5: mapping your journey

From your understanding of the research process, can you map out a network or a chart that will describe your own journey through the process? The examples given are very general; you can make yours more specific to your project. Look out for two essential aspects: the characteristic broadening and narrowing of the subject area as you distil your research down to the essential elements; and the presence of reiterative feedback loops – periodic checking back to theory and evidence.

Step 6: what data will you need?

You have already been reviewing secondary data in your background research. Consider the types of data that you will need to collect in your project. The types of primary and secondary sources you will investigate will do much to determine the characteristics of your research activities, e.g. whether you will be trudging through jungles or sifting through dusty files in a dank cellar. Make sure that what you plan to collect is really relevant and essential to your project, not just of interest. The differences between quantitative and qualitative data are revealed in both the methods of collection and the analysis. A combination of the two is commonly used in social science subjects.

Step 7: choose your research strategy

The three types of research strategy – exploration, testing out and problem solving – are related to the research objectives listed in step 1. Where does your research fit into these? A strategy is a plan. Relate this also to your mapping out of your individual research process, and perhaps add a time and place element to get a framework of what you will actually do. The next chapter will explain in more detail the methods that you can use to carry out this strategy.

Consolidation and assessment

Arrange a tutorial with your tutor or supervisor. You should use this to demonstrate that you have applied the concepts of this chapter to your research project, and have developed your ideas about planning your research and estimating the value of the outcomes. You should also show that you are aware of the obstacles and issues which you will have to confront while carrying out the research.

So, by applying what you have learned in this chapter, and with the help of the steps taken above, clearly state the objectives of your research project in relation to your research problem, and describe how your intended research will be useful. Using correct terminology, set out the steps in the argument that you will pursue, firstly in presenting the research problem, and then in investigating it. Discuss your research strategy and, in principle, how you aim to carry out your research project. As far as you can, explain the practical steps you need to take to make it possible, using a chart or network to illustrate this. Decide on the sorts of data required and how, in general terms, you intend to collect them.

Your tutor will assess whether you can convincingly argue for the quality and value of your research project, and discuss with you your selected approach to its planning. Expect that he/she will examine the appropriateness of what you suggest about the data required and the sources from which they can be obtained. Discuss quantitative and qualitative methods in relation to your research approach.

You will be helped to make decisions about your research approach and your overall plan and possible sequence of activities in relation to the type of research qualification you are aiming at. Obviously, the time frame and complexity allowed for in a PhD project are much greater than those for a Masters dissertation. The tendency is to be too ambitious, so this is a good time to make appropriate decisions to limit the scope of the research before planning a huge menu of research methods, explained in more detail in the next chapter.

Key words

Categorization	Abstractness
Explanation	Intersubjectivity
Prediction	Empirical relevance
Sense of understanding	Primary sources
Control	Secondary sources
Evaluation	

Further reading

Like this one, most books on how to do research will have a section that explains what makes for quality in research and how to go about planning a research project. Here are some books that go into more detail on the desired qualities in research.

Reynolds, P. D. (1977) *A Primer in Theory Construction*. Indianapolis: Bobbs-Merrill.

See the first sections for what qualities scientific research should contain.

Preece, R. (1994) *Starting Research: an Introduction to Academic Research and Dissertation Writing*. London: Pinter.

The first four chapters contain an interesting discussion of the elements of scientific research.

Bryman, A. (2001) *Social Research Methods*, 2nd edn. London: Sage.

Look at the first three chapters for a good introduction to the basics of social research.

Cohen, L. and Manion, L. (1994) *Research Methods in Education*. London: Routledge.

This and later editions are strong on the background to research. Again, see the first few chapters.

Locke, L., Spirduso, W. and Silverman, S. (2004) *Reading and Understanding Research*, 2nd edn. Thousand Oaks, CA: Sage.

Particularly the final chapters which look at different types of research and how to examine the research more critically.

Leedy, P. D. (1989) *Practical Research: Planning and Design*. London: Collier Macmillan.

A bit old, but there are later editions. It was one of my favourites when I did my PhD. Good on explaining different types of research.

And here are some books that give sound practical advice on the planning and execution of research projects.

Phillips, E. M. and Pugh, D. S. (1994) *How to Get a PhD*. Buckingham: Open University Press.

This gives good advice to the research student on many aspects of how to plan the research.

Rudestam, K. E. and Newton, R. (2001) *Surviving Your Dissertation: a Comprehensive Guide to Content and Process*, 2nd edn. Thousand Oaks, CA: Sage.

See Part III for practical advice.

Cryer, P. (2000) *The Research Student's Guide to Success*, 2nd edn. Buckingham: Open University Press.

Continued

Blaxter, L. Hughes, C. and Tight, M. (1996) *How to Research*. Buckingham: Open University Press.

See Chapter 5 for how to plan and manage your project.

Holliday, A. (2001) *Doing and Writing Qualitative Research*. London: Sage.

This is written with great empathy for the practical problems writers face when transferring their research into a written product.

ANSWERS TO EXERCISES

EXERCISE 6.1

The pattern of widening and narrowing continues right through until the completion of the research (Diagram 6.4).

EXERCISE 6.2

1 Factors which determine the temperature at which water boils.

Factors Definition: circumstances, facts or influences which produce a result. Admissibility of data: physical data only, e.g. surrounding air pressure, temperature, type of water container, type and distribution of heat source.

Temperature Definition: measurement of heat content. Admissibility of data: thermometer readings at centre of water mass in degrees Celsius.

Water Definition: H_2O. Admissibility of data: pure distilled water.

Boil Definition: the point at which a liquid begins to be converted to a vapour. Admissibility of data: boiling point determined by constant streams of large bubbles being observed throughout the water mass.

2 The effect of sunshine on plant growth.

Effect Definition: the result of an action. Admissibility of data: observed changes to the plant.

Sunshine Definition: light and other radiation derived directly from the sun. Admissibility of data: measurable in open air (i.e. not in a building) within given limits of visible light rays, ultraviolet and infrared light, gamma radiation.

Plant Definition: member of the vegetable kingdom. Admissibility of data: a specified range of annual green plants grown from seed.

Growth Definition: to show increase in size. Admissibility of data: plant height, spread, girth of main stem, all in millimetres, number of leaves.

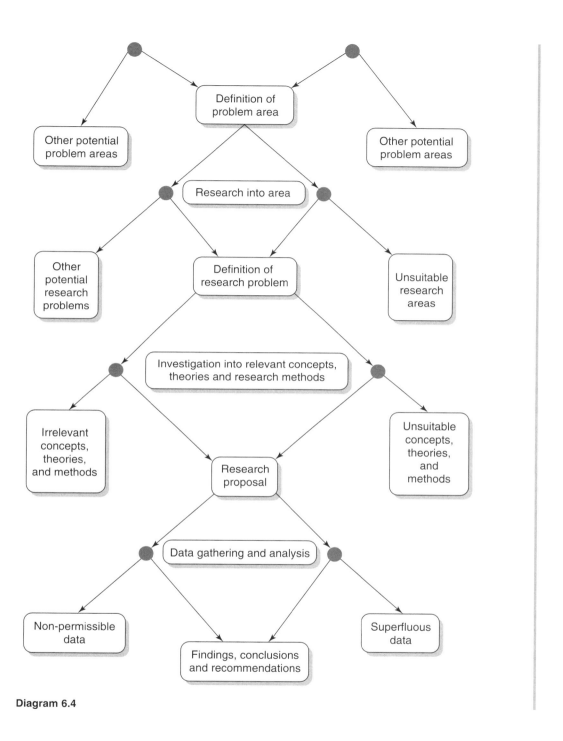

Diagram 6.4

3   The levels of employment in rural areas in Britain.

Levels Definition: a value on a scale. Admissibility of data: proportions of time spent working.

Employment Definition: the state of working for monetary remuneration. Admissibility of data: either self-employed or working for a registered employer.

Rural areas Definition: all areas outside conurbations. Admissibility of data: in areas with settlements of less than 20,000 inhabitants.

Britain Definition: England, Scotland and Wales. Admissibility of data: only data collected from these areas.

EXERCISE 6.3

1   This sounds like a purely quantitative study, i.e. a statistical study seeking correlations between the two variables based on historical data. Qualitative issues could be included.

2   While this could be a purely quantitative study (concerned only with statistics), it is more likely to involve qualitative data and analyses, e.g. investigating what kinds of archaeological sites are interesting to tourists of what kind etc.

3   Qualitative. No indication of anything which can be quantified.

4   Could be either or both.

5   Histories are usually qualitative with sometimes some quantitative elements.

6   This is most likely to be a quantitative study, quantifying insulation levels in different types of construction.

7   This definitely sounds like a quantitative study if the intention is to compare statistical data on urban growth, i.e. rates and profile of growth. It could, however, concentrate on a comparison of the qualitative aspects of urban growth and the reasons for it.

8   This will need a quantitative approach to determine the scientific properties of the paints.

9   Design is much to do with quality, though some aspects of it can be measured quantitatively, e.g. size.

10 Productivity is a quantitative measure, and therefore requires a quantitative approach.

EXERCISE 6.4

1   Obviously it is impossible to give a direct answer to this question here; it is up to you to draw your own conclusions. However, have you considered the following?

(a) Is the process shown as a linear progression or are data collection and analysis concurrent? Which will be appropriate in your study? Some qualitative approaches require a more evolutionary strategy with short feedback loops which connect data collection and analysis.

(b) Do the proposals intend to test a hypothesis or look for a deeper understanding of a situation? The plan of action and type of output are greatly influenced by the aims of the research.

2 Only list those which might be relevant to your research plan, not those which are indicated in the various examples. Use this list for the tasks in the final section of this chapter.

7
Research Methods

Introduction
  Data Collection and Analysis
  Quantitative and Qualitative Research
  Research Strategies
  The Links between Perspectives
Collecting Secondary Data
Collecting Primary Data
  Sampling
  Questionnaires and Diaries
  Interviews: Structured, Semi-Structured and Open
  Standardized Scales and Tests
  Accounts
  Observations and Physical Surveys
  Using the Internet for Primary Research
Combined Data Generation and Analysis
  Experiments
  Models
Analysing Data
  Why Analyse Data?
  Quantitative Analysis
  Qualitative Analysis
Conclusions
The Next Steps: Which Research Methods Will You Use?
Checklist of Activities That Will Progress Your Research
  Consolidation and Assessment
Key Words
Further Reading
Answers to Exercises

- To show the range of research methods available to the researcher.
- To describe the nature of different research methods used for collecting qualitative and quantitative data.
- To indicate appropriate methods of analysing data.

INTRODUCTION

The intention of this chapter is to provide a very brief description of a range of commonly used research methods so that you have a basic idea of the options open to you when you set about planning your research. An essential ingredient of your research proposal will be to suggest appropriate methods by which you will carry out your research, so a prior understanding of the range of methods open to you will help you to decide which might be pertinent to your form of study. Although the range of methods available for research into the natural sciences, the social sciences and the humanities is enormous, the number of methods which could reasonably be explained in this chapter is limited, so only a general indication can be given of some of the principal methods.

It would, at first glance, be easy to cover the subject by neatly dividing it under two headings: methods of data collection, and methods of data analysis. The first part would be a straightforward summary of how to collect data from different sources using different methods, and the second would be a description of techniques of analysis, both quantitative and qualitative. However, it soon becomes evident that both of the activities of data collection and data analysis tend to be inextricably bound up with the research strategies – historical, survey, case study etc. – and cannot easily be discussed without some reference to these. It also becomes obvious that there are often strong links between the type of data collected and the type of analysis appropriate for them. Even the clear distinction between data collection and data analysis can become problematic, as in some cases data collection, collation and analysis go hand in hand, and in others further valuable data are produced by the process of analysis.

So, as an introduction, we will first look briefly at the three perspectives from which one can review research methods, examine the characteristics which make them distinctive, and describe how they interact. The three perspectives are: data collection and analysis, quantitative and qualitative research, and research strategies.

Data collection and analysis

Once the research problem has been formulated, it should become evident what kind of data will be required to study the problem, and also what kind of analysis will be appropriate to analyse the data. The reasons for choosing particular data collection and analysis methods are always determined by the nature of what you want to find out, and the particular characteristics of your research problem, and the specific sources of information. In fact, it will often be appropriate to decide first on the type of analysis, quantitative or qualitative, which will be required to investigate your research problem, and then on the type of data which need to be collected in order to make that analysis.

Note, however, that the categories of data collection and analysis are not always as distinct as they might at first appear. They can, depending on the particular research aims, be closely interlinked. On the one hand, for example in exploratory research, the data may be continuously analysed as they are collected, the analysis giving clues as to the most fruitful area of further data collection and subsequent analysis. On the other hand, when a particular phenomenon is investigated according to a specific predetermined methodology, it might not even be possible to begin the analysis until all the relevant data have been collected.

When considering what data you might require, consider carefully the sources, the availability and the possible methods of collecting the data. When considering analysis, think about the tools, techniques and resources required. The different research strategies have often distinctly different methods for data collection and analysis.

Quantitative and qualitative research

Quite a strong distinction is generally made between quantitative and qualitative research. Not only do the appropriate data have different characteristics, but they also require different techniques for their analysis. Natural science has traditionally concentrated on 'hard' quantitative (positivist) analysis, and this was adopted by the human sciences until its shortcomings became evident. As it became increasingly obvious to some researchers that subjective human feelings and emotions were difficult (or impossible) to quantify, qualitative (anti-positivist) analytical methods were evolved, which took more account of the 'soft', personal data (for a useful discussion of the two approaches, see Cohen and Manion, 1994, pp. 6–12 and 22–40). You are not forced, however, to make a choice between the two approaches in your research project. When appropriate, a mixture of quantitative and qualitative research is possible (see Bryman and Burgess, 1994, Chapter 5 for a discussion of linking qualitative and quantitative data analysis). Within certain limits, all types of research strategy are suitable for quantitative and qualitative research.

Figure 7.1 It became increasingly obvious to some researchers that subjective human feelings and emotions were difficult (or impossible) to quantify

Research strategies

The different types of research (or research strategies or methodologies, as they are often termed) are commonly put into five major categories: experimental, survey, archival analysis, historical and case study (I have added several more in Chapter 3 which expand on this categorization). In some projects, more than one may be used, e.g. historical and case study. Each provides an alternative way, with its own logic, of collecting and analysing empirical evidence. Although each has its own advantages and disadvantages, they can all be used for three customary purposes of research: exploration, description and explanation. The different nature of the various strategies can be clearly illustrated by Box 7.1, which indicates the forms of research question that they can appropriately answer, whether they require control over the events studied, and whether they focus on contemporary events.

Box 7.1 Research strategies

Strategy	Form of research question	Requires control over behaviour or events?	Focuses on contemporary events?
Experimental	How, why, what if?	Yes	Yes
Survey	Who, what, where, how many, how much?	No	Yes
Archival analysis	Who, what, where, how many, how much?	No	Yes/No
Historical	How, why?	No	No
Case study	How, why?	No	Yes

Source: based on Yin, 1994, p. 6

The links between perspectives

It should be evident by now that from whichever perspective one looks at research methods, the other two perspectives must be taken into account. The interlinkages can be simply portrayed in a three-dimensional matrix in Diagram 7.1.

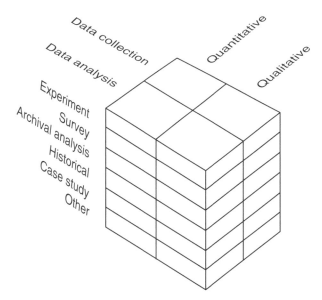

Diagram 7.1 Links between perspectives: matrix diagram

The problem remains of how to provide a clear summary of methods within this matrix, which will enable you to understand the basis of each, and how to help you to decide which methods are likely to be appropriate for your own research project.

We will look first at the pure data collection methods used in literary searches (secondary data) and in archival and historical studies (secondary and primary data) and then at the quest for primary sources normally associated with the survey research strategy and case study research. In all cases, quantitative and qualitative options are discussed, and the important issue of sampling is treated at some length.

Experimental research and associated models are generally interactive in their use and production of data through analysis, so these are considered next. The attributes of a range of pure and quasi-experimental methods are described, as are a diverse range of models suitable for quantitative and qualitative analysis.

The analysis of quantitative data is then considered, particularly statistical techniques, used widely to analyse quantitative data and readily discussed as a distinct analytical method. Statistics are used in the appropriate situations in most of the research strategies, particularly where a large amount of quantitative data is produced and there is a requirement to identify relationships between variables.

The major activities involved in qualitative analytical methods are subsequently described, explaining the essential interplay of data management and theory production, which is a feature of these methods.

COLLECTING SECONDARY DATA

In Chapter 2 of this book, we considered in some detail how to review the literature to form the background to your study. By now you will have gained considerable experience in this method of data collection and recording, but it will probably be useful at this point to go back and check on the main points again. In this chapter, we go on to other types of data collection methods.

When one is doing a historical study (i.e. of any past events or ideas, even the very recent past), three major types of data can be collected. The first is the primary data found in the form of historic artefacts, such as building and ruins, commercial and domestic objects, human and animal remains, works of art etc. The second is primary or secondary data in the form of literary sources, such as histories, commentaries, diaries, letters etc. The third is records, which are contemporary, impersonal recordings of events, situations and states, which may be descriptive or statistical in nature. These, again, may be classified as primary or secondary forms of data, depending on the type of information which you are extracting from them. Any of them can be quantitative or qualitative in nature.

The dividing line between literary sources and records is often difficult to draw sharply. For example, while the Domesday Book (a systematic recording of the inhabitants and contents of every town and village in England in the eleventh century) can be regarded as an impersonal, statistical record, Pepys's diaries, recording the events of the Great Plague and Great Fire of London in the seventeenth century, contain much accurate factual and statistical information interwoven in a narrative full of his own personal views. Artefacts also can sometimes have a literary or record value (consider the hieroglyphics on Egyptian tombs), and historic examples of literature and records are often also regarded as artefacts (as when the paper, watermarks etc. are tested to examine the authenticity of the writings).

One of the main problems faced by the researcher seeking historical and recorded data is that of locating and accessing them. Another is often that of authenticating these sources, and another is the question of interpretation.

Locating historical data is an enormous topic. Activities can involve anything from unearthing city ruins in the desert to rummaging through dusty archives in an obscure library or downloading the latest government statistical data from the Internet. It is difficult to limit a brief description of sources to those which might be relevant to postgraduate student research, as the nature of the detailed subject of research determines the appropriate source and the possible range of subjects is enormous. However, some of the principal sources are shown in Box 7.2.

Box 7.2   Principal sources of secondary information

- *Libraries and archives*   These are generally equipped with sophisticated catalogue systems which facilitate the tracking down of particular pieces of data or enable a trawl to be made to identify anything which may be relevant. International computer networks can make remote searching possible. See your own library specialists for the latest techniques. Apart from these modernized libraries and archives, much valuable historical material is contained in more obscure and less organized collections, in remote areas and old houses and institutions. The attributes of a detective are often required to track down relevant material, and those of a diplomat to gain access to private or restricted collections.
- *Museums and collections*   These often have efficient cataloguing systems which will help your search. However, problems may be encountered with searching and access in less organized and restricted and private collections. Larger museums often have their own research departments which can be of help.
- *Government departments and commercial/professional bodies*   These often hold much statistical information, both current and historic.
- *The Internet*   Rapidly expanding source of information of all types.
- *The field*   Not all historical artefacts are contained in museums. Ancient cities, buildings, archaeological digs etc. are available for study *in situ*. Here, various types of observation will be required to record the required data.

Authentication of historical data can be a complex process, and is usually carried out by experts (one of which you might have to become!). A wide range of techniques is used, for example textual analysis, carbon dating, paper analysis, locational checks, cross-referencing and many others. authentication

Interpretation is an integral part of the analysis of the data, although it can be argued that a correct interpretation of the historical evidence is required before any real analysis can begin. A detailed historical analysis of an event will be worthless if the historical data have been incorrectly interpreted, for example, if the evidence was from a source whose bias was undetected. interpretation

The wealth of purely statistical data contained in the archives, especially those of more recent date, provides a powerful resource for research into many subjects. You will often find, however, that the data recorded are not exactly in the form which you require (for example, when making international comparisons on housing provision, the data might be compiled in different ways in the different countries under consideration). In order to extract the exact data you require you will have to extrapolate from the existing data.

COLLECTING PRIMARY DATA

Survey research depends heavily on the process of sampling and on asking questions, through questionnaires, interviews or observations. You do need to acquire skills to do this properly.

> 'Anyone' can do a bad survey … To do a good survey requires expertise and professionalism at every stage: the design, sampling, questionnaire development, interviewing, analysis and reporting, based on an extensive theoretical framework well grounded in practice and methodological research. (Morton-Williams, 1993, p. 2)

The world is full of potential data. You will, however, only be interested in collecting data which are relevant to your study and specifically required in order to investigate your research problem. Even so, the amount of information you could collect on your specific subject is likely to be enormous, so a method must be used to limit the amount of data you must collect to achieve your aims. The main technique for reducing the scope of your data collection is to study a sample, i.e. a small section of the subject of your study. There are several things one must consider in selecting a sample, so before discussing the different methods of data collection, let us first deal with the issue of sampling.

Sampling

When conducting any kind of survey to collect information, or when choosing some particular cases to study in detail, the question inevitably arises: how representative is the information collected of the whole population?

When we talk about **population** in research, it does not necessarily mean a number of people. 'Population' is a collective term used to describe the total quantity of cases of the type which are the subject of your study. So a population can consist of objects, people or even events, e.g. schools, miners, revolutions. A sample is a selected number of cases in a population.

If you wish to survey the opinions of the members of a small club, there might be no difficulty in getting information from each member, so the results of the survey will represent those of the whole club membership. However, if you wish to assess the opinions of the members of a large trade union, apart from orga-

nizing a national ballot, you will have to devise some way of selecting a **sample** of the members who you are able to question, and who are a fair representation of all the members of the union. Sampling must be done whenever you can gather information from only a fraction of the population of a group or a phenomenon which you want to study. Ideally, you should try to select a sample which is free from bias. You will see that the type of sample you select will greatly affect the reliability of your subsequent generalizations.

There are basically two types of sampling procedure – random and non-random. Random sampling techniques give the most reliable representation of the whole population, while non-random techniques, relying on the judgement of the researcher or on accident, cannot generally be used to make generalizations about the whole population.

Random sampling

The simplest form of random sampling is to represent all the units (sometimes called elements or cases) in a population on slips of paper, put them into a hat, and draw out the slips in a random fashion. As with all samples, the larger the sample, the better. However, for a researcher facing the practicalities of a specific research situation, this example is not very useful, so a set of guidelines is called for.

Firstly, a question should be asked about the nature of the population: is it homogeneous or are there distinctly different classes of cases within it? Different sampling techniques are appropriate for each. The next question to ask is: which process of randomization will be used? The following gives a guide to which technique is suited to the different population characteristics.

Simple random sampling is used when the population is uniform or has similar characteristics in all cases, e.g. a production batch of cars of a particular model from which random samples are selected for testing as to their quality.

When the population is not quite as uniform or one-dimensional as a particular model of a car, simple random sampling is not quite as simple as it sounds. The procedure should aim to guarantee that each element (person, group, class, type etc.) has an equal chance of being selected and that every possible combination of the elements also has an equal chance of being selected. While it is virtually impossible to achieve this in practice, several methods, some using randomly generated numbers, have been devised to produce some form of a fair lottery in which each combination of elements has an equal chance in coming up.

Simple stratified sampling should be used when cases in the population fall into distinctly different categories (strata), e.g. a business whose workforce is divided into the three categories of production, research and management.

simple stratified sampling

With the presence of distinctly different strata in a population, in order to achieve simple randomized sampling, an equally sized randomized sample is obtained from each stratum separately to ensure that each is equally represented. The samples are then combined to form the complete sample from the whole population.

Proportional stratified sampling is used when the cases in a population fall into distinctly different categories (strata) of a known proportion of that population, e.g. a university in which the proportions of the students studying arts and sciences is 61% and 39%.

proportional stratified sampling

When the proportions of the different strata in a population are known, then each stratum must be represented in the same proportions within the overall sample. In order to achieve proportional randomized sampling, a randomized sample is obtained from each stratum separately, sized according to the known proportion of each stratum in the whole population, and then combined as previously to form the complete sample from the population.

In **cluster sampling**, cases in the population form clusters by sharing one or some characteristics but are otherwise as heterogeneous as possible, e.g. travellers using main railway stations. They are all train travellers, with each cluster experiencing a distinct station, but individuals vary as to age, sex, nationality, wealth, social status etc.

cluster sampling

Also known as area sampling, cluster sampling is used when the population is large and spread over a large area. Rather than enumerating the whole population, it is divided into segments, and then several segments are chosen at random. Samples are subsequently obtained from each of these segments using one of the above sampling methods.

Systematic sampling is used when the population is very large and of no known characteristics, e.g. the population of a town.

systematic sampling

Systematic sampling procedures involve the selection of units in a series (for example, on a list) according to a predetermined system. There are many possible systems. Perhaps the simplest is to choose every nth case on a list, for example, every tenth person in a telephone directory or electoral register. In using this system, it is important to pick the first case randomly, i.e. the first case on the list is not necessarily chosen. The type of list is also significant: not everyone in the town owns a telephone or is on the electoral register.

Diagram 7.2 illustrates these sampling techniques.

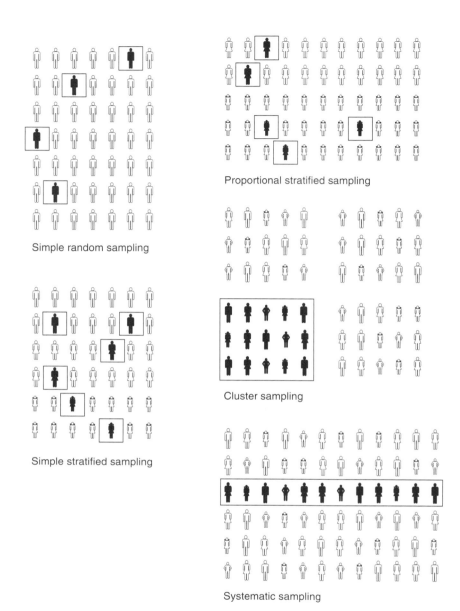

Simple random sampling

Proportional stratified sampling

Simple stratified sampling

Cluster sampling

Systematic sampling

Diagram 7.2 Examples of random sampling methods

Non-random sampling

Although non-random sampling can be useful for certain studies, it provides only a weak basis for generalization.

accidental
sampling

Accidental sampling (or convenience sampling) involves using what is imme-diately available, e.g. studying the building you happen to be in, examining the work practices in your firm etc. There are no ways of checking to see if this kind of sample is in any way representative of others of its kind, so the results of the study can be applied only to that sample.

Used regularly by reporters interviewing on the streets, **quota sampling** is an attempt to balance the sample interviewed by selecting responses from equal numbers of different respondents, e.g. equal numbers from different political parties. This is an unregulated form of sampling, as there is no knowledge of whether the respondents are typical of their parties. For example, Labour respondents might just have come from an extreme left-wing rally.

quota sampling

A useful method of getting information from a sample of the population that you think knows most about a subject is **theoretical sampling**. A study on homelessness could concentrate on questioning people living in the street. This approach is common in qualitative research where statistical inference is not required.

theoretical sampling

Three other methods can be briefly mentioned: *purposive sampling,* where the researcher selects what he/she thinks is a 'typical' sample; *systematic matching sampling,* when two groups of very different size are compared by selecting a number from the larger group to match the number and characteristics of the smaller one; and *snowball techniques,* where you contact a small number of members of the target population and get them to introduce you to others, e.g. of a secret society.

Figure 7.2 Purposive sampling, where the researcher selects what he/she thinks is a 'typical' sample

Having selected a suitable sampling method, the remaining problem is to determine the sample size. There is no easy answer to this problem. If the population is very homogeneous, and the study is not very detailed, then a small sample will give a fairly representative view of the whole. In other cases, you should consider the following.

The greater the accuracy required in the true representation of the population, then the larger the sample must be. The size of the sample also should be in direct relationship to the number of questions asked, the amount of detail required in the analysis of the data, and the number of controls introduced. It is generally accepted that conclusions reached from the study of a large sample are more convincing than those from a small one. However, the preference for a large sample must be balanced against the practicalities of the research resources, i.e. cost, time and effort.

The amount of variability within the population (technically known as the standard deviation) is another important factor in determining a suitable sample size. Obviously, in order that every sector of a diverse population is adequately represented, a larger sample will be required than if the population were more homogeneous.

If statistical tests are to be used to analyse the data, there are usually minimum sample sizes specified from which any significant results can be obtained. A later part of this chapter deals briefly with statistical methods.

A simple method of clarifying the likely size of sample required in a study is to set up a table which cross-references the variability in the population with the number of variables you wish to study. Box 7.3 shows a table for a study of the effect of the number of drinks on driving performance around a course delineated by bollards. Dixon (1987) suggests that for a very simple survey, at least five cases are required in each cell (i.e. $12 \times 5 = 60$). Obviously, if the variables are split into smaller units of measurement, i.e. the numbers of drinks are divided into seven units, then the overall size of the sample must be increased. They also suggest that at least 30 cases are required for even the most elementary kinds of analysis.

Box 7.3   Variables and variability: example

Number of drinks (variables)	Number of bollards collided with (standard deviation of population)		
	Less than 3	3–8	More than 8
0			
2			
4			
6			

Source: adapted from Dixon, 1987, p. 152

Although this table shows a very simple example, the method can be used in more complex cases to provide a guide to an acceptable sample size by clarifying the standard deviation of the population and the number of variables which will be investigated.

…

No sample will be exactly representative of a population. If different samples, using identical methods, are taken from the same population, there are bound to be differences in the mean (average) values of each sample owing to the chance selection of different individuals. The measured difference between the mean value of a sample and that of the population is called the **sampling error**.

sampling error

EXERCISE 7.1

Answer the following questions:

1 Why do researchers use sampling procedures?
2 Why should you not make generalizations about a group by the observation of a single case? Are there instances when this is done? Give one example.
3 (a) What are the two basic types of sampling procedure, and what is the difference between them?
   (b) When is it appropriate to use them?
4 What factors must you examine when deciding on an appropriate random sampling method?
5 What are the critical issues which determine the appropriate sample size?

Thought

Perhaps in your own research project you will not need to do any sampling. However, because the need to select samples is so common it is essential that you understand the principles involved, even if only to argue why you did not find it necessary to use a sampling method. Remember that any form of generalization from particular cases implies that those cases are somehow representative of the wider whole.

Questionnaires and diaries

Asking questions is an obvious method of collecting both quantitative and qualitative information from people. Using a questionnaire enables you to organize the questions and receive replies without actually having to talk to every respondent. As a method of data collection, the questionnaire is a very flexible tool, but it must be used carefully in order to fulfil the requirements of a particular piece of research. While there are whole books on the art of questioning and questionnaires, it is possible to isolate a number of important factors to consider before deciding to use a questionnaire.

Before examining its form and content, we will briefly consider why one might choose this form of data collection, and ways in which the questionnaire can be delivered.

One of the main features of a questionnaire is its impersonality. The questions are fixed, i.e. they do not change according to how the replies develop, and they are the same for each respondent, and the person posing the questions is remote. The responses can be completely anonymous, allowing potentially embarrassing questions to be asked with a fair chance of getting a true reply. Another feature is that there is no geographical limitation with regard to the location of the respondents: they can be anywhere in the world as long as they can be reached by post. Questionnaires can be a relatively economic method, in cost and time, of soliciting data from a large number of people. Time for checking facts and pondering on the questions can also be taken by the respondents, which tends to lead to more accurate information.

There are two basic methods of delivering questionnaires, personally and by post. The advantages of personal delivery are that respondents can be helped to overcome difficulties with the questions, and that personal persuasion and reminders by the researcher can ensure a high response rate. The reasons why some people refuse to answer the questionnaire can also be established, and there is a possibility of checking on responses if they seem odd or incomplete. This personal involvement of the researcher enables more complicated questionnaires to be devised. Obviously, there are problems in both time and geographical location which limit the scope and extent to which this method of delivery can be used.

Postal questionnaires do not suffer from these two limitations. However, the most serious problem is that the rate of response is difficult to predict or control, particularly if there is no system of follow-up. The pattern of non-response can have a serious effect on the validity of the sample by introducing bias into the data collected. Cost is often a determining factor in choosing postal distribution: it is cheap compared with interviewing. It might also be the only method of questioning people spread over a large area or situated in relatively inaccessible regions.

There are simple rules to devising a questionnaire, though it is not always easy to carry them out perfectly. The rules are shown in Box 7.4.

pilot study   A questionnaire should be pre-tested on a small number of people in what is called a **pilot study**. It is best to test it on people of a type similar to that of the intended sample, so as to anticipate any problems of comprehension or other sources of confusion.

When sending out the questionnaire, you should courteously invite the recipients to complete it, and encourage them by explaining the purpose of the survey, how the results could be of benefit to them, and how little time it will take to

1   You must establish exactly which variables you wish to gather data about, and how these variables can be assessed. This will enable you to list the questions you need to ask (and those that you do not!) and to formulate the questions precisely in order to elicit the responses that are required.

2   The language must be unmistakably clear and unambiguous and make no inappropriate assumptions. Leedy gives an illuminating example of a seemingly simple question which is quite ambiguous: 'How many cigarettes do you smoke each day: more than 25, 25–16, 15–11, 10–6, 5–1, none?' (1989, p. 142). There is no problem answering this if you are a regular smoker, but what if you smoke only at weekends, at parties or in the holidays?

3   In order to enhance the response rate, questions generally should be kept simple, and the questionnaires kept as short as possible. This minimizes the effort required by the respondent.

4   Clear and professional presentation is another essential factor in encouraging a good response.

5   Consider how you will process the information from the completed forms. This may influence the layout of the questionnaire, e.g. by including spaces for codes and scoring.

complete. Simple instructions on how to complete the responses are also required. Some form of thanks and appreciation of their efforts should be included at the end. If you needed to be sure of a response from particular persons, you should send a preliminary letter, with a reply-paid response card, to enquire whether the person is willing to complete the questionnaire before you send it (Leedy, 1989, pp. 145–8; see also Moser and Kalton, 1971, Chapter 13; Hague, 1993; and Oppenheim, 1992).

You can think of the use of a *diary* in research as a kind of self-administered questionnaire. The form of text can be totally unstructured or can be a response to a series of questions. Although diaries can provide a huge amount of data for very little effort from the researcher, the content can be quite haphazard depending on the interpretation of the task by the respondent. Bias is especially prone to creep in if the respondents believe that some actions will be taken as a result of the contents, and therefore record events in such a way that might be beneficial to them. It is therefore important to ensure that respondents are clear as to what they have to do, why and when, and that they agree to full co-operation. Confidentiality is obviously a major issue.

A diary method can be used as a substitute for observation where direct observation is difficult or impossible, e.g. in intimate or private situations. It can also be usefully used as a precursor to interviews: the information gained will provide pointers to an appropriate list of questions to be asked in the interview (Robson, 1993, pp. 254–5).

Interviews: structured, semi-structured and open

While questionnaire surveys are relatively cheap and are effective in preventing the personality of the interviewer having effects on the results, they do have certain limitations. They are not suitable for questions which require probing to obtain adequate information, as they should only contain simple, one-stage questions. There are also problems in gaining the required response from the complete sample, especially as the questionnaires tend to be returned by the more literate sections of the population. While interviewing is suitable for quantitative data collection, it is particularly useful when qualitative data are required.

The use of interviews to question samples of people is a very flexible tool with a wide range of applications. There are two main methods of conducting interviews; face-to-face and telephone.

Face-to-face interviews can be carried out in a variety of situations – in the home, at work, outdoors, on the move (e.g. while travelling) – and can be used to question members of the general public, experts or leaders, specific segments of society, e.g. elderly or disabled people, ethnic minorities, both singly and in groups. Interviews can be used for subjects both general or specific in nature and even, with the correct preparation, for very sensitive topics. They can be one-off or, for longitudinal studies, repeated several times over a period to track developments. The interviewer is in a good position to be able to judge the quality of the responses of the subjects, to notice if a question has not been properly understood, and to reassure and encourage the respondent to be full in his/her answers. Visual signs, such as nods, smiles etc., are valuable tools in promoting complete responses.

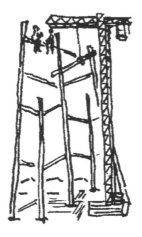

Figure 7.3 Face-to-face interviews can be carried out in a variety of situations

Telephone interviews avoid the necessity of travelling to the respondents, and all the time and problems associated with contacting people personally. With wider telephone ownership, particularly in developed countries, it is often possible to contact a suitable sample of the target population by this method. Surveys can be carried out more quickly than face-to-face, especially if the questionnaire is short (20–30 minutes is the accepted maximum). However, visual aids cannot be used to explain questions, and important visual clues between interviewer and interviewee, e.g. eye contact, smiling, puzzled looks, are absent. Non-response tends to be 5–10% higher on telephone surveys than with equivalent face-to-face surveys (Morton-Williams, 1993, p. 156). It is interesting to note that voice quality is an important factor in successful phone interviews. Interviewers with the highest success rates spoke rapidly and loudly, used standard pronunciation and sounded competent and confident (1993, p. 169).

The structuring of the interview depends on the type of information you wish to elicit. For very precise answers to very precise questions, used for quantitative and statistical analysis, a tightly structured interview is required with closed questions formulated in a method similar to a questionnaire. At the other extreme, if you need to explore a situation and wish to get information which you cannot predict, a very open and unstructured form of interview is appropriate. A semi-structured interview falls between the two, achieving defined answers to defined questions, while leaving time for further development of those answers, and including more open-ended questions. The most important issue when you set up an interview is to know exactly what you want to achieve by it, and what you intend to do with the information gained, and to choose the appropriate structure of interview to achieve this.

Interviews, because of their flexibility, are a useful method of obtaining information and opinions from experts during the early stages of your research project. It is important, however initial your research enquiry, to devise an efficient method of recording what is discussed in the interview and to form a simple structure for organizing the data collected. These early interviews often provide very important information which helps not only to indicate your future research direction, but also to identify and prioritize issues. You should aim to achieve a balance between open questioning to explore issues, and obtaining responses which can subsequently be easily examined and compared.

There is a great difference in technique for conducting interviews 'cold' with the general public and interviewing officials or experts by appointment. In both cases, however, the personality and bearing of the interviewer are of great importance. There is not space here to go into detail about the different techniques which should be acquired for the various interview situations. These are examined in detail in Morton-Williams (1993). What must be stressed, however, is the need for preparation on the part of the interviewer, both in the groundwork (i.e. writing letters for appointments, explaining the purpose of the interview) and in presenting the interview, cultivating confidence, friendliness, good appearance etc. and selecting an appropriate method of recording the responses (tape recording, writing notes, completing forms etc.).

Standardized scales and tests

These can perhaps be seen as versions of structured interviews or of self-completion questionnaires. There is a wide range of standardized scales and tests that have been devised by social scientists and psychologists to establish people's abilities, attitudes, aptitudes, opinions etc. A well known example of one of these is the IQ or intelligence test. The objective of the tests is usually to measure in some way the abilities etc. of the subjects according to a standardized scale, so that easy comparisons can be made. One of the main problems facing the researcher is to select or devise a suitable scale for measuring the often rather abstract concepts under scrutiny, such as attitude to school meals, military service, capital punishment etc.

A common precaution to prevent oversimplification of responses is to ask many questions about the same topic, from a variety of different angles. This form of triangulation helps to build up a more complete picture of complex issues. The use of arbitrary scales should be avoided. It is safer to use well tried and tested standard scales, of which there are several, each taking different approaches according to the results aimed at. To mention a few: the Likert scale, one of the most common, which uses a summated rating approach; the Thurlstone scale, which aims to produce an equal appearing interval scale; the Guttman scale, a unidimensional scale where items have a cumulative property; and the semantic differential scale, where the subjective meaning of a concept to a respondent is gauged, rather than his/her attitude towards it. At this stage you are unlikely to need to know the details of these testing methods, unless they form a central part of your research. If you want to know more, Robson (1993, pp. 255–68) gives a useful succinct introduction and further references.

Accounts

Accounts is a method of qualitative data collection, used mainly in sociological research; it seeks to find information on people's actions and feelings by asking them to give their own interpretation, or account, of what they experience. This form of study is called 'ethnogenic', and is founded on the belief that human beings are plan-making, self-monitoring agents, who are aware of goals and deliberately consider the best ways of achieving them (Cohen and Manion, 1994, p. 205; and if you want a more comprehensive account of the ethnogenic approach see Harré, 1977). Accounts can consist of a variety of data sources: a person's spoken explanations, behaviour (such as gestures), personal records of experiences and conversations, letters and diaries. As long as the accounts are authentic, there should be no reason why they cannot be used as an argued explanation of people's actions.

Since the information must come directly from the respondents, care must be taken to avoid leading questions, excessive guidance and other factors which may cause distortion. Checking the authenticity of the accounts is an important element in this form of data collection. This can be done by cross-checking with other people involved in the events, examining the physical records of the events (e.g. papers, documents etc.) and checking with the respondents during the account gathering process.

The transformation of the collected accounts into working documents which can be coded and analysed is the next procedure to be considered. At this stage, additional checks on the authenticity of the accounts can be made as well as on the reliability of the transformation. The documents can then be analysed qualitatively or quantitatively, depending on the type of research problem and the nature of the enquiry. More details of this process can be seen in Brown and Sime (1981).

Observations and physical surveys

Observation is a method of recording conditions, events and activities through the non-inquisitorial involvement of the researcher. The non-participant researcher takes a detached stance to the phenomena, and aims to be 'invisible', either in fact or in effect (i.e. by being ignored). The participant observer is seen as involved in the process or activity. Observation can also be used for recording the nature or conditions of objects, e.g. buildings. This type of observation is often referred to as a survey, and can range from a preliminary visual survey to a detailed survey using a range of instruments for measurement. As an activity, as opposed to a method, observation is of course required in many research situations, for example, observing the results of experiments, the behaviour of models and even the reactions of people to questions in an interview. Observation can be used to record both quantitative and qualitative data.

Observation can record whether people act differently to what they say or intend. They can sometimes demonstrate their understanding of a process better by their actions than by verbally explaining their knowledge. For example, a machine operator will probably demonstrate more clearly his/her understanding of the techniques of operating the machine by working with it than by verbal explanation.

Observation is not limited to the visual sense. Any sense, e.g. smell, touch, hearing, can be involved, and these need not be restricted to the range perceptible by the human senses. A microscope or telescope can be used to extend the capacity of the eye, just as a moisture meter can increase sensitivity to the feeling of dampness. You can probably think of instruments which have been developed in every discipline to extend the observational limits of the human senses.

On the one hand, observations of objects can be a quick and efficient method of gaining preliminary knowledge or making a preliminary assessment of its state or condition. For example, after an earthquake, a quick visual assessment of the amount and type of damage to buildings can be made before a detailed survey is undertaken.

On the other hand, observation can be very time-consuming and difficult when the activity observed is not constant (i.e. much time can be wasted waiting for things to happen, or so much happens at once that it is impossible to observe it all and record it). Instrumentation can sometimes be devised to overcome the problem of infrequent or spasmodic activity, e.g. automatic cameras and other sensors.

Certain basic hints on how to carry out observations are given in Box 7.5.

Box 7.5   Hints on how to do observations

1   Make sure you know what you are looking for. Events and objects are usually complicated and much might seem to be relevant to your study. Identify the variables that you need to study, and concentrate on these.
2   Devise a simple and efficient method of recording the information accurately. Rely as much as possible on ticking boxes or circling numbers, particularly if you need to record fast-moving events. Obviously, you can leave yourself more time when observing static objects to notate or draw the data required. Record the observations as they happen. Memories of detailed observations fade quickly.
3   Use instrumentation when appropriate or necessary. Instruments which make an automatic record of their measurements are to be preferred in many situations.
4   If possible, process the information as the observations progress. This can help to identify critical matters which need study in greater detail, and others which prove to be unnecessary.
5   If you are doing covert observations, plan in advance what to do if your presence is discovered, to avoid potentially embarrassing or even dangerous situations.

Using the internet for primary research

The use of the Internet to find secondary data has been discussed in Chapter 2. But can it be used to gain primary data? Yes: according to Hewson et al. (2003, p. 78), surveys and questionnaires are the most widely implemented web-based methodology. Although the typical web-based survey involves a structured questionnaire, they maintain that the Internet can be used for the whole range of surveys, from structured questionnaires to unstructured interviews, and even observational studies and experimental designs. However, there is, as yet, little published research on the important factors, such as response rate, bias, non-response, sincerity and completion rates. In the field of marketing, however, there has been plenty of discussion on the subject of maximizing responses.

The attractions of using a web-based survey are that it can potentially reach an enormous number of respondents anywhere in the world, the costs and time involved in distribution and collection of questionnaires are minimized, and analysis of data that are already in electronic format is made easy. Anonymity of the researcher and respondent are also enhanced, which can help to overcome bias engendered by nationality, sex, age etc. and to encourage frankness and higher response rates.

But there are particular problems that must be faced, such as lack of control by the researcher over the quality of the responses that can lead to questions about the reliability and validity of the data. There is also the issue of sampling. The most common approach uses a non-random sampling technique, making announcements on websites or newsgroups to recruit volunteer participants. This raises concerns about the generalizability of the results, as there is little knowledge either of the population or of the sample reached. Better control and more reliable sampling techniques can be applied by using e-mail as the medium of the survey. The problem then posed is how to compile a suitable list of addresses.

E-mail and, even better, 'chatrooms' lend themselves to conducting interviews over the web. Although the extra-linguistic cues are missing in this form of communication, there might be advantages due to the anonymity of the persons taking part in the discussion. As for observation studies, the written medium of the web limits these to mainly linguistic projects focusing on Internet communication itself. Compared with more conventional observation studies, the observer presence bias is removed and the researcher is able to access a wide range of material to locate something suitable for the project. Non-language, behavioural observation research can be devised using simulation, gaming or role-play techniques. The use of webcams for direct observations is as yet limited by technical constraints. Web-based experiments using printed material, video, sound or interactive tasks or games are possible if the design allows the researcher to manipulate the independent variables in order to measure the effect on the dependent variables.

There is not enough space here to consider this medium for research in detail. A host of technical issues must be faced as well as those of challenges to the quality of the research itself. These are all comprehensively explained by Hewson et al. (2003), whose list of ten general principles for use in developing an internet survey is reproduced in Box 7.6.

1   Collect information about participant demographics (gender, education, income, nationality, occupation, and frequency of Internet use).
2   Aim for sampling procedures that allow measurement of sampling frame and response rates.
3   Control access to the survey (for example, by using passwords).
4   Send a preliminary request for participation prior to sending the survey itself.
5   Include an introduction to the survey that gives affiliation details, and provides a professional appearance.
6   Aim for simplicity and clarity in layout and presentation.
7   Keep procedures and software requirements as low-tech as possible given the nature of the study.
8   Undertake extensive piloting across different platforms.
9   Maintain participant anonymity unless it is essential to the study to obtain participant identity.
10   Use server-side scripting (as opposed to the 'mailto:' command) in order to collect data if resources allow. (Hewson et al., 2003, p. 85)

EXERCISE 7.2

1   What is wrong with these questions, designed to be part of a questionnaire?

(a)   Where do you come from?
(b)   How many children do you have? Circle one number: 0, 1, 2, 3, 4.
(c)   Do you like modern architecture? Score your liking by giving a number between 0 and 100: 0 = dislike very much, 100 = like very much.
(d)   When did you last drink a bottle of champagne: yesterday, last week, last month, last year?
(e)   Which one of the following concepts – war, society, public relations, revolution, education – is described in this text: 'the temporary outcome of the attempt to limit the infinite play of differences in the site of the social, to domesticate the potential infinitude of symbiosis corroborated by the principle of indeterminacy of meaning, and to embrace it within the finitude of an order'?

2   What are the main differences between structured interviews, semi-structured interviews, open interviews and accounts?
3   Are sampling techniques used only when aiming to get representative information from a population consisting of people; for example, when making a survey of user attitudes?

Thought

When making generalizations from the conclusions of your research, it is most likely that you have come to your conclusions on the basis of what you have learned from only a few cases amongst all possible cases. It is virtually impossible to examine every case of any phenomenon, so sampling, in one form or other, is one of the most prevalent features of research.

COMBINED DATA GENERATION AND ANALYSIS

As a method of analysing phenomena, and gaining more information about them, it is sometimes possible artificially to create a microcosm of the real world, where only the elements which are regarded as important are included, so that these can be studied in detail by directly manipulating the variables. The laboratory experiment is such a method. There are many other locations where experiments can be carried out, but the laboratory situation is the one which provides the greatest possibilities for control. Use of models is another method of obtaining information about the real world in a controlled situation. In these methods, the collection and analysis of data are inextricably linked. The preliminary data on which the experiments and models are based are used to create new data which, in their turn, can be used for further analysis. Box 7.7 summarizes the difference between experiments and models.

Box 7.7   The difference between an experiment and a model

- An experiment is used to examine actual phenomena, which are controlled in scope and size.
- A model provides an artificial version of the phenomena for study, either by mimicking it at a reduced scale or by abstracting it diagrammatically or mathematically (often using computer techniques).

Experiments are powerful and versatile techniques which can be designed to fulfil virtually any of the analytical functions mentioned in the next main section.

Figure 7.4 Experiments are powerful and versatile techniques

Generally, experiments are designed and carried out in order to examine causes and effects (studying dependent and independent variables), and are used to find explanations for them, e.g. what happens if? And why? The design of the experiments depends on the type of data required, the level of reliability of the data required, and practical matters associated with the problem under investigation.

Checks should be carried out on both experiments and models to test whether the assumptions made are valid. In experiments, a control group is used to provide a 'baseline' against which the effects of the experimental treatment may be evaluated. The control group is one that is identical (as near as possible) to the experimental group, but does not receive experimental treatment (for example, in a medical experiment, the control group will be given placebo pills instead of the medicated pills).

Experiments

Campbell and Stanley (1963, pp. 171–246) divided experiments into four general types as shown in Box 7.8.

Box 7.8   Types of experiments

1   Pre-experimental designs.
2   True experimental designs.
3   Quasi-experimental designs.
4   Correlational and *ex post facto* designs.

Here is a brief summary of the most important experiment designs within each type, with a brief example using the same context to illustrate each. (See Leedy, 1989, Chapter 10; Neale and Liebert, 1986, Chapter 7; Cohen and Manion, 1994, Chapter 8, for a more comprehensive explanation. Most books on research methods have a chapter devoted to experiment design.)

Pre-experiment

- *One-shot case study (after only)*   This is the most primitive type of design where observations are carried out only after the experiment, lacking any control or check. Example: a building material sample is painted and then tested for water absorption; low absorption is observed; conclusion, paint prevents water absorption? (In all these examples, the sample could be multiple, i.e. a group.)
- *One group pre-test and post-test (before–after) design*   Here the group is examined before the experiment takes place. Example: a material sample is

tested for water absorption before painting; after drying it is painted; then it is again tested for water absorption; conclusion, painting reduces absorption in materials?

- *Static group comparison (before–after) design*   Similar to the previous design except that a control group is introduced. Example: two material samples are taken at random; the experimental sample is painted, the control sample is left untreated; both are tested for water absorption and the results compared; conclusion, painting reduces absorption?

It is evident that in these designs, lack of control of the variables can seriously affect the outcomes, e.g. what happens if some of the unpainted material samples do not absorb water?

True experiment

- *Pre-test/post-test control group (before–after) design*   This is the commonest true experimental design. Example: a pair of material samples is selected in the same random procedure; both are tested for water absorption; after drying, one is painted, the other is left untreated; the samples are tested again; the results are compared. Best results are gained if both samples achieve identical results in the pre-test.
- *Solomon four-group (before–after) design*   This is a refinement of the previous design, using four samples, which additionally tests the effects of the pre-test. Example: four material samples are selected in the same random procedure. Two are pre-tested for water absorption; one of these is painted. Of the other two, one is painted; all four are tested for water absorption; the results are compared. It will be detectable if the pre-test wetting of two of the samples affected their subsequent performance by comparing them with those which were not pre-tested.
- *Post-test only control group (after only) design*   This is used when a pre-test is not possible, e.g. in a one-off situation like an earthquake or during a continuous development or, as in this example, if the pre-test would destroy the material. Example: a pair of building material samples (e.g. delicate plaster mouldings) is selected in the same random procedure; one is painted, the other left unpainted; both are tested for water absorption; the results are compared. The validity of this test critically depends on the randomness of the sample.

Quasi-experiment

- *Non-randomized control group, pre-test/post-test design*   When random selection cannot be achieved, the control group and the experimental group should be matched as nearly as possible. Example: two sets of adjacent unpainted panels on a building façade are tested for water absorption; one set is painted, the other left unpainted; both are retested for water absorption and the results compared.

- *Time-series experiment* Repeated identical experiments are made, then one variable is changed to produce a new outcome, and the new experiment is repeated, to check if the variable consistently creates the changed outcome. Example: the water absorption of a sample of an unpainted building material is repeatedly tested; the same sample is painted; the water absorption of the painted sample is repeatedly tested. The danger with this design is that, over time, other unknown factors might affect the results (e.g. the water used in these tests may break down the material in the building sample and make it less absorbent).

- *Control group, time-series experiment* The same process as above, but with a parallel control group which does not undergo the variable change. Example: as above but with a parallel sample which remains unpainted and is used to compare outcomes.

Correlational and ex post facto *designs*

- *Correlational design* This is prone to misuse. After a correlation between two factors is statistically proved, a claim is made that one factor has caused the other. Life is rarely so simple! There may be many other factors that have not been recognized in the research, one or some of which could be the cause or could have contributed to the cause.

- *Ex post facto design* This is not really an experimental approach in that the investigation begins after the event has occurred, so no control over the event is possible. The search for the cause of the event, e.g. a plane crash or the outbreak of an unknown disease, relies on the search for, and analysis of, relevant data. The most likely cause has to be discovered from amongst all possible causes, so there are many opportunities to search in the wrong area! This is a common form of scientific investigation, and needs the skills of a detective in addition to those of a scientist.

Validity

The quality of data gained from true experimental design should genuinely reflect the influence of the controlled variables and should enable generalizations to be made beyond the immediate experimental situation. The level of sophistication of the design and the extent of control determine the **internal validity** of the experimental design, and the extent of the legitimate generalizability of the results gives a rating for the **external validity** of the design.

internal validity

external validity

Cohen and Manion (1994, pp. 170–2) list the factors which cause a threat to internal and external validity, and which are worth summarizing briefly here. Firstly, those affecting *internal validity*:

- *History*   Unnoticed interfering events between pre-test and post-test observations may affect results.
- *Maturation*   When studied over time, the subjects of the experiment may change in ways not included in the experimental variables, e.g. samples deteriorate with age.
- *Statistical regression*   The tendency for extreme results in the tests to get closer to the mean in repeat tests.
- *Testing*   Pre-tests can inadvertently alter the original properties of the subject of the experiment.
- *Instrumentation*   Faulty or inappropriate measuring instruments and shortcomings in the performance of human observers lead to inaccurate data.
- *Selection*   Bias may occur in the samples due to faulty or inadequate sampling methods.
- *Experimental mortality*   Dropout of experimental subjects (not necessarily through death!) during the course of a long running experiment tends to result in bias in what remains of the sample.

And secondly, those affecting *external validity*:

- *Vague identification of independent variables*   Subsequent researchers will find it impossible to replicate the experiment.
- *Faulty sampling*   If the sample is only representative of what (or who) is available in the population rather than of the whole population, the results cannot be generalized to that whole population.
- *Hawthorne effect*   People tend to react differently if they know that they are the subject of an experiment.
- *Inadequate operationalization of dependent variables*   Faulty generalization of results beyond the scope of the experiment (e.g. in the above examples illustrating experimental designs, predicting the effects of painting with any kind of paint while using only one type in the experiment).
- *Sensitization to experimental conditions*   Subjects can learn ways of manipulating the results during an experiment.
- *Extraneous factors*   These can cause unnoticed effects on the outcome of the experiment, reducing the generalizability of the results.

Models

Models are a method of selectively mimicking reality in a form which can be manipulated, in order to obtain data about the effects of the manipulations. Broadbent (1988, p. 91) described the three basic functions of models to be: descriptive, concept structuring and exploratory. He split these basic functions into more detailed ones which include almost the entire list of reasons for doing analysis given in the next section. Box 7.9 shows Broadbent's typology.

1 *Descriptive* Isomorphic, i.e. a true representation in all detail of the object (e.g. a wiring diagram); homomorphic, i.e. a simplified representation showing a selection of features (e.g. a tourist road map).
2 *Concept structuring* Data defining; data collecting; data ordering; data predicting.
3 *Exploratory* Hypothesis testing; hypothesis generating.

In order to make a model, it is necessary to understand the system which lies behind the phenomena in reality, to understand which are the important variables and how they interact. The actual form of the model can be diagrammatic, physical or mathematical. Qualitative models emphasize the relationships between entities without trying to quantify them, while quantitative models not only describe the relationships but also accurately measure their magnitude.

Checks should be carried out on models to test whether the assumptions made in order to set up the model are valid. The results obtained by using a model should also be checked against data collected from the actual case which is being modelled.

Diagrammatic models

A simple method of representing systems is the creation of diagrams. A wide range of techniques can be used to portray various aspects of a system; most of them are qualitative.

- *Multiple cause diagram* Shows the causal links between variables in a system. The links can be sequential or contain loops.
- *Systems map* A 'snapshot' showing the components of a system and its environment, revealing any subsystems and significant overlaps.
- *Influence diagram* Represents the main structural features of a situation and the important relationships (not necessarily causal) that exist among them.
- *Sign-graph diagrams* A development of the multiple cause diagram; it records positive or negative causal links, and situations of positive and negative feedback.
- *Cognitive mapping* A diagrammatic record of a person's thoughts about a particular issue or situation, showing their structure and the connections between ideas and attitudes.
- *Organization charts* Show the paths of command and authorization in an organization.
- *Critical path diagram* Displays the sequence of events and activities in a process, and reveals the critical elements. These are useful in predicting, planning and controlling.

- *Linear responsibility diagram*   A development of the critical path diagram to show responsibilities of, and relationships between, the participants.
- *Technical drawings and maps*   Reduce to two dimensions and simplify actual objects or systems (e.g. London Underground map).
- *Flow chart*   Not so much the portrayal of a system as a step-by-step set of rules to calculate or instruct. This is a form of algorithm.

This is a good place to explain the term **algorithm** – a process or set of rules used for calculation or problem solving, especially using a computer. The detailed work of the Russian mathematician A. A. Markov (*Theory of Algorithms*, 1954) described the main features of different types of algorithm as in Box 7.10.

algorithm

Box 7.10   Main features of an algorithm

1 *Definite*   The prescription for the algorithm is precise and comprehensible.
2 *General*   It is possible to start from the given data, but the data themselves may vary within certain limits.
3 *Conclusive*   The algorithm is oriented towards some desired result, obtained with certainty, provided that the proper kind of data has been fed in.

Algorithms can be portrayed graphically or mathematically (often computer based for ease of use (see Broadbent, 1988, p. 326)). An example is a formula that summarizes the interior conditions that lead to the feeling of climatic comfort, with factors such as air temperature, humidity, air movement, amount of clothing, etc. (see the section on mathematical models below).

Diagramming is commonly used to explore a real-life situation in order to investigate what the important variables in the system are and the manner in which they influence each other. It promotes understanding of complicated situations and interrelationships. The understanding gained can often then be used in the construction of a physical or mathematical model.

Physical models

These are three-dimensional representations of an object or building at a reduced scale. The lavish architectural display model is a familiar spectacle in the developer's boardroom, but is not usually the type of model which is useful for research purposes. Models devised for the purpose of research must be specifically designed to test the variables which are central to the problem being investigated. Thus, a model made to test the acoustics of a concert hall is very different to one made to test mechanical methods of raising and lowering the stage floor elements. They can be qualitative or quantitative in nature.

One of the main problems when using spatial physical models for producing quantitative data is the problem of scaling. It raises the question: do materials and forms of energy behave identically at any scale? Usually, the answer is no. In a model made to test the acoustics of a concert hall, the sound frequency and amplitude of the sound source may have to be scaled down, as may the texture and density of the materials used to line the hall. In mechanical models, the different behaviour of materials at a small scale must be compensated for. To overcome the scaling problem, full-scale prototypes are used where possible.

Mathematical models

These are invariably quantitative models and are divided into two major categories, deterministic and stochastic models. These categories relate to the predictability of the input: deterministic models deal only with predetermined inputs, whereas stochastic models require unpredictable inputs to produce satisfactory results (often produced by using a random number generator). To make this clearer, here are two examples. A mathematical model which calculates the heat loss through walls of different materials and constructions is likely to be a deterministic model: the inputs for the insulation qualities of the materials will be known, as will the temperature difference between inside and outside etc. Another term for this type of model is an algorithm. A model which investigates the effects of a traffic-light control system in a town centre might be designed on a stochastic model, determining the traffic flows from each direction randomly, in order to test the system under widely different and unpredictable conditions.

The computer is an invaluable tool in the construction of mathematical models. Spreadsheet programs provide a systematic two-dimensional framework for devising models, and furnish facilities for cross-calculations, random number generation, setting of variable values, and the build-up of series of formulae.

Scope and limitations of models

The essential qualities of a model are that it should be constructed for a particular purpose and that it should, in some way, reduce the complexity of the real situation. It is important that the purposes of the model and the assumptions on which it is built are clearly enunciated. The scope of applicability should also be described. You should note that the same object or event can be modelled in a number of different ways. However, because each model is devised for a particular purpose, it is potentially dangerous to use it for some other, unrelated, purpose. It could also produce misleading information if it is used beyond the range or area of applicability for which it was designed. Models are never perfect because of the many difficulties faced by the researcher. The main factors which limit the capability of models to accurately mimic reality are as follows.

Figure 7.5 The essential qualities of a model are that it should be constructed for a particular purpose

- *Data limitations* It is obviously impossible to incorporate a relevant variable into a quantitative model if you have no measurement of its values. If you have incomplete or only approximate values, then you will have to rely on guesswork to complete the information. Additionally, if you do not know in which ways the variables interact with each other, then your model will require much conjecture to complete it. However, it is easy to overstate the effects of insufficient information about the variables. If the purpose of the model is to study its behaviour rather than to predict future values of variables, the variables can be substantially changed (say 20% either way) without altering the behaviour significantly.
- *Structural limits* If incorrect assumptions are made about the relevance of the variables and the manner in which they interact, then the model will fail, sooner or later, to accurately reflect reality. For example, the early models of the solar system, devised on the basis of the earth at the centre, failed to represent the future motions of the planets accurately. Thus, it is wrong to assume, however closely the model reflects reality, that it is the 'right one'. It is possible that the effects of other variables, not included in the model, could produce the same results. It is important to check predictions of the model against the field observations of the real situation. However, it is not necessary that the model be perfectly correct in order to be useful.
- *Chaos* It has long been assumed that if a system was accurately modelled, the behaviour of the model would closely reflect reality. Any small errors in the initial settings of the model (say of 1%) would produce only correspondingly small deviations in the results compared with reality (say 1–2%). It is now known that some sorts of systems do not behave in this way, and that tiny changes in the variables' values can result in dramatic subsequent changes. These systems, which are infinitely sensitive to starting values, are called

'chaotic', not so much because they lack order but because they are unpredictable. Chaotic systems are virtually impossible to model in order to make long range predictions (as weather forecasters and investors in the stock market will be quick to tell you).

EXERCISE
7.3

1   What types of experiment do you think it would be possible to carry out in each of the following situations? Describe the different steps that you would take in carrying out the experiment.

(a)   You are a lecturer of art, and you wish to test during one of your lectures how many names of artists the students can remember after having seen named pictures by them during the lecture.
(b)   You have been given a collection of different types of clay brick from around the world, and you want to establish which type of brick is affected by frost after it has been soaked in water. You have a tank of water and a large deep-freeze cabinet at your disposal. Some bricks are baked and others are not.
(c)   You have designed a new type of bed which you maintain makes people sleep longer than other beds. You wish to demonstrate, by a scientific experiment, that this is the case.

2   What kind of models could you use to demonstrate the operations within:

(a)   the solar system
(b)   central government
(c)   a building
(d)   the personal relationships within a family
(e)   a business contract?

3   In the following experiments and models, what sort of data will be needed and what sort of data will be produced? Will it be possible to use the data produced to feed back into the experiment or model in order to increase its precision?

(a)   An experiment to test how long it takes to hard-boil different sizes of freshly laid eggs.
(b)   A physical model of a bed-sitting room with a model set of standard furniture, to investigate how many furniture arrangements are possible in the given space.
(c)   A computer model which mimics the journeys of buses on a bus route in order to investigate when and why they tend to arrive at the bus stop in threes.
(d)   An experiment to test how the framing of glass affects the strength of windows during impact.

Thought

Some of the above examples of models and experiments are rather simplistic in order to keep the answers manageable. However, even in actual research situations, one of the major problems is to try to reduce complex situations or phenomena to manageable formats in order to model them or experiment with them. You must make well argued and often difficult decisions about the choice of important or relevant variables. Another aspect which you will always need to investigate is the availability of resources, both technical and financial. You might find it necessary to beg or borrow the necessary software or equipment!

ANALYSING DATA

Why analyse data?

Little sense can be made of a huge collection of data; therefore an essential part of research is the analysis of the data. This analysis must be carried out in relation to the research problem. You are wasting your time, and that of the eventual readers of your work, if you carry out analysis irrelevant to the aims of your study. You are probably also wasting your time if you amass data which you are unable to analyse, either because you have too much, or because you have insufficient or inappropriate analytical skills or methods to make the analysis. We say 'probably', because research is not a linear process, so it is not easy to predict exactly how many data will be 'enough'. What will help you to judge the type of and amount of data required is to decide on the methods which you will use to analyse them. In turn, the decision on the appropriateness of analytical methods must be made in relation to the nature of the research problem and the specific aims of the research project.

There are several reasons why we analyse data, some of which are the same as the reasons for doing research. These are shown in Box 7.11.

Box 7.11   Main reasons for analysing data

- To measure.
- To make comparisons.
- To examine relationships.
- To forecast.
- To test hypotheses.
- To construct concepts and theories.
- To explore.
- To control.
- To explain.

A large variety of methods is employed to carry out these processes. The more common are summarized below, together with a mention of the above processes for which they may be suitable. You will notice that some methods can be used for more than one process.

A strong distinction is usually made between quantitative and qualitative analysis: many textbooks on research devote different chapters to each, and whole books are written on the techniques involved in each approach. The following descriptions are therefore ordered in this way, although some of the analytical methods can be used both quantitatively and qualitatively. These are mentioned where appropriate.

Quantitative analysis

Quantitative analysis uses the syntax of mathematical operations to investigate the properties of data.

> We can express with numbers what is impossible to state in words. You cannot pile up words and deduce an average from them. You cannot take the square root of a sentence. It is impossible to square a word, a phrase or a paragraph. (Leedy, 1989, p. 173)

Obviously, data which can be analysed in this fashion must be quantitative in nature. The levels of measurement used in the collection of the data, i.e. nominal, ordinal, interval and ratio, are an important factor in choosing the type of analysis which is applicable, as is the numbers of cases involved.

Statistics

There are two meanings to the word 'statistics'. The first is:

> The science of collecting and analysing numerical data, especially in, or for, large quantities, and usually inferring proportions in a whole from proportions in a representative sample. (*Oxford Encyclopedic Dictionary*)

The second refers to any systematic collection or presentation of such facts: for example, population statistics are records of population numbers and makeup. Statistical methods deal purely with quantitative data, or with qualitative data which are expressed in numerical terms.

As you well know by now, one of the primary purposes of scientific investigation is to discover relationships among phenomena in order to explain, predict and possibly control their occurrence. It is in the discovery and quantification of these relationships that statistical methods are a valuable tool. We are talking here about correlational, rather than causal, relationships.

Correlational techniques generally aim to answer three questions about two variables or two sets of data. Does a relationship exist between the two variables or sets of data? If so, what is the direction of the relationship? And what is its magnitude? A wide range of techniques can be used, depending on the nature of the variables being analysed, and they bear exotic names like Kruskal's gamma, Kendall's coefficient of concordance, Guttman's lambda, and the chi-square and Kolmogorov–Smirnov tests. However, there is no reason to be nervous about this for, as Leedy suggested, a simple definition of statistics might be:

> A language that, through its own special symbols and grammar, takes the intangible facts of life and translates them into comprehensible meaning. (1989, p. 179)

You do not even have to be a mathematician to use this special language, as user-friendly computer packages (such as SPSS) will do all the calculations for you. However, you must be able to understand the function and applicability of the various tests to your own sets of data. In this respect, Preece advised:

> For any researcher, the first rule of statistics is 'Always consult a qualified statistician.' The second rule is, 'Know enough about statistics to be able to view the advice critically.' (1994, p. 159)

There is not space (or need) in this book to explain in detail the range of tests and their uses. It will help your understanding, though, if a description of the realm of statistics is provided, and the various branches of the discipline are outlined. Diagram 7.3 portrays the main classes of statistics and their characteristics, and will serve as a guide to the explanations which follow.

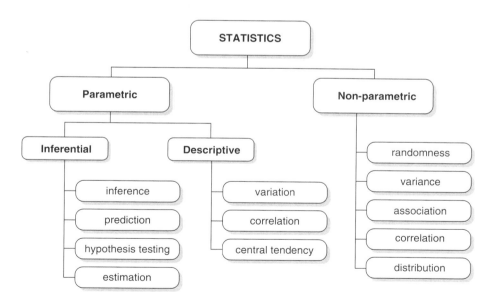

Diagram 7.3   Types of statistics

Parametric statistics

The two major classes of statistics are parametric and non-parametric statistics. An understanding of the meaning of a parameter, which in this context refers to a function of the population, is essential in order to appreciate the difference between these two words. A parameter of a population is a constant feature which it shares with other populations: a common one is the 'bell' curve of the normal frequency distribution. Most populations display a large number of more or less 'average' cases with extreme cases tailing off at each end. For example, most people are of about average height, with those who are extremely tall or small being in a distinct minority. The distribution of people's heights shown on a graph would take the form of the normal or 'Gaussian' curve (Diagram 7.4). Although values vary from case to case, the generality of this type of curve amongst populations is so strong that statisticians take it as a constant – a basic parameter – on which the calculations of parametric statistics are based. For those cases where this parameter is absent, non-parametric statistics may be applicable.

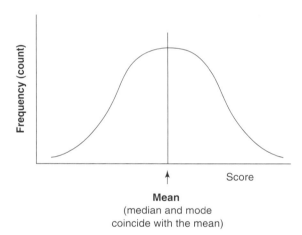

Diagram 7.4 Gaussian curve

The two classes of parametric statistics are descriptive and inferential statistics. **descriptive statistics** **Descriptive statistics** provide a method of quantifying the characteristics of the data, where their centre is, how broadly they spread and how one aspect of the data relates to another aspect of the same data. The 'centre of gravity' of the data, their point of central tendency, can be determined by finding the 'mode' or the 'median' and any one of several 'means'. These measures have their own characteristics and applications and should be chosen with regard to the data being analysed.

The measure of the dispersion (or spread) of the data, how flat or steep the Gaussian curve appears, is an indication of how many of the data closely resemble the mean. The flatter the curve, the greater is the amount of data that deviate from the mean, i.e. the fewer that are close to the average. The horizontal length of the curve also gives an indication of the spread of values and the extent of the extremes represented in the data, while the occurrence of a non-symmetrical curve indicates skewness in the data values.

Apart from examining the qualities of a single set of data, the main purpose of statistical analysis is to identify and quantify relationships between variables. This is the type of research called correlation research. But remember, the mere discovery and measurement of correlations are not sufficient on their own to provide research answers. It is the interpretation of these discoveries which provides the valuable knowledge which will give answers to your research question.

The technical term for the measure of correlation is the **coefficient of correlation**. There are many types of these, the Pearson's *r* being the most common. It is possible to measure the correlation between more than two variables if you use the appropriate tests. However, one must be wary about assuming that, because a strong statistical correlation between variables can be demonstrated, there is necessarily a causal bond between the variables. It may be purely chance or the influence of other factors that, say, leads to areas of high density development in cities having high crime rates. The researcher must carefully question the premises on which such a causal assertion is made, and review the facts to examine if such causality is verifiable in other ways.

coefficient of correlation

Inferential statistics goes beyond describing the characteristics of data and the examination of correlations between variables. As the name implies, it is used to produce predictions through inference, based on the data analysed. What is not so clear from its name is that inferential statistics is also used to test statistically based hypotheses.

inferential statistics

The predictive role is limited to estimating population parameters from sample statistics. This is not as abstruse as it might at first seem. Simply stated, this entails making predictions about the qualities of a total population on the basis

Figure 7.6 A sample of the production is tested in order to estimate the qualities of the total production

of the qualities of a sample. This is an exercise which is commonly carried out in quality control in production processes, where a sample of the production is tested in order to estimate the qualities of the total production. Three parameters (qualities) are commonly estimated: central tendency (proportion of products which are close to the norm, e.g. within permitted size tolerance); variability (e.g. range of sizes occurring); and probability (e.g. the proportion of acceptable products produced).

As with all predictions made from samples, the representative quality of the sample is crucial to accuracy.

Two types of estimate can be made of population parameters from sample statistics: point estimates and interval estimates. Point estimates attempt to pinpoint the population parameter through the sample statistic value (e.g. the standard deviation and average size of a sample of manufactured components, giving an estimate of the standard deviation and average size of the whole production run of the same component). While this produces a precise estimate of the parameters of the population, the values are crucially dependent on the truly representative quality of the sample.

Interval estimates of parameters use the sample statistics to predict the band within which almost all (typically 95% or 99%) of the values will lie. The expected range of the statistical values of the population is established, and if any values fall with a significant frequency (i.e. more than 5% or 1%) outside this range, then this variability will be considered to be caused by something more than mere chance. For example, the range of sizes of a manufactured component is estimated from a sample to be normally within a certain tolerance, e.g. ± 1 mm, when the production machines are running correctly. If more than say 5% of the components are found to be beyond these sizes, then the production is being affected by some unusual influence other than chance (e.g. a fault in the production machine). Obviously, the larger and more representative the sample from which the sample statistics were taken, the more likelihood that the prediction is correct.

null hypothesis   The statistically based hypothesis is commonly referred to as the **null hypothesis**. Inferential statistics are used to test this type of hypothesis. As a very simple example of the principles involved using the above case of the manufactured component, the engineer who designed the production machines could hypothesize that, according to his design, the components will be manufactured within the size tolerance ± 1 mm. Assuming that the machines are properly built and working correctly, if samples taken of the components produced show that 95% of the components fall within the size tolerances (i.e. *no significant difference* is observed between the predicted and the observed parameters: this is where the *null* comes from), then his hypothesis can be seen to be supported. If more samples are taken with the same result, then more support is given. If, however, the sample shows that more than 5% of the components exceed the size tolerance, then there is some cause for this beyond mere chance. The engineer's hypothesis will be rejected. For what reason his hypothesis was proved to be wrong is another matter; perhaps his design was incorrect, or his calculations faulty.

Non-parametric statistics

Not all data are parametric, i.e. samples and populations sometimes do not behave in the form of a Gaussian curve. Data measured by nominal and ordinal methods will not be organized in a curve form. Nominal data tend to be in the dichotomous form of either/or (e.g. this is a cow or a sheep or neither), while ordinal data can be displayed in the form of a set of steps (e.g. the first, second and third positions on a winners' podium). Statistical tests built around discovering the means, standard deviations etc. of the typical characteristics of a Gaussian curve are clearly inappropriate for analysing this type of data. Non-parametric statistical tests have been devised to recognize the particular characteristics of non-curve data and to take into account these singular characteristics by specialized methods. In general, these types of test are less sensitive and powerful than parametric tests; they need larger samples in order to generate the same level of significance.

Tests can be used to compare the qualities of two or more groups or samples (e.g. Wilcoxon matched pairs signed rank test, sign test, Kruskal–Wallis test) or to analyse the rankings made by different judges (Kendall coefficient of concordance, Spearman rank order correlation), or to compare the data from observed and theoretical sources (chi-square test). Detailed information about which tests to use for particular data sets can be obtained from specialized texts on statistics, and of course, your own expert statistical adviser. This is perhaps a good place to warn you that computer statistical packages (e.g. SPSS) will not distinguish between different types of parametric and non-parametric data. In order to avoid producing reams of impressive looking, though meaningless, analytical output, it is up to you to ensure that the tests are appropriate for the type of data you have. (See Preece, 1994, Chapter 7, and Leedy, 1989, pp. 178–211, for more detailed, though straightforward, introductions to statistics; and Siegel and Castellan, 1988, for a comprehensive review.)

Content analysis

This is a specific method of examining records of all kinds (e.g. radio and TV programmes, films etc.), documents or publications. A checklist is made to count how frequently certain ideas, words, phrases, images or scenes appear in order to be able to draw some conclusions from the frequency of their appearance (e.g. the perception of modern architecture in the media). Care must be taken with the selection of the variables to be studied, and the method of their measurement. The data collected can be summarized and collated either on forms or by using statistical tests (see Dixon, 1987, pp. 95–100 for a simple description of the methodology).

Qualitative analysis

By immersing him/herself in the data and then searching out patterns, surprising phenomena and inconsistencies, the researcher can *generate new concepts and theory*, or uncover further instances of those already in existence. The clues to new concepts and theory, though indistinct at first, will be strengthened by repetitions of incidents or words, irregularities (e.g. conflicting views offered by different groups of people), and other signs, such as particular emotions displayed when people say things.

Grounded theory

Devised largely by Glaser and Strauss in the 1960s, grounded theory is frequently quoted as influential in the development of qualitative analysis. It alerted researchers to the desirability of extracting concepts out of data, and to the use of different types of code and their role in concept creation. It is basically concerned with 'the discovery of theory from data' (Glaser and Strauss, 1967, p. 1). A particularly useful explanation of this process is given in Turner (1981). However, it will be worthwhile to include here a short summary of the steps involved to give you an idea of its operation.

The overall aim of the process is to develop a theoretical hypothesis from field data. After collecting some data about the chosen issue and spending some time reflecting on it, the researcher devises a range of categories into which the data can be fitted. This is followed by further research which aims at reinforcing and eventually establishing the meaning and importance of these categories. Subsequent to this, the researcher strives to redefine these categories in a more generalized and abstract form, extending them from the immediate data available. During this process, further thought is given to the interconnections between the categories and to their theoretical implications. The perceived links between categories are tested in hypothetical form in the field (i.e. in the actual research situation). The possible connections between this and other theoretical schemes are investigated. With the further development of the hypotheses, continuing collection of data and theoretical reflection, the developing theory is again tested in the field.

The process consists, therefore, of a continuous comparison of data and theoretical model throughout the research process. The theory is 'grounded' on evidence from the field. However, Bryman and Burgess (1994, p. 221) commented that, although the influences of grounded theory have been powerful, there are few signs in qualitative analytical practice that the iterative interplay of data collection and analysis that lies at the heart of grounded theory has been fully employed, or that there are indications that the theory has been further developed – which would be a sure sign that the theory has been thoroughly employed and examined.

To talk of data 'collection' as a prior stage is inimical to the theoretical assumptions behind qualitative research. The goals of producing theory from data, rather than merely testing prior theory, require the researcher to remain open to patterns, new categories or concepts that may emerge during the process of making data. Hence methods of handling qualitative data must contain ways of catching and developing ideas, exploring fleeting hints, and drawing connections between them and the data from which they derive. (Richards and Richards, 1994, p. 149)

This is not easy to achieve. One of the problems faced by researchers doing qualitative research is the difficulty of coping with the complexity of the huge volume of unstructured data which have to be analysed (e.g. in the form of typescript, field notes, handwritten accounts resulting from unstructured interviews and participant observations). There is a tendency for the data to become more and more sterile as the managing of it becomes more efficient and the files on each topic become larger. The main problem is to sort data into categories without losing the subtle complexities and interlinkages contained within them.

In connection with the developing concepts and theory, it is important to retain very detailed links to the data, in order to support the exploration of ideas and verification of claims. In this respect, remember that all relevant data are valuable, and nothing should be discarded as it might later become useful.

There are practical difficulties in organizing a system which allows for separating the data into categories while at the same time retaining flexibility to enable the theoretical linkages to be explored. Richards and Richards (1994) identified five goals which a data handling system should achieve in order to facilitate theory development, as in Box 7.12.

Box 7.12   Goals for a data system to help theory development

1   It should impose no limit on the number of codes which can be developed, or on the number of times that a fertile piece of text can be coded, and it should provide a method of checking that the codes retain their precise meanings.
2   It should facilitate answering questions about the relationships of categories.
3   Memos about emerging theory should be easily linked with the appropriate data, often present in several categories.
4   It should avoid the problems of segmentation of data, leading to a loss of context, by retaining large segments of text while highlighting the exact text being coded.

Coloured card indexes recording a hierarchical structure of categories and subcategories in the data files, cross-referenced with memos about emerging patterns, can be developed to build up a flexible manual database. However, these aims are more easily achieved with the help of a computer, for which there are now an estimated eleven different software packages. For a review of those available see Miles and Huberman (1994, Appendix), Seidel and Clark (1984, about Ethnograph) and Richards and Richards (1994, about NUDIST: Non-Numerical Unstructured Data Indexing, Searching and Theorizing).

But even with the help of the computer, it will continue to be the main task of the researcher to construct theories by creating 'mental maps, abstracted webs of meaning, that the analyst lays over bits of data to give them shape without doing violence to them' (Miles and Huberman, 1994, p. 83).

Commonalities in qualitative analysis

Unlike the well established statistical methods of analysing quantitative data, qualitative data analysis is still in its early stages. The certainties of mathematical formulae and determinable levels of probability are not applicable to the 'soft' nature of qualitative data, which are inextricably bound up with human feelings, attitudes and judgements. Unlike the large amounts of data which are often collected for quantitative analysis, which can readily be managed with the available standard statistical procedures conveniently incorporated in computer packages, there are no such standard procedures for codifying and analysing qualitative data. According to Turner (1994, pp. 208–13), it is perhaps not even desirable that there should be homogeneous, classifiable types of qualitative analysis; researchers must structure their analytical approaches to fit the nature of the data with which they are faced.

However, there are common steps which have to be made in all qualitative data analysis. Bryman and Burgess (1994, pp. 6–8) identified two general processes: the building of typologies and taxonomies, and the generation of concepts and theory. Robson (1993, p. 401) went further to provide a list of tactics for drawing conclusions from qualitative data. These also fall into the two processes above: counting, patterning, clustering and factoring into the first; and relating variables, building of causal networks and relating findings to general theoretical frameworks into the second. Miles and Huberman (1994, pp. 10–12) added a third component in their definition of the components of analysis, the three concurrent flows of activity being data reduction, data display, and conclusion drawing and verification.

The inclusion of data display is important. The unwieldy mass of information that normally provides the basis for analysis, even when coded, clustered, summarized etc., cannot be easily understood when presented as extended text. Information in text is dispersed, is sequential rather than concurrent, and is bulky and difficult to structure. The mind is not adept at processing large amounts of information, but prefers to simplify complex information into patterns and easily understood configurations. Using suitable methods to display the data (in the form of matrices, graphs, charts and networks) aids not only in the reduction and ordering of the data, but also in its analysis. Miles and Huberman advocate 'more systematic, powerful displays and urge a more inventive, self-conscious, iterative stance toward their generation and use' (1994, p. 11).

Preliminary analysis during data collection

When conducting extended field research it is important to maintain an analytical attitude to the type and amount of data being collected, and to acknowledge the assumptions and hypotheses that brought you to this stage. It will be easier to structure the information whilst the details are fresh in the mind, to identify gaps and to allow new ideas and hypotheses to challenge your assumptions and biases. Raw field notes, often scribbled and full of abbreviations, and tapes of interviews or events, need to be processed in order to make them useful. Much information will be lost if this task is left for weeks or months.

The process of data reduction and analysis should be a sequential and continuous procedure, simple in the beginning stages of the data collection, and becoming more complex as the project progresses.

To begin with, one-page summaries can be made of the results of contacts, e.g. phone conversations, visits. A standardized set of headings will prompt the ordering of the information: contact details, main issues, summary of information acquired, interesting issues raised, and new questions resulting from these. Similar one-page forms can be used to summarize the contents of documents.

Typologies, taxonomies and coding

As the data accumulate, a valuable step is to organize the shapeless mass of data by building typologies and taxonomies, that is, by identifying differences in the data and thereby forming subgroups within the general category. Using these new typologies helps to clarify the relationships among concepts.

> Even the simplest classification, like Whyte's (1955) 'street corner' and 'college' boys, or Jenkins's (1983) 'lads', 'citizens' and 'ordinary kids', can help to organize amorphous material and to identify patterns in the data. Differences between the components of such classification in terms of behaviour patterns are important in generating the kinds of linkage that will form the basis for the development of theory. (Bryman and Burgess, 1994, p. 7)

The development of a **coding** system is an important aspect of forming typologies, as it facilitates the organization of copious data (in the form of notes, observations, transcripts, documents etc.) and provides a first step in conceptualization. Codes are labels or tags used to allocate units of meaning to the collected data. This helps to prevent 'data overload' resulting from mountains of unprocessed data in the form of ambiguous words.

coding

Miles and Huberman (1994, p. 57) formulated four general categories of code: descriptive, interpretive, explanatory and astringent. More specifically, Lofland

(1971, pp. 14–15) devised a classification of 'social phenomena' on which it would be possible to build a coding scheme. His six classes are: acts, activities, meanings, participation, relationships and settings. The process is analytical, requiring you to review, select, interpret and summarize the information without distorting it. It is normal to compile a set of codes before doing the fieldwork, based on the background study, and then to refine it during the data collection.

Coding is rarely regarded by different researchers as exactly the same kind of activity. However, two essentially different types of coding can be distinguished, one used for the retrieval of text sequences, the other devised for theory generation. The former refers to the process of cutting out and pasting sections of text from transcripts or notes under various headings. The latter is a more open coding system used as an index for ideas: reflective notes or memos, rather than merely bits of text.

While the process of identifying segments of records for orderly copying and filing under topics might be seen as an onerous, boring and essentially clerical activity, Richards and Richards (1994) maintained that actually this judgement obscures the fact that much of the activity involved in coding for retrieval is a theorizing process. The analytical decision to create a particular code has a defining effect on what you will find in your collated data: 'data control methods must be processes of analysis, not merely of data disposal' (1994, p. 149).

Coding is an important part of much qualitative research, and you will have to refer to more specialist texts for details of its development and application (see Miles and Huberman, 1994, pp. 55–72; Strauss and Corbin, 1990; Strauss, 1987). Several computer programs used for analysing qualitative data (such as Ethnograph and NUDIST) also have facilities for filing and retrieving coded information. They allow codes to be attached to the numbered lines of notes or transcripts of interviews, and for the source of the information/opinion to be noted. This enables a rapid retrieval of selected information from the mass of material collected.

Pattern coding, memoing and interim summary

The next stage of analysis requires us to begin to look for patterns and themes, and explanations of why and how these occur. This requires a method of pulling together the coded information into more compact and meaningful groupings. Pattern coding can do this by reducing the data into smaller analytical units such as themes, causes/explanations, relationships among people and emerging concepts, to allow the researcher to develop a more integrated understanding of the situation studied. This will generally help to focus later fieldwork and lay the foundations for cross-case analysis in multi-case studies by identifying common themes and processes.

Miles and Huberman (1994, pp. 70–1) describe three successive ways that pattern codes may be used. The newly developed codes are provisionally added to the existing list of codes and checked out in the next set of field notes to see whether they fit. Next, the most promising codes are written up in a memo (described below) to clarify and explain the concept so that it can be related to other data and cases. Finally, the new pattern codes are tested out in the next round of data collection.

Generating pattern codes is surprisingly easy as it is the way by which we habitually process information. However, it is important not to cling uncritically onto initially developed patterns, but to test and develop, and if necessary reject, them as your understanding of the data develops, and as new waves of data are produced.

To develop a greater understanding of events and to make more sense of the relationships between codes, short analytical descriptions can be compiled based on the evolving ideas of the researcher reacting to the data and the development of codes and pattern codes. Compiling **memos** is a good way to explore links between data and to record and develop intuitions and ideas. This can be done at any time – but is best done when the idea is fresh! Remember that memos are written for yourself, and so the length and style are not important, but it is necessary to label them so that they can be easily sorted and retrieved. The activity of memoing should continue throughout the research project; you will find that the ideas become more stable with time until a 'saturation' point is achieved, i.e. the point where you are satisfied with your understanding and explanation of the data.

memo

Data collection in qualitative research is inherently more flexible and less predictable than with quantitative research. Therefore it is essential, at probably about one-third way through the data collection, to seek to reassure yourself and your supervisors/sponsors by checking the quantity and quality of what you have found out so far, your confidence in the reliability of the data, and the presence and nature of any gaps or puzzles that have been revealed, and to review what still needs to be collected in relation to your time available. This exercise will result in the production of an **interim summary**, that is a provisional report (10–25 pages are usually sufficient).

interim summary

This report will be the first time that everything you know about a case will be summarized, and presents the first opportunity to make cross-case analyses in multi-case studies and to review emergent explanatory variables. Remember however that the summary is provisional, and perhaps will be sketchy and incomplete. It should be seen as a useful tool for reflecting on the work done, for discussion with your colleagues and supervisors, and for indicating any changes that might be needed in the coding and in the subsequent data collection work. In order to check on the amount of data collected about each research question, a data accounting sheet can usefully be compiled. This is a table that sets out the research questions and the amount of data collected from the different informants, settings, situations etc. Shortcomings can thereby easily be identified.

Further techniques during data collection

Three other useful techniques for analysis during the data collection period are described by Miles and Huberman (1994, pp. 81–9). These are vignettes, prestructured case analysis and sequential analysis. Some very brief remarks about these will be useful.

A *vignette* is a short, contextually rich narrative story that is used to encapsulate a typical event or attitude in a straightforward, direct way. It results in a vivid, compelling and persuasive interpretation of an issue, an abstraction rather than a representation of an original event. It can be used in interim reports to formulate core issues and also in longer case reports in order to highlight important subjects.

Prestructured case analysis is used to streamline data collection and to produce good comparability between data sets from different cases by collapsing the processes of data collection, analysis and report writing into one evolving procedure. It assumes that the research questions are closely specified and that the conceptual framework is well developed.

The method consists of compiling a standard case report outline and data display formats before data collection begins. The collected information from each case can then be 'slotted into' the prepared framework. The case reports are filled in, edited and refined as the information is collected, enabling the reports to be finalized almost as soon as the data collection is complete. In this way, coding can be applied to raw field notes and entered straight into the selected displays, obviating the need to compile coded write-ups. Any shortage of information is easily detected, and can be noted for future collection. Because the process of analysis direct from the field is difficult to illustrate, various forms of triangulation should be used to verify the results obtained.

Sequential analysis allows the researcher to review and deepen understanding of the findings at particular points during the research project, and to inform the data gathering process in the next stage. It helps to develop a progressively profound focus on evolving important issues as the data gathering can become more targeted on vital questions. Each session of sequential analysis should involve discussion with your supervisor and critical colleagues, to help you to review and, if necessary, reorient your analysis of the facts and theory development.

Main analysis during and after data collection

The traditional text-based report tends to be a lengthy and cumbersome method of presenting, analysing, interpreting and communicating the findings of a research project. Not only is it forced by its nature to present the evidence and arguments sequentially, but it also tends to be bulky and difficult to grasp quickly because information is dispersed over many pages. This presents a problem for the writer, as well as for the final reader, who rarely has time to browse backwards and forwards through masses of text to gain full information, let alone compare a series of such reports. Graphical methods of data display and analysis can largely overcome these problems and are useful for exploring and describing as well as explaining and predicting phenomena. They can be used equally effectively for one-case and cross-case analysis (see Miles and Huberman, 1994, for a detailed guide to a wide range of displays).

Box 7.13   Categories of displays

- Matrices
- Networks

Graphical displays fall into two categories: matrices and networks (Box 7.13). The two-dimensional arrangement of rows and columns in **matrices** can summarize a substantial amount of information. They can easily be produced informally in a freehand fashion to explore aspects of the data, to any size, and computer programs in the form of databases and spreadsheets can aid in their production. Matrices can be used to record variables such as time, levels of measurement, roles, clusters, outcomes and effects (Diagram 7.5). Latest developments allow the formulation of three-dimensional matrices.

matrices

A **network** is made up of blocks (nodes) connected by links. These maps and charts can be produced in a wide variety of formats, each with the capability of displaying different types of data. Flow charts are useful for studying processes or procedures. Not only are they helpful for explanation, but their development is a good device for creating understanding. Organization charts display relationships between variables and their nature, e.g. formal and informal hierarchies. Causal networks are used to examine and display the causal relationships between important independent and dependent variables, causes and effects.

networks

These methods of displaying and analysing qualitative data are particularly useful when you compare the results of several case studies, as they permit a certain standardization of presentation, allowing comparisons to be made more easily across the cases.

The information can be displayed in the form of text, codes, abbreviated notes, symbols, quotations or any other form that helps to communicate compactly. The detail and sophistication of the display can vary depending on its function and on the amount of information available; displays are useful at any stage in the research process.

The different types of display can be described by the way that information is ordered in them. *Time ordered displays* record a sequence of events in relation to their chronology. A simple example of this is a project programme giving names, times and locations for tasks of different kinds. The scale and precision of

TASKS....INITIATION AND DESIGN PHASE	grade of difficulty	PET	NVT	GL	DU	LTM	DCH	HOL	FUS	BA
investigation of situation, inception	low	R	P	P	P	P	P	P	R	P/R
formulation of brief	med	R	P/R	P	P	D/P	P	P	P/R	P/R
source land	low	R	P	P	P	P	P	P	P/R	P/R
survey site	high	P	P	N	P	P/R	P	P	P	P
design site layout	med	P	P	N	T	D	P	P	P/D	P
design house plan layout	high	P/R	P/R	P	P	D	P	P	D	P
3D house design	high	P	P	P	P	P/D	P	P	D	P
construction design	high	P	P	P	P	P	P	P	D/P	P
structural design	high	P	P	N	P	P	P	P	P	P
planning and building regs applications	high	P	P	P	P	P	P	P	P	P
costing and programming	high	R	P	P	P	P	P	P	P	P
find funds	med	R	P	T	P	T	P	P	P	P/R
find self-builders	low	R	T	P	T	T	P	P	R	R/P
select self-builders	med	R	R	P	T	R/P	P	P	R	R/P
select professionals	low	R	P	P	P	R/P	P	P	P/R	P/R

Key: skill requirement

R   required skill of self-builders
D   deskilling of task to reduce skill requirement
T   training provided to instil skill required
P   professional person allocated to task
N   no requirement for skill and task within the scope of the project

Key: skill difficulty grade

LOW   no particular skills, though some instruction necessary
MEDIUM   basic skills requiring limited training and practice
HIGH   sophisticated skills requiring extended training and practice

Diagram 7.5   Matrix example: measures taken to reduce the initial skill requirements of the self-builders, initiation and design phase

timing can be suited to the subject. Events can be of various types, e.g. tasks, critical events, experiences, stages in a programme, activities, decisions etc. Some examples of types of time ordered displays are:

- *Event listing*   A chronological presentation of concrete or significant events in the various strands of a situation, commonly using a matrix with the time registered in columns left to right. Networks can also be used to indicate the flow of events or states (e.g. levels of knowledge, confidence etc.).
- *Critical incident chart*   This lays the stress on the incidents that have been critical in a process. Here the time element can be indicated by the rows.

- *Event state network*   Useful to help to make sense of a large number of events by displaying them in a series of boxes in chronological order, some running parallel or in series, and to test one's ideas about what is making things happen and why. Computer programs such as Inspiration and Meta Design make the creation and manipulation of these networks quick and easy.
- *Activity record*   A display that analyses steps in accomplishing a task, showing the sequential activities required to realize each stage.
- *Decision modelling*   Commonly used to analyse a course of action, employing a network with yes/no routes from each decision taken.
- *Time ordered matrix*   Similar to events listing, but with a more general content, i.e. not necessarily events.
- *Time ordered meta-matrix*   A cross-case chronological display enabling comparisons to be made between the timing of case events.
- *Scatterplots over time*   Another cross-case technique, this time looking for clustering of cases at two or more distinct times during an extended event or programme.
- *Composite sequence analysis*   Used to compare the trajectory of events in several cases, e.g. developments in the careers of a number of professionals.

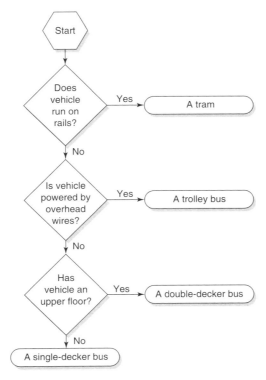

Diagram 7.6   Network example: a decision tree model sorting out public transport vehicles

Conceptually ordered displays concentrate on variables in the form of abstract concepts related to a theory and the relationships between these. Examples of such variables are motives, attitudes, expertise, barriers, coping strategies etc. They can be shown as matrices or networks to illustrate taxonomies, content analysis, cognitive structures, relationships of cause and effect or influence. Here is a selection of different types:

- *Conceptually or thematically clustered matrix*   Helps to summarize the mass of data about numerous research questions by combining groups of questions that are conceptually or thematically connected, either from a theoretical point of view, or as a result of groupings that can be detected in the data.
- *Taxonomy tree diagram*   Useful to break down concepts into their constituent parts or elements.
- *Cognitive map*   A descriptive diagrammatic plotting of a person's way of thinking about an issue, showing important concepts and non-hierarchical links between them. Useful to understand somebody's way of thinking or to compare that of several people.
- *Effects matrix*   Plots the observed effects of an action or intervention. These may be intermediate and/or final effects on principal dependent variables. A necessary precursor to explaining or predicting effects.
- *Decision tree modelling*   This helps to make clear the sequence of decisions resulting in an action, by setting up a network of sequential yes/no response routes (Diagram 7.6). The trees resulting from several cases can be combined into a composite tree to generalize the model.
- *Causal models*   These are used in theory building to provide a testable set of propositions about a complete network of variables with causal and other relationships between them, based on a multi-case situation. A preliminary stage in the development of a causal model is to develop causal chains, i.e. linear cause/effect lines (Diagram 7.7).

Role ordered displays show people's roles and their relationships in formal and informal organizations or groups. A role defines a person's standing and position by assessing their behaviour and expectations within the group or organization. These may be conventionally recognized positions, e.g. judge, mother, machine operator; or more abstract and situation dependent roles, e.g. motivator, objector. People in different roles tend to see situations from different perspectives: a strike in a factory will be viewed very differently by the management and the workforce. A role ordered matrix will help to systematically display these differences or can be used to investigate whether people in the same roles are unified in their views.

Partially ordered displays are useful in analysing 'messy' situations without trying to impose too much internal order on them. For example a context chart can be designed to show, in the form of a network, the influences and pressures that bear on an individual from surrounding organizations and persons when making a decision to act. This will help to understand why a particular action was taken.

A very different function can be carried out by a checklist matrix: to examine the components of a complex variable during and after fieldwork. A variable seen as crucial to the study (e.g. commitment) may have several components and appear in different guises depending on the role and situation of the subjects. The use of this type of matrix will enable these disparate aspects to be collated and compared in a systematic way.

A partially ordered meta-matrix is useful when making a preliminary analysis across cases. With data collected on several cases amounting to perhaps hundreds of pages of field notes, an oversight can be gained by compiling a condensed 'master display' from individual case displays that use common codes and standardized displays. This will involve partitioning and clustering data and help you to note patterns and themes as the table develops through several iterations.

Case ordered displays show the data of cases arranged in some kind of order according to an important variable in the study. This allows you to compare cases and note their different features according to where they appear in the order.

A case ordered meta-matrix does this by simply arranging case matrices next to each other in the chosen order to enable you to simply compare the data across the meta-matrix. The meta-matrix can initially be quite large if there are a number of cases. A function of the analysis will be to summarize the data in a smaller matrix, giving a summary of the significant issues discovered. Following this a contrast table can also be devised to display and compare how one or two variables perform in cases as ordered in the meta-matrix.

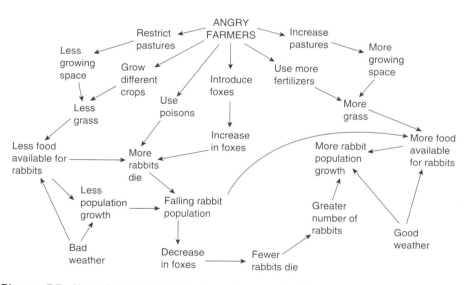

Diagram 7.7   Network example: multiple cause diagram of rabbit control system

Cases might not be equally spaced out sequentially but may be bunched in groups with similar characteristics. A scatterplot showing values across two particular variables will reveal if the results show any grouping characteristics.

EXERCISE
7.4

1 Consider the following different types of data and state if you consider them to be amenable to quantitative or qualitative analysis, or both.

   (a) A collection of scripts taken from semi-structured interviews with 150 prisoners, asking them about their attitudes to the regime of discipline in the prison.
   (b) The results of a questionnaire sent to all UK solicitor practices, asking them about their fee income, insurance premiums, turnover and staffing levels.
   (c) Observations noted of traffic movements at a busy traffic intersection during a period of one week.
   (d) A pile of historic documents found in an attic, consisting of letters, diaries and financial accounts, all to do with the building of a stately eighteenth century country home.
   (e) A survey of government statistics about homelessness throughout the twentieth century.

2 What is the essential difference between parametric and non-parametric statistics?
3 Could you use inferential statistics to prove that smoking causes cancer? If you think you could, how; and if not, why not?
4 Qualitative analysis appears to be more of a creative art than a science. Do you think that this is true? State your reasons for agreeing or disagreeing in two or three sentences. What are three or four essential differences in method which distinguish it from quantitative analysis?
5 Describe which form of display may be suitable to usefully show the following:

   (a) The management structure of a government department.
   (b) The attitudes of parents in different social classes to private schooling and state schooling.
   (c) To explain what one has to do to change the wheel of a car.
   (d) The results of introducing into a factory a new pay system based purely on productivity.

Thought

It is quite obvious that you can learn a lot about the different methods of data analysis, but you should ask yourself how much you really need to know in detail in order to define, at this stage, what you will be doing in your research project. In many cases, particularly if you are doing an MPhil with transfer to PhD, you will only be able to decide on your exact methodology after your background research has been completed.

CONCLUSIONS

The three perspectives of research with which we began this discussion, i.e. data collection/analysis, qualitative/quantitative research and research strategies, interlace in a three-way matrix. This complex combination provides a large number of choices of research methods from which you, as a prospective researcher, must make a selection appropriate to your research problem.

It is evident that, even within one research project, there may be several research methods which could be justifiably applied to different aspects of the same research problem. Each enables a different aspect of the problem to be investigated and analysed. Data collection and analysis may not just happen once: there is often a repeated sequence of collection and analysis, for example:

> collection of historical data → analysis → hypothesis for case study → data collection → analysis

This chapter can only be a very brief introduction to some of the more common methods available. In the course of your background research it will be necessary to investigate more thoroughly the particular methods which have been used in contexts similar to your own study, and to evaluate them in order that you can select those which are appropriate. Detailed study can then be made of the selected methods.

THE NEXT STEPS: WHICH RESEARCH METHODS WILL YOU USE?

The aims of this section are:

- to determine the type of data which you should collect in order to investigate your research problem
- to decide on the appropriate methods for collecting the data
- to investigate appropriate methods of data analysis
- to examine what can be achieved by using these techniques.

Checklist of activities that will progress your research

Step 1: quantitative or qualitative research or both?
Review the sort of data you will be collecting and the type of analysis you will want to subject them to. Do they fall into one or the other category, or do they contain elements of both? It is important for you to recognize the difference

between the two types of research because their fundamental assumptions are different. How can you recognize the difference? Try the tests in the next steps.

Step 2: test for quantitative research
Two features distinguish quantitative research: the use of precise measurement, and the use of quantities expressed as numbers capable of being analysed by statistical methods or other computational methods. Once you start counting how many, measuring how much, you are doing quantitative research!

Step 3: test for qualitative research
Qualitative research is any research that does not conform to the description in step 2 (well, almost). Qualitative research usually is to do with people and their activities, and is concerned with variables that cannot be quantified on an interval or ratio level. Data in the form of words, either written or spoken, are a common feature, but data could also be of sounds or actions (e.g. music or dance).

Step 4: devise your research strategy
Check Box 7.1, on research strategies, to help define your research strategy. Decide the types of question you will be asking. You might decide that the list of strategies is not sufficiently complete (see Chapter 3) or you might add your own, based on another source. Also, you might use more than one in order to cover your topic.

Step 5: link it all up
Make a chart or a diagram of the different threads to your research, considering the different perspectives you will be using to study them. Use the three perspectives shown in Diagram 7.1, i.e. strategies, data collection/analysis, and quantitative/qualitative approaches. Note that in some instances you can collect qualitative data and analyse them quantitatively, and vice versa. This exercise will help to consider the type of actions you will need to take in your research project.

Step 6: collecting data
Make a list of all the types of data that you will need to collect in order to answer our research questions. Try to order them in categories of secondary and primary data. Then decide where you might find these data – the data source. In the case of secondary data, will you be able to test their authenticity? In the case of primary data, will you need to select a sample? In both cases, will it be possible for you to get access to the required data?

Step 7: what sort of sample?
If you do not need to select a sample, you can leave out this step. Firstly, consider what your population is, and if possible, what are its characteristics (e.g. homogeneous,

stratified etc). Next, select an appropriate sampling method. As you can see, there is a lot of factors apart from accurate representation that will influence your choice, such as manageable numbers, locations, accessibility, practicality, timing etc. At this stage you do not have to be too precise about your methods (unless you are doing a proposal for a PhD direct), but you will need to indicate that you are aware of the issues involved.

Step 8: choose your data collection methods
Reflect on your list of data required from step 6. For each item on the list, decide on the best method to use in order to acquire the data. You might end up with a variety of methods. Consider the practical consequences of these. Now is a good time to assess the practicality of what you propose.

Step 9: choose your data analysis methods
The methods of data analysis you select will depend on the nature of the data and what you want to find out from them. Consider the list of the reasons in Box 7.10 for why we analyse data. Your background reading will help you to ascertain what methods have been used successfully in previous, similar research. Again, practicality will be an important factor, e.g. will you need expensive equipment or special computer resources?

Step 10: combining data collection and analysis
Perhaps the research into your subject does not divide so neatly into two separate sequences of data collection and analysis. If not, formulate an appropriate strategy for combining these activities. Normally, the collection and analysis still use different methods, but these are alternated so as to provide mutual feedback at regular intervals. You will have to convince that your planned activities are both appropriate and practicable.

Step 11: draft your plan of work
A reality check! Now that you are clearer about what you want to do and how you will do it, the question of whether you can fit it into the time needs to be answered. A simple bar chart showing a list of activities with their time allowance set within the overall time available is all that is required here. Do not forget to add in time taken for learning new techniques, writing up, holidays, travel, conferences etc. This will enable you to check that you are not being unrealistic in your ambitions. Ask yourself: is the time allocated to each task reasonable? If not, now is the time to make adjustments. This might entail reducing the scope of the research, cutting down on case studies, limiting the size and complexity of surveys, simplifying experiments, and reducing the amount of analysis to the bare essentials.

Consolidation and assessment

When you are ready, arrange a tutorial with your tutor or supervisor. The main point of this consultation is to discuss the research methods you have selected to use in your research project, and to explain why you think they are appropriate and what you hope to achieve by using them. Use the information you have gained from this chapter on methods of data collection and analysis and different research strategies to explain how your research problem can be tackled in a realistic way.

You should explore how the research methods might be practically carried out, their scope and level of complexity, while considering what resources will be needed to produce and analyse the data. Consider particularly the relationships between collection and analysis of data: can the former be completed before commencing the latter, or will they have to be carried out in tandem? Contemplate whether you will need to select samples during your research and, if so, what will be the important considerations in your case. Surmise how using these particular methods will reinforce your argument, and discuss the possible advantages and disadvantages of alternative approaches.

Explain your draft plan of work, which demonstrates how the various methods you will use form a logical sequence, and point out any difficulties you anticipate which might affect the timing, such as availability of people or information, access to equipment and software, travel and financial resources, and the need to acquire new knowledge and skills.

Key words

Authentication	Pilot study
Interpretation	Internal validity
Population	External validity
Sample	Algorithm
Simple random sampling	Descriptive statistics
Simple stratified sampling	Coefficient of correlation
Proportional stratified sampling	Inferential statistics
Cluster sampling	Null hypothesis
Systematic sampling	Coding
Accidental sampling	Memo
Quota sampling	Interim summary
Theoretical sampling	Matrices
Sampling error	Networks

Further reading

There are hundreds of books about data collection methods and sampling techniques, and about all the ways to analyse data. In addition to these are the examples of the previous theses done in your subject, which you can consult for the nature of data collected and their use of methods.

The first set of books listed here looks in more detail at the different aspects of sampling and data collection. For more choice, look up key words such as sampling, questionnaires, survey research etc. in your library catalogue. The next set is about quantitative analysis; the third about qualitative analysis; the fourth about experiments and models; and the last about using the Internet for research. Again, consult your library catalogue for specific textbooks.

Sampling and data collection

To start with, here are some books on research in general. For some I have pointed out the sections on data, data collection, sampling etc. which are useful because of their brevity. Look at the contents pages of the others for the relevant sections, which cover other aspects of the research process too.

Seale, C. (ed.) (2004) *Researching Society and Culture*, 2nd edn. London: Sage.

See chapter by Clive Seale and Paul Filmer on 'Doing social surveys'.

Holliday, A. (2001) *Doing and Writing Qualitative Research*. London: Sage.

Consult Chapters 6 and 7 for what counts as data and writing about data.

Fowler, F. J. (2001) *Survey Research Methods*, 3rd edn. London: Sage.

This book goes into great detail about all aspects of the subject of doing surveys. Good on sampling, response rates, methods of data collection – particularly questionnaires and interviews. Use it selectively to find out more about the particular methods you want. This book will also be useful later for analysis, and has a section on ethics too.

Robson, C. (1993) *Real World Research: a Resource for Social Scientists and Practitioner-Researchers*. Oxford: Blackwell.

Part III gives valuable information and advice on the tactics of data collection using a wide range of methods. See pp. 255–68 for an explanation of standard scales. See pp. 51–63 and Chapter 6 for case study research. Later editions are also available.

Aldridge, A. (2001) *Surveying the Social World: Principles and Practice in Survey Research*. Buckingham: Open University Press.

Continued

Another comprehensive book; find what you need by using the contents list and index.

Bryman, A. (2004) *Social Research Methods*, 2nd edn. Oxford: Oxford University Press.

One of the most popular standard handbooks for social research students.

Greenfield, T. (2002) *Research Methods for Postgraduates*, 2nd edn. London: Arnold.

A wide range of authors give tips on all aspects of postgraduate research. Easy to navigate as the chapters are nicely divided into discrete topics.

Fink, A. (1995) *The Survey Kit*. London: Sage.

Nine volumes covering all aspects of survey research! This must be the ultimate.

Some books specifically on questionnaires, in order of usefulness:

Peterson, R. A. (2000) *Constructing Effective Questionnaires*. London: Sage.

Gillham, W. E. and William, E. C. (2000) *Developing a Questionnaire*. London: Continuum.

Dillman, D. A. (2000) *Mail and Internet Surveys: the Tailored Design Method*, 2nd edn. Chichester: Wiley.

Frazer, L. (2000) *Questionnaire Design and Administration: a Practical Guide*. Chichester: Wiley.

And a few on interviewing, again in order of usefulness at your stage of work:

Keats, D. M. (2000) *Interviewing: a Practical Guide for Students and Professionals*. Buckingham: Open University Press.

Jaber, F. (ed.) (2002) *Handbook of Interview Research: Context and Method*. London: Sage.

Wengraf, T. (2001) *Qualitative Research Interviewing: Biographic, Narrative and Semi-Structured*. London: Sage.

And a couple on sampling:

Schaeffer, R. L. (1996) *Elementary Survey Sampling*, 5th edn. Belmont, CA: Duxbury.

Fink, A. (1995) *How to Sample in Surveys* (*The Survey Kit*, vol. 6). London: Sage.

And a couple on case studies, simplest first:

Nisbet, J. D. and Watt, J. (1982) *Case Study*. Rediguide no. 26. Oxford: TRC Rediguides.

Yin, R. K. (2003) *Case Study Research: Design and Methods*, 3rd edn. Thousand Oaks, CA: Sage.

Quantitative research

For a straightforward introduction to statistics, see:

Diamond, I. and Jeffries, J. (2000) *Beginning Statistics: an Introduction for Social Scientists*. London: Sage.

This book emphasizes description, examples, graphs and displays rather than statistical formulae. A good guide to understanding the basic ideas of statistics.

For a comprehensive review of the subject see the following. I have ordered these in order of complexity, simplest first. The list could go on for pages with ever increasing abstruseness. You could also have a browse through what is available on your library shelves to see if there are some simple guides there.

Wright, D. B. (2002) *First Steps in Statistics*. London: Sage.

Kerr, A., Hall, H. and Kozub, S. (2002) *Doing Statistics with SPSS*. London: Sage.

Byrne, D. (2002) *Interpreting Quantitative Data*. London: Sage.

Bryman, Alan (2001) *Quantitative Data Analysis with SPSS Release 10 for Windows: a Guide for Social Scientists*. London: Routledge.

Siegel, S. and Castellan, N. J. (1988) *Nonparametric Statistics for the Behavioural Sciences*. New York: McGraw-Hill.

Seale, C. (ed.) (2004) *Researching Society and Culture*, 2nd edn. London: Sage.

For a good guide on how to interpret official statistics, look at the chapter by Don Slater in Seale (2004).

Qualitative analysis

As you would expect with this big and complex subject, there is a myriad of books dedicated to explaining all aspects. In the list below, I have tried to explain a bit about each book and how it may be of use to you. I have ordered them in what I think is going from simplest to most sophisticated.

Robson, C. (1993) *Real World Research: a Resource for Social Scientists and Practitioner-Researchers*. Oxford: Blackwell.

A resource book, and should be used as such. Good for getting more detailed information on most aspects of data collection and analysis. Read the recommendations at the beginning on how to use the book.

Flick, U. (2002) *An Introduction to Qualitative Research*, 2nd edn. London: Sage.

Continued

Useful sections on analysing verbal and visual data, with practical advice on documentation, coding, interpretation and analysis. The well organized layout will enable you to be selective in picking out what is relevant to you.

For a really comprehensive though incredibly dense and rather technical guide to qualitative data analysis, refer to:

Miles, M. B. and Huberman, A. M. (1994) *Qualitative Data Analysis: an Expanded Sourcebook*, 2nd edn. London: Sage.

This has a lot of examples of displays that help to explain how they work, but is technically sophisticated so you might find it difficult initially to understand the terminology in the examples. Once you get into it, it could provide you with valuable techniques for managing and analysing text-based data.

And a few more books if you don't find what you want in the above. Your library catalogue will list many more. Try a search using key words, such as data analysis, with management, education or whatever your particular subject is, to see if there are specific books dedicated to your particular interest.

Silverman, D. (2001) *Interpreting Qualitative Data: Methods for Analysing Talk, Text and Interaction*, 2nd edn. London: Sage.

Holliday, A. (2001) *Doing and Writing Qualitative Research*. London: Sage.

A general guide to writing qualitative research aimed at students of sociology, applied linguistics, management and education.

Schwandt, T. (1997) *Qualitative Enquiry: a Dictionary of Terms*. Thousand Oaks, CA: Sage.

To help you understand all the technical jargon.

Coffey, A. and Atkinson, P. (1996) *Making Sense of Qualitative Data: Complementary Research Strategies*. London: Sage.

Modelling and experimentation

Another huge subject with a huge choice of books. I have divided the list below into different sections.

Here are some books on modelling, a subject that soon gets immersed in mathematical formulae, though there are computer packages that take much of the sweat out of calculations. I have ordered them in levels of increasing detail and complexity. Look in your library catalogue to see if there are any devoted to your own subject.

Marker, D. (2002) *Model Theory: an Introduction*. London: Springer.

Edwards, D. (2001) *Guide to Mathematical Modelling*, 2nd edn. Basingstoke: Palgrave.

Morgan, B. J. (2000) *Applied Stochastic Modelling*. London: Arnold.

Edwards, D. (2000) *Introduction to Graphical Modelling*, 2nd edn. New York: Springer.

Examples of modelling applied to specific subjects:

Oppenheim, N. (1980) *Applied Models in Urban and Regional Analysis*. London: Prentice-Hall.

Hedman, J. (2002) *IT and Business Models: Concepts and Theories*. Malmö: Liber Ekonomi.

Samuel, A. E. (1999) *Introduction to Engineering Design: Modelling, Synthesis and Problem Solving*. Oxford: Butterworth-Heinemann.

Some books dedicated to experimental methods. Again, check out under your own subject headings.

Cohen, L. and Manion, L. (1994) *Research Methods in Education*. London: Routledge.

Chapter 8 gives a comprehensive explanation about experiments. Most books on research methods have a chapter devoted to experiment design.

Lewis-Beck, M. S. (ed.) (1993) *Experimental Design and Methods*. London: Sage.

Dean, Angela (1999) *Design and Analysis of Experiments*. New York: Springer.

Montgomery, Douglas C. (1997) *Design and Analysis of Experiments*, 4th edn. New York: Wiley.

Wheeler, A. J. (1996) *Introduction to Engineering Experimentation*. London: Prentice-Hall.

About algorithms, for a simple explanation see the first below, but for more technical guides, much to do with computing, see the others.

Broadbent, G. (1988) *Design in Architecture: Architecture and the Human Sciences*. London: Fulton, p. 326.

Bateman, R. (2002) *The DSP Handbook: Algorithms, Application and Design Techniques*. Harlow: Prentice-Hall.

Harel, D. (1992) *Algorithmics: the Spirit of Computing*, 2nd edn. Wokingham: Addison-Wesley.

Continued

Internet

Here is a couple of good books about using the Internet to do research, particularly for doing surveys. They discuss the viability of the Internet as a research tool, the equipment required, how to design a survey, and what can go wrong, and provide some case studies as examples.

Hewson, C., Yuyle, P., Laurent, D. and Vogel, C. (2003) *Internet Research Methods: a Practical Guide for the Social and Behavioural Sciences.* London: Sage.

Mann, C. and Stewart, F. (2000) *Internet Communication and Qualitative Research: a Handbook for Researching Online.* London: Sage.

ANSWERS TO EXERCISES

EXERCISE 7.1

1 In order to be able to study a manageable number of cases. The sampling procedures help to ensure that the cases actually studied are representative of the whole population.

2 The single case is unlikely to be representative of the whole group, unless the group is very homogeneous in the aspect studied. There are situations when studying a single case is not only useful, but unavoidable. For example, when only one fossilized skeleton of a type of dinosaur has been discovered, many generalizations have been made about other possible dinosaurs of the same type, even in the absence of other skeletons.

3 (a) Random and non-random sampling. Random sampling relies on pure chance to select cases, which eliminates any possible influence of the researcher. Non-random sampling consists of selecting cases on the basis of convenience, even though there might be an attempt to achieve an element of representativity.

   (b) Random sampling must be used whenever possible if you wish to make generalizations from your collected data. When the numbers in the population are very small, when time is very short or it is impossible to gain access to the full range in the population, then non-random sampling may be used, with inherent limitations on the validity of generalizations made from the sample.

4 You must examine the nature of the population: is it homogeneous, or does it consist of strata? If the latter, what is the nature of the strata? Alternatively, the population may consist of clusters. Appropriate sampling techniques must be chosen in each case.

5 The required size of the sample depends on the nature of the population and the detail of the survey. Great variability within the population and detailed information requirement demand large samples. If great accuracy is needed, then the sample also needs to be large. If the population is very homogeneous and the survey limited in scope, then a small sample will suffice. Minimum sample sizes are normally stipulated for different statistical tests. Take account also of the practical limits imposed by the project.

EXERCISE 7.2

1   (a)   Too vague. Do you want to know which street, town, country or continent the person has come from?

    (b)   What reply can people give if they have 5 or more children? You could add the category 'more than 4' to cover this eventuality.

    (c)   The gradation in the scale is too fine. What is the difference between 54% and 56%? It is meaningless. A five-point scale is common: like very much, like, neither like nor dislike, dislike, dislike very much. Another may be added: don't know!

    (d)   This assumes that you have drunk a bottle of champagne within the last year. Not everyone is so lucky!

    (e)   Too complicated! Unless you are aiming this questionnaire at a very specialist and knowledgeable sample, the responses will be pure guesswork.

2   The main difference between all the four different kinds of personal data collection is the amount of control that the researcher has in determining the questions, and hence the type of answers which are expected. The most directed kind is the structured interview, where the respondent is strongly guided to limit him/herself to answering the series of questions posed by the researcher. At the other extreme, accounts are elicited from respondents with prompts, rather than questions, in order to encourage them to speak freely with as little direction from the researcher as possible. Semi-structured and open interviews fall between these two extremes.

3   No. When talking about a 'population', we are not only talking about people. A sample can be taken from a population of objects, events, situations and phenomena.

EXERCISE 7.3

1   (a)   Assuming that you want to keep all of your students in your lecture, a true experiment will not be possible. A one-shot case study (testing the students after the lecture) is possible, but takes no account of what they might already know. The one-group pre-test/post-test design would be better (testing the students before and after the lecture and comparing their increase in artist recognition).

    (b)   Much depends on whether you have several bricks of the same type which you can choose from randomly. If so, you could carry out a true experiment using a control group (pre-test/post-test control group). I suppose you would have to assume that any unbaked bricks that dissolved when you soaked them, would also not stand up to frost!

    (c)   Difficult, as there are so many uncontrollable variables which determine how long people sleep. Try setting up a pseudo-experiment and give a sleeping drug to the participants sleeping in your bed!

2 (a) Mechanical (physical), mathematical, diagrammatic.

(b) Diagrammatic.

(c) Physical, diagrammatic (including computer generated).

(d) Diagrammatic.

(e) Diagrammatic, possibly mathematical.

3 (a) Input data: egg size. Output data: time. No feedback.

(b) Input data: room geometry, furniture number and type with sizes, minimum spaces required around furniture in use. Output data: room arrangements. Feedback: possible changes to the space needs of using furniture through overlaps.

(c) Many inputs: speed of buses, position of bus stops, state of traffic etc. Output data: behaviour of buses relative to each other. Feedback: many possibilities to explore changes in input data suggested by results, e.g. change bus speed, alter bus stops etc.

(d) Input: glass type and strength, type and shape of framing, method of fixing glass, type of impact. Output: resistance to impact data. Feedback: different and more efficient combinations of the input values might be suggested by the output data.

EXERCISE 7.4

1 (a) The large number of scripts suggests that some quantitative analysis is possible, assuming that there is some standardization in the questions, and hence in the replies to them. Qualitative analysis would have to be used to assess the wider range of opinions given.

(b) This appears to be a purely qualitative study.

(c) Quantitative at first sight. It does depend, though, on what data are collected.

(d) Both quantitative and qualitative analysis are possible here.

(e) Again, this looks like a quantitative study, though it is possible that some qualitative analysis could be made by inference.

2 Parametric statistics are used to study data which conform to a common parameter, normally the Gaussian curve. Non-parametric statistics do not conform to a common parameter.

3 It is difficult (impossible?) to prove anything with statistics! You could, however, support an argument with statistical analysis which suggests correlations between variables which you claim demonstrate a connection between smoking and cancer.

4 I agree that you do have to use your creative and imaginative faculties when doing qualitative analysis, but your arguments must be backed up with logic and a coherent set of evidence. The use of human abilities to simplify, order and theorize complex, open-ended

social phenomena is essential for gaining an understanding of our everyday existence. However, this is not to say that science is devoid of creativity. Some of the greatest discoveries have been made on an intuitive basis, and only later supported by empirical data.

Unlike quantitative analysis, qualitative analysis must rely less on systematic experiment and testing than on continuous comparison of data. Concepts and theories are more likely to be developed during, and as a result of, this continuous comparison, rather than being formulated at the outset of the research. Quantitative analysis has the potential of providing precise answers, which qualitative analysis lacks. However, qualitative analysis can deal with subjective data that cannot be precisely measured.

5 (a) A network in the form of an organization chart would show the hierarchical structure. A role ordered display would also add information on the type of relationships between the roles.

   (b) A simple matrix could be used here to plot types of school vertically and social classes horizontally, giving fields to record the data on attitudes with each combination.

   (c) A network in the form of an activity record would clearly show the sequence of steps required to complete the task successfully.

   (d) An effects matrix would help to show how this change affected the work in the factory, and even if necessary the levels of pay.

8

Honesty and Research Ethics

Introduction
Honesty in Your Work
   Intellectual Ownership and Plagiarism
   Citation and Acknowledgement
   Responsibility and Accountability of the Researcher
   Data and Interpretations
   Where Do You Stand? Epistemology
Situations that Raise Ethical Issues
   Research Aims
   Means and Ends
   Ethics in Relation to Other People
   Participants
   Carrying Out the Research
   Dissemination
Ethics Policies, Permissions and Committees
   Organizations
   Ethics Committees
Conclusions
The Next Steps: Plan Your Code of Ethics
Checklist of Activities That Will Progress Your Research
   Consolidation and Assessment
Key Words
Further Reading
Answers to Exercises

AIMS

- To establish honesty and responsibility in research work.
- To consider ethics in research projects.
- To ensure the ethical treatment of research participants.
- To check the ethics of all research methods used.
- To understand the purposes of research organizations and ethics committees.

INTRODUCTION

Although there always was a keen awareness of ethical issues in professional research, increasing attention is being awarded to research carried on at student level. This is particularly the case for students doing research degrees, where carrying out the research goes beyond being an educational exercise and is likely to be of wider significance and to be disseminated to the public at a professional level.

There are two perspectives from which you can view the ethical issues in research. One is concerned with the values of honesty and frankness and personal integrity, the other with those of ethical responsibilities to the subjects of research, such as consent, confidentiality and courtesy.

Whilst the principles underpinning ethical practice are fairly straightforward and easy to understand, their application can be quite difficult in certain situations. Not all decisions can be clear-cut in the realm of human relations. It is therefore important that you discuss the ethical issues thrown up by your research with your supervisors and others who are specialists in this field. If you will be working with human participants, it is likely that you will have to obtain some kind of ethical approval from your university or organization. It is necessary for you to find out what conditions apply in your situation.

HONESTY IN YOUR WORK

Firstly, consider those issues which are concerned with research activities generally, and the conduct of researchers in particular. Honesty is essential, not only to enable straightforward, above-board communication, but to engender a level of trust and credibility to promote debate and the development of knowledge. This applies to all researchers, no matter what their subject. Although honesty must be maintained in all aspects of the research work, it is worth focusing here on several of the most important issues.

Intellectual ownership and plagiarism

plagiarism

Unless otherwise stated, what you write will be regarded as your own work; the ideas will be considered your own unless you say to the contrary. The worst offence against honesty in this respect is called **plagiarism**: directly copying someone else's work into your report, thesis etc. and letting it be assumed that it is your own. Using the thoughts, ideas and works of others without acknowledging their source, even if you paraphrased into your own words, is unethical. Equally serious is claiming sole authorship of work which is in fact the result of collaboration or amanuensis ('ghosting').

Figure 8.1   The worst offence against honesty is called plagiarism

Citation and acknowledgement

citation

Obviously, in no field of research can you rely entirely on your own ideas, concepts and theories; therefore standard practices have been developed to permit the originators of the work and ideas to be acknowledged within your own text. This is called **citation**. These methods of reference provide for direct quotations from the work of others and references from a wide variety of sources (such as books, journals, conferences, talks, interviews, TV programmes etc.), and should be meticulously used. You should also acknowledge the assistance of others and any collaboration with others.

The 'Harvard' system of referencing is explained in Chapters 2 and 9. There are other recognized methods which differ in detail. Very often, editors will insist on the use of a particular form of referencing for their publications. There are software programs (e.g. ProCite) which are accurate and time-saving utilities that enable you to convert your list of references almost instantaneously from one form to another and act as a database for all your references and appended notes.

Responsibility and accountability of the researcher

You do have responsibilities to fellow researchers, respondents, the public and the academic community. Apart from correct attribution, honesty is essential in the substance of what you write. Accurate descriptions are required of what you have done, how you have done it, the information you obtained, the techniques you used, the analysis you carried out, and the results of experiments – a myriad of details concerning every part of your work.

Data and interpretations

There is often a temptation to be too selective in the data used and in presenting the results of the analysis carried out. Silently rejecting or ignoring evidence which happens to be contrary to one's beliefs constitutes a breach of integrity. What could be of vital importance in developing a theory could be lost. For example, the hypothetico-deductive method depends on finding fault in theoretical statements in order not only to reject them but to refine them and bring them nearer to the truth. History is full of instances of scientific fraud. Here are two recent cases. The first is a proven case of tampering with medical records in order to mislead others, reported in *The Times* on 7 June 1995. This was a particularly dangerous kind of fraud, which might have led to untested and potentially harmful treatments being carried out on pregnant women. *The Times* on 19 June 1995 reported the reaction of the academic establishment, and the estimates of the incidence of medical fraud. This is summarized in Box 8.1.

Box 8.1   Fraud through fabrication and lying

Gynaecologist's research fraud prompts need for 'fraud squad'

Calls were made by the Royal College of Physicians to set up a 'research fraud squad' after an eminent gynaecologist was ordered to be struck off the medical register because he fabricated research work and lied about performing a pioneering operation.

(Continued)

The public should be assured that scientific research was free of bogus research claims. Science must be seen to be conducted with integrity and honesty, and any transgressions should not be covered up by the professions. Reliable estimates of fraud in medical science are difficult to come by, but enough concern is expressed by scientists to warrant immediate action. A central body made up of experts and other influential people will be established to co-ordinate investigations.

The case which prompted this call was that of Mr Pearce, who invented research findings in ectopic pregnancies on the basis of non-existent trials. He obtained signatures on his fabricated reports from colleagues who were not able to verify his work. Later, he claimed to have successfully conducted the first operation to successfully transfer an ectopic pregnancy. He was found guilty of creating a web of lies in an internal enquiry and was struck off the medical register to protect the public.

The great danger of scientific fraud is that researchers follow in good faith the techniques and treatments described as being successful in published papers. The dangerous consequences of this to patients and to the development of knowledge are obvious. The problem is compounded by the reluctance of medical institutions to investigate suspected instances of fraud because of a fear that their reputations may be damaged. (*The Times,* 19 June 1995)

The second case is an attack on one of the most revered intellectuals of our time for suspected falsification of evidence, as reported in *The Times* on 5 June 1995 and summarized below in Box 8.2.

Jung was a fraud, claims Harvard scholar

Richard Knoll, a prize winning academic at Harvard University, claims that he can prove that Carl Jung, a founder of psychoanalysis, was a fraud. He believes that the proof that he falsified evidence to promote his theories lies in archives of the Library of Congress, but that access to them has been blocked by the Jung family. Jung developed a theory that humanity shares archetypal images in its collective unconscious, and asserted that this was supported by evidence collected by one of his assistants, J. J. Honegger, in 1909. According to Honegger, a male patient he interviewed, known now as Solar Phallus Man, reported that he saw a vision of the sun with a phallus. This image was similar to those found in the ancient Greek cult of the god Mithras, thus proving, according to Jung, that this archetypal image had persisted throughout the ages.

Box 8.2

Knoll claims that Jung deliberately falsified the research notes in order to substantiate his claims. Because the mythology of Mithras was being popularized at that time in Germany, Jung changed the dates on the notes to before the publication of popular books on this subject in order to counter any possible assertions that the man had read about the solar phallus and recalled it during the interview. This makes Jung, according to Knoll, 'the most influential liar of the 20th century'. (*The Times*, 5 June 1995)

It is difficult, and some maintain that it is impossible, to be free from bias. However, distorting your data or results knowingly is a serious lapse of honesty. Scientific objectivity should be maintained (or attained as nearly as is practical). If you can see any reason for a possibility of bias in any aspect of the research, it should be acknowledged and explained. If the study involves personal judgements and assessments, the basis for these should be given. The sources of financial support for the research activities should be mentioned, and pressure and sponsorship from sources which might influence the impartiality of the research outcomes should be avoided.

It is good practice to admit to limitations of competence and resources. Promising more than you can deliver can be seen as not only foolhardy but also dishonest.

Read the accounts in Boxes 8.1 and 8.2 about instances of proven and suspected scientific fraud and answer the following questions:

EXERCISE 8.1

1   What type of fraud was Mr Pearce convicted of (Box 8.1)?
2   What dangers might have resulted from the misinformation which he disseminated?
3   What safeguards incorporated into scientific method are intended to overcome the possibility of this kind of deception?
4   Is the call for a 'fraud squad' realistic? Give reasons for your opinions. What difficulties do you think it would face?
5   Is the lie which Richard Knoll accuses Jung of perpetrating in Box 8.2 of the same type as the medical case cited in Box 8.1? What are the differences, if any?
6   What do you think are the reasons which make some researchers lie? Why do they not do it more often?

Where do you stand? epistemology

There are often lively debates about how research should be carried out, and the value and validity of the results resulting from different approaches. The theoretical perspective or **epistemology** of the researcher should be made clear at the outset of the research so that the 'ground rules' or assumptions that underpin the research can be understood by the readers and, in some instances, the subjects of the research.

Although others might disagree with your epistemology, at least it will be clear to all as to what it is. In many subjects it will initially be a challenging task to become aware of and to understand all the current and past theoretical underpinnings to relevant research. One of the principal functions of doing background research is to explore just this aspect, and to come to decisions on theory that will form the basis of your research approach. You will have the opportunity to make this clear in your research proposal.

Doucet and Mauthner stressed the need, while doing qualitative research, to reflect on the intertwined ethical, methodological and epistemological processes in order to attain a high degree of 'epistemic responsibility' through 'knowing well' and 'knowing responsibly' (2002, p. 139). They maintained that the reflexivity of a researcher should take into account those theoretical, epistemological and ontological models that inform and influence our knowledge construction, and argued that it was important to maintain relationships with participants who conflicted with those models, particularly during the data analysis processes. Data analysis is an ethical issue and data analysis methods are not ethically neutral. They are founded on both ontological and epistemological assumptions.

SITUATIONS THAT RAISE ETHICAL ISSUES

Now let us consider **ethics** in terms of the personal relationships often involved in research projects. Social research, and other forms of research which study people and their relationships to each other and to the world, need to be particularly sensitive about issues of ethical behaviour. As this kind of research often impinges on the sensibilities and rights of other people, researchers must be aware of necessary ethical standards which should be observed to avoid any harm which might be caused by carrying out or publishing the results of the research project.

Research aims

The aims of the research can be analysed from an ethical viewpoint. Is the research aimed merely at gaining greater knowledge and understanding of a phenomenon? If so, this kind of quest, seen in isolation, has little or no ethical consequences: the expansion of scientific knowledge is generally regarded as a good thing. But what might be done with the knowledge gained? The developers of the atomic bomb relied on the research in nuclear physics. Research in genetics resulted in the ability to clone a sheep, and in the future, perhaps humans.

Genetically modified crops are seen by some as a potential saviour for farmers in Third World countries, and by others as a great danger to our ecology. Is it the responsibility of the researchers in exploratory research to predict what might be developed as a result of their discoveries? The ethical debate around genetic research, stem cell research and many other innovative advances is grappling with these issues. Is the argument by some scientists, that if they do not do the work then others will, good enough to overcome ethical scruples?

The aims of applied research are more easily subjected to ethical investigation. A series of questions can be posed to tease out the ethical issues. Firstly, are the aims clearly stated? Are the aims likely to be achieved by the outcomes of the research? Will the results of the research benefit society, or at least not harm it? Will there be losers as well as gainers? You will have to argue that the aims of your research are in accordance with the ethical standards proscribed by your university or organization.

It might not be easy to persuade everyone about the benefits that might accrue from your research because of the variety of viewpoints and vested interests. For example, research into how sweatshop workers in developing countries could assert power to gain better working conditions might be regarded by the factory owners as subversive and a threat to the economy and the stability of society.

Aims that are too ambitions, that cannot be achieved by the planned research, can be seen as a form of deception, or at least of self-delusion. It is necessary to be realistic. The intention to achieve the stated aims is a sort of promise that needs some credibility of being fulfilled. There are always risks in doing research: the future cannot be predicted, but wild speculation and rash promises have no place in academic or professional research. Not only are the subjects of your research relying on the feasibility of the outcomes, but so too are the funders or other supporters of the project.

Means and ends

How the aims, however laudable, are achieved should also be examined from an ethical viewpoint. 'No gain without pain' is a popular expression – but can this approach be justified in a research project? There are many famous controversies that surround this issue, for example the horrific medical experiments on detainees carried out by Mengele in Nazi Germany, the results of which are reputed to have been transported to the USA after the war to inform the development of defence methods; or, on a quite different level, the experiments on animals for development and testing of medicines; or the research at the British Common Cold Research Centre, which used to induce a cold in volunteers in the attempt to find a cure; or the growing of test areas of GM crops on open farmland.

There might be several ways that the research aims can be achieved. You should look at the alternatives to see if there are any ethical implications in the choice. Also, examine if there might be unintended or unexpected side effects of your methods. If the only means of achieving a beneficial end is at the expense of discomfort or inconvenience, is it the sufferers that are likely to be the beneficiaries? Whatever the situation, the nature and the extent of the 'pain' must be assessed, consent must be obtained from the participants, and of course, clearance must be given by the relevant ethical committee.

Ethics in relation to other people

Quite obviously, research ethics are principally concerned with the effects of research on people, and importantly, on those people who get involved in the research process in one way or another. It is the researcher who plans the project that has the responsibility to predict what the effect will be on those people that he/she will approach and involve in the research, as subject, participant, respondent, interviewee etc.

Before going into details about the process of the research, it is worth discussing briefly the important influences of terminology used during the research:

1 in the way you use language in your written work
2 in relation to people and their roles.

Let us look at the use of language first. According to an Open University (1993) guide to language and image, there are five aspects to be aware of when writing, as given in Box 8.3.

Box 8.3   What to be aware of when writing

- *Age*   Avoid being patronizing or disparaging.
- *Cultural diversity*   Avoid bias, stereotyping, omission, discrimination.
- *Disability*   Avoid marginalizing, patronizing.
- *Gender*   Avoid male centricity, gender stereotyping.
- *Sexual orientation*   Avoid prejudice, intolerance, discrimination.

The aim is to be as neutral as possible in the use of terminology involving people – who and what they are, and what they do. So many words and phrases are in common use that make unwarranted assumptions and assertions about people, or are at least imprecise and possibly insulting. Acceptable terminology changes with time, so you should be aware that what is used in some older literature is not suitable for use now. You require to be constantly aware of the real meaning of terms, and their use within the particular context. In order to test you on your awareness, try the following exercise.

Read the following extracts from a fictitious report about the results of a survey and consider the suitability of the terminology used with regard to people. Suggest better alternatives to the words you find to be discriminatory, derogatory or too imprecise.

Report

The research project was centred on comparing the opinions on street crime of a large range of people, from old folk in care homes to youngsters on the street. The results of the research are summarized as follows.

The old dears were, in general, most influenced by what they saw on the news on television. Half of the normal ones feared going out after dark alone, and almost all of the disabled, such as the blind, the deaf, the wheelchair bound and those with a mental handicap, would not go out unless accompanied.

Middle age professional people such as businessmen, doctors, headmasters etc. were not afraid to walk through the city centre at night, though took simple precautions such as putting their wallets into their trouser pockets instead of in their coat pockets.

Of the lower class people, it was generally charwomen, deliverymen, 24 hour shop sales-girls and waiters who felt particularly vulnerable, as they tended to be out late at night.

Policemen on the beat were aware of some problems in town centres at the weekends, but most laymen thought that street crime was a problem at all times. British people in particular blamed the violence on other ethnic groups, such as the blacks and other immigrants.

When asked if street violence was a youth issue, youngsters generally said no, blaming it instead on druggies, homosexuals and tramps. They complained about the intolerance of geri-atrics who did not respect their way of life. A typical young person was likely to think himself more streetwise than any other age group, citing quick-wittedness and agility as his main attributes.

How will you present yourself in the role of the researcher? As a student researcher, you can present yourself as just that, giving the correct impression that you are doing the research as an academic exercise that may reveal useful information or understanding, but do not have the institutional or political backing to cause immediate action. If you are a practitioner embarking on research, e.g. a teacher researcher, a nurse researcher or a social worker researcher, then you have a professional status that lends you more authority and possibly power to instigate change. This might influence the attitude and expectations of the people you involve in your project.

The words **subject**, **participant**, respondent, interviewee and other similar labels have shades of meaning that suggest or denote relationships with the researcher and status in the research project.

subject
participant

> The word 'subject' perhaps carries the implication that something is being done *to* them, while the term 'participant' implies that something is carried out in conjunction *with* them. During the research process, the distinction could be quite important. (Oliver, 2003, p. 4)

How one behaves with people during the research sends out strong signals and might raise unforeseen expectations. Stopping people in the street and asking them a set of standardized questions is unlikely to elicit much engagement by the subjects. However, if you spend a lot of time with a – perhaps lonely – old person, delving into her personal history, the more intimate situation might give rise to a more personal relationship that could go beyond the simple research context. How 'friendly' should you become? Even more expectations can be raised if you are working in a context of deprivation or inequality: will the subjects begin to expect you to do something to improve their situation?

Thus the place and the degree of involvement are important factors in the characteristics of the research. Making observations in a public place will not result in the subjects of the research being affected by your demeanour, but the more private and individual the context, the more attention will have to be paid to one's personal attitude and behaviour.

Your status and role might put you in a dominant position that affects the free action of the participants in the research. If you are an employer researching your staff, a teacher with a project about your students, or a doctor or nurse investigating your patients, it might be difficult for the participants to refuse to co-operate or withhold information or give true opinions. Perhaps, as a 'wealthy' Westernized person engaged in research in a deprived rural Third World area, you might be accorded additional respect and authority. Care must be exercised not to take advantage of these situations.

Thus practitioner researchers, both student and professional, face particular problems in avoiding any confusion between their roles as practitioners and as researchers. Their concern must be how to 'manage' their responsibilities towards clients, students, patients etc., fellow practitioners, organizational bodies, other researchers and academic institutions, in ways that all parties should consider ethical. The main issues of concern are those of confidentiality and negotiation within the research process, access to subjects, seeking informed voluntary consent, and whether or not to emphasize the role of practitioner when carrying out research (Bell and Nutt, 2002, pp. 70–5).

Participants

Participants, subjects, respondents or whatever term you wish to use for the people you will approach for information in your research, need to be treated with due ethical consideration, both on their own part and on the part of the information they provide. There is a series of issues that need to be considered when you use human participants. Here are some comments on a range of these to take into consideration.

Choosing participants

In some cases, participants choose themselves whether to take part in a survey. If you simply drop off a questionnaire at their house, they are quite free to fill it in or not, assuming that there is nothing in the questionnaire that threatens or otherwise affects a free choice. There are situations, however, where pressure, inadvertent or not, might be exerted on participants. Enlisting friends or relatives – people who feel they have an obligation to help you despite any reservations they may have – could result in a restriction of their freedom to refuse. Leaving too little time for due consideration might also result in participants regretting taking part.

Figure 8.2 The subjects of your study are obviously not in a position to choose whether they are observed or not

When you are making observations in a public place, the subjects of your study are obviously not in a position to choose whether they are observed or not. Measures must be taken to protect their anonymity (e.g. if photographed). If you cannot do this, you must approach the subjects to give them the choice of featuring in your research or not.

If the choice of participants is made by others, e.g. by a 'gatekeeper' (someone with overall responsibility for a group of people, usually within an organization), the basis on which the choice is made should be agreed, and assurance gained that the participation is voluntary. Issues of bias should be considered, e.g. the head-teacher might only want the best pupils to be questioned, or the factory owner might only allow access to compliant workers. Alternatively, the boss might bring pressure to bear on a participant to take part against his/her will. Consider whether any restrictions imposed by the gatekeeper will compromise the research.

Freedom from coercion: reward or not?

Obviously dishonest means of persuasion, for example, posing as an official, making unrealistic and untrue promises, allowing the belief that you have come to help, being unduly persistent, and targeting people in vulnerable situations, must be avoided. Although it is easy to detect crass instances of these, you could employ them almost inadvertently if you are not alert to people's situations and reactions.

The question of whether, what and how much to reward the participants is one that is not often posed in research student projects, as the financial means are rarely sufficient to cover such incentives beyond perhaps the inclusion of reply-paid envelopes. However, in funded research this could be a real issue. Some commensurate recompense for time and inconvenience can usually be justified. Rewards that might unduly influence the decision of the participants to take part are not suitable, nor are those that might influence their responses to questions. You will have to justify the need for and nature of any rewards in your proposal.

Informed consent, written consent

An important aspect of the decision of the participants to take part or not is the quality of the information they receive about the research, enabling them to

informed consent

make a fair assessment of the project so that they can give **informed consent**. The form that this information takes depends on the type of respondent, the nature of the research process and the context.

There may be several layers of consent required. When working within an organization, the managers or other people with overall responsibilities may need to be consulted before the individual participants. There could be a conflict of interest between the management and those of the employees. It must be made clear and agreed at all levels how the investigation will be conducted, how confidentiality will be maintained, and what issues are to be discussed. This is a particularly sensitive matter in cases where criticism may be made of persons, organizations or systems of work or conditions. There must be some obvious form of protection for those making criticisms and those at the receiving end.

Clarity, brevity and frankness are key attributes in providing information on which consent is based. Verbal explanations may suffice in informal situations, though a written résumé on a flyer could be useful. Questionnaires should always provide the necessary written information as an introduction. In many cases, the wording of any information may have to be simplified in order that the non-technical person can understand; do not try to impress with technical jargon. The participant needs to know: who is doing the research, what are its aims and objectives, what the participant is being asked to do and why, how the information given will be used, and what steps are being taken to ensure confidentiality and anonymity. Time may be needed for the participant to consider the implications of taking part, and perhaps also for consulting others.

The form of consent must also be considered. Is verbal consent sufficient? Normally it is when doing informal interviews in public places, and the questions are not too intimate or controversial. In the case of a simple questionnaire, the fact that the respondent has completed it and returned it is usually sufficient.

When dealing with organizations, written consent is always required, not least by yourself, to cover you against any possible future difficulties. In more complex forms of data gathering, e.g. experiments, trials, extended interviews etc., it is good practice to get written confirmation from the participants that they understand what is required and agree to take part.

Getting consent from vulnerable people (this includes children, some old people, the illiterate, foreign language speakers, those that are ill, and even the deceased) requires particular consideration, depending on the circumstances. The level of understanding must be assessed, and those that are responsible for the vulnerable people must be consulted. There are often difficult decisions to be made. Special help to aid understanding might be given, but not to the point of condescension or social labelling. The assistance of an intermediary might be appropriate, such as a translator, relative or carer. In some cases, those responsible for the care of the vulnerable people may be in the position to give consent on their behalf. It is a good idea to consult at an early stage with people experienced in these issues, and with those responsible for vetting the ethical standards of the proposed research.

Notwithstanding any agreement to take part in a research project, participants must have the right to terminate their participation at any time. There could be many reasons why a participant may want to stop taking part in the research: there may be aspects of the research that they did not fully understand, unwanted implications that appeared, discomfort or embarrassment, or just too much bother. No reason need be given for the termination, and it should be accepted immediately, however inconvenient to the researcher.

Carrying out the research

Potential harm and gain

Ethical research is aimed at causing no harm and, if possible, producing some gain, not only in the wider field, but for the participants in the project. A prediction must be made by the researcher about the potential of the chosen research methods and their outcomes for causing harm or gain. The implications of involving people in your research are not always obvious, so if there are issues about which you are not certain, you should consult with experts in the field who have had more experience.

What sort of precautions should be taken? Find out how you can avoid risk to participants by recognizing what the risks might be, and choosing methods that minimize these risks. For example, psychological harm can be caused by investigations into tragic or uncomfortable experiences, particularly if the subjects are still very much emotionally involved with the event. Assuming that there is good reason for making these investigations, there may be ways to minimize the harm by consulting people who are not so immediately affected by the event. Also, participants might be reassured about the benefits to others of the research; perhaps further such events might thus be prevented. It may help to have a relative or friend present to support the participant.

Other types of harm to avoid are those arising not so much from the encounter with participants, but from the results of the investigation. Could what is revealed in any way be harmful to the reputation, dignity or privacy of the subjects? Could it in any way alter the status quo to the disadvantage of the participants, e.g. by unjustifiably raising their expectations or by souring their relationships with other people?

Figure 8.3 Particular care must be taken when the researcher is working in an unfamiliar social situation

Particular care must be taken when the researcher is working in an unfamiliar social situation, e.g. in an institution or amongst people of a different cultural or ethnic background. It may be that because the mores are not well understood, offence can be committed inadvertently. Language barriers can also lead to mis-understandings, as can religious differences. The best way to reduce the risk of harm in these circumstances is to carefully weigh up the areas of doubt to get advice and guidance on measures to avoid potential pitfalls. Being aware of the problems goes half-way to solving them!

One way to ensure that individuals or groups of participants are not impli-cated in any way in the findings of the research is to devise systems to ensure anonymity and confidentiality in the material accessible by other people. This relates not only to the published work, but also to your collected data that might be accessed by others. There is more about this subject in the later section on dissemination.

Interviews and questionnaires

When recording data, particularly from interviews and open questions, there is a danger of simplifying transcripts, and in the process losing some of the meaning. By cleaning up, organizing, ignoring vocal inflections, repetitions and asides etc., you start to impose your own view or interpretation. This is difficult to avoid, as the grammar and punctuation of written text impose their own rules which are different from those of verbal forms. Losing subtleties of humour can misrepresent emotional tone and meaning. Alldred and Gillies pointed out that speech is a 'messy' form of communication, and by writing it down we tend to make an account 'readable' and interpret 'what was meant' (2002, pp. 159–61).

It is easy to impose one's own particular assumptions, e.g. in interviews, especially when questioning people of different background, culture or social status. Is the content of your interview based perhaps on white, Western assumptions, or other assumptions inherent in your own cultural milieu? As an example, Alldred and Gillies related how the notion of personal decision making and individualism which underpinned interview questions about the nature of parenthood and agency made little sense to a couple from Bangladesh, who were being asked to narrate themselves as Westernized modernist subjects (2002, pp. 155–7).

Participant involvement: experiments, observations, groups

If your research entails close communication between you, the researcher, and the participants, the issues of getting involved and the question of rapport are raised. How will those involved understand your actions, and are these in balance with your judgement about your own practice? Your intentions for your research might be to gain as much revealing information as possible, and by 'doing rapport' or faking friendship you might encourage the interviewee to open up. The intimacy between researcher and respondent can resemble friendship. This raises the question: is it taken so far as to deceive in order 'to encourage or persuade interviewees to explore and disclose experiences and emotions which – on reflection – they may have preferred to keep to themselves or even "not-to-know"' (Duncombe and Jessop, 2002, p. 120)?

Sensitive material

Research into human situations, whether in the workplace, in social settings, in care institutions or in education, can throw up information that is of a sensitive nature. This means that the information is such that if revealed, it could do damage to the participants or to other people. Revelations about the treatment of individuals due to the actions of others or due to the workings of an organization may call for action on the part of the researcher that is outside the remit of the project. If, for example, a pupil complains to you about being bullied or an employee claims to be the victim of discrimination, what attitude should you adopt about taking action to remedy the unfair situation? What should you do if someone admits to cheating or an even more serious misdemeanour? Should you report the information to the relevant management or authority, or should you keep it confidential? Sometimes, the researcher is seen by participants as someone who could help or who has special knowledge or power to influence the situation.

Every case must be judged individually, and careful thought must be given to the implications of divulging the information to any third party. It may be possible to give advice to the participant about who to contact for help, such as a school tutor, trade union or ombudsman. It is not advisable to get personally involved as this could lead to unforeseen and unfortunate consequences that could not only cause harm to the participant and other people, but endanger the integrity of yourself and the research project. Take advice from your supervisor or ethics officer if the decisions are difficult.

Honesty, deception and covert methods

An ethically sound approach to research is based on the principle of honesty. This precludes any type of deception and the use of covert methods. However, it may be argued that some kind of information which could be of benefit to society can only be gained by these methods, because of obstruction by people or organizations that are not willing to risk being subjected to scrutiny. Injustices might be brought to light that are otherwise obscured by lack of information, such as discrimination, unfair working practices or the neglect of duties. If the argument is based on the principle of doing good without doing harm, it must be recognized that the prediction of the outcomes of the research are speculative. How can one be sure of the benign consequences of the actions? The risks involved are such as to make the use of deception and covert methods extremely questionable, and even in some cases dangerous (one need only think of the risks run in cases where investigative journalists have infiltrated a gang of football hooligans and other criminal organizations in order to uncover their covert operations).

EXERCISE 8.3

This exercise involves you looking up a web page and considering the ethical issues involved in a particularly controversial psychological experiment carried out by psychologist Stanley Milgram at Yale University in the 1950s and 1960s. He wanted to see how far people would be willing to turn up the dial, if ordered to do so, on a machine that pretended to give electrical shocks to people in the next room. He was surprised how many people were willing to go all the way, even though some broke down in tears after hearing fake screams coming from the other room.

The web address is http://www.wadsworth.com/psychology_d/templates/student_ resources/0155060678_rathus/ps/ps01.html (sorry about the length!) based on Milgram (1963), with the permission of Alexandra Milgram. This is a detailed account of why and how the experiment was carried out, and there is a set of questions at the end on the ethical issues raised. I reproduce those that are directly related to ethics.

1 Milgram's methods made the subjects extremely uncomfortable. Do you believe that his research was ethical? Why or why not?
2 Milgram undertook his research in the late 1950s and early 1960s, before ethics review committees were established. These committees weigh the value of proposed research against its potential harm. If you were proposing the research to such a committee, what arguments could you make in its favour? If you were a member of such a committee, what arguments might you make to block the research?
3 Can you think of a way in which Milgram's research might have been conducted without deceiving the subjects?
4 Milgram 'debriefed' subjects after they participated in the study. That is, he explained that they did not really shock anyone. Debriefing is intended to protect subjects from harm. If you had participated in the study, which would you have found more stressful: belief that you had or had not shocked anyone? Why?

Using assistants or delegating tasks

You may be in the lucky situation where you can call on assistance to carry out some of the fieldwork, particularly if you are doing funded research. Your ethical responsibilities will be of course delegated to your assistants, so you must be sure that they are aware of these. A thorough training in what they should do (and not do) is essential so as to avoid problems arising from ignorance and confusion. Regular feedback from the assistants is essential to ensure standards are maintained.

Storing and transmitting data

The data that you have collected will often be sensitive, i.e. will contain confidential details about people and/or organizations. It is therefore important to devise a storage system that is safe and only accessible to you. Paper-based and audio data should be locked away, and computer databases should be protected by a password. If it is necessary to transmit data, take measures to ensure that the method of transmission is secure. E-mails and file transfers can be open to unauthorized access, so precautions should be taken to use the securest transmission method available.

The Data Protection Act 1998 covers virtually all collections of personal data in whatever form and at whatever scale in the UK. It spells out the rights of the subjects and the responsibilities of the compilers and holders of the data. You can search for a copy of this on the UK government website www.open.gov.uk and equivalent regulations on sites in other countries (e.g. www.open.gov.au for Australia, www.usgovsearch.northernlight.com for the USA – a pay-site).

Analysing the data and getting results

One might assume that, once the necessary data have been acquired in an ethical fashion, the analysis of those data is an ethics-free activity. After all, you are only trying to make sense of the data and to reveal the hidden 'truths' by applying standard analytical techniques that are known for their reliability. However, Doucet and Mauthner conclude that:

> Data analysis is an ethical issue because it exposes power and privilege in relation-ships, decision-making around maintaining or curbing relationships with research subjects, and the potential for profound relational violations. In arguing that data analysis processes are theoretically infused we also suggest that data analysis methods are not neutral techniques, Rather, they are methods that embrace both methodological and epistemological assumptions. (2002, p. 139)

They stress the importance of maintaining relationships with research subjects during the analysis stage, particularly those that do not 'fit' into your theoretical, epistemological and political frameworks. Specifically in qualitative research, the combination of influences from your own personal life, your choice of the academic texts that frame your research and analysis, and the institutional context will guide you towards a particular way of 'seeing' and 'hearing' respondents' accounts (Doucet, 1998). The way to gain clarity and accountability in the analysis stages is to be as transparent as possible about your personal and theoretical attitudes, which have a bearing on the analytical and interpretive parts of the research. This requires a high degree of reflexivity about one's own cultural assumptions, theoretical stance and personal attitudes, and knowledge of other ways that the analysis could be approached.

Checking data and drafts

What are your responsibilities in relation to the data that you have collected from respondents? To what extent should you allow participants to see your observation notes, interview transcripts etc.? Oliver (2003, p. 63) draws the distinction between raw data and data that have been subjected to some interpretation or analysis. He suggests that it would be reasonable to allow a respondent to have a copy of the tape of their recorded interview or their completed questionnaire (i.e. raw data), but not transcripts or observational data, as these have been subjected to a level of coding, selection or analysis that renders them the intellectual property of the researcher. It is not practical to let respondents read and edit large amounts of primary data owing to the delays this would cause, and as they are unlikely to have the necessary skills to judge their validity and accuracy.

It is normal practice to produce drafts of your work in order for you and others to check it for spelling and grammatical errors and for structure and content. It is appropriate to pass the drafts on to colleagues or supervisors for comment, with the proviso that the content is kept confidential, as at this stage it is not ready for publication and dissemination. It is generally not appropriate, however, to allow sponsors to make comments on a draft because of the danger that they may demand changes to be made to conclusions that are contrary to their interests. This could undermine the intellectual independence of the findings of the report.

Dissemination

If you are doing a research degree, the first stage of dissemination is the submission of the thesis for examination. In some countries, the examination at PhD level is a very public affair. The candidate must present the thesis to a panel of examiners, who question the examinee in front of a large invited audience, members of which can also pose questions. Mercifully, this is not generally the case in the UK, where the viva is much more intimate. After your successful completion of a thesis or dissertation, there will be standard procedures, depending on your university or college, for making your work available to the public.

You may wish to disseminate your work further by publishing the results in the form of conference or journal papers, a website or other types of publication. As this process inevitably involves reducing the length of the material, and perhaps changing the style of the writing for inclusion into professional journals or newspapers, you must be careful that the publication remains true to the original. Oversimplification, bias towards particular results or even sensationalization may result from targeting a particular readership.

In most cases, the intellectual ownership of sponsored research remains with the researchers. Apart from any specific agreements between the researchers and sponsors, dissemination is the concern of the authors of the research report. Oliver (2003, p. 121) suggests one situation where the sponsor may wish to see the final report before dissemination. If the findings of the report are contrary to the sponsor's interests, or the sponsor disagrees with the conclusions, seeing the report will enable them to formulate a statement in reply that can be disseminated at the same time as the report. This will leave the readers to make their own judgements.

The question of authorship in team efforts needs to be addressed. Agreement should be reached between those that contributed to the research and production of the report as to who should be listed as authors and in which order the names should occur. Acknowledgement should be made to others who contributed substantially to the work, and to the sponsors. This may not be an easy process in larger projects where many people have been involved at various stages of the work and in various capacities (see Townend, 2000, pp. 92–6).

Participants might request to be informed about the outcomes of the research. This raises certain questions about the ownership of the final report. If the report has been commissioned by a sponsor it could, depending on the contract, be their property and you might have no right to disseminate it to others without permission. If the results of the research are published in the public domain, however, there is no reason why the participants should not be sent a copy of the article or paper. In some cases, a short summary of the findings might suffice.

Disposing of records

When the data have been analysed and are no longer needed, a suitable time and method for disposal should be decided. Ideally, the matter will have been agreed with the participants as a part of their informed consent, so the decision will have been made much earlier. However, this issue might not be as easy as it appears. There are several reasons why you might want to keep confidential data for longer than needed for your immediate project. You may want to keep the data in case there are any queries about them at a later date, or if you expect to use them as the basis of further publications. Perhaps you only used a part of the collected data, and wish to use some more of them for another project. You might even know another researcher who could make good use of the data you have collected.

There are several precautions that can be taken when faced with these issues. If the conditions about disposal of data were agreed with the participants, and you wish to change the conditions, you should contact the participants again to ask if they object to your new proposals. This might cause practical problems of finding the participants again, in which case a pragmatic solution should be sought that protects the interests of the participants. One basic policy is to ensure that all the data are anonymous and non-attributable. This can be done by removing all labels and titles that could lead to identification.

When destroying data, make sure that they are disposed of in such a way as to be completely indecipherable. This might entail shredding documents, formatting disks and erasing tapes.

ETHICS POLICIES, PERMISSIONS AND COMMITTEES

Organizations

All organizations that are involved in research with human participants will have set up a code of practice for their researchers. To see typical examples of these types of guidelines, you can refer to the web page produced by the British Educational Research Association (www.bera.ac.uk/guidelines.htms) or the British Sociological Association statement of ethical practice (www.britsoc.co.uk/index).

Your university will certainly have set up its own code of practice. As an indication of what you might expect, Box 8.4 gives an abbreviated version of the Oxford Brookes University (2003) code. Do, though, refer to your own organization's code when preparing your own ethical policy.

Box 8.4   Ethical standards for research involving human participants

Code of Practice

1   *Introduction*   The integrity of any research depends not only on its scientific rigour, but also on its ethical adequacy. Ethical issues are many and varied, and may be quite complex. All research should be guided by a set of fundamental ethical principles to ensure the protection of human participants.

Underpinning the standards are the ethical imperatives of *do no harm* (nonmaleficence) and *do good* (beneficence). Consideration of risks versus benefits must be weighed up by researchers. In medical research physically invasive procedures are easily defined, but what constitutes risk in social research is sometimes less clear-cut. Questionnaires, observation and interviews can all be potentially intrusive and provoke anxiety in participants, or worse, involve psychological risk. Certain groups are particularly vulnerable and may succumb to pressure, while some are unable to give informed consent and are therefore less able to protect themselves.

The following standards have been developed to guide staff and students undertaking research involving human participants. They are intended to cover general principles, but they may not address all situations, and the researcher should seek further advice from their School's Research Ethics Officer, the University Research Ethics Committee and their profession's code of practice for research ethics as appropriate.

2   *No research should cause harm, and preferably it should benefit participants* A judgement must be made as to whether a particular intervention is likely to affect the well-being of participants and any potential risks should be identified. Procedures must be justified, explaining why alternative approaches involving less risk cannot be used. The potential benefits of the research to participants, the scientific community and/or society must be clearly stated. Any cultural, religious, gender or other differences in a research population should be sensitively and appropriately handled by researchers at all stages.

3   *Potential participants normally have the right to receive clearly communicated information from the researcher in advance*   Most research procedures should be explained on an information sheet that is easily comprehensible by the potential research participant. The information sheet should set out: the purpose of the investigation; the procedures; the risks and the benefits, or absence of them, to the individual or to others in the future or to society; a statement that individuals may decline to participate and also will be free to withdraw at any time without giving a reason; and an invitation to ask questions. The information sheet should also provide contact details of the School's Research Ethics Officer so that participants may report any procedures that seem to violate their welfare.

4   *Participants should be given plenty of time to study the information sheet, and consult relevant parties*   Participants should not be pressured to participate in a study. Promises of compensation and care for damage, injury or loss

(Continued)

Box 8.4

of income should not be considered inducements. Inducements (other than reimbursement for travel expenses or in some cases time) should usually be avoided. Risks involved in participation should be acceptable to participants and they must be free to withdraw from the study at any time.

5 *Participants in a research study have the right to give their informed consent before participating*   Participants should understand the purpose and nature of the study, what participation in the study requires, and what benefits are intended to result from the study. Voluntary informed consent, in writing, should usually be obtained, though consent may be implied by the completion and return of many social survey questionnaires. It is the researcher's responsibility to seek ongoing consent during the course of a study. Individual consent may be unnecessary for some unintrusive research activities, for example studies involving observation of public behaviour.

6 *Where third parties are affected by the research, informal consent should be obtained*   When third parties, for example spouses, teachers or health care professionals, are directly involved in the care, education or treatment of the potential participants, they should be fully informed and consent should also be obtained from them, in written form if the proposed research is likely to interfere with the treatment or care being provided.

In certain situations, if participants are affiliated to organizations such as educational institutions, businesses, or hospitals, it may be necessary to gain permission to conduct the research project and follow any relevant policies, procedures or guidelines.

7 *The consent of vulnerable participants or their representatives' assent should be actively sought by researchers*   If the involvement of children in a research study is justified, then parents or other legal guardians have the right to be informed and to give their assent for inclusion of the child in the study. To the extent that it is feasible, the willing consent of participants who are children should also be sought. Generally, children over age 16 may be assumed to be capable of giving informed consent, but this will vary depending on the nature of research and special guidance may need to be sought.

In cases where people are unable to comprehend the implications of research, for example people with dementia, assent to participate may have to come from a representative, such as a legal guardian or immediate relative. Witnessed consent is required for vulnerable participants who have intellectual or cultural difficulties in speech or understanding, but who are deemed capable of giving consent.

The quality of the consent of participants who are in a potentially dependent relationship with the researcher (e.g. students, employees and patients) requires careful consideration, as willingness to volunteer may be unduly influenced by the expectation of advantageous benefits.

8 *Honesty should be central to the relationship between researcher, participant and institutional representatives*   The deception of participants should be avoided. If deception is necessary, the reasons should be explained to participants after the study. The use of covert observation, e.g. one-way mirrors, must be justified.

Box 8.4

9 *Participants' confidentiality and anonymity should be maintained* Researchers should take precautions to protect confidentiality of participants and data. When personal identifiers are used in a study, researchers should explain why this is necessary and how confidentiality would be protected. Researchers should deal with all data so as not to compromise the personal dignity and privacy of the participant. Any information which may identify the participant may not be revealed without the participant's adequate prior consent in writing.

All information obtained in the course of a research project should be considered privileged information and should not be publicly disclosed and identify any individual or organization (except if subpoenaed by a court).

Procedures for protecting the confidentiality of participants should be followed and include:

- securing individual confidentiality statements from all research personnel
- coding data with numbers instead of names
- using codes for identification of participants when transcribing audiotapes
- storing data with any identifying information in a locked file with limited access
- using pseudonyms for participants, agencies and geographical settings in the publishing of reports
- disposing of information that can reveal the identity of participants or places carefully, e.g. burning or shredding.

10 *The collection and storage of research data by researchers must comply with the Data Protection Act 1998* Researchers should follow the University's Data Protection Policy and Guidelines and be aware of the risks to anonymity, privacy and confidentiality posed by all kinds of personal information storage and processing. Measures to prevent accidental breaches of confidentiality should be taken (see section 9), and in cases where confidentiality is threatened, relevant records should be destroyed.

Participants must be informed of the kinds of personal information which will be collected, what will be done with it, and to whom it will be disclosed. 'Consent to process' may need to be obtained where information collected from individuals is to be used later for research purposes.

Provisions for data security at the end of a project must be made. Where the researcher leaves the University, this responsibility should usually rest with the relevant School.

11 *Researchers have a duty to disseminate their research findings to all appropriate parties* Participants and relevant stakeholders should be offered access to a summary of the research findings. Reports to the public should be clear and understandable, and accurately reflect the significance of the study.

Source: Oxford Brookes University, *Ethical Standards for Research Involving Human Participants: Code of Practice*, 2003

Ethics committees

The role of ethics committees is to oversee the research carried out in their organizations in relation to ethical issues. It is they who formulate the research ethics code of conduct and monitor its application in the research carried out by members of their organizations. Your university or other institution will probably have a system which makes it possible for its research committee to do its job. This, inevitably, involves filling in forms.

In order to help researchers decide whether their research proposals should be submitted for approval by the school research ethics officer or committee, your university will also provide an ethics review checklist that can be adapted for the particular circumstances of the research in each subject area. Obtain one of these to check whether your activities will necessitate ethics approval. Examples of questions you might expect in the checklist are in the 'next steps' section later in this chapter.

If you answer 'yes' to any of the questions, you will have to submit your proposal using the appropriate ethics approval application form to your school research ethics officer. It is advisable, when any doubt arises in relation to the above, to always forward your proposal to the school research ethics officer for him/her to review.

The forms will ask a series of questions on a range of ethical issues and will require detailed information on your research methods. You will have to justify why you have selected the particular methods proposed and to explain how you will deal with all the attendant ethical issues. Box 8.5 gives a guide, taken from the Oxford Brookes University consent form guidelines (http://www.brookes.ac.uk/research/ethics/ethicscode/html), to what you will probably need to include.

Box 8.5 Checklist of issues for ethics consent form

- Title of the study.
- Purpose of the study.
- Why participant was selected.
- Description of procedures, purpose, length of time required and how participant will be involved.
- Discomforts, inconveniences expected.
- Risks, if any.
- Benefits, if any.
- Withholding standard care/treatment or an alternative, if any.
- Compensation to be expected, if any.
- How confidentiality, anonymity and privacy will be maintained.
- Right of participant to refuse to participate or withdraw at any time for any reason.

Box 8.5

- Sources for information and assurances that researcher will provide further and ongoing information (e.g. name and contact phone number of the researcher).
- Signature of the researcher and the participant or the participant's representative.
- Signature of the witnesses where appropriate.

Source: Oxford Brookes University

The research committee will then review your forms, and all being well, give you clearance to continue with the research. If there are issues that are not clear or not fully dealt with, the committee will want to have clarification before giving consent.

If you are embarking on a research degree, this process commonly occurs immediately after you have submitted your research proposal and are registered to do the degree. Similarly, if you are doing a Masters degree dissertation, seek ethics approval if necessary after your research proposal has been approved. For contract research, answering the ethical issues will normally be part of preparing the initial research proposal. In any case, the ethics consent should be obtained before any fieldwork or contact with participants has begun. It is up to you to ensure that you have clearance from the relevant bodies, including other organizations if they are involved (e.g. National Health Service, school, company) before you begin the research work.

When applying principles to any practical activity, there are often conflicts and dilemmas; the application of ethical standards in research activities is no exception. You will have to be able to argue that you have taken reasonable, best possible measures to conform to high standards of research ethics.

Figure 8.4 Forms of behaviour and etiquette desirable in the civilized pursuit of knowledge

But beyond the moral obligations of research, there are forms of behaviour and etiquette desirable in the civilized pursuit of knowledge which should be observed when communicating with people. A considerate and courteous attitude to people will also help to improve their readiness to assist you and provide you with the information you require. Remember that you are relying on their co-operation and generosity to make your research possible, and this should be acknowledged in your attitude and behaviour.

You should devise a systematic method of making requests for information, interviews, visits etc., together with one for confirmation of appointments, letters of thanks, and some follow-up and feedback where appropriate. More detailed consideration has been given in Chapter 7, where research techniques and methods were discussed.

CONCLUSIONS

The value of research depends as much on its ethical veracity as on the novelty of its discoveries. How can we believe in the results of a research project if we doubt the honesty of the researchers and the integrity of the research methods used? It is easy to cheat and take short cuts, but is it worth it? The penalties resulting from discovery are stiff and humiliating. It is also easy to follow the simple guidelines on citation which avoid violations of intellectual property, and which also enhance your status as being well read and well informed about the most important thinkers in your subject.

To treat participants in your research with respect and due consideration is a basic tenet of civilized behaviour. Official concern about the ethical issues in research at any level that involves human subjects is growing. This means that there is a greater need to analyse the methods used in research in detail and to account for the decisions made when seeking official approval. Admittedly, the issues can become quite complicated, with no clear-cut solutions. It is therefore important that you consult with others, especially advisers appointed for that purpose.

Miller and Bell suggest that keeping a constant record of decisions made is a good safeguard against sloppy thinking and inadvertent overlooking of ethical issues:

> Using a research diary to document access routes and decisions made throughout the research process is one practical way of developing an ethics checklist. This practice of regular reflection helps ensure that ethical and methodological considerations are continually reassessed. (2002, p. 67)

This chapter has presented a brief overview of the principal ethical issues in research, and what actions you need to take to ensure that your research will be ethically sound and that you have obtained the necessary clearances from relevant authorities.

THE NEXT STEPS: PLAN YOUR CODE OF ETHICS

Sound ethical procedures are the basis of good research. The extent to which ethical issues impinge on your work depends on how and how much you will be working with people (and perhaps animals?). Beyond the basic ethical matters of honesty etc. you will have to make an assessment of how you will tackle the problems of fair dealing, gaining consents, providing information, privacy and anonymity etc. Obtain the guidelines and an ethics application form from your ethics department to see what questions you will have to answer. You may be surprised at the extent of information you will need to give!

This is bound to raise a lot of issues and questions, some of which you will not be able to resolve yet. You will need to record what ethical issues are presented by your research, to be able to discuss how you have come to your conclusions about ways of overcoming problems, and to list issues that you think important but have not resolved. This will provide a good basis for discussion with your supervisors and ethics advisers to help you compile a set of priorities for further investigation and clarification.

The aims of this section are:

- to consider the ethical aspects of the project
- to find solutions to ethical problems
- to consult with others on unresolved issues
- to be in a position to apply for approval (if necessary) from the ethics committee or other responsible body.

Checklist of activities that will progress your research

By taking simple precautions you can ensure that your research complies with every aspect of the expected ethical standards. By following the steps below, you will check that you have considered the most important factors. There are a lot of things to consider if your research is going to involve human participants and you have to submit your planned methods and explain your decisions to the ethics committee for their approval.

Step 1: check your methods of citation

In order to make sure that you cannot be accused of plagiarism, check that you have not used other people's ideas or writing in such a way as to deceive the reader about the real author of the work. If you have used the ideas and words of others, which is in no way reprehensible, make sure that you have rigorously followed a system of citation and reference. Check that your citations make it easy for the reader to identify the relevant section of text, and that the reference list is consistent in its order of information, punctuation, use of italics, inverted commas etc. Remember that even if you do not know the author of the work (which is often the case on websites and in newspaper articles) you should still acknowledge the source so as not to pass it off as your own work.

Step 2: clarity of data presentation, analysis, outcomes and conclusions

This is about being open and honest about what you do, what you find out and how you interpret it. This is all rather in the future, as your work is still at the beginning. But it is obviously a big issue and will permeate the whole of your work. It requires you to cultivate an open and honest attitude, especially when things do not turn out as expected. There is no shame in finding the unexpected; in fact this is what research is about. Even if your theories are proved wrong, your assumptions are without ground and your findings are inconsistent, there is always something to be learned for you and others. At least they will not have to make the same mistakes as you to learn the lesson. Check that you have used non-sexist, non-ageist, non-cultural etc. terminology throughout your writing.

Step 3: what ethical issues are involved?

Will your research involve human participants? If not, then you can read through the following with interest rather than to find out what to do. If it does involve human participants, first ensure that your intended actions comply generally with all the standard ethical issues as discussed above. Here is a short checklist:

- your relationship to participants
- how you choose participants
- how you inform participants and what the information consists of
- assurance of the right to terminate
- guarantee of confidentiality and anonymity
- gaining of permissions from organizations
- impartiality in data collection
- impartiality in data analysis
- management of sensitive information
- freedom from deception and cover methods
- adequate training of assistants
- careful management of data and eventual disposal
- feedback to participants
- forms of dissemination that ensure no harm is done
- responsibilities to funders.

Then go through the following steps to make sure that you pick up all aspects that need special attention.

Step 4: vulnerable participants

Will the study involve participants who are particularly vulnerable or unable to give informed consent (e.g. children, unconscious patients, people under 18 or with learning difficulties, difficulties in understanding or communicating)? You will have to take special measures to ensure that those responsible for them are fully informed and give permission on their behalf, and that the participants do not get confused or harmed in any way.

Step 5: children

If the participants are school children, will you be able to obtain permission to involve children under sixteen from the school or parent? If not, what are the reasons? You will need to justify your approach. In the UK, any person employed to work with children needs to get an official character clearance. Find out what the situation will be with regard to your intended work.

Step 6: medical procedures

Will the research involve medical procedures? You will need to be qualified to carry these out, and they should be approved by knowledgeable experts. A rigorous risk assessment will have to be carried out. Similar precautions are required if drugs, placebos or other substances (e.g. food substances, vitamins) are to be administered to the study participants, or blood or tissue samples are to be obtained. In all cases, the proposed procedures will have to be painstakingly explained and evaluated.

Step 7: pain or discomfort or potential harm

Is pain or more than mild discomfort likely to result from the study? There will have to be good reasons why this should be so, and how the level of pain or discomfort can be predicted and monitored. What if the study involves invasive, intrusive or potentially harmful procedures of any kind (e.g. manipulation, aromatherapy oils, exercise routines, splints, specialized equipment)? Again, you will have to argue for the benefits of this type of research outweighing the possible harm, and the lack of alternative, more benign, risk-free methods. This is equally necessary if it is predicted that the research could induce psychological stress or anxiety, cause harm or have negative consequences for the participants (beyond the risks encountered in their normal lifestyles). Prolonged or repetitive testing could also lead to fatigue and psychological or even physical harm.

Step 8: financial inducements

Will financial inducements (other than reasonable expenses and compensation for time) be offered to participants? The worry is that the results could be affected by a form of bribe that puts the participant under pressure to provide the desired answers. For most poor postgraduate students, this issue is unlikely to be relevant!

Step 9: deception

Will the study involve deception of participants, their carers, dependants, support networks or others, in any way (e.g. omitting or giving false information about the researcher's background, reason for study or anticipated outcomes)? This is usually not permissible, but perhaps, in certain circumstances, covert methods are the only way to get unsullied data. This is a really problematic issue, as one of the most important principles of ethical research is that participants are fully informed about the research as far as it affects them. You will have to have very good reasons why deception is necessary, and examine what possible effects may result when the truth is revealed.

Step 10: right to remain anonymous

Are there problems with the participants' right to remain anonymous, or to have the information they give not be identifiable as theirs? This could possibly lead to embarrassment and much worse (in some cases even threat to life), so this right should not be abused. If anonymity cannot be assured, then the participant must be made aware of this before agreeing to take part in the research.

Step 11: right to withdraw

The right to withdraw from the study at any time is a basic condition of ethical research. Will it be withheld, or not made explicit? It may be very inconvenient for the researcher if participants withdraw without warning, but this should be the prerogative of voluntary participation. Why should you not allow this?

Step 12: access to groups

Will the study require access to groups or individuals because of their membership of a group, organization, place of study or dwelling place (e.g. university students, self-help group, nursing home, police force, National Health Service)? If so, several issues will need to be addressed, such as gaining permission from the organizations and complying with their regulations. You will even perhaps need to get ethics clearance from them.

Step 13: confidential information

Do you require access to confidential information? This could be perhaps health records, prison or conviction records, even school or university grades. Obviously, because such records are confidential, they are only allowed to be given to certain authorized people or organizations. How will you get access to them, and how will you ensure that they remain confidential? These are questions you will certainly have to answer.

Step 14: special circumstances

Are there any other special circumstances? This is a 'catch-all' question. Consider if there is any situation in which the ethical rules might be transgressed. Research is a very complex business, with decisions to be made that cannot be clear-cut. Become aware of the shades of interpretation that can be made in human situations, and the network of responsibilities that are incurred when doing research that impinges in some way or other on fellow human beings. Constant alertness and sensitivity are required to detect any possible problems; it helps to always consult with others as they might see matters quite differently to yourself.

The questions in the above, from step 2 onwards, are compiled from lists provided by the ethics officers in a range of schools in Oxford Brookes University. The students are instructed that if they answer 'yes' to any of them, they will have to fill in an ethics application form for approval by the University Ethics Committee. It is likely that you will have a similar system at your university or college. Check it out!

Consolidation and assessment

Arrange a tutorial with your tutor or supervisor. Consider the issues of ethics and privacy, and describe any aspects of them which you think will have a particular bearing on the type of research you are proposing. You may find this checklist useful (Burnett et al., 1994, p. 15):

- Whose interests are involved?
- Is there any risk of damaging or embarrassing participants?
- What issues of confidentiality are involved?
- What issues of law and professional conduct need to be checked out?
- What are the effects of this research and/or publication on the participants?
- What are the effects of this research and/or publication on other interested parties?

Key words

Plagiarism   Subject
Citation   Participant
Epistemology   Informed consent
Ethics

Further reading

Although ethical behaviour should underlie all academic work, it is in the social sciences (as well as medicine etc.) that the really difficult issues arise. Researching people and society raises many ethical questions that are discussed in the books below. The first set of books is aimed generally at student and professional researchers, and the second set contains examples of more specialized books – though the issues remain much the same for whoever is doing research involving human participants. The general books are as follows.

Robson, C. (1993) *Real World Research: a Resource for Social Scientists and Practitioner-Researchers*. Oxford: Blackwell.

Two sections that are short and useful: pp. 29–34, 470–5.

Oliver, P. (2003) *The Student's Guide to Research Ethics*. Maidenhead: Open University Press.

This is an excellent review of the subject, going into detail on all aspects of ethics in research, and providing useful examples of situations where ethical questions are raised. It demonstrates that there are not always simple answers to these questions, but suggests precautions that can be taken to avoid transgressions.

Laine, M. de (2000) *Fieldwork, Participation and Practice: Ethics and Dilemmas in Qualitative Research*. London: Sage.

The main purposes of this book are to promote an understanding of the harmful possibilities of fieldwork; and to provide ways of dealing with ethical problems and dilemmas. Examples of actual fieldwork are provided that address ethical problems and dilemmas, and show ways of dealing with them.

Mauthner, M., Birch, M., Jessop, J. and Miller, T. (eds) (2002) *Ethics in Qualitative Research*. London: Sage.

This book explores ethical issues in research from a range of angles, including: access and informed consent, negotiating participation, rapport, the intentions of feminist research, epistemology and data analysis, tensions between being a professional researcher and a 'caring' professional. The book includes practical guidelines to aid ethical decision making rooted in feminist ethics of care.

Geraldi, O. (ed.) (2000) *Danger in the Field: Ethics and Risk in Social Research*. London: Routledge.

Read this if you are going into situations that might be ethically hazardous.

Townend, D. (2000) 'Can the law prescribe an ethical framework for social science research?', in D. Burton (ed.), *Research Training for Social Scientists*. London: Sage.

There are also books about ethics that specialize in certain fields. Here are some examples. You could search out some in your subject perhaps.

Bryson, B. (1987) *The Penguin Dictionary of Troublesome Words*, 2nd edn. Harmondsworth: Penguin.

Whitbeck, C. (1998) *Ethics in Engineering Practice and Research*. Cambridge: Cambridge University Press.

Graue, M. E. (1998) *Studying Children in Context: Theories, Methods, and Ethics.* London: Sage.

Royal College of Nursing (1993) *Ethics Related to Research in Nursing.* London: RCN Research Advisory Group.

Burgess, R. G. (ed.) (1989) *The Ethics of Educational Research.* London: Falmer.

Rosnow, R. L. (1997) *People Studying People: Artefacts and Ethics in Behavioural Research.* New York: Freeman.

EXERCISE 8.1

1   Tampering with medical records to support his claim to have performed a pioneering operation. He also pretended to have conducted extensive research trials into ovarian diseases.

2   Other obstetricians and gynaecologists might have tried to perform the same reputed operation with possible dangerous results, and have based treatments on the evidence put forward by the reputed research trials.

3   Several safeguards are there, but they are not, on their own, defence against fraud. Claims must be substantiated with accessible and reliable evidence (though as seen in the article, this evidence can sometimes be maliciously altered), and the research methods used must be open to scrutiny and repeatable (after several deaths, the success of the operation methods will be questioned!). While many types of experiment can be repeated without harmful effects, even if they are not successful, in medicine this is definitely not the case.

4   It is difficult to imagine how a 'fraud squad' could operate in a direct and active way without the inside help of members of the research community. As it appears to be a small (though perhaps important) problem with little obvious effects on society, general policing or detective work like that used in financial fraud is unlikely to be appropriate. However, a system which provides anonymous and discreet consultation with the 'squad' by researchers who suspect fraud within their department might alert the authorities to criminal activities.

5   The accusation is that Jung falsified documents which he used as evidence to support his argument. This is similar to the type of falsifying of which Mr Pearce was convicted. The greatest difference is that the accusation against Jung cannot be substantiated because the evidence lies in an archive in the Library of Congress to which access has been refused by the Jung family. If the accusation is true, it might be difficult to assess whether anybody has been physically or mentally harmed by the fraud (in Mr Pearce's case, this would have been much simpler). However, if true, the credibility of Jung's other writings will be put in question, and the evidence he puts forward to support all his theories will need to be closely investigated.

6   It must be very tempting to 'bend' the evidence if it does not quite fit your radical theory, which you think will make you respected as a leader in your field of research. Ambition is a powerful emotion. There are several reasons why scientists do not lie: they are, like most people, honest; professional disaster awaits those who are found out; and scientific advance is not achieved only by 'proving' new theories, because the falsifying of an existing hypothesis or theory also counts as a scientific success.

EXERCISE 8.2

Here are the words I found inappropriate, with suggestions for suitable terminology to replace them.

old folk, old dears   These are condescending terms. Use 'older people' or possibly 'senior citizens'.

the normal ones   This implies that disabled people are not normal people! Use 'able-bodied people' or 'people without disabilities'.

the disabled   Not acceptable any more as it is depersonalizing. Use 'disabled people' or 'people with disabilities'. Remember that this does not necessarily mean old people.

the blind   A vague term without the personal element. Alternatives are 'blind or partially sighted person', 'someone with visual impairment', 'people with little or no sight'.

the deaf   A vague term again. Add the personal element, and if possible whether partially deaf or profoundly deaf. Some people use 'the deaf' as a term for a linguistic minority rather than a disabled group.

the wheelchair bound   Substitute with 'wheelchair users' or 'people with impaired mobility'.

mental handicap   'Handicap' is seen as a discriminatory term. Use 'learning difficulties' or 'learning disabled'.

businessmen   Is it only the men who are mentioned here? Probably not. Use 'business person', 'manager' or 'executive'.

headmasters   The same gender question applies here. Use 'headteacher'.

putting their wallets into their trouser pockets   This assumes that all the previous professions are male occupations. Rephrase to include female terms or non-gender terms such as 'purse' and 'inside pocket'.

lower class   Seen by many as derogatory and demeaning. Use 'working class', though this is rather old-fashioned, or 'people with lower earnings'.

charwomen, deliverymen, salesgirls and waiters, policemen, laymen   Again, these are gender specific when this is probably not intended. Use non-gender terms such as 'cleaners', 'couriers', 'sales assistants', 'waiting staff', 'police officers', 'lay persons'.

British people   As used here, this implies that these are a white ethnic group – patently not true. Use instead 'white people'.

the blacks   Depersonalized. Use 'black people' or, if more precision is required, use 'African' (although note that not all Africans are black), 'Afro-American' or 'Afro-Caribbean'. People of Asian origin are not necessarily included in the black ethnic category: use the term 'Asians', or 'of Asian origin'. This is a complicated issue as there is a multiplicity of races and mixtures of origins. It is best to avoid overgeneralizations: be as precise as possible.

other immigrants   This implies that 'the blacks' are necessarily immigrants. This is of course not the case in a multicultural society.

druggies, homosexuals and tramps If these are the terms used by the young people, this should be made explicit. 'Drug dealers' or 'drug users' is more precise, 'gay persons' overcomes the use of medical terminology that is usually associated with males, and perhaps 'vagrants' is a less derogatory term.

geriatrics A medical term for a branch of medicine. Use 'older people'.

typical young person … himself … his Ignores the female gender of this category of people. Use 'him/herself', 'his/her', or the now quite grammatically acceptable 'their' even if it is in the singular.

EXERCISE 8.3

Here are my brief thoughts. I am sure that you will have a range of reactions that are worth discussing with your colleagues. It is unlikely, though, that your research will take such a radical experimental direction.

1   In defence of Milgram's methods is the fact that no physical harm was incurred by any of the subjects. Despite the thorough debriefing after the experiment, I question whether the anguish suffered by the participants caused by their situation was trivial and whether the psychological effects of the experience might not have been harmful in the longer term. I would definitely have felt very cheated and angered had I been a participant in that research.

2   For:

(a)   This is the only way to discover facts about this important issue.
(b)   Full precautions are taken to explain to the participants that they have been deceived and that no pain at all was administered.
(c)   The participants are allowed to stop the experiment at any stage.

Against:

(a)   An experiment based on deception is basically unethical. Other methods must be devised to gain the required data.
(b)   The participants are put into a situation that inevitably causes them stress beyond what they should be asked to bear.
(c)   The longer term effects on the participants cannot be gauged. Trauma might result in post-traumatic stress. The experiment does not include follow-up monitoring.

3   It is difficult to see how participants could be subjected to a similar situation without the need for deception, and still have to make such onerous choices of action. The whole point of the exercise was to measure the extent to which ordinary people go against their normal principles when faced with authority. Perhaps nowadays, a computer simulation might be used to create a scenario that involves this type of conflict of interests.

4   Assuming that I behaved like most of the other participants, my main shock would have been my willingness to inflict pain against my normal natural inclinations. I would have been very relieved that I had not, after all, caused harm to anyone, but I would have felt angry that I had been exploited in this way.

9

Preparing the Research Proposal and Starting to Write

Introduction
The Recipe For a Successful Research Proposal
   Types of Research Proposal
   The Main Ingredients and Sequence
   Finalizing your Proposal
   Proposals for Funded Research
How to Get Started with Writing
   The Writing Process
   Forming the Structure and Preparing an Outline
   Retrieving and Organizing Notes
   Drafting and Redrafting
   Presentation
   Bibliographies, References and Footnotes
Conclusions
The Next Steps: Your Research Proposal
Checklist of Activities That Will Progress Your Research
   Consolidation and Assessment
Further Reading
Answers To Exercises

- To explain the necessary ingredients of a research proposal.
- To provide a step-by-step guide to writing a successful proposal.
- To assist you to start writing the introductory chapters of your thesis.

INTRODUCTION

This, the last chapter of the book, will culminate in the writing of your research proposal which will provide a foundation for your thesis or research project. You will need to use all the understanding which you have acquired and skills you have developed in the previous chapters in order to accomplish this task. You will have to clarify in your own mind exactly what your specific area of study will be, and explain it in a compact and logical form so that anyone who reads your proposal will be able to understand the character and value of your intended work. Because submitting your proposal is a part of the formal process of attaining a research degree or applying for project funding, you will have to abide by the relevant university or funding body's regulations with regard to the suitability of your proposed research and the form of the research proposal. This chapter will help you to achieve this.

You will notice that the exercises in this chapter aim to help you to examine aspects of your own work in preparation for writing your proposal. There are obviously no right or wrong answers to these questions, so the answers at the end of the chapter tend either to provide a list of points for you to check against what you have written, or to urge you to consult with your tutor or supervisor to discuss the outcome of the exercise.

Of course, gaining approval for your intended work as described in your proposal is only the beginning of the process of research. The main effort will be in carrying out the research. Although this book is not intended to be a practical guide to help you to do this, it does conclude with some useful hints as to how to approach the problem of writing and presenting your thesis or report. You will no doubt be faced with many new situations during your subsequent work, but the preparatory work which you have done during reading this book should help you to beat a path through the complex and often frustrating process of completing your research project.

In order to be fully aware of what is required of you if you are doing a research degree, it is essential that you carefully read your university research degree regulations, a copy of which you should have received when you first registered. If you are doing a major assignment or a project, follow the detailed guidelines in your assignment or project instructions. If you are preparing a proposal for a funding application, then read the detailed instructions prepared by the funding body given to you with the application forms.

THE RECIPE FOR A SUCCESSFUL RESEARCH PROPOSAL

Proposals for research tend to follow a defined pattern. They all have these features in common: an explanation, in a compact and precise fashion, of the nature of the research; why it is needed; how it will be done; the likely outcomes; and, in most cases, exactly what resources are required to carry it out. According to Locke et al. (1993, pp. 3–5), there are three main functions of a proposal, as shown in Box 9.1.

Box 9.1   Main functions of a research proposal

- A means of communication from the researcher to those who will assess, approve and possibly fund the work.
- A plan for action to describe the scope, aims, step-by-step procedures and expected outcomes of the work.
- A contract that will form the basis of agreement between the parties involved, e.g. the researcher, supervisors, funders, institutions (e.g. university or college); the signed agreement cannot be substantially altered without the agreement of all the parties.

There are, of course, differences in the nature of research projects and this will affect the exact nature of the proposal. However, keep in mind that any proposal is a type of promise, so it is advisable not to 'promise mountains and deliver molehills'!

Types of research proposal

The types of proposal that we are particularly concerned with in this book are those prepared for academic research degrees, MPhil and PhD, for major projects or dissertations that are the culmination of many postgraduate degrees and diplomas, and for applications for funded research projects.

Three forms of study are possible when doing a research degree: MPhil; MPhil transferring to PhD; and PhD direct. The emphasis in proposals for research for each of these is different, so it is necessary to be aware of the essential features of each programme of research.

MPhil

According to a typical example of university research degree regulations:

> The MPhil shall be awarded to a candidate who, having critically investigated and evaluated an approved topic and demonstrated an understanding of research methods appropriate to the chosen field, has presented and defended a thesis by oral examination to the satisfaction of the examiners.

The type of research required for this qualification must be such that it will demonstrate that the student has substantially mastered the main techniques of research. While no original contribution to knowledge is required, in order for the research to be of any significance there must be sufficient exploration and analysis of the data to provide a new perspective or understanding of a situation, and to suggest issues which would benefit from original research.

MPhil transferring to PhD

The MPhil stage, as described above, provides the foundation for the original research of the PhD stage. How the two stages will be accomplished, the one following from the other, must be clearly described. There must be evidence, not only of the need for the work, but that it will result in an original contribution to knowledge.

Again, typical university research degree regulations might state:

> The PhD shall be awarded to a candidate who, having critically investigated and evaluated an approved topic resulting in an independent and original contribution to knowledge and demonstrated an understanding of research methods appropriate to the chosen field, has presented and defended the thesis by oral examination to the satisfaction of the examiners.

PhD direct

Normally, students undertaking this route will have already completed an MPhil or a Masters degree, or have demonstrated substantial expertise and previous research in the chosen subject. This research must be shown to provide a suitably defined problem which can be investigated in order to produce a thesis which provides an original contribution to knowledge. If you are contemplating to go by this route, or any of the others for that matter, do read the relevant sections of your own university research degree regulations.

In all cases, the research projects should not only have merits for the insights which result, but also be suitable vehicles by which the student learns and practises the theoretical and methodological aspects of the research process, while demonstrably remaining within the practical and financial resources of the student.

Proposals for major projects, dissertations or theses that form the culmination of many postgraduate degrees and diplomas will be similar to those of an MPhil research project, but because of the shorter time-span allowed for the project the aims and objectives are likely to be more restricted. You might also be more closely directed as to the topic of the research.

The other type of research proposal considered in this chapter is that for funded research. The description of the research process itself will be similar to that of the academic proposals, but in addition there must be a detailed description of the finance required to fund the work, staffing arrangements, timetable, dissemination and publication arrangements.

The main ingredients and sequence

Academic research proposals are usually composed of the following elements: the title, aims of the research, the background, the research problem, possible outcomes, outline of methods and selected bibliography. This sequence is usual, but small variations are possible.

It is a good idea, at the first attempt, to write a preliminary draft of the proposal while concentrating your attention exclusively on the orderly sequence of statements and ignoring grammatical and stylistic considerations. Once you have achieved a sound structure you can spend time refining your composition without danger of a subsequent major reconstruction.

It helps to look at proposals written by other students or researchers in the past, but be careful to analyse them for their form rather than content so as not to be influenced by their particular subject or problem.

The title

The function of the title is to encapsulate in a few words the essence of the research. Although, in academic proposals, you are not committed to using the same title in the thesis (the emphasis of the study may alter during the work), it should accurately reflect your intentions at this stage.

As one of the main purposes of the title is an aid to retrieval, it typically contains all the essential key words that someone might use in an attempt to locate the kind of study you are proposing. These words are likely to include the main variables, the type of research tasks, the theoretical basis and the purpose of the study. In the title 'The implications of the 1998 Labour and Conservative policies on the economics and management of day-care centres', the independent variables are Labour and Conservative policies, and the dependent variables are economics and management; the type of research task is implied as a comparative study; the theoretical basis is one of prediction of effects of policies; and the purpose of the study is to predict their effects on day-care centres.

As important as words which indicate the subject are those which delineate it, e.g. in time, place and type. A good title often has a structure which progresses from the general to the specific, for example 'Access and servicing of city centre shops in regeneration areas in the UK'. A shorter title, such as 'City centre shopping problems', which might describe a similar study, sounds far too vague and lacks the key words. However, unnecessarily long titles should be avoided: two lines should be enough. You can leave out such phrases as 'an investigation into', 'a study of', 'aspects of', as these are obvious attributes of a research project.

EXERCISE 9.1

Write a list of key words which summarize the main aspects of your intended work. Don't be afraid at first of writing too many. In order to reduce your list you can eliminate those which are repeated or non-essential, or possibly combine words to form more general concepts. When you have reduced the list to the essential words, form a sentence with them to create a title that appears to satisfy both technical and aesthetic standards. Check in the answers at the end of the chapter to see if you have included all the essential relevant points.

Aims of the research

This serves as an introduction to the heart of the project. It should be possible to state the aims of the research in two or three sentences. If you cannot do this, you have probably not thought sufficiently about what you are actually going to do. It should be evident that the aims are delineated sufficiently so that it is possible to achieve them with the available resources and time.

EXERCISE 9.2

Write a list of the aims of your research. Think of as many as you can which you believe are relevant to your project. When you have done this, consider each one carefully by asking the questions:

1 How will the aim be achieved – methods, resources, skills, time? Is it realistically possible to achieve it?
2 What results are required for it to be achieved?
3 Is the aim central to your study?
4 Are there any overlaps between the aims? Keep them discrete.
5 Is there a sequence or hierarchy which links one aim to another? If so, are they in the correct order?
6 Are there too many aims to be realistically achievable?

Make notes answering questions 1, 2 and 3 about each aim on your list.

The background

It is necessary to explain, to the reader of your proposal, the context from which the research problem emerges. You should be able to demonstrate that you are aware of the major factors which surround your problem, and of any significant literature which relates to it. It is also the function of this introduction to capture the interest of the reader.

NB

Some of the factors which make up the context might be of a physical nature, such as building types (e.g. schools, prisons), materials (e.g. historical artefacts, household products), situations (e.g. the playground, the street, the countryside) or organizations (e.g. local government, secret society, local community), while others might be more conceptual, such as the economy, legislation, development policy etc. More abstract are theoretical concepts such as power, poverty and Marxism. In order to keep the description as short as possible, use references to relevant literature which, if known or followed up by the reader, give a full account of the concept or situation mentioned. It is quite difficult to pitch the level of your text so that any intelligent reader understands the factors from which your problem emerges, while at the same time persuading the expert that you are conversant with details of the principal issues. Do not assume that the reader knows anything about your subject.

The efficient use of references is crucial in keeping the proposal short. By quoting the references to publications you can refer to whole theoretical positions, approaches and movements in just a few words. In addition to this, the inclusion of relevant literature demonstrates your knowledge of the significant personalities and positions in your subject.

There should be a flow in the text of the background section which reads in the form of a progressive account, where every issue raised can be seen to contribute to an argument which leads inexorably to the research problem. This is the case in all types of research proposal. However, for MPhil and MPhil with later transfer to PhD, and in initial studies and exploratory projects, it is recognized that, subsequent to the approval of the proposal, much of the initial research work consists of a deeper investigation into the relevant literature and nature of the research problem. But in applications for limited dissertations, PhD direct, transfer from MPhil to PhD and many funded research projects, it is expected that the background has already been thoroughly researched and it is from the conclusions of this work that the research problem has been precisely formulated.

The research problem

The research problem must be the focus of the proposal and, in fact, of the whole research project. It is the culmination of the background work and the initiator of the specific research tasks. It must be very clear from the text of the proposal what the nature of the problem is, how it was identified, and why it is a significant problem which needs to be researched. There has been enough written in previous chapters about the nature of research problems (see particularly Chapter 1). It is also essential that you check carefully that the description of your problem complies with the required university regulations, course requirements or conditions of the funding body, and with the relevant form which defines how your application should be set out.

The problem may be expressed in abstract terms initially, but through the statement of sub-problems you should indicate how it can be investigated practically. You might, particularly when applying to do PhD direct, or transferring from MPhil to PhD stages, or when applying to do funded research, state the exact hypotheses or questions which will direct the original research. Although the problem may be expressed in abstract terms, it is a mistake to express it in general terms. To limit the scope of the research to what is practicable, the problem must be very precisely defined and delimited. It will help in this respect if you carefully define your terms and state the assumptions you are making.

To prepare your argument which leads up to the statement of your research problem, make a list of the issues you will address in your account of the context. The issues should be summarized in a few words, as you are concerned only with the skeletal structure of your proposal at this stage. Put them in an ordered sequence so that it is possible to progress from one issue to the next in a logical fashion. Keep the list brief, but make sure that it is complete (i.e. covers all the essential issues). You will probably not get the order right at the first attempt, so do not hesitate to experiment with different sequences with the help of the word processor or by writing each issue on a separate slip of paper and then rearranging the slips.

Write out your research problem in one sentence at the end of the list (you may elaborate on it later if necessary). Check that in your sequence the issues all relate to the problem and lead logically towards it. If there are gaps in the logic of the argument, add linking issues. If the argument leads to a different problem, either change the problem or re-examine the issues you have listed, and their order.

When you think that the argument is cogent, you can put some 'flesh' on the 'bones' in the text by making full sentences and adding references.

Outline of methods

This part of the proposal explains briefly what you are going to do in order to carry out your research, based on your chosen research approach. In proposals for funded research this may need to be described in great detail. If you are applying for MPhil/PhD, then the description should be in two parts: the first, what you will do to complete the MPhil stage, and the second, how you will develop this in the PhD work. The first of the two parts should therefore have as its last topic the precise formulation of the research problem. This will be researched as described in the second (PhD) part of the methods description. In the case of single projects, MPhil and PhD direct applications, obviously only one continuous explanation is required.

Every proposal is different in its description of methods, as these have to be specifically chosen to collect and analyse data effectively on the specific research problem, and to produce the type of outcomes aimed at. However, one common feature is likely to be a review of the literature relevant to the research topic. Other review activities may be through consultation with experts and specialists in the subject, and perhaps with people involved in other ways. It is generally relevant to distinguish between the methods of data collection and data analysis, although in some cases, particularly in qualitative research, these may go hand in hand.

It may be important that you indicate how you will be able to access certain types of information. If there are obvious problems in access, describe how you will go about solving them. If you have privileged access to obscure or restricted information, this should be reported, as should the fact that you have resources to cover the cost of research in your own country, or if relevant, abroad.

It is the convention to explain the methods to be used in the form of a list, without numbering the items. This enables you to be very concise. A very detailed account of methodology is not generally required: you should limit

Figure 9.1 If you have privileged access to obscure or restricted information, this should be reported

yourself to an indication of the range of methods required and the general scale of the procedures and why you are using those methods. Always answer the questions: which method, how will you carry it out, and why? The answer to the question 'why' is often left out, with disastrous results. Use the list in Box 9.2 to check for the inclusion of relevant tasks.

Box 9.2   Checklist for outline of methods

- Literature search and critical analysis.
- Consultation with experts.
- Identification of research population(s) or situations.
- Sampling (if relevant) – size of sample(s), location of sample(s), number of case studies.
- Data collection methods – questionnaires, interviews, study of documents, observations etc.
- Analytical methods – quantitative, qualitative and combination of both.
- Evaluation of results of analysis.

In the case of an MPhil/PhD application, some of these methods will be used in both the MPhil and the PhD stages of the work. With the PhD direct and most funded research projects, you may have to describe separately the methods used to investigate each sub-problem, or sub-hypothesis, as these are likely to vary considerably.

Possible outcomes of the research

Since the proposal is a type of contract to deliver certain results, it is a mistake to 'promise mountains and deliver molehills'. Although you cannot predict exactly what the outcomes will be (if you could, there would be little point in carrying out the research), you should try to be quite precise as to the nature and scope of the outcomes and as to who might benefit from the information. Make sure that the outcomes relate directly to the aims of the research which you described at the beginning of the proposal. You can be more general when describing the overall significance of the outcomes, when you make the point quite directly about the importance of what you are proposing to do in your chosen subject. Note that in PhD proposals and most funded research there is a need to indicate what will be the original contribution to knowledge. These outcomes may be a contribution at a practical and/or a theoretical level.

Prepare a list of methods suitable for your own research, going from the general to the particular, i.e. from background research to detailed research and evaluation. Check that they read in a logical order and that, although brief, they are informative enough to indicate types of method appropriate to the subject researched.

EXERCISE 9.4

Culminate your list of methods with a statement which lists the possible outcomes of the research and another which specifies why, and how, the intended research is important.

Finalizing your proposal

By now you have certainly thought a lot about what your research problem is, and how you are going to do your research, and you have probably written several drafts describing your intentions. Now you must write your research proposal in full, following the required structure and including all the information required on the appropriate form.

Box 9.3 summarizes what to do and how to do it, with reference to the parts of this book that deal with the different aspects. You might not have to start at the beginning if you are already clear about the area of your research, but you will have to clearly define the research problem, even if you are pretty sure about the subject of your research. If you are doing a proposal for a PhD direct, it is assumed that you are already very knowledgeable about your specific research topic and that you will be able to go almost straight into the original research work. To be able to do this you will need to give a much more detailed explanation of your research methods and a more comprehensive timetable.

Box 9.3   Checklist for finalizing your proposal: what to do, how to do it and where to find the guidance

What you need to do	How to do it	See
Do background investigations to identify research area	Consider your own expertise and interests. Read books, newspapers, journals etc. on a relevant range of subjects. Keep your eyes and ears open for possible important/ controversial issues. Ask people who have expert knowledge if they know of work that needs to be done in their area	Chapter 1: 'Starting your own research'; 'The research problem'; 'Types of research degree'
Concentrating on the research area, define a research problem and develop it into a research question or hypothesis. Based on this, formulate the title of your research project	Review what constitutes good research. Do a more focused literature search within the chosen area to identify a researchable problem. Examine what research has already been done so as to find the gap in knowledge that you can fill. Formulate a research question or hypothesis that presents the problem in a compact form. You might also break the question/ hypothesis into sub-questions/hypotheses in order to make it less abstract and general. A title for the project should flow naturally from these. You will probably need to discuss this with your supervisor or tutor several times as you work to focus and refine the problem	Chapter 1: 'The research approach'; 'Research problem definition' Chapter 5: 'Hypotheses: do you need them?' Chapter 6: 'Good research'
Create an argument as to why this question needs to be addressed	Draw on your background reading and experience to cover the following issues: • nature and extent of problem • existing research and identification of gap in knowledge • why it is important to do this research	Chapter 2: 'Doing a literature review' Chapter 4: 'Argument'
Explain how your research will help to address the research problem	Work backwards by first considering what outcomes are desirable to help in solving the problem. Then check that you will be able in practice to achieve the desired outcomes. Then argue why and how these outcomes will be useful, and who is likely to benefit	Chapter 3: 'Types of research'
Decide how the research problem can be practically researched	You will have to work out the following: • what information you will need • where/whom you will get it from • how you can get it • what you will do when you have got it • who you will need to consult • what equipment you might need.	Chapter 6: 'Quantitative and qualitative data'; 'Planning a research project'

Box 9.3

What you need to do	How to do it	See
	Apart from obvious answers to these issues based on your knowledge of the problem, reports on previous research in subjects close to yours will give invaluable information based on other people's experience	
Now find out what information collection techniques (research methods) will be the most suitable to help you acquire this information. You will probably need more than one	This requires a closer look at the nitty-gritty aspects of research methods. There are a huge number of books that comprehensively describe a large number of data collection methods. At this stage you should avoid getting bogged down in detail, but check that the types of methods chosen are suitable and practicable in your circumstances. Describe them briefly and explain the type of information each will produce. Check out the ethical issues, if any	Chapter 7: 'Collecting secondary data'; 'Collecting primary data' Chapter 8: 'Honesty in your work'; 'Situations that raise ethical issues'; 'Ethics policies, permissions and committees'
Explain what analytical research methods will be suitable. Again, you might need several different methods, depending on the type of data, and what you need to discover from them	Consult the research textbooks for data analysis methods. These are often divided into qualitative and quantitative methods. You might need both. Indicate which data will be analysed using which method. Unless you are doing a PhD direct, you really only need to outline the methods selected and explain the nature of the results aimed at	Chapter 7: 'Analysing data'; 'Combined data generation and analysis'
Describe briefly the expected nature of the outcomes and how the conclusions will be presented. This will depend on whom you aim to address	You should refer back to the reason for doing the research in the first place and the research problem addressed. Do not try to predict the actual outcomes, but explain what form they will take. It is also a good idea to stress their importance at the same time, and if a PhD, the original contribution to knowledge. Check what the requirements are for presenting your work. Although this research project might be an academic exercise, it is a pity if all your work is wasted by not being read by those who might make good use of it	University regulations
Present a timetable of the projected work	This will be assessed for practicality, so ensure that you are realistic in what you can do in the time allotted. A simple bar chart or a dated list will be sufficient	Chapter 6: 'Planning a research project' Chapter 9: 'The writing process'

The cogency of the argument is of paramount importance. A good way to start is to make a series of short statements in which you summarize the main aspects of your research project, and which follow each other to form an argument. Do not concentrate on grammatical perfection or formal elegance at this stage. A series of concise notes will do. You have already done this as far as the exposition of the research problem in Exercise 9.3, so build on what you have achieved already. You will have to add what approach you will take to research the problem and discuss alternative methodologies which might appropriately be used.

Keep conferring with your tutor or supervisor as you refine the structure of the argument and develop your successive drafts of the proposal. Make sure that other members of staff and/or colleagues also see your work; different comments are essential. Remember, however, that it is you who must decide what you want to do in the research, so be prepared to discuss it further with your tutor if you do not agree with some of the comments or recommendations made by others.

The completed proposal must be fitted onto the official registration form for the university's research degrees committee or funding body, or must conform to the requirements of the course or project in which you are taking part. Normally, there is limited space on the forms, and often you must ensure that your proposal is not longer than can be comfortably fitted onto two sides of A4. This is not easy, but is a very good discipline in writing a dense argument. Where possible, use the references as a shorthand to describe theoretical approaches.

Though there can be no standard or total guidance on how applications should be completed, given the wide range of types of research and students' backgrounds which have to be encompassed, nevertheless you may find the list of typical questions in Box 9.4 of use in completing a form devised for application to register for a research degree. Almost all of the points on the list will be relevant to more limited academic research projects as well as funded projects. Careful consideration of the questions should assist in both completing the form and achieving the successful approvals.

Whichever way the form is designed and in whichever sequence the various sections follow each other (e.g. the aims of the investigation, the background, relationship to previous work, proposed plan of work etc.), when preparing to complete the form you must think of the overall structure in terms of:

background (relation to previous work) → *problem definition* → *problem solution* (aim) → *methodology* (plan of work)

After a logically structured research approach has been devised, it must then be resequenced to fit into whichever format the form stipulates.

The following questions are those that the research committee might ask themselves when they are reviewing your proposal. Use them as a checklist when devising your proposal to make sure that you answer them all as appropriate.

1 Do the overall layout and structure of, and terms used in, the application demonstrate the intellect and training of a highly educated mature candidate who has recently completed a lengthy course (with its extensive background of reading) in research methods, theories and practice?

2 Do the qualifications, training, experience and previous published research papers of the applicant (if any) provide an adequate and sound basis for the research proposal?

3 Does the title of the proposed research exactly identify and delineate the area of the investigation/study proposed?

4 Are the aim(s) of the investigation/study clearly related to the problem(s) outlined in the background to the research?

5 Does the research clearly identify the problem(s) which it undertakes to investigate/study?

6 Does the application show:

   (a) an adequate knowledge of the general background to the problem – giving references to the main literature/publications on the subject

   (b) an adequate knowledge of the specific problem area – giving references to the specific literature/publications on the subject

   (c) an adequate and up-to-date knowledge, by reference, of other research in the same subject area that either has been completed or is in progress at present

   (d) an adequate basis for any tentative hypotheses/propositions which are used to structure the methodology (plan of work)?

7 Does the application give adequate reasons/arguments to show that the proposed specific area of research constitutes a worthwhile study as:

   (a) a contribution to knowledge, or

   (b) a contribution to development of theory in the subject, or

   (c) a contribution to either theoretical or practical methodology?

8 Does the proposed plan of work:

   (a) show how the research will be structured

   (b) show how the research will be phased

   (c) clearly differentiate between deskwork and fieldwork

   (d) show how the research will be carried out

   (e) show the techniques and methods that will be used and the reasons why these techniques and methods were chosen

(Continued)

Box 9.4

(f) show that the work proposed is practicable and realistic within the time available – including the period for writing up the thesis?

9 If the research involves gaining access to the data and facilities of government departments or other organizations or institutions:

(a) What evidence is there that such access/co-operation will be available?
(b) Are the result(s) of the research expected to have any general or specific practical applications, e.g. design guidance or government policy?

10 Does the research involve any problems of ethics/confidentiality and, if so, how will they be overcome?

11 If the research involves investigation overseas, does the application

(a) outline the knowledge/techniques/methods that are required to be learnt/understood in the home country prior to the investigation abroad
(b) illustrate an understanding of the part that different cultural values/factors/variables may play in the research and its findings?

12 If the application includes the possibility of transfer subsequently to a PhD, is the potential extension of the MPhil part of the research into the original research work required of a PhD logically structured and connected?

13 Are the facilities detailed in the investigation adequate and do they include:

(a) computing
(b) libraries – both general and specialist?

14 Collaborating institution:

(a) Does the application involve collaborating with another institution? If not, do the experience, expertise and background of the supervisor(s) as well as the type of research involved render the use of a collaborating institution unnecessary?
(b) Where a collaborating institution is proposed, is there attached a letter of acceptance from the institution concerned?

15 Does the programme of related activities include reference to:

(a) completion of the research methods course
(b) courses/lectures that are being attended or will be attended
(c) computer course(s) completed
(d) any other relevant courses/studies?

16 Are adequate details of the second supervisor(s) and adviser(s) listed in the application? Where the second supervisor(s) has not previously supervised a university student, is a CV (clearly illustrating the expertise etc. necessary to the subject area) attached to the application?

Proposals for funded research

In addition to the information required in a research proposal for an academic degree, a proposal to do funded research requires further information covering costs, personnel, timetabling, outputs and other issues. It is important, when preparing such a proposal, that you argue a case for awarding the money and demonstrate that the researchers are likely to make good use of the funds. You should take care to apply only to funders who are likely to be interested in your work, or to organizations whose terms of reference specifically cover your research topic. Nearly all research funders provide clear information on their specific areas of interest. It is a waste of your time to attempt to gain their backing for research into subjects that they are unable or unwilling to support.

Costs

When seeking funding, a clear and comprehensive account of all the costs which will be incurred is obviously of vital importance. There are many categories of costs; these are often listed in the application forms issued by funding bodies. The main categories are: personnel remuneration, travel and subsistence, capital equipment (e.g. computers, printers, measuring instruments and experimental equipment), overheads (e.g. universities charge for the use of their facilities), consumables (e.g. stationery, telephone). Your own university or organization will probably have clear budgeting guidelines and will be able to provide help in setting up a spreadsheet if necessary.

Personnel

The funders are interested in the competence of those proposing to do the research, and of those whom they wish to employ to help them in order to be assured that the team will be capable of carrying out what they propose. CVs of the main members of the research team will usually be required. It is important to get the right balance of managers and workers, and the requisite skills and capabilities. Some funders insist on a partnership between academic and industrial/ commercial organizations. In this case the roles of the various members of the partnership must be spelt out.

Successful project management and organization are becoming increasingly important issues in the selection process. Indicate the intended management structure, the relevant experience of the responsible managers, research quality assurance procedures and other relevant budgetary and monitoring devices.

Timetabling

This shows when the various operations will be carried out and in which sequence, and how long the project will take overall. A bar chart showing the various tasks and their timing is a useful way to summarize the programme, together with a written description of what is involved in each task. A sequence of milestones with a description of what will be produced at each will give a reliable monitoring guide. Take into account any risk factors and build in some fallback solutions, particularly if the risks are overt and an inherent part of the project.

Outputs

There is little point in carrying out funded (or, for that matter, any other) research if the outcomes are not disseminated to those who might benefit from them. The proposed outputs could be in the form of articles, reports, papers, books, pamphlets, guides, conferences, computer programs etc. How the outputs will be made available to potential readers/users will also be of interest.

Your intellectual property rights should also be considered here. Your aim should be to retain as many rights as possible. However, in more commercial work this can become a complicated issue and you will probably need to gain expert advice and be involved in discussions with the other participants and the promoter.

Successful proposals

There is increasing competition in the research and consultancy environment. The process has become more subject to the time limited, programmatic priorities of funding bodies, and to increasing emphasis on the relevance to industry and the economy. The ways in which applicants convey their interest and expertise, register and enter the competition are important criteria used by promoters in the selection of participants and allocation of funds.

It is essential that researchers are aware of how the research agendas are set. To be best informed, get yourself on relevant circulation lists which will supply you with information, calls for expressions of interests, research conferences and other dissemination events. Consult with the sponsoring or commissioning bodies for details and opinions. For inside information, find out if any of the staff in your organization are members of an advisory or steering research group of the commissioning body: they should know more details about the research relevant agenda. Consult also with research directors in your organization; they will have had plenty of experience in making applications. And do not hesitate to show the drafts of your proposal to colleagues in order to get opinions about the clarity and strength of your argument. Strict submission deadlines are usually enforced, so do give yourself enough time to develop the proposal and to get support and approval from all parties involved in order to avoid last minute panics: it inevitably takes longer than you think at first!

Submitted proposals are generally reviewed and evaluated blind (that is, without knowing who the submitter is) by a selected panel or committee, often with the help of specialist advisers drawn in to ensure that this type of peer review is thorough. These specialists may be competitors or colleagues in your field of interest. They will be looking for the bids of the highest quality, based on solid and dependable research approaches that break new ground in areas of current concern, and that are feasible within the projected framework, using the personnel proposed.

Judith Margolin (1983, pp. 233–4) noted that a large proportion of applications for funded research are rejected. She devised a list of ten reasons why proposals are turned down, which provides a useful tool for a critical appraisal of your own proposal and is shown in Box 9.5. The list has been adjusted to show which items apply to academic as well as to funded research proposals, and which apply only to proposals for funded research.

Box 9.5 Reasons that proposals fail

Reasons relevant to all research proposals:

1 There is an inadequately presented statement of need. It is perceived by the assessor either as not significant or as one of such magnitude that it is clearly impossible for the lone researcher to come to any useful conclusions in view of his/her limited resources (or, in the case of funded research, a few grant dollars would barely make a dent in the problem).
2 The objectives are ill-defined and are put forward as vague goals or personal aims.
3 The procedures are confused with the objectives.
4 There is a lack of integration within the text among components of the pro-posal (e.g. aims and objectives do not match).
5 The individual has adopted a poor approach and appealed on an emotional or a political rather than a factual or a theoretical basis.
6 Not enough information is provided about the details of the project.

Reasons which apply only to applications for funded research:

7 The funder does not accept proposals from unaffiliated individuals.
8 The funder knows that the proposed idea has already been tried and failed.
9 The funder approves of the concept but believes that the applicant is not the proper individual to conduct the project or that the institution with which the applicant is affiliated is not suitable.
10 The idea costs too much.

Boxes 9.6 and 9.7 give two examples of successful proposals that clearly explain the intended research, making good use of subheadings for each aspect of the project. The first is for a PhD, the second for an MPhil research degree.

Box 9.6   Sample proposal 1

GENDER, WORK AND POVERTY IN INDIA

Justification and thematic priorities

The ESRC thematic priority on 'social inclusion and exclusion' raises questions about the relations between economic growth and processes of social inclusion which are increasingly framed in a world of global interdependence. This research will investigate a set of research questions at the heart of the growth/social-inclusion relationship in the context of India, since South Asia is where global poverty is most concentrated. The population of India will render the research results relevant to a large population, and there are important policy lessons to be learned from the experiences of the Indian state in poverty reduction. The Department for International Development White Paper on development (1997) put poverty reduction at the centre of all UK development policy, and DFID is committed to gender equity in development. The second thematic priority which this research addresses is 'economic performance and development', in particular 'the relationship between economic growth and development and patterns of deprivation and inequality'.

The current thematic focus on social inclusion and exclusion aims to deepen our understanding of the nature of contemporary poverty and processes of marginalization. *Work* is pivotal to many understandings of poverty, well-being and social exclusion, as well as to prescriptions for poverty reduction, as exemplified in both the New Poverty Agenda and many Women in Development policies which emphasize labour-intensive growth and greater participation by women in employment (World Bank, 1990; UNDP, 1995). Social exclusion approaches also focus on employment-based inclusion for vulnerable or excluded groups (Gore et al., 1995), and assume that well-being will be enhanced by employment, since work leads to income, social approval and self-esteem. Gender analysts have, however, questioned the pathways through which work leads to well-being, for example, through 'time-famine' experienced by poor women due to long working days, cultural disapproval of women in employment, and gender conflict within households. Furthermore, questions about the effects on the poor of labour-intensive work that is also effort intensive have been raised by Breman (1996). It is important for development policy to unpack assumptions about work and social exclusion, and the proposed research would provide an in-depth case study investigation that would contribute to this.

Research context

The most appropriate case study within India, which would offer a depth of previous studies, is the Employment Guarantee Scheme (EGS) in the state of Maharashtra, which is the state programme that best exemplifies the labour-intensive approach of the proponents of the New Poverty Agenda. The EGS was adopted by the state government of Maharashtra in 1974 and now comprises the single largest poverty reduction scheme of any state in India (Ravallion, 1990). It offers a guarantee of employment to any rural adult at a wage rate aimed to be low enough in order to

Box 9.6

self-target the poor. The work typically consists of unskilled manual labour on small scale rural public works, such as roads, irrigation facilities and reforestation, and the explicit labour-intensive nature of the scheme is maintained via a labour–capital ratio in expenditures of at least 60:40. I am currently employed on a research project which involves a field visit to the EGS, my supervisors have extensive contacts in India and I expect to be attached to a research institute in Mumbai during the fieldwork for this research.

Usefulness of the research and user groups

This research will be useful to two sets of users: first, to other academics and development analysts who are concerned with theorizing well-being, work, gender and development; and second, to development policy makers at a range of levels from project staff to policy specialists in bilateral and multilateral aid agencies, and NGOs. I am visiting the US at Easter 1999 to collect materials and discuss this research with policy analysts in the UNDP, World Bank and IFPRI, and will be taking account of their comments in the research design. DFID has a core interest in poverty and gender research to inform policy and I will consult widely within DFID.

The research will have direct and indirect implications for policy, for example, ascertaining which forms of employment-based intervention might best enhance well-being, which interventions might threaten the well-being of poor individuals, how the burdens and benefits of interventions are distributed, and how interventions need to disaggregate by gender in employment-based policies for social inclusion and poverty reduction. The conceptual refinements in capability and embodiment theories will also aid academics working on the conceptual underpinnings to contemporary labour-based poverty reduction policies.

Research objectives and conceptual framework

The broad research objective is to explore the social processes by which labour-intensive work translates (or does not) into personal well-being, and social inclusion, for poor women and men (more detailed research questions are set out below). The research will be grounded in two conceptual approaches; the capabilities approach to well-being, and notions of embodied subjectivities which have been developed in gender analysis. Combining these two approaches is novel and will hopefully result in fresh insights.

The capabilities approach (Sen, 1983) has increasingly come to replace traditional poverty assessments that were in terms of household income, production or calorie levels. The capabilities approach suggests the need to trace through the links from an individual's 'endowments' to their command over commodities, consumption and 'decision-making' which thereby transforms entitlements into personal well-being, in other words a focus on the social processes which generate well-being, rather than on poverty as a condition.

(Continued)

Box 9.6

The concept of embodiment, which grows out of the recent social theories of the body, is broadly taken to mean the display, maintenance and management of the body (Turner, 1996) and has arisen due to an increasing recognition that our life experiences, subjectivities and agency emerge from our bodies' habitual relations to the world (Annandale, 1998). Research on embodiment in the west has tended to focus on 'abnormal' bodies, such as the anorexic, and on sexualities. However, a concept of embodiment seems a very useful approach to poverty analysis as it attends to the endowment which poor rural people rely on more than any other – their bodies; that is their physical endowments, their labour entitlements, their extended entitlements to the labour of others (or their products), their capabilities and functionings and their achievement of well-being (Jackson and Palmer-Jones, 1998).

Research questions

The proposed research will address the following linked research questions:

1   How do the income/goods earned in the EGS connect to improved *economic well-being* for poor women and men? What gender differences are there in these connections? Here I will locate the EGS work as one element of a livelihood portfolio, which includes other elements, and look at how the food and income gains from the EGS contribute directly and indirectly towards poverty reduction, and how these effects are mediated by gender.
2   How does the effort intensity of EGS work affect the *bodily well-being* of gendered subjects? Does labour-intensive work, which is also effort intensive, such as in the EGS, have unrecognized negative effects on the bodily condition of the poor? How are these effects gender differentiated? Here I will study the social backgrounds (of caste, class, gender and age) of EGS participants, and the everyday realities of participation of differently gendered bodies in the EGS will be explored to understand possible health effects and hazards for poor people with stunted or wasted bodies. I will also consider questions of agency: e.g. do poor people, whose bodies are frequently stunted or wasted, nevertheless manage their bodily condition to limit the negative effects of high energy-intensive work? What practical and discursive strategies are used for this end, and how do they vary by gender? I plan to investigate how far participants exercise choice in relation to participation, and agency in how they manage the effects of heavy labour on their bodies, through working practices and social relations both within the scheme and outside it.
3   How does the experience of employment in the EGS produce *social inclusion* of the poor, and how are these effects gender differentiated? Further research questions will focus on the socio-cultural evaluations of work, the deployments of discourses about work in intra-household bargaining and resource allocation, and the wider symbolic significance of money/goods in changing gender relations, and move between levels of analysis from household to community.

Box 9.6

I will also examine the ways the scheme is implemented to understand who obtains access and who is excluded, and what the terms and conditions of social inclusion are.

The empirical study of this major poverty reduction policy will be used to develop a broader gendered analysis of the policy implications of employment-based social inclusion initiatives.

Timetable

October 1999 to Summer 2000: UK, literature reviewing, research training courses, language training.

Summer 2000 to December 2000: first fieldwork period in India.

December 2000 to January 2001: UK, analysis of initial data and supervision.

February 2001 to Summer 2001: second fieldwork period in India to refine and complete data collection.

Summer 2001 to Summer 2002: UK, writing-up period.

Sources and methods

During the first year of research I will focus on analysis of secondary data and materials. Relevant literature available in the UK will be reviewed to refine the research design and questions and to learn from existing studies. Visits to IFPRI and UNDP (April–May 1999) necessary for my current research job will also be a useful source of information from international institutions. Other secondary data used will be EGS statistics, Maharashtra employment figures, the Indian census and Indian-based literature. The predominant source of information for the research will come, however, from the primary data collected during fieldwork.

Attempting to explore people's embodied experiences of work and well-being is best approached through qualitative methodologies which will include life histories, participant observation, semi-structured interviews and key informant interviews. I plan to interview EGS personnel, and observe the detail of its implementation, as well as labour contractors and unions. A major part of the study will be interviews with a number of male and female EGS participants and work with them to understand how the EGS is situated within their livelihoods, social relations and life courses, and how they perceive well-being. This work will be supplemented with studies of non-EGS workers, local labour markets and livelihood systems. I will try to ensure rigour in the qualitative work by triangulation, and a thorough contextualization of respondents' voices. These methods will require me to build trust between respondents and myself, which will involve language study, a period for integration into the community upon which the research is focused, and collaboration with local researchers.

(Continued)

Box 9.6

Ethical considerations

This research will be based on studying a group of vulnerable poor people, and awareness of their rights to confidentiality and privacy will be important, as will a sensitivity to making demands on their time. I intend to approach these issues through informed consent, thorough explanations of the research, guarantees of confidentiality and anonymity in the thesis, acceptance of reluctance or refusals in interviews, and a serious attention to building co-operation over time. I also think it important to recognize the assistance of local assistants and scholars and be mindful of my own positionality. I will ensure that copies of research outputs are distributed within India and that Indian policy makers are consulted on the research.

References

Annandale, E. (1998) *The Sociology of Health and Medicine: a Critical Introduction.* Cambridge: Polity.

Breman, J. (1996) *Footloose Labour.* Cambridge: Cambridge University Press.

Gore, C., Rogers, G. and Figueiredo, J. (1995) 'Social exclusion: rhetoric, reality and responses'. International Institute for Labour Studies.

Jackson, C. and Palmer-Jones, R. (1998) 'Work intensity, gender and well-being'. DP 96. Geneva: UNRISD.

Ravallion, M. (1990) 'Reaching the poor through rural public employment: a survey of theory and evidence'. Discussion Paper 94. Washington, DC: World Bank.

Sen, A. (1983) 'Economics and the family'. *Asian Development Review*, 1 (2): 14–26.

Turner, B. (1996) *The Body and Society*, 2nd edn. London: Sage.

UNDP (1995) *Human Development Report*, 1995. Oxford: Oxford University Press.

World Bank (1990) *World Development Report*, 1990. Oxford: Oxford University Press.

(This was a successful PhD proposal by Louise Waite, Norwich University. Now she is Dr Waite at Leeds University.)

Box 9.7   Sample proposal 2

THE IMPACT OF INTRODUCING COGNITIVE BEHAVIOURAL THERAPY ON NURSING PRACTICE IN ACUTE AREAS OF A MENTAL HEALTH CARE

Aims of the investigation:

1   To introduce a psychological model to nurses working on acute in-patient units of a Mental Healthcare Trust.
2   To ascertain and explore nurses' perceptions of their role and clinical competencies in an in-patient area using a CBT framework.
3   To evaluate the impact of CBT techniques on nurses' perceived and actual clinical effectiveness in their work areas.

Box 9.7

Proposed plan of work, including its relationship to previous work, with key references

Introduction

Several nurses with recognized specialist training and skills were employed to help develop clinical nursing practice within the Trust (OMHT). The main aims of the role as a Clinical Nurse Specialist (CNS) is to provide specialist post-basic education and clinical supervision to other nurses. Two of the outcomes sought are: (1) continual improvement of nursing practice and clinical effectiveness, (2) personal development of the nurse practitioner. In the process of developing the role of CNS in Cognitive Behavioural Therapy (CBT) for the OMHT, one of the challenges identified was establishing an effective way to introduce speciality skills into nursing practice with different cultural characteristics to each of the five units offering acute in-patient care. While each unit has different ideologies and values in their approach to nursing care, they share the same function in the patients they treat. The first action taken by the author from 1990 to 1993 was to have a nurse seconded from an acute unit of OMHT working with the Clinical Nurse Specialist group for a period of one year. The nurse was introduced to all specialist theories and had experience working with patients using the differing models of treatment. The second clinical practice development was a CBT training group. The membership comprised a staff nurse from each of the five acute units. During the CBT training the members were also encouraged to identify research questions within their practice with relevance to all five units and suited to the CBT process and elements of an action research paradigm.

From reflective journals based on open-ended questions on topics such as attitude to level of functioning in their role and with patients etc., there were a number of outcomes (Dodd, 1995). These outcomes were not formally investigated. Both of the clinical developments produced similarities. The main areas this research seeks to investigate based on the results are: (a) present nursing practice does not use a standard nursing model, (b) nurses *initially* believed themselves to be less effective with patients, (c) the behaviour in some of the patients was experienced as threatening and insoluble, (d) nurses believed they were not always skilled to deal with certain groups of patients even though their skills were evident, (e) negative assumptions (irrational beliefs) and thoughts were triggered which made them question their role, believe they were deskilled and inadequate to be clinically effective, (f) nurses were not identifying their own distress, comparing themselves negatively to their colleagues, (g) their own self-evaluation was negative, affecting their ability to procure job satisfaction, and they felt on the fringes of the team, fearing the team would identify them as inadequate in their role and be critical of them as nurses, (h) their behavioural response was to contain patient behaviour functioning in a custodial manner rather than work in a psychological method. A preliminary study demonstrated and confirmed that nurses believed the existing nursing models were not always relevant in psychiatry.

(Continued)

Box 9.7

In relation to research, none of the interviewed nurses read or used research material and they were unaware if any colleagues participated in this exercise. No nurse interviewed had or was likely to initiate research within their practice. The main reasons were lack of time and insufficient knowledge of research. These findings are similar to those in studies elsewhere (Bostrom et al., 1989; McKenna, 1990; Marsh and Brown, 1992; McKenna, 1994).

There is a lack of theory underpinning nursing practice in the acute units of the Trust. The outcomes of the clinical developments demonstrate a lack of confidence and a negative self-evaluation of nursing staff who were participating in the projects. The second clinical development integrated a theoretical understanding of a psychological treatment into an established nursing practice. Recognizing their own perceptions of themselves whilst in their role as a nurse was an integral component of the CBT training. The nurses learnt how to challenge and correct their perceptions if they were negative and interfered with their confidence and self-esteem. The impact improved understanding of the patients, the nurses became more efficient in their role, they supported their colleagues, and they felt more potent and skilled to deal with most difficulties that acute areas offer.

Cognitive behavioural therapy

Over the past three decades, cognitive behavioural therapy (CBT) has become one of the predominant forces in psychotherapeutic practice (e.g. Mahoney, 1988; Arkowitz and Hannah,1989). The publication of a book specifically devoted to in-patient applications of Beck's model of cognitive therapy is further evidence of the growth of this approach (Thase and Wright, 1991; Beck, 1993; Wright et al., 1993). The concerns world-wide appear to seek cost containment and more efficient treatments for in-patients. Indeed in this country the government has moved toward community care and Trust status confirming these changes in attitudes and treatment (HMSO, 1989). Some of the advantages of cognitive therapy that have fuelled its development is short-term format, established efficacy, compatibility with biological psychiatry, and evidence of relapse prevention effects (Wright et al., 1993). Nurses may be introduced to basic knowledge of CBT in their training or through a locally based postgraduate course. Unfortunately the practice of CBT by the majority of CBT trained nurses is in specialist areas usually attached to Departments of Psychology or Psychotherapy or working in Primary Care. There is little opportunity or facilities for in-patient staff to develop such skills (Friedberg and Fidaleo, 1992). Cognitive behavioural therapy is widely researched as an effective psychological treatment for patients with mental health problems (Hackman, 1993). Some of the principles governing this therapy are: collaborative alliance with the patient; the patient, where appropriate, setting their own targets or goals in treatment; treatments are specified in operational terms and evaluated with a variety of objective, valid and reliable measures, providing the practitioner and the patients with empirical data on the effectiveness of the interventions utilized. This results in a continuous dialogue between clinical practice and research,

Box 9.7

ensuring that theoretical research and clinical issues interact in a unique way (Hackman, 1993). Meyer (1993) and Titchen and Binnie (1993) describe how action research supports the systematic development of knowledge born of practice which complements the CBT model and approach.

Theoretical framework

Building on the informal information derived in clinical developments, this study will further investigate the impact of CBT on nursing practice in mental healthcare. The study will be developed through the CBT developmental model (Fennell, 1989). This model is similarly described elsewhere for research as a 'multi component view of attitude' in Fishbein and Ajzen (1975) based on a conception by Rosenberg and Hovland (1960). The developmental model suggests that attitudes are predispositions to early life events that are operated from the unconscious by stimuli pertinent to those attitudes. The attitude will trigger cognitions which are the perceptual evaluation of the stimulus (Fennell, 1989). Beck et al. (1979) suggest these cognitions influence how we feel emotionally and physiologically. Our behaviour is then based upon the cognitive evaluation and subjective attribution of belief and the emotional impact on the person. This process is well described in the outcomes of the pilot project. It was apparent that the influences of CBT training had an impact on some of the group which influenced their attitudes and beliefs and therefore their clinical behaviour. The therapeutic model is deemed appropriate for this study, as it is introducing the construct for self-understanding and the therapeutic process and it links together theory and practice as well as the areas this study seeks to examine. The study will explore the impact of the CBT tools and techniques on the nurses' perceptions within their role and clinical behaviour, i.e. what they do with patients while working in the acute areas, and ascertain if the nurse is more clinically effective.

Operational definitions

Clinical effectiveness   This is defined as patients' perceptions of the impact of nurse interventions on their psychological, emotional and physical health. These will be rated by a patient/nurse rating scale.

Competencies   This is defined as clinical decision making as portrayed in the case notes, care plans and clinical supervision.

Irrational beliefs (IB)   This is the 'cognitive' term that describes attitudes, assumptions, basic beliefs that are not in the conscious awareness, yet govern our responses to outside stimuli. If irrational, then one's response may be dysfunctional.

Design

This study will use a combination of qualitative and quantitative methods to identify nurses' attitudes and perceived role. Two quantitative instruments will be modified for this study. There will be four components involved in the study design:

(Continued)

(1) exploratory, in which reflective journals will record uncensored thoughts, emotions and behaviour of subjects and provide themes to formulate semi-structured interviews; (2) modification of the IB instrument based on the literature and the exploratory phase; (3) test IB instrument for reliability and validity; (4) a pilot study on five subjects and five comparison subjects, using the IB and second quantitative instrument. Phase 4 includes the CBT training intervention. The didactic period will be six weekly workshops followed by ongoing weekly supervision until the group terminates. Key areas that will be taught are: assessment, conceptualization (Persons, 1990), Socratic questioning, and the application of CBT tools and measures to practice.

Sample

The purposive sample for this study will be nurses working on in-patient acute mental health areas of a Mental HealthCare NHS Trust. The five participants will be chosen for their interest in using CBT and represent each of the five acute in-patient areas. A comparison group of five will be randomly selected from nurses of similar grade/position working on the in-patient areas and not undertaking the CBT training intervention. The sample for this study is small owing to the nature of clinical practice development and introducing theory into practice. The process is prolonged for the subjects because the nature of training and supervision required is to ensure safe and effective practice. Finally, the research is undertaken within the context of the CNS role and not as an independent researcher.

Instruments

The study will use a range of instruments.

1 Reflective journals will allow subjects to free associate and record their thoughts, feelings and behaviour within their work area pertaining to their role and clinical practice.
2 Semi-structured interviews using Socratic (open-ended) questioning based on the themes contained in the reflective journals, e.g. thoughts of being deskilled and inadequate, being negatively evaluated by colleagues etc.
3 An IB of the nurses' questionnaire modified from the *Irrational Belief of Therapists* (Wright, 1985). This instrument consists of a number of items that subjects will score on a 10-point scale of 1–10. The questionnaire will be tested for reliability and validity as part of this research. The IB scale is used in therapist training to aid in recognition of assumptions that may interfere with the therapeutic alliance and clinical behaviour.
4 A patient/nurse scale which will be developed from the patient/therapist scale, also a tool used in therapist training which supplies feedback from patients, giving the opportunity of collaboration to patients not assertive in session and aiding the therapist in refining their clinical skills (Beck et al., 1979). This scale will

Box 9.7

be completed by the patients for each formal one-to-one session. The subjects will give it to the patient(s) who will rate their perceptions on a scale of 1–10 based on a number of items relating to the clinical behaviour of the nurse. The scale is organized into key domains: appropriate use of CBT tools; the nurse being clear and rational about interventions; and the characteristics and behaviour of the nurses in session. It is anticipated that the scale will be introduced periodically throughout the training and clinical intervention. This instrument will be used to collect data in relation to clinical behaviour and efficacy.

Data collection

(1) Reflective journals will be completed at the subjects' convenience. This may take up to 30 minutes per entry at most, depending on the events of the shift. (2) Following completion of the journals over a one month period, they will be examined and help to form the semi-structured interviews. The subjects will be seen in their area of practice for the interviews. (3) The IB scale will be administered before and after the CBT training intervention. (4) The patient/nurse scale will be administered for a one week period at differing stages throughout the training and supervised clinical practice. It is anticipated that each subject will have twelve to fifteen ratings per week. Collection of the scales will be during the group meeting where the participants discuss, compare and share their experiences and values with the researcher. (5) The IB and patient/nurse scales will be given to the five randomly selected groups of nurses of similar grade/position working on the in-patient areas at the same time as the subjects.

Analysis

The reflective journals will be examined for themes that reflect attitudes/beliefs, e.g. perfectionism, expectations, responsibility and fears of failure. The journals will be compared to identify similarities among the subjects. Semi-structured interviews will be conducted to clarify the themes from the reflective journals into statements (beliefs) and consequences, e.g. 'If I make a mistake then I will damage the patient.' These will be used to modify the IB scale. The IB scale is not recognized as a formal research instrument; therefore as part of this study the instrument will be tested for reliability by test–retest, internal consistency and interrater reliability, and for validity through criterion-related validity and concurrent validity. The subject scores from the IB will be compared pre and post CBT training intervention. The IB scores will be compared to the IB scores of the comparison group pre and post CBT intervention. The patient/nurse scale scores will be examined to ascertain any improvement as the subjects progress through the training and clinical practice and will be correlated with any significant changes in the subject IB scores. These scores will also be compared to those of the comparison group.

(Continued)

Box 9.7

Ethics

The study will be forwarded to Nursing Research Committee by March 1996. Subjects will be assured of confidentiality. Recorded data necessary for reports will be given anonymity. Subjects will be assured that the purpose of this study is to enhance their clinical practice and development and is not an assessment for any managerial appraisal or to their detriment. A full information sheet will be given to outline these assurances.

Plan

(1) Registration, form group and consent of participation, March 1996. (2) Reflective journals and semi-structured interviews, April/May 1996. (3) Modify and test IB, June 1996. (4) Administer IB, initiate CBT training intervention and patient/nurse scale, weekly supervision, assess adequate CBT working knowledge of project group, September 1996. (5) Clinical behaviour for appropriate period, apply patient/nurse scale periodically, begin September 1996. (5) Apply IB. (6) Data analysis, case report, publish findings, November 1997.

Budget

This project has the financial support and clinical collaboration of the Oxfordshire Mental Health NHS Trust. This is demonstrated by the covering letter attached.

References

Arkowitz, H. and Hannah, M. T. (1989) 'Cognitive, behavioural, and psychodynamic therapies'. in A. Freeman, K. M. Simon, L. E. Beutler and H. Arkowitz (eds), *Comprehensive Handbook of Cognitive Therapy*. New York: Plenum.

Beck, A. T. (1993) *Cognitive Therapy: Past, Present, Future*. New York: Guilford.

Beck, A. T., Rush, J. and Emery, G. (1979) *Cognitive Therapy for Depression*. New York: Guilford.

Bostrom, A. C., Malnight, M., MacDougal, J. and Hargis, D. (1989) 'Staff nurses' attitudes toward nursing research: a descriptive survey', *Journal of Advanced Nursing*, 14, pp. 915–922.

Dodd, H. (1995) *Staff Nurse Development Project Annual Report*. Published for OMHT internally.

Fennell, M. J. V. (1989) 'Depression', in K. Hawton, P. M. Salkovskis, J. Kirk and D. M. Clarke (eds), *Cognitive Therapy for Psychiatric Problems: a Practical Guide*. Oxford: Oxford University Press.

Fishbein, M. and Ajzen, I. (1975) *Belief, Attitude, Intention and Behaviour*. Philippines: Addison-Wesley.

Friedberg, R. D. and Fidaleo, R. A. (1992) 'Training inpatient staff in cognitive therapy', *Journal of Psychotherapy: an International Quarterly*, 6, 2, pp. 105–112.

Box 9.7

Hackman, A. (1993) 'Behavioural and cognitive psychotherapies: past history, current applications and future registration issues', *Journal of the British Association for Behavioural and Cognitive Psychotherapies*, Supplement 1, pp. 2–72.

HMSO (1989) *Working for Patients*. London: HMSO.

Mahoney, M. J. (1988) 'The cognitive sciences and psychotherapy: patterns in a developing relationship', in I. Dobson (ed.), *Handbook of Cognitive Behavioural Therapies*. New York: Guilford.

Marsh, J. M. and Brown, T. L. (1992) 'The measurement of nurses' attitudes towards nursing research and the research environment in clinical settings', *Journal of Clinical Nursing*, 1, pp. 315–322.

McKenna, H. P. (1990) 'The perception of psychiatric-hospital ward sisters/charge nurses towards nursing models', *Journal of Advanced Nursing*, 15, pp. 1319–1325.

McKenna, H. P. (1994) 'The attitudes of traditional and undergraduate nursing students toward nursing models: a comparative survey', *Journal of Advanced Nursing*, 19, pp. 527–536.

Meyer, Julienne E. (1993) 'New paradigm research in practice: the trials and tribulations of action research', *Journal of Advanced Nursing*, 18, pp. 1066–1072.

Persons, J. B. (1990) *Cognitive Therapy: a Case Conceptualisation*. London: Norton.

Rosenberg, M. J. and Hovland, C. I. (1960) 'Cognitive, affective, and behavioural components of attitudes', in C. I. Hovland and M. J. Rosenberg (eds), Attitude, Organization and Change. New Haven, CT: Yale University Press.

Thase, M. E. and Wright, J. H. (1991) 'Cognitive behaviour therapy manual for depressed in-patients: a treatment protocol outline', *Behaviour Therapy*, 22, pp. 579–595.

Titchen, A. and Binnie, A. (1993) 'What am I meant to be doing? Putting practice into theory and back again in new nursing roles', *Journal of Advanced Nursing*, 18, pp. 1054–1065.

Wright, J. H. (1985) 'Irrational belief of therapists'. Unpublished document.

Wright, J. H., Thase, M. E., Beck, A. T. and Ludgate, J. W. (1993) *Cognitive Therapy with In-patients: Developing a Cognitive Milieu*. New York: Guildford.

(This was a successful MPhil proposal by Harry Dodd at Oxford Brookes University. Now he is a Consultant Cognitive Behavioural Psychotherapist at Warneford Hospital in Oxford.)

Read Boxes 9.6 and 9.7 analytically, paying particular attention to the structure of the proposal, and locating the following features of each:

EXERCISE 9.5

- title of the research
- aims
- literature review and explanation of the theory and history to support the research
- method of citation

- exposition of the research questions or problems
- research methods used to investigate the questions or problems
- ethical issues
- programme of work
- organization of list of references.

Compare these with what you have written by making the same analysis of your proposal. How does it match up?

Thought

So now you should be at the point where you can submit your proposal and are really clear about what you will be doing over the next few months. In response to the common question asked when people find out that you are a researcher – 'Oh yes, so what is your research about?' – you will be able to respond with the question, 'Do you want the five second answer, the five minute answer or the five hour answer?'

HOW TO GET STARTED WITH WRITING

After your proposal has been accepted by your course leader, your university's research degree committee, or the funding body to which you applied – what comes next? It is very easy to relax at this point, having exerted great efforts to sort out and describe your intended research. After a short pause for breath, you should now regard your proposal as your springboard to doing the research proper, and take the first steps in carrying it out.

The description of methods provides a succinct action list which you can now start to implement. What you should do first really depends on what is on the list. However, there are two preliminary tasks which will help you to organize your work:

1 Devise a structure plan of your thesis, dissertation or report (or at least of the introductory chapters).
2 Devise a detailed timetable of your actions for the next year or so if you are doing a research thesis, or for the duration of a shorter research project.

The most usual item at the head of the plan of work is to continue background reading and consultations and critical analysis of the literature. When you submitted your proposal, you should have completed much of the necessary reading and preliminary information collection, so you should be able to start writing a draft of your introductory chapters. It is an acknowledged fact that committing yourself to beginning your thesis or report is not easy or comfortable. Preece described the psychological problems of starting the task of writing:

> One common reaction is that the student becomes overwhelmed, not to say mentally paralysed, by the seemingly daunting prospect of writing so many words. (1994, p. 210)

However, there are two good reasons why you should begin your research project in this way. Firstly, the process of writing forces you to review your notes and to assess their suitability for use in the argument which you will be developing in your chapters, and may also reveal gaps in the information you have collected. Secondly, it tests the adequacy of the argument which must form the foundation of your research.

It is difficult for your supervisor to comment in any detail on your work if it is not written down. However, the writing process is not easy and requires considerable discipline and organization. It has often been noted that professional authors invariably work regular office-type hours at their word processors and do not sit around waiting for inspiration! Inspiration comes through active engagement in the writing process, and feeds on the efforts required to organize and create written work. However, do remember to take appropriate breaks to avoid the stresses and strains caused by using the computer for long periods. You can use these breaks to give yourself time to think quietly about your work. Once you have successfully written a few sections of text, the task will no longer seem to be so daunting.

Figure 9.2 Professional authors invariably work regular office-type hours at their word processors

The writing process

According to Freeman and Meed (1993, p. 53), all writing involves a number of stages, as shown in Box 9.8.

Box 9.8	Stages of writing

- Identifying what kind of writing you must do (the task), and what it is for (the reader).
- Deciding how to tackle it: this can involve choosing a topic or analysing a question.
- Collecting information you will need: this may involve doing research or reading.
- Preparing an outline for what you will write.
- Writing a first draft and submitting it to others for comment.
- Editing and redrafting to refine it.
- Giving a final check before handing it or sending it to the reader.

Whenever you want to produce a piece of writing, you have to ask yourself whether to write something that merely describes a situation or an event, or to argue about a particular point of view or a research problem, saying, for example, that there is a relationship or not between X and Y. So you will be faced with either a descriptive or an argumentative approach. Smith and Smith (1994, p. 116) define a descriptive approach as one in which you have to list important issues. Your own point of view is often not required at all, although you may wish to comment on and compare the issues. On the other hand, an argumentative approach is one in which you have to state your own point of view, and to defend it by giving supporting arguments.

Forming the structure and preparing an outline

There is no single right way of setting about your writing task. Before you start writing, however, it is essential to devise a structure for the work, and then to prepare an outline of what you want to write. The best approach depends on the nature of the piece (a short article, a chapter of an extended thesis, a densely argued conference paper etc.). Consider the following advice offered by various authors, and select and adapt it to help you to organize the 'skeleton' of the particular writing task you are facing.

Many reports are written with the intention of answering a question or a series of questions. When formulating the structure of your report, you can start by setting out the question or questions you are trying to answer. You may start off by formulating a large number of questions and in this way break down the major problem posed by the subject into a series of questions or sub-problems. You have to select the significant issues and reject those of only peripheral importance. The much reduced list of questions can then be arranged to form a preliminary plan of your report, and consideration of how you will answer these questions will prompt you to devise a logical arrangement for the components of your report. According to Newman:

The final questions must clearly be of such a nature that they will fit into a pattern or structure which can form the outline of the essay. From the answers to these questions your aim must be to construct a coherent, logical pattern of ideas and arguments that will form the structure or backbone of your essay or paper. Into this structure the data which you have discovered can then be fitted to 'flesh out' and support your theme, argument or thesis. (1989, pp. 20–1)

There are other ways of planning a piece of written work. A plan was defined by Freeman and Meed (1993) as a series of headings with an idea or two under each heading. The headings should do no more than cover the points you intend to write about. The priority in the plan is logical order. This does not mean that there is one and only one order which you can consider but it does mean that your final order must justify itself and be clear to the reader. One way of doing this is to look at the material you have collected and decide which are the main points you wish to cover (1993, p. 59). Your plan would then look like Box 9.9.

Box 9.9   Plan of written work

- An introduction: to define your terms and indicate how you intend to tackle the topic.
- A list of main sections, summarized in the form of topic headings.
- A summary or conclusion: to recall the issues raised in the introduction, draw together the points you made in the main sections and explain the overall significance of your conclusions.

Fairbairn and Winch (1991) elaborated on the above points. They advised that in preparing an outline, you should consider carefully what you want to say about the topic. How should you best introduce what you want to say? How will you conclude? What are the central points of your argument? Each word should add something to the sense of the sentence and each sentence should add something to the thrust of the paragraph of which it is a part. Each paragraph should make a coherent contribution to what you write about your topic. They also advise you to pursue your argument as in Box 9.10 (1991, pp. 34–5).

Box 9.10   Setting up and pursuing your argument

1   Begin by thinking about what it is you want to say, including what conclusions you wish to reach. Write down a brief statement of the gist of what you intend to communicate, perhaps listing the main points to be made.
2   Work out the best order for presenting your main points. Make a skeleton of your essay.

(Continued)

---

3 Check that the ideas you want to present follow on from one another. If they don't, add linking ideas.

4 Check whether any examples you have listed are adequate to illustrate the main points you wish to make.

5 Decide on how you will introduce your piece. Write the draft introduction. Avoid long-windedness: introductions should do no more than engage the reader by giving some kind of 'trailer' for what is to come.

6 Write a draft of the remainder of the essay.

7 Write the conclusion or concluding paragraphs. At this point you may wish to emphasize some points or recapitulate the main threads in your arguments; or you may wish to indicate areas into which you have not entered because to do so would have taken more space than you had available. Paradoxically, it will often be worth thinking about what you wish to conclude before even beginning to set pen to paper in preparing your initial plan, since this might influence what you decide to include and exclude from the main body of your essay.

Thought

Bear in mind the following useful points also made by Fairbairn and Winch (1991, p. 25). When you are planning a piece of writing, particularly if it is to be an important one such as an article, an essay or an extended thesis, your text can be reread and analysed over and over again. On each occasion different aspects and interpretations may occur to the reader. Although your reader will be able to formulate ideas in his/her own mind about what you are saying or meaning, he/she will usually not be able to ask you any questions at the time of reading. You will therefore need to ask yourself the questions your reader might be inclined to ask, in order to save him/her the fruitless task of asking and not being able to get an answer. Do not be afraid of patronizing your readers by supplying information, references or arguments that you think are 'obvious', because they may not be obvious to him/her.

Retrieving and organizing notes

In order to write, you will need to refer to the information you have assimilated from the literature over the previous months. By now you will have collected a substantial amount of relevant information that you have ordered in some way so that it remains coherent, manageable and controllable. Supposing you have used a card system: then you could have utilized a box of the appropriate size for the cards and divided it into sections by means of slightly larger cards, each section being reserved for one of the subject areas that you have decided on. You might find it necessary to transfer cards between subject area divisions. You can do this easily if you have followed the advice given earlier about only inserting one item of information on each card; now you realize the advantage of reserving one card for one idea or item of information. You will understand that cards often need to be cross-referenced to other information cards. For this reason you should devise a simple system of numbering the cards (Newman, 1989, pp. 24–5).

Figure 9.3 You should devise a simple system of numbering the cards

If, on the other hand, you have put all your notes in the form of 'records' into a computer database, you will find it easy to sort out and select notes through the search facility, which allows you to retrieve notes which contain particular key words, or which refer to a particular subject or author. Again, there is much to recommend the practice of keeping the records short and devoted to only one subject. The cards referred to subsequently in this text are equivalent to the 'records' which you saved and subsequently retrieved from the database.

In drafting an outline of your essay, report or chapter, begin by retrieving the relevant notes already saved. This should not be very difficult; gradually start feeding the information into the planned sections of your work, which is quite simple if you have initially well organized your information notes into sections related to the relevant subject areas, and if the overall plan of your work has been broken down into a number of small and manageable subject divisions.

The information collected on cards (or records) and organized under specific subject areas has been assembled piecemeal over a period of time. In addition, during information collection you will have written out and recorded your own ideas as they occurred to you, and inserted these cards into the appropriate subdivision of your material. By considering all the relevant notes, you must develop a clear idea of the overall structure of your argument. You should take out the information cards in each section (or print out the relevant records) and sift and rearrange them in an order that provides the basic facts and ideas needed for each section of your argument. You might in fact discard some cards as no longer relevant to your work (1989, pp. 24–5). Now it is time to think and write.

Drafting and redrafting

Once you have identified your arguments, formed the structure, prepared an outline and collected and ordered the information you need, you are ready to start writing. Do not worry if you do not get it right the first time. Remember that you start with a first draft which you then revise (often many times). Freeman and Meed (1993, p. 61) outlined the advantages of drafting as in Box 9.11.

Box 9.11   Advantages of drafting

- You do not have to get it right first time, and this sometimes makes it easier to start writing.
- You do not have to start at the beginning: the introduction can be difficult to write, so it might make sense to start in the middle.
- You can change the order if it does not work in practice.
- You do not have to worry about getting your style and spelling right first time: you can come back and correct later.

In addition, according to Newman (1989, p. 31), the main asset offered by a first draft is that it gives an opportunity to revise the text. It does this in two ways. Firstly, you can circulate the draft text amongst your tutors or supervisors with a view to gaining their expert comment on the draft as a whole and in its particular details. But, most important of all, it gives you the opportunity to think again. Having written the first draft you should leave it alone for a few days and get on with some other work. When you return to it later you may well be amazed at the faults in structure and in detail that leap to the eye as you examine it (see also van Dalen, 1979, pp. 430–1).

You should regard redrafting as a normal activity, not an admission of failure. Writing and developing ideas always takes time, and until you have made an initial draft, you and others cannot review your work and change and improve it. There are several reasons why you may wish to redraft your work: the length may be wrong, the arguments may not be really clear, there are spelling and grammatical mistakes, or you have developed or changed your ideas since you originally wrote them. You may also have spotted repetitions or omissions, or you want to adjust the text to fit better with new material that you have subsequently written.

Writing can be seen as a reiterative process, particularly when the work is long and complicated. How often should you redraft? This depends on the length, complexity and duration of the research work. Short reports can sometimes be drawn up in one go and revised as a whole. With longer texts, a chapter by chapter approach is normally used initially, and then the whole work is looked at and adjusted to ensure continuity and completeness. For a very condensed piece of work, such as a research proposal or an academic paper, inexperienced writers may have to redraft five, ten or even twenty times to reach the required standard. For more experienced writers writing less crucial texts, perhaps only one or two redrafts will be necessary.

In drafting and redrafting your work you should use the best technology available to you. This means one of two things: a typewriter, pen, scissors, sticky tape, correcting fluid and lots of energy for retyping, or a word processor (Fairbairn and Winch, 1991, p. 42).

In the 'scissors and sticky tape' method you should annotate the draft with which you are working with any changes you wish to make to the text, including noting places where you want to rearrange by moving sentences or even whole chunks about. You may want to write yourself notes about research that you now believe is necessary. Correcting fluid can come in handy for making minor changes to text, allowing you to remove text and write in changes more neatly. If you have decided to move several chunks of text to different places you will probably find it useful to cut up the relevant pages and stick them together in the new order before retyping. This is useful for small amounts of text (lecture notes, posters etc.) or as a preliminary method of sorting your notes, but is now not acceptable for longer works.

It is necessary to have access to a computer for later and longer drafts, and it is essential that you develop your skills in using a word processor program. A word processor allows you to create and revise successive drafts without rewriting or retyping large chunks of text each time. It allows you to move text about, and to delete and replace words, phrases, sentences and longer passages, as in the

Figure 9.4   The 'scissors and sticky tape' method of working is not now acceptable for longer works

scissors and sticky tape method, but more swiftly and neatly. You should keep a copy of the original text on disk in case you are unhappy with changes you make. Since the word processor displays your redrafting only on a screen (VDU or visual display unit), it is essential to remember to save your work regularly onto disk, to avoid losing hours of work should the power be interrupted or you make a silly mistake on the keyboard. Do make the effort to learn how to use the facilities built into the word processing package, e.g. spell check, search, replace, formatting, use of fonts, blocking and changing, printing etc. Use the 'online help' facility if you get stuck, and don't hesitate to ask your more experienced colleagues for advice.

Paragraphs

I suggest that at the first draft stage you should aim to write one paragraph (or perhaps more if necessary) for each of the headings in your outline. But you need to be careful about paragraph content and construction: see Box 9.12.

Box 9.12   Paragraph construction

- Each paragraph should contain one main idea – from your outline.
- The first sentence should, if possible, introduce this idea.
- Other sentences should support the main idea by explaining it more, giving examples or linking it to other paragraphs.
- It is very dangerous to introduce a second idea as this will almost certainly confuse the reader.

Ideas and evidence

When you are writing your report, you will often wish to put forward other people's ideas as well as your own. It is therefore essential that you express these ideas clearly and concisely and give credit where it is due: for example, if you quote from a book or an article, make reference to the title, author and publisher. Exactly how you should do this is described later in this chapter. Ideas should always be backed up with evidence, whether from your own research or as quotations from other sources from your reading. Bald statements of fact will not be accepted unless they are general currency (e.g. that the world orbits the sun).

Introduction and conclusion

According to Newman (1989, p. 33), if you are writing a self-contained report, the introductory section should comply with the points in Box 9.13.

1   State precisely the area of study. This is very important; you can hardly be criticized for failing to cover something outside the area of research you have defined.
2   Explain why the research is being carried out.
3   Draw attention to the originality and the conclusions.
4   Point to the inadequacy of the work so far carried out in this area of research.
5   Describe the methods of research.
6   State what special difficulties have been encountered.

When you feel that you have reached a reasonable structure for your report, try to draft an introductory section to your report, which will be continually improved and gradually rewritten as the research progresses. Writing the conclusion is more complex. Newman (1989, pp. 33–4) suggests that a clear distinction should be made at an early stage of the research between, on the one hand, the possible conclusions that may emerge or the hypotheses that are being tested (which must necessarily be delineated as a part of the structure) and, on the other hand, the actual research-based conclusions which can be written only when the research has actually been carried out. The conclusion should also include an assessment of the soundness of the whole written report, with perhaps suggestions of how further research in the same subject area might be carried forward.

When writing an individual chapter in a thesis or a report, similar considerations apply to the introduction and conclusions, but these must be tailored to the specific needs and content of the chapter, while referring to, and making connections with, the other chapters. It is difficult to make all the connections before other chapters are written, so be prepared to review the work as a whole when the full draft has been completed in order to forge these connections.

Illustrations

At the first draft stage, you should also think about whether, and how, you should illustrate what you write. Depending on what you are writing, you may wish to draw your own pictures – diagrams, charts, maps, graphs or tables – or to include copies of pictures from other sources. Box 9.14 gives criteria for illustrations.

Any illustrations should:

- be relevant to what you are saying
- be clear and simple to understand
- add usefully to what is already there
- be cross-referenced and explained in the text
- be clearly labelled and, if from other sources, fully referenced.

Quotations

When you are drafting your research report, make sure that you utilize only necessary quotations; over-weighting your report with them might possibly diminish its originality, and consequently its value. According to van Dalen (1979, p. 423), interlarding a report indiscriminately with quotations and footnotes is a cultural affectation that some inexperienced writers assume to conceal shoddy workmanship. He adds that pasting numerous quotations into an authority-laden mosaic does not create an acceptable research report. Strings of these passages reveal that you are little beyond the note-taking stage of your work. A research report is a creative effort – a synthesis of what you have read, observed and mentally ordered into a new pattern – rather than a mere compilation of other people's work. You may use quotations, but use them sparingly and purposefully.

If you wish to refer to another person's work by citing his/her words directly, you should give a precise location for them, i.e. include the page number of the book/article. This will test the quality of your information storage and retrieval system: many a frustrating hour or even day has been spent in looking for the precise location of an essential quotation months or years after it was noted! If you are citing less than a certain number of words (say up to 30) you should put the quotation within your text, using quotation marks to show to the reader that you are borrowing these words from another person. If you have longer quotations, begin a new line, perhaps use single spacing and perhaps a different font, and indent the quoted passage slightly from both sides. The use of quotation marks is not then necessary. The reference should follow the quotation, strictly following the requirements of the chosen citing system (more about this later in the chapter).

Punctuation

When you are drafting, use punctuation which helps the readers to understand the message you intend to convey. Punctuation is an indication of the way in

Figure 9.5 The use of punctuation can also help to indicate meanings that in speech are conveyed by tone of voice, gesture, stress on particular words or syllables, pauses and so on

which you should speak the text, so it is often a good test to read it out aloud, which will check that the punctuation helps to indicate meanings conveyed by tone of voice, gesture, stress on particular words or syllables, pauses and so on. On the other hand, its overuse can also cloud meaning.

You should make sure that you are able to make correct use of the following: full stop, capital letters, comma, semicolon, colon, question mark, exclamation mark, apostrophe, brackets, inverted commas and hyphen. You should also learn to paragraph appropriately and to use indentation to make certain sections of your work stand out. The use of the dash – for example, in making an aside – is also worth learning. For further information, including description, function, use and examples of the above-mentioned types of punctuation, you can refer to Fairbairn and Winch (1991, pp. 52–61) and other books treating the use of punctuation in texts.

The short summary in Box 9.15, based on guidance notes prepared by Margaret Ackrill (1994) for architectural research students at Oxford Brookes University, will give you the main points to consider.

Box 9.15   Use of punctuation

1   *Commas* are the smallest interruption to continuity, to enable the reader to pause. They mark off one thing from another to prevent ambiguity and mis-reading. They are not needed before the last item of a simple list which is usually preceded by 'and'. Try reading the following without a comma, to see why one is necessary: 'After eating the lions yawned and then dozed.'

2   *Semicolons* give a greater break, and usually separate two points of equal significance, e.g. 'The buses were late; the trains usually ran on time.'

3   *Colons* give an even bigger gap and precede a clause or phrase which explains or expands what has just been said, e.g. 'The weather was unusual for April: never since the beginning of records had it been so cold and sunless.'

4   *Exclamation marks*, unless part of a quotation, are not appropriate for a thesis.

5   *Quotation marks* are needed around all short (say less than 30 word) direct quotations. Single marks are used, except for a quotation within a quotation, when double ones surround the inner quotation. If the end of the quotation is the end of your sentence, a full stop should be used outside the final quotation mark if the quotation itself is not a full sentence, but inside if it is. Omissions within a quotation should be shown by three dots (ellipsis): when omissions spread over a full stop, some writers show the full stop before or after the three dots as appropriate. Long quotations, i.e. those spreading over say more than 30 words, should be indented, possibly typed in single-space type, and not surrounded by quotation marks.

6   *Brackets* set off something in parenthesis, something said in an undertone, e.g. 'The building (considering its mode of construction) was in a good state.' Round brackets should be used unless the parenthesis is something you have inserted within a quotation, when square brackets [ ] should be used.

Spelling

Spelling is very important. If you use a word processor, it is common courtesy now to use the spell checker on your draft before submitting it to someone to read, to avoid them unnecessary time and effort correcting obvious spelling errors. Even when the spelling errors are pointed out after reading a draft, many of the same errors sometimes reappear in a subsequent draft. Some students fail to take the time to check their work thoroughly. It is worthwhile getting somebody to read your writing with the intention of pointing out spelling errors and even places where he/she is unsure whether you have spelled a word correctly; you can check the queried spelling in a dictionary or the spell checker in your word processing program.

When drafting and revising your work you should, according to Fairbairn and Winch (1991, p. 95), learn to read it in two ways. Firstly, you should be able to read it as if you have never read it before at the level of content. Does it make the points it is supposed to make? Does it make them succinctly and clearly? Secondly, you should read your work in order to attend to format – to spelling, punctuation, grammar and so on.

Some of the most common spelling mistakes arise from confusions between words that sound the same but are spelled differently and mean different things. A little thought should help you to avoid these confusions in spelling. Words that sound the same but have different meanings are called homophones. If you use a word processor, look out for spelling mistakes caused by typing too fast. All word processors nowadays include a facility for spell checking; however, these have their limitations. For example, you might type a word which is correctly spelled but, because it not the right word, does not give any meaning to the sentence. When you use the spell checker on your word processor, it will not point out this word because for it the word is spelled correctly; for example, if you typed 'of' instead of 'for', the spell check will not reveal your mistake. Mistakes such as these may remain in your final draft unless you habitually read your work carefully for spelling mistakes before deciding it is finished.

Presentation

As your drafts become more refined, you need to start thinking about how the text and illustrations will be presented. There are conventions which help to keep presentation clear and consistent. Here are some of them as summarized in Ackrill (1994).

Tables

A table should follow the first reference to it in the thesis. If it will not fit into the remaining space on a page, place it at the end of the paragraph in which it is first mentioned. All tables should have a title and be numbered within each chapter. The third table in Chapter 2, for instance, should be shown as Table 2.3.

A separate list of tables should appear after the list of contents at the beginning of the thesis.

Where the table is not your own work, the source should be given at the foot of the table, in the same form as the references.

A two-line gap must be left before the table number and title, and a similar gap at the end of the table. If the source is cited, this gap is after the named source. Where tables are unwieldy, they go into an appendix. Consult your tutor or supervisor about how they should be numbered.

The number and title of a table may appear at the side or in the centre of the page. Wording may be in capitals, or with capitals for important words, or with no capitals. But all positioning and lettering must be consistent throughout the thesis or report.

Figures

Figures (i.e. small graphs or charts) are presented in the same way as tables, except that they must have their own set of numbers, e.g. Figure 3.1.

Numbering

All chapters must be numbered, and sections within chapters may also be numbered, e.g. the first section in Chapter 2 can be numbered 2.1, and subsections within it 2.1.1, 2.1.2 etc.

The items in any lists should be consecutively numbered or otherwise indicated, e.g. by bullets. They should be in the same grammatical form, e.g. all beginning with a noun, or a participle, or an infinitive. Initial capital letters and punctuation should follow a consistent system. The lists themselves do not need to be numbered by chapter in the same way as the figures and tables.

Bibliographies, references and footnotes

When reviewing the literature relating to your research project, you should, if at all possible, include recent information. This by no means implies that older information is not relevant, but the review should be up to date. A review of the literature that had no entries less than two years old, for example, would be suspect, and could show a serious gap or deficiency (Wiersma, 1986, p. 77).

When information is reported from a source, it must be adequately referenced. It is important that whenever you cite others, you make available sufficient information to enable the reader to look up such work for him/herself. Below is a brief description, based on Ackrill (1994), of two widely acceptable methods, either of which you can safely adopt. Neither, in my experience, has ever been questioned by an examiner or a reviewer.

Note, though, that a number of alternative formats are used in academic publishing. Different journals adopt their own particular systems, and insist that their authors comply with them. It is possible to convert your bibliographies from one format to another very easily if you use a suitable computer program (such as ProCite or EndNote) when you compile your initial bibliography.

Bibliographies

All reports and theses must include a bibliography. The bibliography is a list of all written materials found useful in writing the report or thesis. It must include everything from which direct quotations are made, or to which the text refers, or which is the source of reasonably specialized information. It does not normally include entries in encyclopedias.

The bibliography lists works in alphabetical order of their authors, with the last name appearing first. Whenever you read something useful, make an index card giving the authors' names, and indicating whether the first and any other names appear on the title page in full, or are referred to only by initials. Then record the name of the book or article, the journal in which the latter was published, together with its volume and issue number, the date of publication (including the month of an issue, or the date of a newspaper article), the name of the publisher and the date of publication. The page or pages of an article should also be noted, e.g. pp. 34–48. The presentation of this information in the bibliography should take one of the two forms explained below.

References

References should be given for all direct or indirect quotations, and in acknowledgement of someone's opinions, or of a source of factual information which is not general knowledge. The first method illustrated here, which I will call method A, is more commonly found in British publications. The second, method B, is an adaptation of the Harvard system, more commonly found in United States publications. Whichever method is adopted, it should be followed in detail. Examples of the two methods are given in Box 9.16.

Method A

A reference is shown in the text by a number in round brackets. Except when a dash is used, punctuation marks always precede a reference number, e.g. '… of this learned work. (27)' and not '… of this learned work (27).'

In a thesis, a separate set of numbers beginning with (1) should be used in each chapter: in a short report, numbers may run consecutively throughout. At the end of the chapter (or report) the works to which the numbers refer are listed. Each entry begins with the author's last name in capitals, followed by the other names or initials of the writer, as they appear on the title page of the work in question. A comma or semicolon separates the name from the title of the book or article; be consistent whichever you choose. Titles of books and articles have the main words beginning with capitals; subordinate parts of a title, often in smaller print on the title page, should be marked off from the main title by a semicolon. Titles of books are in italics; titles of articles are not in italics but are enclosed in single quotation marks. The title of an article is followed by the name of the journal, and this name is in italics and followed by the volume issue number, and, in round brackets, the date of publication, and the page or pages on which the information is found. After the title of a book, its place of publication, name of publisher and date of publication are given, and enclosed in one set of round brackets. The page or pages containing the information are then given.

In addition to these references, a bibliography is needed at the end of a thesis using method A. The bibliography, of course, includes all sources given as references, and in addition, works of general use for the thesis. The form of name, title etc. is the same as for chapter references, except that individual pages are not given. However, the pages which an article occupies in a journal are given, e.g. pp. 283–325.

Method B

A brief reference is given in the text by an entry enclosed in round brackets, and a longer version of the reference is given in the bibliography. There is no list of references at the end of chapters.

The entry in the text consists of the last name of the writer, followed by the year of publication and the page number. Should the bibliography include more than one work written in a given year by a given author, the works are lettered a, b, c etc., and this letter follows the year of publication, e.g. (Huxtable, 1976b, p. 43).

The entry in the bibliography begins with the author's last name in capitals followed by a comma, and other names in full if these are known, or indicated by initials if they are not. The year of publication and if necessary a, b etc. follow, enclosed in round brackets. The title of the book or article is then given, with only the first letter of the first word and of other words which normally take capitals (e.g. place names) in capitals. The title of a book is in italics, but not that of an article. The name of the journal in which an article appeared then follows, and is in italics; volume and issue number, and the month of publication, and the page or pages which an article covers are given, e.g. pp. 21–3. The entry for a book ends with the place of publication and the name of the publisher.

Footnotes

Footnotes, in the literal sense of notes at the foot of the page, should be avoided if possible. Where a non-English word is used, explain its meaning in the text when first mention is made of it. If the definition (e.g. of a technical or professional term) is so long that it interrupts the flow of the thesis, it may be put in a note at the bottom of the page. A superscript (1) after the term in the text and preceding the explanation at the bottom of the page is all that is needed.

Method A

End of chapter book reference:

> 1.   NORRIS, A. B.: *Why It Doesn't Fall Down: a Study of Single Span Architecture* (London, Lothbury Press, 1984) p. 52.

End of chapter article reference:

> 1.   BLENKINSOP, Peter J.: 'Nothing Is for Nothing: the Cost of Open Space' *Journal of Architectural Economics* Vol. 14 No. 3 (August 1985) pp. 46–7.

Method B

Bibliographical entry (at end of thesis) of a book title:

> NORRIS, Algernon George (1984). *Why it doesn't fall down: a study of single span architecture*. London, Lothbury Press.

Bibliographical entry (at the end of thesis) of article title:

> BLENKINSOP, Peter John (1985). Nothing is for nothing; the cost of open space. *Journal of Architectural Economics* Vol. 14, No. 3, August, pp. 46–59.

For further refinements – e.g. multiple authors – see Parsons (1973) for method A, and Chicago University Press (1969) for method B.

EXERCISE 9.6   In order to check that you remember the points made above about good writing, see if you can spot and correct the mistakes in the following text. There are about 60 mistakes – in punctuation, spelling, form of quotations, citation and referencing, and in the bibliographic referencing. The corrected text is given in the answers section.

USA and the british colonies; simplified building techniques

The simplification of building techniques has a long history Efforts were continually being made through using industrialised techniques, to reduce costs and to minimise the skills required to construct permanent buildings, particularly in situations where building materials and skills were scarce (Blomeyer and Tietze, pp.7–10).

From the latter part of the 18th century the need for permanent quickly bilt houses in the new settlements of the British colonies gave rise to a continuous development of pre-fabricated building systems which could be easily exported from Britain and erected in a short time by inexperienced labour the design of these houses developed quickly from a rudimentary example of a framed canvas for-roomed structure brought to Australia from Britain in 1788 by captain arthur phillip, which unfortunately proved 'not perfectly impervious to either wind or weather (Freeland et al., 1969, p.16), to the widely advertised, fully prefabricated and packed timber 'Manning Portable Cottage', which was exported in large numbers in the early 1840s (Herbert, 1978, p.14–15). The Manning cottage was: '… designed for ease of erection. It was completely fabricated in the carpenter's shop and required little or no site work other than the building of foundations and the assembly of components. The structure required no fashioning of joints, no cutting of timber, no nailing – "whoever can use a common bed-wrench can put this cottage up." The design was tailored to the limited resources of skill and tools available to the emigrant (Herbert, 1978, pp.10–11).'

The advent of machined widely available timber sections and the mass production of nails in the muddle of the 19th century, led to the pioneering 'Balloon Frame' timber construction system in America, which enabled the rapid building of settlements using standardised timber sections and frame configurations with simple weatherboard cladding (Giedion, 1962, pp.345–350).

> A man and a boy can now (1865) attain the same results, with ease, that twenty men could on an old-fashioned frame. (Woodward, 1896, pp.152–164)

Giedion suggested that 60–80% of all houses in the United States used balloon frame construction (Giedion; 1962; pp.344), while a contemporary commentator observed

> If it had not been for the knowledge of the balloon frame, Chicago and San Francisco could never have arisen, as they did, from little villages to great cities in a single year (Robinson, 1855).

Iron was also used to simplify the building of houses, espically after the development of economic methods of manufacturing corrugated iron (Herbert, 1978, pp.33–39).

In 1849 the Californian gold rush and the sudden increased of emigration to Australia provided markets for pre-fabricated structures and … the iron houses of E. T. Bellhouse of Manchester could be seen in profusion in San Francisco. White, 1965, p.13.

The use of timber and iron in combination was developed further to provide easily erected; prefabricated and sometimes re-locatable, buildings; such as housing, hospitals and stables for the army in the Crimea during 1849–56.

The High Orchard Saw Mills at Gloucester produced prefabricated huts by the hundred, for use in Britain and for shipping out to the Crimea.

> The efficiency of production and dispatch was impressive. A thousand men operated the factory by day and night, in shifts. As the barracks were completed they were packed into portable packages, each numbered in accordance with the code contained in the instruction sheet … In one month, from mid-December 1854 to me-January 1855, 1,500 huts for enlisted men and 350 for officers were thus completed and dispatched, via France, to the battlefront. From the initial order in mid-November, until

mid-January, a total of 3,250 units were constructed, crated, and shipped out to the British and French armies. (Herbert, 1978, p.78)

A report to the War Department in 1856 confirmed that the Gloucester huts answered the requirements that it should be easy to transport on ship, easy to erect on land that is, within the capability of the regiment's own skills and easy to repair, using improvised parts (Report of a Board of Officers, 1856).

The military continued to be interested in developing prefabricated quickly erctable and relocatable buildings and one result of investigations by a First World War Canadian engineer officer called Captain Nissen into simplifying and speeding up the construction of simple shelters led to the ubiquitous Nissen Hut. This type of corrugated iron barrel-vaulted hut could be erected: after a short introductory training session, by four men in four hours on any foundation. And big enough to provide sleeping space for 24 people widely used for temporary housing. After the second world war, these shelters were often still in use after more than ten years (Blomeyer and Tietze, p.17–18).

Bibliography

BLOMEYER, G. R., and TIETZE, B. (1984). Die andere bauarbeit: zur Praxis von Selbsthilfe und kooperativem Bauen. Stuttgart, Deutsche Verlags-Anstalt.

FREELAND, J. M. et al (1969). *Rude timber buildings in Australia.* London; Thames and Hudson

GIEDION, S. (1962). *Space, Time and Architecture Oxford*, Oxford University Press.

HERBERT, G. (1978). *Pioneers of prefabrication: the British contribution in the nineteenth century.* Johns Hopkins University Press, Baltimore.

ROBINSON, S. (1855). *New York Tribune* 18 Nov. Quoted in Woodward (1896), p 151.

R. B. White, (1965) *Prefabrication: A History of Its Development in Great Britain.* London, HMSO.

Woodward, G. E. (1896). *Woodward's Country Homes.* New York, Harding.

Thought
It must have been fairly obvious to you during this exercise that correct spelling and punctuation and consistent citing and referencing are extremely important in making a text possible to understand and, even better, clear and simple. The corrected text also demonstrates the amount of information (i.e. source, page numbers etc.) that you have to append to your notes when you are making them from the books and articles which you read. Be sure to note all the information you require to satisfy the citation and referencing requirements when writing your thesis.

CONCLUSIONS

The research proposal is the most important document you have to prepare before writing the thesis or report itself. Although it does not irrevocably commit you to a particular detailed course of action, the effort and time which you expend in its preparation, and the vigorous thought which is required to formulate your intended project, make it unlikely that you will want to drastically change the direction of your research after your proposal has been approved. In the case of funded research, it will probably be difficult to make any significant changes anyway. This is not to suggest that no alteration in your course will take place. Particularly with very long courses of study, such as the MPhil/PhD course, it is impossible at the proposal stage to predict in detail how the outcome of the MPhil work will affect the research to be carried out at PhD level. You have the opportunity when submitting the transfer document to provide a review of the findings of the MPhil stage of the research and to outline the proposed PhD research on the basis of your conclusions.

Apart from the proposal serving as an essential guide to setting up your plan of work and starting your writing, you will find that it is useful to refer back to it at regular intervals during the research work. When you are deeply involved in the minutiae of detailed practicalities, it will help to refresh your memory about the overall objectives of the research, and to see how your present task is a stage in the context of the whole project.

THE NEXT STEPS: YOUR RESEARCH PROPOSAL

The culmination of this book is the production of your research proposal. If you have understood the issues raised in the preceding chapters, and have related them to your research into the background and important current issues of your topic, you should be quite clear about the nature of your research problem and the methods you will use to undertake the research. The real challenge which faces you now is to form a tight and compact argument which justifies the importance of your project and demonstrates its practicability within your resources, while at the same time conforming with the regulations relating to the research degrees, course objectives or project description.

The aim of this section is the completion of a sound research proposal.

Checklist of activities that will progress your research

Step 1: specific course related guidance
Before you finalize your proposal, make sure that you are aware of any specific course related guidance or instructions. This will save you making changes later. For funded research, carefully read the conditions that come with the application forms and guidance given by the funding institution.

Step 2: type of research degree

You should be aware by now about the requirements of the type of degree that you are undertaking, e.g. Masters, MPhil, MPhil with transfer to PhD, or PhD direct. Remember that your proposal should respond to these requirements. If you are in any doubt, consult with your tutor or supervisor.

Step 3: get the right forms

'If you are alive, you have to fill in forms' noted my son when he went to university. There is a form for everything, including for research proposals. There are likely to be standard forms on which to submit your proposal. You will be required to include not only your proposal text, but also personal details and administrative information (such as your sponsors, supervisors, advisers etc.). Find out who must sign the forms, the submission procedure and timing.

Step 4: finalize the title of your study

Remember that the title is the shortest summary of your work, and the most used for searching in databases. Ensure that it contains the main concepts of your study and any limitations to its scope, but remains sufficiently precise to distinguish it from other works.

Step 5: your list of aims

This should not be more than four or five long, so the aims need to be focused and sufficiently varied to cover the range of objectives you are aiming at. Exercise 9.2 will have prepared you for this. Check that the research problem and expected outcomes correspond to the aims: it is best to use the same terminology to ensure this.

Step 6: your background and literature review

It is easy to write too much here, as a result of your extensive background research! Concentrate on forming a succinct argument that persuades about the need for the investigation based on the context of existing knowledge (or lack of it) and on previous research. Provide enough information for any intelligent person to understand the main factors discussed and the state of the debate: the research committee are not necessarily academics in your field. For PhD direct, make sure that you include your own published and unpublished work on the subject and any relevant experience you may have: you are expected to have completed the MPhil-type research as preparation for this project.

Step 7: your research problem

The research problem is the linchpin of the proposal, which is generated by your discussion of the background and in turn generates the outline of research methods. It is essential that its formulation is tightly constructed so as both to focus the work and to limit it in scope. There is no room for vagary.

Step 8: outline of methods

You can do this in list form if you like. If you are doing an MPhil with transfer to PhD, divide the sequence into two parts, MPhil stage and PhD stage. You will use the MPhil stage to clarify and further define the research problem and select the specific research methods for the PhD stage. For a PhD direct, you will be expected to be absolutely clear about the problem and which research methods you will employ to investigate it. Particularly important are the details about data analysis and how you intend to achieve the aims of the research.

Step 9: timetable

A timetable showing the succession of stages and the time they will take is an essential tool for any research project, however small. Use one of these to demonstrate the practicality of what you are proposing. If you are doing a funded research programme, you will also have to include 'milestones'. These are intermediate points in the project where progress is reviewed and staged payments are made.

Step 10: the rest of the proposal application form

Read carefully all the sections that you need to fill in and make sure they are complete. You may need to co-operate with the course administrator to complete details about supervisors and to get the appropriate signatures. Make sure you leave enough time for this; it might take several days to liaise with the people concerned. For funded research, quite detailed particulars of collaborators will be required and it can be a lengthy process to compile all the necessary information.

The research committees will have regular dates for their meetings, research funders will have deadlines for submissions, and Masters courses will also stipulate when the proposals have to be submitted. Make advance preparations so as to make sure that you do not have a panic at the last moment.

Step 11: ethics approval

If there are ethical issues concerning research involving human participants, make sure that you comply with the procedures of your institution and any other that might be involved. More form filling!

Consolidation and assessment

You will need to arrange a whole series of tutorials with your allotted tutor or supervisor and also other members of staff and/or colleagues as you work from one draft of the proposal to the next. Ten to twenty drafts are not unusual for an extended project, so make sure that the correction and development of each draft are quick (if possible on a daily basis) so that the issues remain fresh in your mind, and you do not get bogged down in minutiae.

When you have completed the proposal to an acceptable standard, pencil in all the information required on a copy of the application form for typing by yourself or a secretary. The actual proposal text can be printed, rather than typed, on the form from your floppy disk. In some cases it is possible to obtain an electronic copy of the form which is easy to complete using a word processor.

After having submitted your proposal, and while waiting for the result, you can take comfort in the fact that the skills you have learned whilst reading this book will be a good preparation for your research project which, because of your lucid and thorough proposal, is about to be approved!

Further reading

There are books that are solely dedicated to writing academic proposals of all kinds. The principles are the same for all of them; it is the extent and detail that vary. All are reasoned arguments to support a plan of action. If you want to read more, or find different approaches to proposal writing, you can explore some of these books; you will undoubtedly find something useful. I have put them in order of complexity, simplest first, though you may want to look at a more subject specific book first. Every book on how to do dissertations and theses will also have a section on writing a proposal; you will undoubtedly have seen some of these by now.

Writing good English is not that easy, particularly if English is not your first language. I have suggested a few books that will help you to check that you present your work as clearly and correctly as possible.

Jay, R. (2000) *How to Write Proposals and Reports that Get Results*. London: Prentice-Hall.

Vithal, R. (1997) *Designing Your First Research Proposal: a Manual for Researchers in Education*. Lansdowne: Juta.

Locke, L. F., Spirduso, W. W. and Silverman, S. J. (1993) *Proposals That Work: a Guide for Planning Dissertations and Grant Proposals*, 3rd edn. London: Sage.

Silyn-Roberts, H. (2000) *Writing for Science and Engineering. Papers, Projects and Proposals: a Practical Guide*. Oxford: Butterworth-Heinemann.

Coley, S. M. and Scheinberg C. A. (1990) *Proposal Writing*. London: Newbury Park in co-operation with the University of Michigan.

Meador, R. (1984) *Guidelines for Preparing Proposals*. Chelsea, MI: Lewis.

A bit old, but this one is good on motivation. Read this to get the full story.

Jay, R. (1995) *How to Write Proposals and Reports that Get Results*. London: Pitman.

Really aimed at managers, but we all have to manage! Good practical advice on all aspects of writing.

Here is lots of advice on writing. I have put them in order of accessibility and level of academic stage aimed at.

Hall, G. M. (ed.) (1998) *How to Write a Paper*, 2nd edn. London: BMJ Publishing.

Bowden, J. (1991) *How to Write a Report: a Step-by-Step Guide to Effective Report Writing*. Plymouth: How To Books.

Oliver, Paul (2003) *Writing Your Thesis*. London: Sage.

Murray, R. (2002) *How to Write a Thesis*. Buckingham: Open University Press.

Berry, R. (2000) *The Research Project: How to Write It*, 4th edn. London: Routledge.

Woods, P. (1999) *Successful Writing for Qualitative Researchers*. London: Routledge.

Really thorough on all aspects of writing: getting started and keeping going, organization, alternative forms of writing, style, editing etc.

Mounsey, C. (2002) *Essays and Dissertations*. Oxford: Oxford University Press.

A compact, easy-to-read guide to writing, in the 'One Step Ahead' series. Other titles in the same series might also be useful: *Editing and Revising* by Jo Billingham, *Punctuation and Spelling* by Robert Allen, and *Words and Writing Reports* by John Seely.

The following are two examples of books that specialize in writing about particular subjects. I suggest you do a search for similar books in your own subject, which is easily done using key words (such as 'writing' and 'geography', for example).

Hamilton, A. (1988) *Writing Matters*. London: RIBA Publications.

Part 1 deals with writing in general; after that it gets more into writing for architects.

Fabb, N. and Durant, A. (1993) *How to Write Essays, Dissertations and Theses in Literary Studies*. Harlow: Longman.

Especially for those who specialize in writing about writings.

And here are two books to help you sort out the finer points of writing in English:

Evans, H. (2000) *Essential English*. London: Pimlico.

Get your spelling and grammar and construction right with this.

Trask, R. L. (2001) *Mind the Gaffe: the Penguin Guide to Common Errors in English*. London: Penguin.

See whether you make common mistakes.

For citing and referencing, first consult your own library about any guidance handouts they might produce. These should be ideally suited to your needs. If you really need more information, then here are some books:

Bosworth, D. (1992) *Citing Your References: a Guide for Authors of Journal Articles and Students Writing Theses or Dissertations*. Thirsk: Underhill.

British Standards Institution (1990) *Recommendations for Citing and Referencing Published Materials*. BS 5605. London: BSI.

University of Chicago Press (1993) *The Chicago Manual of Style*, 14th edn. Chicago: University of Chicago Press.

University of Northumbria at Newcastle (2000) *Frequently Asked Questions about Reference and Citation: Harvard Method*. Retrieved 16 January 2001 from http://www.unn.ac.uk/central/isd/subj/harvard.htm

Li, X. and Crane, N. (1996) *Electronic Styles: a Handbook for Citing Electronic Information*, 2nd edn. Medford: Information Today.

And this one is for some light relief!

Fine, A. (1996) *How to Write Really Badly*. Illustrated by P. Dupasquier. London: Mammoth.

ANSWERS TO EXERCISES

EXERCISE 9.1

Have you got key words referring to the following aspects? If yes, are they really needed? If no, have you missed something important?

- specific place, e.g. specific country or city

- general place or situation, e.g. rural, urban, building/social context (school, home, factory), the natural environment, local government

- context, e.g. social, political, economic

- time, e.g. dates, past, contemporary

- measures, e.g. effectiveness, impact, performance, values, relationships between, appraisal, influences, implications

- concrete concepts, e.g. steel, interior planting, local regulations, houses, professional practices, environmental legislation, crime figures

- theoretical concepts, e.g. wealth, leisure, disability, heritage, conservation, ecology, education, access, housing, the environment.

EXERCISE 9.2

This list, together with your answers to the questions, is good material for discussion with your tutor. Why not make an appointment to see him/her? Bring along the list of key words which you have selected in Exercise 9.1 together with the title which you have composed.

EXERCISE 9.3

The result of this exercise will be the first draft of your proposal (without the description of methods, which you can write only after you know exactly what the research problem is!). Show this to your tutor, and discuss and revise it several times before you go on to the methods section. The process of regular consultation with various members of tutorial staff is essential at this stage, so that your thinking about your intended research develops rapidly and along the right lines.

EXERCISE 9.4

This is a preparation for the plan of work in your proposal that describes the methods you will use. You will need to discuss this with your tutor or supervisor. The main aspects to check are the appropriateness of the methods in relation to what you want to find out, and the practical issues involved (access to sources of information, necessary equipment, time requirements, costs, travel etc.). It is best to set out this section broadly following the sequence in which the work will be carried out. You must show that you have a good understanding of what is involved in carrying out the methods you propose and the reasons why you are going to use them. In an extended study, e.g. a PhD thesis, it is likely that part of your plan will be to find out more about appropriate methods and to refine or adapt them for application to your particular subject.

The last part of this exercise will help you to focus on the essential aspects of your project and the reasons why you are undertaking such a major task. Do not hesitate to discuss these with your colleagues and supervisors. It is also particularly useful to get the reactions of people who are not familiar with your field of study in order to test the clarity of the contents and the language.

EXERCISE 9.5

You do not really need an answer from me here, as you are by now completely competent to do this kind of analysis. The point of the exercise is to make you look afresh at your own proposal, as if it were another example of the kind shown in Boxes 9.6 and 9.7, so that you can analyse it from a purely technical and structural standpoint. Are all the ingredients of a successful proposal there, and are they presented clearly in order to build up a good argument for doing the research? Can it convince the research committee that the project is practical and can be completed within your resources of time, skills, equipment and finance?

EXERCISE 9.6

The following is the correct text, which I have marked with the places where the mistakes occurred.

USA and the British colonies: simplified building techniques

The simplification of building techniques has a long history. Efforts were continually being made through using industrialised techniques, to reduce costs and to minimise the skills required to construct permanent buildings, particularly in situations where building materials and skills were scarce (Blomeyer and Tietze, 1978, pp. 7–10).

From the latter part of the 18th century, the need for permanent, quickly built houses in the new settlements of the British colonies gave rise to a continuous development of prefabricated building systems which could be easily exported from Britain and erected in a short time by inexperienced labour. The design of these houses developed quickly from a rudimentary example of a framed canvas four-roomed structure brought to Australia from Britain in 1788 by Captain Arthur Phillip, which unfortunately proved 'not perfectly impervious to either wind or weather (Freeland et al., 1969, p. 16)' to the widely advertised, fully prefabricated and packed timber 'Manning Portable Cottage', which was exported in large numbers in the early 1840s (Herbert, 1978, pp. 14–15). The Manning Cottage was:

long quotation

designed for ease of erection. It was completely fabricated in the carpenter's shop and required little or no site work other than the building of foundations and the assembly of components. The structure required no fashioning of joints, no cutting of timber, no nailing – whoever can use a common bed-wrench can put this cottage up. The design was tailored to the limited resources of skill and tools available to the emigrant. (Herbert, 1978, pp. 10–11)

The advent of widely available machined timber sections and the mass production of nails in the middle of the 19th century led to the pioneering 'balloon frame' timber construction system in America, which enabled the rapid building of settlements using standardised timber sections and frame configurations with simple weatherboard cladding (Giedion, 1962, pp. 345–350). short quotation 'A man and a boy can now (1865) attain the same results, with ease, that twenty men could on an old-fashioned frame (Woodward, 1896, pp. 152–164).'

Giedion suggested that 60–80% of all houses in the United States used balloon frame construction (Giedion, 1962, p. 344), while a contemporary commentator observed:

> If it had not been for the knowledge of the balloon frame, Chicago and San Francisco could never have arisen, as they did, from little villages to great cities in a single year. (Robinson, 1855)

Iron was also used to simplify the building of houses, especially after the development of economic methods of manufacturing corrugated iron (Herbert, 1978, pp. 33–39).

indent quotation

> In 1849 the Californian gold rush and the sudden increase of emigration to Australia provided markets for pre-fabricated structures and … the iron houses of E. T. Bellhouse of Manchester could be seen in profusion in San Francisco. (White, 1965, p. 13)

The use of timber and iron in combination was developed further to provide easily erected, prefabricated and sometimes relocatable buildings, such as housing, hospitals and stables for the army in the Crimea during 1849–56.

The High Orchard Saw Mills at Gloucester produced prefabricated huts by the hundred, for use in Britain and for shipping out to the Crimea.

space

> The efficiency of production and dispatch was impressive. A thousand men operated the factory by day and night, in shifts. As the barracks were completed they were packed into portable packages, each numbered in accordance with the code contained in the instruction sheet … In one month, from mid-December 1854 to mid-January 1855, 1,500 huts for enlisted men and 350 for officers were thus completed and dispatched, via France, to the battlefront. From the initial order in mid-November, until mid-January, a total of 3,250 units were constructed, crated, and shipped out to the British and French armies. (Herbert, 1978, p. 78)

A report to the War Department in 1856 confirmed that the Gloucester huts answered the requirements that they should be easy to transport on ship, easy to erect on land (that is, within the capability of the regiment's own skills), and easy to repair, using improvised parts (Report of a Board of Officers, 1856).

The military continued to be interested in developing prefabricated, quickly erectable and relocatable buildings, and one result of investigations by a First World War Canadian engineer officer called Captain Nissen into simplifying and speeding up the construction of simple shelters led to the ubiquitous Nissen Hut. This type of corrugated iron barrel-vaulted hut could be erected, after a short introductory training session, by four men in four hours on any foundation, and was big enough to provide sleeping space for 24 people. Widely used for temporary housing after the Second World War, these shelters were often still in use after more than ten years (Blomeyer and Tietze, pp. 17–18).

Bibliography

BLOMEYER, G. R. and TIETZE, B. (1984). *Die andere Bauarbeit: zur Praxis von Selbsthilfe und kooperativem Bauen.* Stuttgart, Deutsche Verlags-Anstalt.

italics

FREELAND, J. M., COX, P. S. and STACEY, W. (1969). *Rude timber buildings in Australia.* London, Thames and Hudson.

GIEDION, S. (1962). *Space, time and architecture.* Oxford, Oxford University Press.

HERBERT, G. (1978). *Pioneers of prefabrication: the British contribution in the nineteenth century.* Baltimore, Johns Hopkins University Press.

ROBINSON, S. (1855). *New York Tribune* 18 Nov. Quoted in Woodward (1896), p. 151.

WHITE, R. B. (1965). *Prefabrication: a history of its development in Great Britain.* London, HMSO.

WOODWARD, G. E. (1896). *Woodward's country homes.* New York, Harding.

Key Words Glossary

Abstractness
A characteristic of research findings that make them independent from specific time and place. Such research findings are useful as they can be applied to other situations.

Accidental sampling
Also called convenience sampling. A non-random sampling technique that involves selecting what is immediately available, e.g. studying the building you happen to be in, examining the work practices of your firm.

Algorithm
A process or set of rules used for calculation or problem solving, especially using a computer. It can be expressed graphically or, more often, as a mathematical formula. An example is a formula that summarizes the interior conditions that lead to the feeling of climatic comfort, with factors such as air temperature, humidity, air movement, amount of clothing etc.

Analogy
A comparison of two different types of thing in order to detect the similarities between them. It may be possible to infer that they possess further undetected similarities.

Argument
A type of discourse that not only makes assertions but also asserts that some of these assertions are reasons for others. Argument is often based on the rules of logic in order to provide a solid structure.

Assertive discourse
A type of discourse that contains assertive statements, e.g. this man is bald.

Associational statements
Make an assertion that two concepts are associated in some way, positively or negatively, or not associated at all. The word 'correlation' is often employed to refer to the degree of association.

Authentication

Checking on historical data to verify whether they are authentic. Typical techniques used are textual analysis, carbon dating, paper analysis, cross-referencing etc.

Axiomatic theory

A theory that comprises an initial set of statements (axioms) or self-evident truths, each independent of the others, and from which it is possible to logically derive all the other statements (propositions) of the theory. A good example of one of these is Pythagorean geometry.

Bibliographic database

An electronic list of bibliographic information. Databases may be on CD-ROM, or online on the Internet. Many of these are available through university and other libraries and can be searched using key words, subjects, authors, titles etc.

Bibliography

A list of key information about publications. These can be compiled on particular subjects or in relation to a particular piece of academic work. There are standard systems for compiling bibliographies, e.g. Harvard. Libraries usually compile their own bibliographies to guide students to literature in their particular subject.

Categorization

Involves forming a typology of objects, events or concepts. This can be useful in explaining what 'things' belong together and how.

Causal process theory

An interrelated set of definitions and statements which not only define the theory, but describe when and where the causal processes are expected to occur, and explain the causal processes or mechanisms by identifying the effect of the independent variables on the dependent variables.

Causal statements

These make an assertion that one concept or variable causes another – a 'cause and effect' relationship. This can be deterministic, meaning that under certain conditions an event will inevitably follow, or if the outcome is not so certain, probabilistic, meaning that an event has a certain chance (which may be quantifiable) of following.

Citation

A reference to a source of information or quotation given in a text. This is usually in abbreviated form to enable the full details to be found in the list of references.

Class

A set of persons or things grouped together or graded or differentiated from others. Classes can be formed by collection or division. Classes can be divided into subclasses to form a hierarchy.

Cluster sampling

Selection of cases in a population that share one or some characteristics, but are otherwise as heterogeneous as possible, e.g. travellers using a railway station. Also known as area sampling when random segments are chosen from a large area of population distribution.

Coding

The application of labels or tags to allocate units of meaning to collected data. This is an important aspect of forming typologies and facilitates the organization of copious data in the form of notes, observations, transcripts, documents etc. It helps to prevent 'data overload' resulting from mountains of unprocessed data in the form of ambiguous words. Coding of qualitative data can form a part in theory building. Codes can also be allocated to responses to fixed choice questionnaires.

Coefficient of correlation

The measure of a statistical correlation between two or more variables. There are many types of these, the Pearson's *r* being the most common.

Concept

General expression of a particular phenomenon, or words that represent an object or an idea. Concepts can be concrete, e.g. dog, cat, house; or abstract, independent of time or place, e.g. anger, marginality, politics. We use concepts to communicate our experience of the world around us.

Conceptual scheme theory

Conceptual schemes that designate, or even proscribe, what constitute the characteristics of 'social facts'.

Consistency

A quality of argument concerned with the compatibility of beliefs, i.e. a set of beliefs that can be shown to be consistent with each other is said to be consistent.

Control

Having the ability to determine the influences on variables in a phenomenon, for example in an experiment. The crucial issue in control is to understand how certain variables affect one another, and then be able to change the variables in such a way as to produce predictable results. Not all phenomena can be controlled, as many are too complex or not sufficiently understood.

Critical rationalism

An approach usually associated with Popper. It maintains that rival theories can be judged against specific, unchanging, universal criteria, which are divorced from or set beyond the influences of time or society.

Critical realism

A non-empirical (i.e. realist) epistemology that maintains the importance of identifying the structures of social systems, even if they are not amenable to the senses. This will enable the structures to be changed to ameliorate social ills.

Deduction

The inferring of particular instances from a general law, i.e. 'theory then research' approach.

Descriptive statistics

A method of quantifying the characteristics of parametric numerical data, e.g. where the centre is, how broadly they are spread, the point of central tendency, the mode, median and means. These are often explained in relation to a Gaussian (bell) curve.

Directive (language)

Language used for the purposes of causing or preventing overt action.

Discourse

Communication in the form of words as speech or writing or even attitude and gesture. Discourse analysis studies the way people communicate with each other through language in a social setting, where language is not seen as a neutral medium for transmission of information, but is loaded with meanings displaying different versions of reality.

Empirical generalization

A generalization based on several empirical studies that reveal a similar pattern of events. All concepts in an empirical generalization must be directly measurable.

Empirical relevance

The measure of the correspondence between a particular theory and what is taken to be objective empirical data.

Epistemology

The theory of knowledge, especially about its validation and the methods used. Often used in connection with one's epistemological standpoint – how one sees and makes sense of the world.

Ethics

The rules of conduct. In this book, particularly about conduct with other people and organizations, aimed at causing no harm and providing, if possible, benefits.

Evaluation

Making judgements about the quality of objects or events. Quality can be measured either in an absolute sense or on a comparative basis.

Existence statements

These claim that instances of a concept exist in the real world, and provide a typology or a description.

Experience

Actual observation or practical acquaintance with facts or events that results in knowledge and understanding.

Explanation

One of the common objectives of research.

Expressive (language)

Language used to express emotions and feelings.

External reality

Acceptance of the reliability of knowledge gained by experience to provide empirical evidence.

External validity

The extent of the legitimate generalizability of the results of an experiment.

Falsification

The process by which a hypothesis is rejected as a result of true observational statements which conflict with it.

Formal fallacies

These occur due to some error in the structure of the logic used, causing the chain of reasoning to be defective.

Generality

The assumption that there can be valid relationships between the particular cases investigated by the researcher and other similar cases in the world at large.

Hypothesis

A theoretical statement which has not yet been tested against data collected in a concrete situation, but which it is possible to test by providing clear evidence for support or rejection.

Hypothetico-deductive method

Synonymous with scientific method. Progress in scientific thought by the four-step method of: identification of a problem, formulation of a hypothesis, practical or theoretical testing of the hypothesis, rejection or adjustment of the hypothesis if it is falsified.

Index journal

Catalogues of the bibliographic details of journal articles without further details apart from perhaps key words.

Induction

The inference of a general law from particular instances. Our experiences lead us to make conclusions from which we generalize.

Inferential statistics

Statistical analysis that goes beyond describing the characteristics of the data and the examination of correlations of variables in order to produce predictions through inference based on the data analysed. Inferential statistics are also used to test statistically based hypotheses.

Informal fallacies

These occur when: the ambiguities of language admit error to an argument, something is left out that is needed to sustain an argument, irrelevant factors are permitted to weigh on the conclusions, or unwarranted presumptions alter the conclusion.

Informative (language)

Language used to communicate information.

Informed consent

Consent given by participants to take part in a research project based on having sufficient information about the purposes and nature of the research and the involvement required.

Interim summary

A short report prepared about one-third of the way through data collection in qualitative research in order to review the quantity and quality of the data, confidence in their reliability, and the presence and nature of any gaps or puzzles that have been revealed, and to judge what still needs to be collected in the time available.

Internal validity

A measure of the level of sophistication of the design and extent of control in an experiment. The values of data gained should genuinely reflect the influences of the controlled variables.

Interpretation

An integral part of the analysis of data that requires verification and extrapolation in order to make out or bring out the meaning.

Interpretivism

The standpoint that recognizes the 'embedded' nature of the researcher, and the unique personal theoretical stances upon which each person bases his/her actions. It rejects the assertion that human behaviour can be codified in laws by identifying underlying regularities, and that society can be studied from a detached, objective and impartial viewpoint by the researcher. Attempts to find understanding in research are mediated by our own historical and cultural milieu.

Intersubjectivity

Agreement between people about the meaning of concepts used in statements, attained by precise definition of the concepts. Put another way: inter-observer agreement about the veracity of an operational definition. Intersubjectivity is also promoted by the use of appropriate logical systems such as mathematics, statistics and symbolic logic.

Interval level (of measurement)
The use of equal units of measurement, but without a significant zero value, e.g. the Fahrenheit or Celsius temperature scales.

Journal of abstracts
Catalogues of the bibliographic details of journal articles together with summaries of articles (indicative or informative abstracts). These often are devoted to specific subject areas.

Law
Statement that describes relationships that are so well supported by evidence, and engenders such strong confidence in their reliability, that they are considered to express the 'truth' in the cases to which they apply.

Levels of abstraction
The degree of abstraction of a statement based on three levels – theoretical, operational and concrete, the last being the least abstract.

Levels of measurement
The four different types of quantification, especially when applied to operational definitions, namely nominal, ordinal, interval and ratio.

Library catalogue
Bibliographic details of items in a library. The databases are now usually accessed by computer as online public access catalogues (OPACs).

Logical truth
Logically true statements can be divided into three varieties: trivial (obvious), true by necessity (according to rules, e.g. mathematical) and true by definition (conforming to unambiguous definition).

Matrices
Two-dimensional arrangements of rows and columns used to summarize substantial amounts of information. They can be used to record variables such as time, levels of measurement, roles, clusters, outcomes, effects etc. Latest developments allow the formulation of three-dimensional matrices.

Memo
Short analytical description based on the developing ideas of the researcher reacting to the data and development of codes and pattern codes. Compiling memos is a good way to explore links between data and to record and develop intuitions and ideas.

Model
(a) A term used to describe the overall framework that we use to look at reality, based on a philosophical stance (e.g. postmodernism, poststructuralism, positivism, empiricism etc.).

(b) A simplified physical or mathematical representation of an object or a system used as a tool for analysis. It may be able to be manipulated in order to obtain data about the effects of the manipulations.

Networks
Maps or charts used to display data, made up of blocks (nodes) connected by links. They can be produced in a wide variety of formats, each with the capability of displaying different types of data, e.g. flow charts, organization charts, causal networks, mind maps etc.

Nominal level (of measurement)
The division of data into separate categories by naming or labelling.

Null hypothesis
A statistically based hypothesis tested by using inferential statistics. A null hypothesis suggests no relationship between two variables.

Operational definition
A set of actions that an observer should perform in order to detect or measure a theoretical concept. Operational definitions should be abstract, i.e. independent of time and space.

Order
The condition that things are constituted in an organized fashion that can be revealed through observation.

Ordinal level (of measurement)
Ordering data by rank without reference to specific measurement, i.e. more or less than, bigger or smaller than.

Paradigm
The overall effect of the acceptance of a particular general theoretical approach, and the influence it has on the scientist's view of the world. According to Kuhn, normal scientific activity is carried out within the terms of the paradigm.

Parsimony
Economy of explanation of phenomena, especially in formulating theories.

Participant
Someone who takes part in a research project as a subject of study. This term implies that the person takes an active role in the research by performing actions or providing information.

Pilot study
A pre-test of a questionnaire or other type of survey on a small number of cases in order to test the procedures and quality of responses.

Plagiarism

The taking and use of other people's thoughts or writing as your own. This is sometimes done by students who copy out chunks of text from publications or the Internet and include it in their writing without any acknowledgement to its source.

Population

A collective term used to describe the total quantity of cases of the type which are the subject of the study. It can consist of objects, people and even events.

Prediction

One of the common objectives of research.

Primary sources

Sources from which the researcher can gain data by direct, detached observation or measurement of phenomena in the real world, undisturbed by any intermediary interpreter. It is a matter of philosophical debate as to what extent the detachment and undisturbed state are possible or even desirable.

Problem area

An issue within a general body of knowledge or subject from which a research project might be selected.

Proportional stratified sampling

Used when cases in a population fall into distinctly different categories (strata) of a known proportion of that population.

Proposition

A theoretical statement that indicates a clear direction and scope of a research project.

Quantification (of concepts)

Measurement techniques used in association with operational definitions.

Quota sampling

An attempt to balance the sample by selecting responses from equal numbers of different respondents. This is an unregulated form of sampling as there is no knowledge of whether the respondents are typical of their class.

Ratio level (of measurement)

A scale with equal units of measurement and containing a true zero equal to nought – the total absence of the quantity being measured.

Reasoning

A method of coming to conclusions by the use of logical argument.

Relational statements

These impart information about a relationship between two concepts. They form the bedrock of scientific knowledge and explain, predict and provide us with a sense of understanding of our surroundings.

Relativism

The stance that implies that judgement is principally dependent on the values of the individuals or society and the perspectives from which they make their judgement. No universal criteria can be 'rationally' applied, and an understanding of decisions made by individuals or organizations can only be gained through knowledge of the historical, psychological and social backgrounds of the individuals.

Reliability

In relation to human perception and intellect, the power of memory and reasoning to organize data and ideas in order to promote understanding.

Research problem

A general statement of an issue meriting research. It is usually used to help formulate a research project and is the basis on which specific research questions, hypotheses or statements are based.

Research question

A theoretical question that indicates a clear direction and scope for a research project.

Sample

The small part of a whole (population) selected to show what the whole is like. There are two main types of sampling procedure: random and non-random.

Sampling error

The differences between the random sample and the population from which it has been selected.

Scientific method

The foundation of modern scientific enquiry. It is based on observation and testing of the soundness of conclusions, commonly by using the hypothetico-deductive method. The four-step method is: identification of a problem, formulation of a hypothesis, practical or theoretical testing of the hypothesis, rejection or adjustment of the hypothesis if it is falsified.

Secondary sources

Sources of information that have been subject to interpretation by others, usually in the form of publications.

Sense of understanding

A complete explanation of a phenomenon provided by a wider study of the processes that surround, influence and cause it to happen.

Set of laws theory
A theory that comprises a set of separate, though interrelated, laws.

Simple random sampling
A method used to select cases at random from a uniform population.

Simple stratified sampling
A method that recognizes the different strata in the population in order to select a representative sample.

Statement
An assertion based on a combination of concepts.

Subject
The participant in a research project. The term implies a passive role in the project, i.e. that things are done to the subject in the form of a test or an experiment.

Sub-problem
A component of a main problem, usually expressed in less abstract terms to indicate an avenue of investigation.

Symbol
A sign used to communicate concepts in the form of natural or artificial language.

Systematic sampling
A sampling method that selects samples using a numerical method, e.g. selection of every tenth name on a list.

Term
A word used to express a definite concept. Terms can be primitive, which cannot be described by using other terms, or derived, which can.

Theoretical sampling
Selection of a sample of the population that you think knows most about the subject. This approach is common in qualitative research where statistical inference is not required.

Theory
A system of ideas based on interrelated concepts, definitions and propositions, with the purpose of explaining or predicting phenomena.

Validity
The property of an argument to correctly draw conclusions from premises according to the rules of logic.

Venn diagram
A diagram of overlapping circles used to analyse arguments.

References

Ackrill, M. (1994) 'A few notes to assist you with the presentation of your report/thesis'. Unpublished.

Alldred, P. and Gillies, V. (2002) 'Eliciting research accounts: re/producing modern subjects?', in M. Mauthner, M. Birch, J. Jessop and T. Miller (eds), *Ethics in Qualitative Research*. London: Sage. Chapter 8, pp. 148–65.

Barr Greenfield, T. (1975) 'Theory about organisations: a new perspective and its implications for schools', in M. G. Hughes (ed.), *Administering Education: International Challenge*. London: Athlone.

Beardsley, M. C. (1975) *Thinking Straight: Principles of Reasoning for Readers and Writers*. Englewood Cliffs, NJ: Prentice-Hall.

Beck, R. N. (1979) *Handbook to Social Philosophy*. New York: Macmillan.

Bell, L. and Nutt, L. (2002) 'Divided loyalties, divided expectations: research ethics, professional and occupational responsibilities', in M. Mauthner, M. Birch, J. Jessop and T. Miller (eds), *Ethics in Qualitative Research*. London: Sage. Chapter 4, pp. 70–90.

Bhaskar, R. (1989) *Reclaiming Reality: a Critical Introduction to Contemporary Philosophy*. London: Verso.

Blaxter, L., Hughes, C. and Tight, M. (1996) *How to Research*. Buckingham: Open University Press.

Booth, W. C., Colomb, G. G. and William, J. M. (1995) *The Craft of Research*. Chicago: University of Chicago Press.

Borg, W. R. (1963) *Educational Research: an Introduction*. London: Longman.

Broadbent, G. (1988) *Design in Architecture: Architecture and the Human Sciences*. London: Fulton.

Brown, J. and Sime, D. J. (1981) 'A methodology of accounts', in M. Brenner (ed.), *Social Method and Social Life*. London: Academic.

Bryman, A. (1988) *Quantity and Quality in Social Research*. Aldershot: Avebury.

Bryman, A. and Burgess, R. G. (eds) (1994) *Analysing Qualitative Data*. London: Routledge.

Burnett, A., Sheehy, J. and Digby, A. (1994) *Theory, Methodology and Techniques of Research in the Humanities: 1. Research Design*. Oxford: EMU Oxford Brookes University.

Campbell, D. T. and Stanley, J. C. (1963) 'Experimental and quasi-experimental designs for research on teaching', in N. L. Gage (ed.), *Handbook of Research on Teaching*. Chicago: Rand McNally.

Campbell, D. T. and Stanley, J. C. (1966) *Experimental and Quasi-Experimental Designs for Research*. Boston: Houghton Mifflin.

Chalmers, A. F. (1982) *What Is This Thing Called Science?*, 2nd edn. Milton Keynes: Open University Press.

Chicago University Press (1969) *Manual of Style for Authors, Editors and Copy-Writers*, 12th edn. Chicago: Chicago University Press.

Cohen, L. and Manion, L. (1994) *Research Methods in Education*. London: Routledge.

Collier, A. (1994) *Critical Realism: an Introduction to Roy Bhaskar's Philosophy*. London: Verso.

Copi, I. M. (1982) *Introduction to Logic*, 6th edn. New York: Macmillan.

Dixon, B. R. (1987) *A Handbook of Social Science Research*. New York: Oxford University Press.

Dominowski, R. L. (1980) *Research Methods*. Englewood Cliffs, NJ: Prentice-Hall.

Doucet, A. (1998) 'Interpreting mother-work: linking methodology, ontology, theory and personal biography', *Canadian Woman Studies*, 18 (2, 3): 52–8.

Doucet, A. and Mauthner, N. (2002) 'Knowing responsibly: linking ethics, research practice and epistemology', in M. Mauthner, M. Birch, J. Jessop and T. Miller (eds), *Ethics in Qualitative Research*. London: Sage. Chapter 7, pp. 123–45.

Duncombe, J. and Jessop, J. (2002) ' "Doing rapport" and the ethics of "faking friendship"', in M. Mauthner, M. Birch, J. Jessop and T. Miller (eds), *Ethics in Qualitative Research*. London: Sage. Chapter 6, pp. 107–22.

Fairbairn, G. J. and Winch, C. (1991) *Reading, Writing and Reasoning: a Guide for Students*. Buckingham: SRHE and Open University Press.

Fearnside, W. W. and Holther, W. B. (1959) *Fallacy*. Englewood Cliffs, NJ: Prentice-Hall.

Feyerabend, P. (1981) 'How to defend society against science', in I. Hacking (ed.), *Scientific Revolutions*. Oxford: Oxford University Press. pp. 157–67.

Foucault, M. (1972) *The Archaeology of Knowledge*. London: Tavistock.

Fox, D. J. (1969) *The Research Process in Education*. New York: Holt, Rinehart and Winston.

Freeman, R. and Meed, J. (1993) *How to Study Effectively*. London: Collins Educational.

Freese, J., Powell, B. and Steelman, L. C. (1999) 'Rebel without a cause or effect: birth order and social attitudes', *American Sociological Review*, 64 (April): 207–31.

Glaser, B. G. and Strauss, A. L. (1967) *The Discovery of Grounded Theory: Strategies for Qualitative Research*. Chicago: Aldine.

Godwin, D. (1994) 'Science's social standing', *The Times* 30 September, pp. 17–19.

Goetz, J. P. and LeCompte, M. D. (1984) *Ethnography and Qualitative Design in Educational Research*. London: Academic.

Gottschalk, L. (1951) *Understanding History*. New York: Knopf.

Hacking, I. (ed.) (1981) *Scientific Revolutions*. Oxford: Oxford University Press.

Hague, P. N. (1993) *Questionnaire Design*. London: Kogan Page.

Harré, R. (1972) *The Philosophies of Science*. Oxford: Oxford University Press.

Harré, R. (1977) 'The ethnogenic approach: theory and practice', in L. Berkowitz (ed.), *Advances in Experimental Social Psychology*, vol. 10. New York: Academic.

Hewson, C., Yuyle, P., Laurent, D. and Vogel, C. (2003) *Internet Research Methods: a Practical Guide for the Social and Behavioural Sciences*. London: Sage.

Hill, J. E. and Kerber, A. (1967) *Models, Methods and Analytical Procedures in Educational Research*. Detroit: Wayne State University Press.

Hodges, W. (1977) *Logic*. Harmondsworth: Penguin.

Hughes, J. A. (1990) *The Philosophy of Social Research*, 2nd edn. Harlow: Longman.

Hughes, J. A. and Sharrock, W. W. (1997) *The Philosophy of Social Research*, 3rd edn. Harlow: Longman.

Hyland, K. (1999) 'Academic attribution: citation and the construction of disciplinary knowledge', *Applied Linguistics* 20: 341–67.

Jenkins, R. (1983) *Lads, Citizens and Ordinary Kids: Working Class Youth Styles in Belfast*. London: Routledge and Kegan Paul.

Kerlinger, F. N. (1970) *Foundations of Behavioral Research*. New York: Holt, Rinehart and Winston.

Kidder, L. A. and Judd, C. M. (1986) *Research Methods in Social Relations*, 5th edn. New York: Holt, Rinehart and Winston.

Krantz, H. and Kimmelman, J. (1992) *Keys to Reading and Study Skills*, 4th edn. Fort Worth, TX: Harcourt Brace Jovanovich, College.

Kuhn, T. S. (1970) *The Structure of Scientific Revolutions*, 2nd edn. Chicago: University of Chicago Press.

Lakatos, I. (1970) 'Methodology of scientific research programmes', in I. Lakatos and A. Musgrave (eds), *Criticism and the Growth of Knowledge*. Cambridge: Cambridge University Press. pp. 91–196.

Leedy, P. D. (1989) *Practical Research: Planning and Design*, 4th edn. London: Collier Macmillan.

Llobera, J. (1998) 'Historical and comparative research', in C. Seale (ed.), *Researching Society and Culture*. London: Sage.

Locke, L. C., Spirduso, W. W. and Silverman, S. J. (1993) *Proposals That Work: a Guide for Planning Dissertations and Grant Proposals*. Newbury, CA: Sage.

Lofland, J. (1971) *Analysing Social Settings: a Guide to Qualitative Observation and Analysis*. Belmont, CA: Wadsworth.

Margolin, J. B. (1983) *The Individual's Guide to Grants*. London: Plenum.

Markov, A. A. (1954) *Theory of Algorithms* (trans. J. J. Schorr-Kon 1962). Jerusalem: Israel Programme for Scientific Translation.

Mauthner, M., Birch, M., Jessop, J. and Miller, T. (eds) (2002) *Ethics in Qualitative Research*. London: Sage.

Medawar, P. B. (1969) *Induction and Intuition in Scientific Thought*. London: Methuen.

Medawar, P. B. (1984) *The Limits of Science*. Oxford: Oxford University Press.

Mikellides, B. (1990) 'Colour and psychological arousal', *The Journal of Architectural Planning and Research*, 7 (1): 13–18.

Miles, M. B. and Huberman, A. M. (1994) *Qualitative Data Analysis: an Expanded Sourcebook*. London: Sage.

Milgram, S. (1963) 'Behavioral study of obedience', *Journal of Abnormal and Social Psychology*, 67: 371–8.

Mill, J. S. (1973) *A System of Logic, Ratiocinative and Inductive: Books I–III and Appendices*. London: Routledge and Kegan Paul.

Miller, T. and Bell, L. (2002) 'Consenting to what? Issues of access, gatekeeping and "informed" consent', in M. Mauthner, M. Birch, J. Jessop and T. Miller (eds), *Ethics in Qualitative Research*. London: Sage. Chapter 3, pp. 53–69.

Morton-Williams, J. (1993) *Interviewer Approaches*. Aldershot: Dartmouth.

Moser, C. A. and Kalton, G. (1971) *Survey Methods in Social Investigation*. Aldershot: Dartmouth.

Mouly, G. J. (1978) *Educational Research: the Art and Science of Investigation*. Boston: Allyn and Bacon.

Neale, J. M. and Liebert, R. M. (1986) *Science and Behaviour: an Introduction to Methods of Research*, 3rd edn. New York: Prentice-Hall.

Newman, R. J. (1989) *Study and Research: a Systematic Approach for All Students*. Oxford: Bookmarque.

Ó Dochartaigh, N. (2001) *The Internet Research Handbook: a Practical Guide for Students and Researchers in the Social Sciences*. London: Sage.

Oliver, P. (2003) *The Student's Guide to Research Ethics*. Maidenhead: Open University Press.

Open University (1993) *An Equal Opportunities Guide to Language and Image*. Milton Keynes: Open University.

Oppenheim, A. N. (1992) *Questionnaire Design, Interviewing and Attitude Measurement*. London: Pinter.

Oxford Brookes University (2003) *Ethical Standards for Research Involving Human Participants: Code of Practice*. http://www.brookes.ac.uk/research/ethics/ethicscode/html

Parsons, C. J. (1973) *Theses and Project Work*. London: Unwin.

Phillips, E. M. and Pugh, D. S. (1994) *How to Get a PhD*. Buckingham: Open University Press.

Pinter, H. (1998) *Various Voices: Prose, Poetry, Politics 1948–1998*. London: Faber and Faber.

Pirie, M. (1985) *The Book of the Fallacy: a Training Manual of Intellectual Subversives*. London: Routledge and Kegan Paul.

Preece, R. (1994) *Starting Research: an Introduction to Academic Research and Dissertation Writing*. London: Pinter.

Quine, W. V. O. (1969) *Ontological Relativity and Other Essays*. New York: Columbia University Press.

Reynolds, P. D. (1971) *A Primer in Theory Construction*. Indianapolis: Bobbs-Merrill.

Reynolds, P. D. (1977) *A Primer in Theory Construction*. Indianapolis: Bobbs-Merrill.

Richards, L. and Richards, T. (1994) 'From filing cabinet to computer', in A. Bryman and R. G. Burgess (eds), *Analysing Qualitative Data*. London: Routledge. pp. 146–72.

Robson, C. (1993) *Real World Research: a Resource for Social Scientists and Practitioner-Researchers*. Oxford: Blackwell.

Salmon, W. C. (1984) *Logic*, 3rd edn. Englewood Cliffs, NJ: Prentice-Hall.

Seidel, J. V. and Clark, J. A. (1984) 'The Ethnograph: a computer program for the analysis of qualitative data', *Qualitative Sociology*, 7: 110–25.

Siegel, S. and Castellan, N. J. (1988) *Nonparametric Statistics for the Behavioral Sciences*. New York: McGraw-Hill.

Silverman, D. (1998) 'Research and social theory', in C. Seale (ed.), *Researching Society and Culture*. London: Sage.

Slater, D. (1995) 'Analysing cultural objects: content analysis and semiotics', in C. Seale (ed.), *Researching Society and Culture*. London: Sage.

Smith, M. and Smith, G. (1994) *A Study Skills Handbook*, 4th edn. Oxford: Oxford University Press.

Stephens, S. S. (1946) 'On the theory of scales of measurement', *Science*, 677–80.

Strauss, A. L. (1987) *Qualitative Analysis for Social Scientists*. Cambridge: Cambridge University Press.

Strauss, A. L. and Corbin, J. (1990) *Basics of Qualitative Research: Grounded Theory Procedures and Techniques*. Newbury Park, CA: Sage.

Swales, J. and Feak, C. (2000) *English in Today's Research World: a Writing Guide*. Michigan: University of Michigan Press.

Townend, D. (2000) 'Can the law prescribe an ethical framework for social science research?', in D. Burton (ed.), *Research Training for Social Scientists*. London: Sage.

Turner, B. A. (1981) 'Some practical aspects of qualitative data analysis: one way of organising the cognitive processes associated with the generation of grounded theory', *Quantity and Quality*, 15: 225–47.

Turner, B. A. (1994) 'Patterns of crisis behaviour: a qualitative enquiry', in A. Bryman and R. Burgess (eds), Analysing Qualitative Data. London: Routledge. pp. 192–215.

Uzzell, D. (1995) 'Ethnographic and action research', in M. G. Breakwell, S. Hammond and C. Fife-Shaw (eds), *Research Methods in Psychology*. London: Sage.

van Dalen, D. B. (1979) *Understanding Educational Research: an Introduction*, 4th edn. New York: McGraw-Hill.

van Dijk, T. A. (1994) 'Discourse and cognition in society', in C. Crowly and D. Michell (eds), *Communication Theory Today*. Cambridge: Polity. pp. 107–26.

Walliman, N. (1993) 'A study of recent initiatives in group selfbuild housing in Britain'. PhD thesis, Oxford Brookes University.

Weber, M. (1949) *The Methodology of the Social Sciences* (trans. and ed. E. A. Shils and H. A. Finch). Glencoe, IL: Free.

Whyte, W. F. (1955) *Street Corner Society*, 2nd edn. Chicago: University of Chicago Press.

Wiersma, W. (1986) *Research Methods in Education: an Introduction*, 4th edn. Boston: Allyn and Bacon.

Williams, M. and May, T. (1996) *Introduction to the Philosophy of Social Research*. London: UCL Press.

Yin, R. K. (1994) *Case Study Research: Design and Methods*. London: Sage.

Zohar, D. and Marshall, I. (1993) *The Quantum Society*. London: Bloomsbury.

Index

A

abstract, 8, 11, 13, 46, 52,
    61, 65, 70, 96–100, 103,
    108, 109, 140, 150, 152,
    162, 213, 214, 223, 229,
    235, 260, 286, 308, 318,
    376, 377, 380, 431, 434,
    435, 437
  concept, 46, 70, 97, 98,
      103, 286, 318
abstractness, 236
accounts, 14, 32, 122, 126,
    252, 286, 287, 290, 309,
    320, 331, 339, 352
action research, 254, 255,
    256, 393, 395, 399
aims of research, 95, 249
algorithm, 297, 298
analogy, 173, 174, 177, 185
analysis
  archival, 271
  content, 123, 318
  discourse, 97, 123
  qualitative, 93, 246, 273,
      302, 308, 310, 320,
      325, 332, 333
  quantitative, 142, 205, 310,
      320, 325, 332
  statistical, 72, 89, 118, 285,
      305, 332
  systems, 120, 144
analytical
  reading, 16, 147
  review, 83
  survey, 116
archival analysis, 271

argument, 10, 13, 14, 18, 21,
    24, 35, 39, 42, 43, 44,
    46, 61, 69, 75–88, 124,
    127, 147, 148, 152–179,
    183, 191, 201, 203, 208,
    216, 222, 223, 226, 227,
    230, 260, 262, 324, 332,
    341, 350, 367, 376, 377,
    380, 382, 386, 401, 403,
    405, 406, 419, 420, 426,
    431, 433, 436, 438
Aristotle, 10, 168, 191
assertive discourse, 152, 153
assessment, 75, 82, 95, 99,
    100, 114, 123, 128, 133,
    142, 144, 183, 207, 219,
    229, 244, 258, 288, 346,
    361, 363, 396, 398, 409
association, 105, 116, 117,
    140, 150, 151, 429, 436
associational statement, 150,
    151, 179
axiomatic theory, 109, 111

B

background
  cultural, 122
  information, 35, 38,
      40, 51
  investigation, 40, 380
  literature, 37
  reading, 30, 93, 136, 137,
      176, 211, 323,
      380, 400
  social, 18, 197, 243,
      390, 436

theoretical, 80, 82, 107,
    112, 235
  to research, 188, 263
Baskhar, 208, 209
bibliographic
  aids, 51, 53
  database, 52, 55, 84,
      87, 88
  format, 75
bibliography, 56, 66, 74, 75,
    85, 374, 414, 415
Blake, 17

C

card index, 309
catalogue, 51, 52, 86, 87,
    112, 274, 325, 434
category, 71, 90, 137, 148,
    149, 170, 172, 173, 234,
    311, 330, 368, 369
causal
  process, 109, 110, 430
  process theory, 109
  statement, 151
cause, 12, 17, 63, 115, 117,
    118, 119, 141, 151, 158,
    209, 211, 216, 230,
    235, 236, 287, 294,
    295, 296, 307, 318,
    343, 350, 352, 354,
    355, 363, 430, 437
  and effect, 17, 117, 118,
      119, 151, 318, 430
chaos, 135, 144
citation, 81, 84, 336, 360,
    361, 399, 416, 418

class, 15, 73, 90, 114, 127, 129, 134, 153, 164, 166, 171, 172, 173, 183, 184, 214, 276, 343, 368, 390, 436
classification, 95, 107, 150, 172, 173, 184, 311, 312
cluster sampling, 277
coding, 123, 255, 311, 312, 313, 314, 327, 352, 357
coefficient of correlation, 29, 305
coercion, 20, 345
common mistakes, 7, 28, 424
comparative, 16, 42, 47, 102, 112, 115, 131, 143, 210, 235, 248, 257, 374, 399, 432
  entity, 102
  measurement, 102
comparison, 15, 29, 45, 115, 123, 127, 159, 173, 188, 200, 205, 212, 220, 228, 247, 266, 293, 308, 332, 396, 397, 429
  of differences, 115
  of sets of data, 29
computer
  course, 384
  program, 25, 75, 257, 312, 315, 386, 414
  technique, 291
  terminal, 51
concept
  abstract, 46, 70, 97, 98, 103, 286, 318
  concrete, 97, 425
  measurement, 98
  of research, 7
  quantification of, 101, 151, 302
  theoretical, 98, 99, 100, 101, 103, 125, 142, 143, 144, 152, 376, 425, 435
conceptual, 32, 106, 110, 139, 213, 214, 247, 254, 255, 256, 314, 376, 389
  model, 106
conclusions, 9, 10, 11, 13, 16, 19, 24, 25, 28, 42, 43, 52, 60–64, 70, 75, 76, 77, 91, 113, 116, 119, 121, 132, 155, 156, 157, 159, 163, 164, 169, 171, 176, 177, 188–193, 215, 216, 222, 223, 230, 231, 239, 244, 251, 259, 266, 280, 290, 307, 310, 353, 361, 362, 376, 381, 387, 403, 409, 419, 433, 436, 437, 438

conclusion indicators, 76, 153, 155, 176
consent, 335, 342, 344, 346, 347, 356, 357, 358, 359, 365, 398, 433
consistency, 21, 72, 89, 161, 397
construction, 29, 110, 134, 164, 183, 184, 248, 252, 266, 297, 298, 340, 408, 411, 417, 418, 424, 426, 427
content analysis, 123, 318
control, 17, 22, 105, 115, 117, 118, 119, 122, 124, 126, 127, 163, 205, 234, 235, 236, 260, 271, 272, 282, 289, 291, 292, 293, 294, 298, 301, 302, 331, 431, 433
  data, 312
  of variables, 119
  quality, 257, 306
  samples, 119
correlation, 42, 45, 103, 105, 112, 116, 117, 119, 151, 155, 179, 254, 294, 305, 307, 324, 429, 431
  coefficient of, 29, 305
  degree of, 29, 131, 132
costs, 15, 42, 54, 73, 81, 121, 158, 170, 256, 257, 258, 289, 385, 387, 416, 425, 426
covert methods, 350, 364
critical
  path diagram, 297
  realism, 208, 209
cultural
  background, 122
  context, 120
  exchange, 123
  meaning, 123
reality, 202, 207
research, 142
texts, 123

D
data
  analysis, 33, 34, 41, 128, 246, 269, 320, 321, 323, 328, 340, 352, 362, 366, 377, 381, 421

collection, 25, 33, 42, 136, 246, 251, 259, 266, 269, 270, 273, 275, 281, 282, 287, 308, 311, 312, 313, 314, 321, 322, 323, 324, 325, 327, 331, 362, 377, 378, 381, 391, 433
  display, 310, 314, 315
  interpretation of, 28, 122
  measurement, 104
  primary, 241, 242, 243, 273, 288, 322, 352, 391
  secondary, 49, 241, 242, 261, 273, 288, 322, 391
  sets of, 29, 45, 119, 302, 303
database, 50, 52, 54, 57, 66, 67, 68, 69, 74, 75, 84, 85, 86, 256, 257, 258, 309, 337, 405, 430
deduction, 10, 11, 160, 190, 193, 210, 216, 222
deductive
  argument, 159, 160, 163, 164, 171, 230
  reasoning, 11, 191, 222, 251
definition
  dictionary, 96, 97
  of research, 239
  of research problem, 239
  operational, 98, 99, 100, 101, 105, 125, 136, 138, 143, 144, 434, 436
dependent variable, 109, 117, 151, 289, 295, 315, 318, 374, 430
derived term, 95, 96
diagram, 25, 38, 135, 164, 165, 166, 172, 238, 239, 296, 297, 318, 322, 438
  Venn, 164, 165, 166, 167, 168, 171, 176, 178, 183, 438
diaries, 244, 273, 274, 281, 283, 286, 320
Dilthey, 17
discourse, 97, 123, 124, 126, 127, 148, 149, 152, 153, 154, 162, 175, 178, 429
  analysis, 97, 123
  assertive, 152, 153
  scientific, 174
display, 38, 297, 304, 310, 315, 317, 318, 319, 320, 390, 408, 435
  time ordered, 316

dissemination, 255, 257, 258, 352, 353, 362, 374, 386
drafting, 405, 406, 407, 410, 412

E
editing, 72, 89, 402, 423
email, 289
empirical, 9, 11, 12, 106, 107, 109, 111, 112, 162, 203, 211, 212, 236, 237, 243, 260, 271, 332, 391, 394, 431, 432
relevance, 236
research, 111
empiricism, 94, 435
epistemology, 187, 339, 340, 366, 431
estimate, 70, 89, 156, 216, 245, 306
ethical standards, 340, 341, 347, 359, 361
ethics, 325, 335, 340, 342, 350, 351, 354, 355, 358, 359, 360, 361, 364, 365, 366, 381, 384
ethics committee, 335, 354, 358
ethnogenic, 112, 122, 286
evaluation, 77, 82, 112, 113, 119, 120, 121, 125, 142, 143, 145, 197, 234, 235, 257, 258, 259, 378, 379, 393, 394, 395
evidence
empirical, 12, 109, 112, 260, 271, 432
historical, 275
existence statement, 149, 150
experience, 9, 10, 11, 12, 15, 17, 25, 31, 71, 94, 100, 107, 114, 115, 126, 128, 162, 183, 191, 193, 203, 229, 242, 250, 251, 254, 273, 286, 347, 369, 380, 383, 384, 385, 386, 390, 393, 413, 420, 431, 432
experiment, 19, 41, 115, 117, 118, 190, 193, 203, 291, 292, 293, 294, 295, 300, 301, 329, 331, 332, 350, 367, 369, 377, 431, 432, 433, 437
experimental research, 118, 121, 122
explanation, 19, 20, 21, 24, 56, 89, 105, 120, 131, 132, 135, 143, 163, 234, 235, 271, 287, 292, 308, 313, 315, 325, 329, 372, 377, 379, 399, 416, 435, 437

F
external
reality, 12, 18, 38, 41
validity, 294, 295

fallacy, 169, 170, 171, 172, 176, 178, 183, 184
formal, 169
informal, 169
falsification, 194, 195, 196, 338
feminist, 77, 112, 122, 123, 209, 366
research, 123, 366
theory, 209
figures, 73, 80, 90, 91, 131, 243, 391, 413, 425
population, 188
flow chart, 435
footnotes, 410
formal fallacies, 169
Foucault, 17, 124

G
generality, 13, 18, 38, 304
Goethe, 17
grounded theory, 308

H
historical
records, 53
research, 53, 113, 114
honesty, 335, 336, 337, 338, 339, 350, 360, 361, 381
hypothesis, 11, 93, 107, 110, 111, 112, 118, 131, 132, 143, 189, 193, 194, 211, 212, 213, 214, 215, 216, 217, 218, 222, 223, 227, 228, 230, 231, 267, 296, 306, 307, 308, 321, 324, 367, 379, 380, 432, 433, 435, 437
formulation of, 217
null, 212
hypothetical construct, 98
hypothetico-deductive method, 190, 195, 196, 210, 217, 221, 337, 437

I
idealism, 17
ideas, 10, 12, 13, 17, 18, 32, 34, 37, 39, 43, 44, 56, 59, 60, 64, 66, 69, 75, 76, 78, 82, 85,

94, 110, 122, 131, 136, 147, 158, 176, 201, 209, 210, 254, 261, 273, 296, 307, 309, 311, 312, 313, 317, 327, 336, 361, 403, 404, 405, 406, 408, 434, 436, 438
illustrations, 63, 409, 412
independent variable, 109, 117, 122, 151, 289, 292, 295, 374, 430
index, 51, 52, 54, 57, 58, 61, 66, 71, 312, 325, 354, 414
card, 309
indicator, 56, 99, 155, 179, 180, 215
induction, 160, 163, 190, 191, 192, 193, 210, 216, 226, 227
inductive
argument, 159, 160, 162, 163, 173, 174, 177, 191
reasoning, 11, 191, 196
inferential statistics, 304, 305, 320, 435
informal fallacy, 169
informed consent, 346, 354, 355, 356, 362, 366, 392
instrumentation, 34, 111, 241, 244, 288
intellectual
ownership, 353
property, 352, 360, 386
interim summary, 312, 313
internal validity, 294
Internet, 50, 52, 55, 57, 58, 87, 88, 257, 274, 288, 289, 290, 325, 326, 329, 330, 430, 435
interpretation, 8, 16, 18, 28, 72, 89, 93, 100, 114, 118, 120, 122, 123, 132, 135, 196, 203, 220, 241, 243, 251, 274, 275, 283, 286, 305, 314, 327, 349, 352, 364, 437
of data, 28, 122
interpretivism, 17, 204, 208, 210, 229
intersubjectivity, 100, 188, 236, 237
interval level of measurement, 103
interviews, 36, 47, 62, 69, 116, 127, 128, 130, 133, 188, 210, 252, 253, 255, 256, 275, 284, 285, 286, 289, 290,

309, 311, 312, 320, 325,
331, 336, 346, 347, 349,
355, 360, 378, 391, 392,
396, 397, 398
introduction, 34, 36, 75, 80, 133,
139, 155, 187, 225, 233,
252, 263, 270, 286, 290, 321,
326, 346, 375, 392, 403, 404,
406, 409

J

journal, 19, 50, 51, 52, 53, 55, 67,
74, 86, 353, 414, 415, 433, 434
electronic, 55

K

Kant, 17
Kierkegaard, 17
knowledge
    contribution to, 22, 23, 38, 373,
        379, 381, 383
    nature of, 7, 187, 196, 210, 222,
        224, 247
    scientific, 11, 19, 20, 43, 44, 108,
        150, 197, 202, 224, 234,
        236, 340, 436
Kuhn knowledge, 17, 111, 178,
    197, 198, 199, 201, 210, 226,
    228, 435

L

language, 8, 9, 52, 76, 95, 96,
    97, 122, 123, 124, 147, 148,
    149, 152, 162, 168, 169, 205,
    209, 241, 283, 289, 303, 342,
    347, 391, 422, 425, 431, 432,
    433, 437
law, 93, 107, 109, 111, 112, 365,
    366, 431, 433
    set of laws theory, 109
level
    of abstraction, 98, 150, 177
    of measurement, 104, 434, 436
library, 31, 41, 50, 51, 52, 53, 55,
    58, 64, 68, 75, 83, 84, 85,
    86, 256, 274, 325, 327, 328,
    424, 434
    catalogue, 41, 51, 52, 64, 83, 86,
        325, 328
literature review, 23, 31, 34, 49, 50,
    75, 78, 80, 81, 82, 83, 85, 86,
    147, 176, 222, 391, 420

logic, 57, 58, 76, 119, 148, 153,
    156, 159, 160, 161, 163,
    169, 171, 178, 191, 193,
    199, 207, 215, 226, 251,
    271, 332, 377, 429,
    432, 438
    of discovery, 199
logical
    indicator, 153, 154, 155,
        157, 179
    rigour, 236
    truth, 162, 163

M

map, 38, 39, 77, 78, 261, 296,
    297, 318
    mental, 310
mathematical
    model, 205, 297, 298
    proof, 16
    proposition, 163
    sign, 95
mathematics, 20, 44, 95, 237, 434
matrix, 272, 310, 315, 316, 317,
    318, 319, 321, 333, 434
measurement, 41, 47, 70, 71, 91,
    98, 99, 100, 101, 103, 104,
    105, 107, 117, 125, 135, 138,
    141, 143, 144, 152, 214, 220,
    235, 242, 245, 264, 280, 287,
    290, 299, 305, 307, 322, 399,
    434, 435, 436
    concept, 98
    levels of, 101, 104, 302, 315, 434
memo, 313
methodology, 9, 12, 36, 41, 64, 82,
    93, 123, 137, 145, 198, 231,
    251, 254, 255, 256, 270, 288,
    307, 320, 378, 382, 383
mistakes, 28, 75, 113, 151, 168,
    362, 406, 412, 416, 426
model, 44, 74, 94, 121, 122, 126,
    127, 134, 144, 145, 198, 207,
    209, 254, 276, 291, 296, 297,
    298, 299, 300, 301, 318, 392,
    393, 394, 395
    causal, 318
    evaluation, 120
    mathematical, 205, 297, 298
    physical, 298, 300
    social, 125, 126, 127
    theoretical, 308

N

network, 44, 55, 67, 88, 261, 262,
    315, 317, 318, 333, 364
    causal, 310, 435
    computer, 219, 220, 274
nominal level of measurement,
    101, 102, 105
non-parametric statistics, 304, 320
non-random sampling, 278,
    330, 429
notes
    field, 255, 309, 311, 313,
        314, 319
    taking, 62, 64, 65, 87
null hypothesis, 212, 213, 306, 435
numbering, 51, 238, 378, 405

O

objectives of research, 233, 234,
    236, 432, 436
objectivity, 17, 114, 123, 339
observation, 11, 12, 36, 47, 107,
    110, 114, 115, 116, 121, 122,
    127, 128, 189, 190, 191, 192,
    193, 194, 195, 196, 197, 203,
    204, 222, 227, 229, 237, 241,
    242, 246, 255, 274, 281, 283,
    287, 288, 289, 352, 355, 356,
    391, 432, 435, 436, 437
operational definition, 98, 99, 100,
    101, 105, 125, 136, 138, 143,
    144, 434, 436
order
    alphabetical, 414
    rank, 102, 103, 307
ordered displays, 315, 318, 319
ordinal level of measurement,
    103, 105
outcomes, 16, 24, 25, 41, 117, 120,
    125, 132, 143, 144, 177, 189,
    212, 214, 229, 236, 242, 245,
    248, 249, 254, 261, 293, 294,
    315, 339, 341, 347, 350, 353,
    362, 363, 372, 374, 377, 379,
    380, 381, 386, 393, 394, 395,
    420, 434
outline, 78, 80, 314, 374, 378,
    381, 384, 398, 399, 402,
    403, 405, 406, 408,
    419, 420
    of methods, 374, 378
outputs, 385, 386, 392

P

paradigm, 111, 112, 198, 199, 202, 217, 228, 393, 399, 435
paragraphs, 19, 89, 110, 404, 408
parameters, 36, 47, 54, 57, 120, 143, 202, 305, 306
parametric statistics, 304, 307, 332
parsimony, 13, 18, 38, 107
participant, 127, 128, 129, 246, 255, 287, 290, 309, 342, 343, 345, 346, 347, 348, 350, 355, 356, 357, 358, 359, 363, 364, 369, 391, 437
personnel, 52, 357, 385, 387, 391
perspective, 55, 100, 128, 132, 144, 198, 203, 206, 222, 272, 340, 373
philosophy, 77, 78, 125, 139, 187, 188, 209, 217, 224, 225
   of research, 139, 187
physical model, 298, 300
physical survey, 287
pilot study, 72, 283, 396
plagiarism, 54, 336, 361
planning, 28, 30, 32, 37, 38, 63, 81, 233, 240, 250, 251, 259, 261, 262, 263, 269, 296, 403, 404
population, 71, 72, 73, 89, 90, 91, 98, 116, 129, 158, 188, 275, 276, 277, 279, 280, 281, 284, 285, 289, 290, 295, 302, 304, 305, 306, 323, 330, 331, 355, 378, 388, 430, 436, 437, 438
positivism, 16, 17, 94, 187, 188, 202, 205, 208, 435
post structuralism, 435
prediction, 105, 117, 118, 134, 135, 212, 234, 235, 260, 306, 347, 350, 374
   prediction studies, 117
pre-experiment, 119, 292
preliminary analysis, 40, 253, 319
premise, 10, 153, 154, 155, 156, 157, 163, 169, 176, 179
   indicators, 154
presentation, 124, 155, 158, 169, 223, 283, 290, 302, 315, 316, 362, 412, 414

primary
   data, 241, 242, 243, 273, 288, 322, 352, 391
   sources, 132, 242, 243, 273
primitive term, 95, 96, 97
probability, 12, 151, 192, 212, 306, 310
problem
   area, 28, 30, 31, 32, 37, 38, 39, 40, 177, 221, 234, 239, 243, 383
   definition, 32, 380, 382
   of induction, 191, 192
   of scaling, 298
   of writing, 371
   solving, 198, 250, 261, 297, 429
   sub-, 13, 33, 34, 35, 39, 46, 223, 229, 376, 379, 402
programme of work, 13, 25
proposal, 35, 47, 75, 80, 125, 128, 131, 132, 134, 137, 142, 143, 144, 222, 257, 258, 323, 346, 358, 359, 371, 372, 374, 375, 376, 377, 379, 380, 382, 383, 385, 386, 387, 392, 399, 400, 419, 420, 421, 422, 425, 426
proposition, 29, 112, 159, 218, 222, 223
   hypothetical, 9
   mathematical, 163
punctuation, 67, 349, 361, 410, 411, 412, 413, 414, 416, 418
purposive sampling, 279

Q

qualitative
   analysis, 93, 246, 273, 302, 308, 310, 320, 325, 332, 333
   data, 246, 261, 266, 284, 286, 287, 302, 309, 310, 312, 315, 322, 328, 380, 431
   research, 21, 116, 139, 233, 246, 247, 270, 271, 279, 309, 312, 313, 321, 322, 328, 340, 352, 377, 433, 438
quantification, 101, 103, 104, 105, 136, 151, 184, 302, 434, 435
quantitative
   analysis, 142, 205, 310, 320, 325, 332

data, 269, 271, 273, 284, 298, 302, 310
model, 296, 298, 299
research, 21, 116, 117, 246, 247, 313, 321, 322
quasi-experiment, 119, 205, 273, 292
question, 9, 12, 13, 14, 16, 18, 24, 25, 27, 28, 29, 31, 32, 33, 35, 37, 41, 44, 50, 60, 61, 66, 69, 70, 72, 76, 89, 99, 103, 107, 129, 132, 137, 149, 174, 179, 189, 192, 199, 200, 217, 218, 222, 223, 224, 227, 228, 229, 234, 244, 266, 274, 275, 276, 283, 284, 298, 305, 322, 323, 346, 349, 353, 364, 367, 368, 369, 378, 380, 393, 400, 402, 411, 414, 436
   research, 24, 34, 100, 110, 112, 217, 271, 272, 305, 313, 314, 318, 322, 380, 388, 389, 390, 393, 400, 437
questionnaire, 69, 71, 72, 73, 89, 99, 129, 137, 253, 257, 258, 275, 281, 282, 283, 284, 285, 288, 290, 320, 331, 344, 345, 346, 352, 396, 435
Quine, 18, 107
quota sampling, 279
quotation, 81, 410, 411, 415, 430
   mark, 410, 411, 415

R

random
   number generation, 298
   sampling, 276, 281, 324, 330, 437
rank, 102, 103, 172, 307, 435
ratio, 101, 104, 143, 144, 151, 302, 322, 389, 434
ratio level of measurement, 101, 104, 151, 322
reading
   analytical, 16, 147
   background, 30, 93, 136, 137, 176, 211, 323, 380, 400
   instrumental, 242

reality
  cultural, 202, 207
  external, 12, 18, 38, 41
  social, 188, 205, 229
reasoning, 9, 10, 11, 12, 153, 156,
  168, 169, 174, 198, 222, 247,
  260, 432, 436
  deductive, 11, 191, 222, 251
  inductive, 11, 191, 196
reconciliatory approach, 203
redrafting, 39, 69, 402, 406,
  407, 408
references, 14, 19, 51, 52, 53, 58,
  63, 68, 74, 75, 78, 81, 83, 84,
  85, 86, 114, 125, 178, 251,
  254, 280, 286, 336, 337, 376,
  377, 382, 383, 393, 400, 404,
  413, 415, 430
relational statement, 150
relational studies, 117
relativism, 19, 197
reliability, 12, 18, 19, 38, 99, 100,
  111, 119, 123, 128, 134, 192,
  227, 241, 242, 243, 244, 245,
  248, 276, 287, 289, 292, 313,
  352, 396, 397, 432, 433, 434
research
  approach, 7, 21, 24, 33, 35, 37,
    93, 117, 136, 137, 138, 189,
    217, 220, 221, 223, 224,
    246, 250, 259, 262, 340,
    377, 380, 382, 387
  definition, 219
  design, 33, 34, 224, 389, 391
  methods, 23, 37, 137, 189, 215,
    222, 238, 239, 262, 269,
    270, 272, 292, 321, 324,
    329, 335, 347, 358, 360,
    367, 373, 379, 381, 383,
    384, 420, 421
  objectives, 127, 219, 246,
    250, 261
  problem, 7, 13, 22, 23, 25, 27–42,
    45, 46, 49, 50, 58, 63, 64, 75,
    78, 80, 82, 86, 93, 110, 136,
    137, 155, 176, 189, 202,
    203, 211, 214, 217–224,
    229, 234, 246, 248, 251,
    262, 270, 275, 287, 301,
    321, 324, 374, 375, 376,
    377, 379, 380, 381, 382,
    402, 419, 420, 421, 425

process, 8, 9, 23, 24, 25, 49, 50,
  118, 233, 236, 238, 242,
  255, 256, 261, 308, 315,
  325, 342, 343, 344, 346,
  360, 373, 374
proposal, 34, 35, 36, 80, 83, 85,
  125, 137, 239, 244, 245,
  269, 340, 358, 359, 371,
  372, 374, 376, 379, 383,
  385, 387, 407, 418, 419, 420
qualitative, 21, 116, 139, 233,
  246, 247, 270, 271, 279,
  309, 312, 313, 321, 322,
  328, 340, 352, 377,
  433, 438
quantitative, 21, 116, 117, 246,
  247, 313, 321, 322
question, 24, 34, 100, 110, 112,
  217, 271, 272, 305, 313,
  314, 318, 322, 380, 388,
  389, 390, 393, 400, 437
skills, 248
strategy, 177, 221, 261, 262,
  271, 322
respect, 61, 69, 98, 103, 125,
  128, 130, 173, 260, 303, 309,
  336, 343, 344, 360, 377
responsive evaluation,
  120, 121
retrieving notes, 65
role ordered display, 333

S

sample, 45, 47, 72, 73, 85, 91, 116,
  119, 125, 127, 131, 143, 241,
  252, 253, 254, 255, 275, 276,
  277, 279, 280, 281, 282, 283,
  284, 285, 289, 292, 293,
  294, 295, 302, 305, 306,
  322, 323, 330, 331, 378,
  396, 436, 437, 438
sampling
  cluster, 277
  error, 281
  random, 276, 281, 324, 330, 437
  stratified, 277, 324, 436, 437
scale, 11, 14, 38, 45, 70, 73, 94,
  101, 102, 103, 104, 116, 121,
  135, 136, 137, 143, 220, 223,
  254, 266, 286, 291, 297, 298,
  315, 331, 351, 378, 389, 395,
  396, 397, 398, 436

scanning, 60, 62, 84
scientific
  enquiry, 12, 18, 20, 43, 109, 120,
    187, 189, 190, 191, 193,
    196, 197, 210, 220, 221,
    228, 229, 251, 437
  knowledge, 11, 19, 20, 43, 44,
    108, 150, 197, 202, 224,
    234, 236, 340, 436
  method, 7, 12, 13, 14, 16, 17,
    18, 20, 21, 36, 38, 44, 114,
    187, 189, 195, 202, 204,
    217, 221, 222, 229, 246,
    247, 248, 339, 433
scope, 9, 21, 22, 30, 34, 35, 39, 45,
  46, 78, 93, 109, 110, 114, 116,
  125, 136, 137, 176, 212, 213,
  219, 222, 249, 256, 262, 275,
  282, 291, 295, 298, 323, 324,
  330, 372, 377, 379, 420, 436
search engine, 54, 55, 57, 257
secondary
  data, 49, 241, 242, 261, 273,
    288, 322, 391
  sources, 51, 242, 243,
    244, 261
semiotics, 123, 124
sense of understanding, 95, 109,
  150, 235, 236, 436
sequential analysis, 314
set of laws theory, 109
social
  construct, 18, 19, 20, 21, 43,
    44, 247
  context, 19, 124, 424
  facts, 188, 189, 203, 204, 431
  phenomena, 115, 203, 207,
    312, 332
  problems, 28
  reality, 188, 205, 229
  science, 18, 20, 74, 77, 98, 103,
    106, 107, 110, 117, 123,
    189, 202, 203, 204, 205,
    207, 208, 222, 226, 245,
    247, 260, 261, 269, 329,
    365, 366
  survey, 69, 70, 89, 91, 246, 356
  system, 18, 97, 206, 431
  theory, 124
sociology, 12, 13, 15, 18, 19, 20,
  43, 44, 128, 203, 204, 209,
  246, 247, 328, 392

spelling, 57, 352, 406, 412, 416, 418, 424
standardised, 344, 417, 426
statement
 observation, 191, 196, 197, 227
 of intent, 219, 222
 theoretical, 105, 108, 110, 111, 112, 197, 337, 433, 436
statistics
 inferential, 304, 305, 320, 435
 non-parametric, 304, 320
 official, 56, 188, 189, 327
 parametric, 304, 307, 332
stratified sampling, 277, 324, 436, 437
structure, 46, 61, 65, 66, 76, 78, 85, 89, 101, 107, 128, 130, 144, 152, 157, 161, 169, 190, 205, 209, 214, 285, 296, 309, 310, 311, 320, 333, 352, 374, 377, 379, 382, 383, 385, 399, 400, 402, 403, 405, 406, 409, 417, 426, 429, 432
 of argument, 161
sub-
 class, 430
 hypotheses, 214, 223
 problems, 13, 33, 34, 35, 39, 46, 223, 229, 376, 402
 questions, 13, 218, 380
subjectivity, 17, 93
survey
 analytical, 116
 physical, 287
 research, 273, 325, 326
 social, 69, 70, 89, 91, 246, 356
 technique, 116
 telephone, 285
 visual, 287

syllogism, 10, 168
symbol, 57, 94, 95, 96, 140
symbolic, 205, 237, 247, 390, 434
 interactionism, 205, 247
 logic, 237, 434
systems
 analysis, 120, 144
 map, 296

T
tables, 409, 412, 413
taxonomy, 318
technical
 drawing, 297
 term, 93, 153, 159, 305
theoretical
 concept, 98, 99, 100, 101, 103, 125, 142, 143, 144, 152, 376, 425, 435
 statement, 105, 108, 110, 111, 112, 197, 337, 433, 436
theory
 grounded, 107, 254, 255, 275, 308, 389
 of research, 37
 social, 124
time ordered display, 316
timetable, 25, 374, 379, 381, 400, 421
title, 24, 50, 51, 52, 60, 61, 64, 67, 68, 69, 74, 136, 142, 143, 144, 245, 374, 375, 380, 383, 408, 412, 413, 414, 415, 416, 420, 425
 of books etc, 50-52, 64, 69
 of research, 24

truth, 12, 17, 18, 20, 21, 43, 108, 109, 111, 147, 159, 162, 163, 178, 192, 193, 194, 197, 200, 239, 241, 337, 364, 434
typology, 95, 149, 150, 234, 430, 432

V
validity, 61, 90, 107, 111, 134, 160, 161, 162, 163, 164, 166, 168, 171, 175, 188, 227, 244, 245, 249, 282, 289, 293, 294, 324, 330, 339, 352, 396, 397, 432, 433
value
 of concepts, 95
 of research, 360
 statistical, 306
variable, 54, 117, 119, 134, 151, 215, 235, 294, 298, 299, 319, 430
 dependent, 109, 117, 151, 289, 295, 315, 318, 374, 430
 independent, 109, 117, 122, 151, 289, 292, 295, 374, 430
Venn diagram, 164, 165, 166, 167, 168, 171, 176, 178, 183, 438
vignette, 314

W
Weber, 17, 202, 203, 206, 207, 229, 247
Wittgenstein, 17, 123
World Wide Web, 53, 54, 55, 56, 57, 424
writing
 a proposal, 422
 notes, 286
 process, 381, 401